Energiepolitik u
Energy Policy and Climate Protection

Reihe herausgegeben von
Lutz Mez, Berlin, Deutschland
Achim Brunnengräber, Berlin, Deutschland

Diese Buchreihe beschäftigt sich mit den globalen Verteilungskämpfen um knappe Energieressourcen, mit dem Klimawandel und seinen Auswirkungen sowie mit den globalen, nationalen, regionalen und lokalen Herausforderungen der umkämpften Energiewende. Die Beiträge der Reihe zielen auf eine nachhaltige Energie- und Klimapolitik sowie die wirtschaftlichen Interessen, Machtverhältnisse und Pfadabhängigkeiten, die sich dabei als hohe Hindernisse erweisen. Weitere Themen sind die internationale und europäische Liberalisierung der Energiemärkte, die Klimapolitik der Vereinten Nationen (UN), Anpassungsmaßnahmen an den Klimawandel in den Entwicklungs-, Schwellen- und Industrieländern, Strategien zur Dekarbonisierung sowie der Ausstieg aus der Kernenergie und der Umgang mit den nuklearen Hinterlassenschaften.
Die Reihe bietet ein Forum für empirisch angeleitete, quantitative und international vergleichende Arbeiten, für Untersuchungen von grenzüberschreitenden Transformations-, Mehrebenen- und Governance-Prozessen oder von nationalen „best practice"-Beispielen. Ebenso ist sie offen für theoriegeleitete, qualitative Untersuchungen, die sich mit den grundlegenden Fragen des gesellschaftlichen Wandels in der Energiepolitik, bei der Energiewende und beim Klimaschutz beschäftigen.

This book series focuses on global distribution struggles over scarce energy resources, climate change and its impacts, and the global, national, regional and local challenges associated with contested energy transitions. The contributions to the series explore the opportunities to create sustainable energy and climate policies against the backdrop of the obstacles created by strong economic interests, power relations and path dependencies. The series addresses such matters as the international and European liberalization of energy sectors; sustainability and international climate change policy; climate change adaptation measures in the developing, emerging and industrialized countries; strategies toward decarbonization; the problems of nuclear energy and the nuclear legacy.
The series includes theory-led, empirically guided, quantitative and qualitative international comparative work, investigations of cross-border transformations, governance and multi-level processes, and national "best practice"-examples. The goal of the series is to better understand societal-ecological transformations for low carbon energy systems, energy transitions and climate protection.

Reihe herausgegeben von
PD Dr. Lutz Mez
Freie Universität Berlin

PD Dr. Achim Brunnengräber
Freie Universität Berlin

Weitere Bände in der Reihe http://www.springer.com/series/12516

Joshua Posaner

Held Captive by Gas

The Price of Politics in Gazprom's Long-Term Contracts with Central European Buyers (2009 to 2014)

Springer VS

Joshua Posaner
Berlin, Germany

Dissertation Freie Universität Berlin, 2016

D 188

ISSN 2626-2827 ISSN 2626-2835 (electronic)
Energiepolitik und Klimaschutz. Energy Policy and Climate Protection
ISBN 978-3-658-27517-4 ISBN 978-3-658-27518-1 (eBook)
https://doi.org/10.1007/978-3-658-27518-1

Springer VS

This Springer VS imprint is published by the registered company Springer Fachmedien Wiesbaden GmbH part of Springer Nature.
The registered company address is: Abraham-Lincoln-Str. 46, 65189 Wiesbaden, Germany

This book is dedicated to my parents.

Acknowledgements

This book was completed during two periods of intensive writing between February and September 2015 and April and July 2016, following earlier fieldwork, data collection and drafting through 2014 in Budapest and Berlin. It was revised in April 2019 in Berlin.

Thanks must go to PD Dr. Lutz Mez for supervising the first draft of this work as a PhD thesis, and to Prof. Dr. Miranda Schreurs, Prof. Dr. a.D. Hajo Funke, and Dr.phil Ursula Stegelmann for providing much needed advice along the way.

Special thanks must also be reserved for Professor Andreas Goldthau, who provided invaluable feedback on an earlier draft version of this work and has been a great source of inspiration and intellectual clarity along the way.

Additionally, Artak Galyan, Stefan Roch, Vija Palkalkaite, Olga Löblová, Reka Vizi- Magyarosi, Wojciech Jakóbik, Andras Szirko, Andras Deák, Jacopo Maria Pepe, Sandu-Daniel Kopp, Marco Wedel, Heinrich Schulz, Andrej Nosko, Juraj Kuruc and Anca Gurzu are also owed gratitude for their assistance and feedback during drafting.

Many others provided help and insight in the development of this project, not least Professor Jonathan Stern, whose expertise on the global gas markets is unrivalled.

Editing and formatting assistance from Chris Fenwick proved indispensable in the completion of this manuscript, as did earlier graphical wizardry from Doug Kitson in London.

Professionally, Therese Robinson, James Batty and Tom Hoskyns are all owed apologies for the delayed articles while I rushed to complete this text in its first draft.

Institutionally, I would also like to thank the staff at the Free University in Berlin where my doctoral studies were based, and the team at the Central European University in Budapest who hosted me for a research stay in winter 2013/2014.

Though the colleagues, friends, and experts listed above provided much to improve this text, any remaining mistakes are the reserve of the author alone.

There is far too much in the realm of gas supply contracts and their connection to politics that remains cloaked from the view of analysts. If nothing else, this text aims at least partially to improve understanding of a once overlooked area of the European gas supply system and to provide a snapshot of a small energy battle that took place in Europe's core at its most fierce – that of the small-states vying for their energy independence against the former hegemon to the East.

Berlin, April 2019 Joshua Posaner

Contents

1 Introduction ... 1

1.1 The puzzle ... 4
1.2 State of research ... 14
1.3 Structure ... 20

2 Research design ... 23

2.1 Potential explanations ... 27
2.2 Theoretical framework ... 31
2.2.1 Domestic structure ... 32
2.2.2 Party cleavages ... 35
2.3 Methodology ... 39
2.4 Case selection ... 44

3 Energy security ... 55

3.1 Securitising energy ... 56
3.1.1 The Eurasian gas system ... 60
3.1.2 Institutional economics ... 65
3.2 Historical context: 1945–1989 ... 69
3.2.1 'Brotherhood' corridor ... 70
3.2.2 Sands, steppes and lowlands ... 73
3.2.3 Golden age of gas ... 76
3.2.4 Plotting pipelines ... 78
3.3 European market context ... 83
3.3.1 Oil-indexation vs. hub-based pricing ... 89
3.3.2 EU regulatory landscape ... 93

4 Poland ... 97

4.1 Orenburg and Yamburg: 1989–1993 ... 100
4.2 Yamal and the Contract of the Century: 1994–1999 ... 103
4.3 'Little' and 'big' Nordic contracts: 2000–2004 ... 106
4.4 The 'Molotov–Ribbentrop' pipeline: 2006-2010 ... 112
4.5 Towards an Energy Union: 2011–2014 ... 116
4.6 Poland policy review ... 124
4.7 Poland policy conclusions ... 132

5 Czech Republic ... 137

5.1 The 'Brotherhood' bridge: 1989–1995 ... 142
5.2 Norwegian corridor: 1996–2005 ... 146
5.3 'Gas Wars': 2006–2009 ... 150

5.4 Reversing the flow: 2010–2014 ... 155
5.5 Czech Republic policy review ... 161
5.6 Czech Republic policy conclusions ... 166

6 Slovakia ... 171

6.1 Post–Velvet Divorce: 1993–1998 ... 175
6.2 State sell-off: 1999–2005 ... 177
6.3 Crisis mode: 2006–2009 ... 179
6.4 Brotherhood reversed: 2010–2014 ... 183
6.5 Slovakia policy review ... 190
6.6 Slovakia policy conclusions ... 195

7 Hungary ... 199

7.1 Back to Europe: 1989–1997 ... 203
7.2 Enter Orbán: 1998–2004 ... 207
7.3 The drama of Nabucco: 2005–2009 ... 211
7.4 Orbánistan and the pipeline graveyard: 2010–2014 ... 218
7.5 Hungary policy review ... 224
7.6 Hungary policy conclusions ... 229

8 Evaluation ... 233

8.1 Aggregating contract evidence ... 234
8.2 Dependence as proxy for price ... 237
8.3 Politics as a variable ... 241
8.4 Re-appraising the 'energy weapon' ... 245

9 Conclusion ... 249

9.1 Results ... 250
9.2 Further research ... 255
9.3 Policy outcome ... 256

Bibliography ... 259

List of Abbreviations

ANO	Alliance of the New Citizens (Slovakia)
APERC	Asia Pacific Energy Research Centre
AWS	Solidarity Electoral Action (Poland)
BACI	Bidirectional Austrian–Czech Interconnector
bcm	billion cubic metres
BIM	bilateral monopoly
CDC	Caspian Development Corporation
CEE	Central and Eastern Europe
CEGH	Central European Gas Hub
CIS	Commonwealth of Independent States
COMECOM	Council for Mutual Economic Assistance
CPP	Český plynárenský podnik
ČSSD	Czech Social Democratic Party
CV	conditional variable
DEÚS	Democratic Union of Slovakia
DV	dependent variable
ECSC	European Coal and Steel Community
ECT	Energy Charter Treaty
EPH	Energetický a Průmyslový Holding
EU	European Union
FGSZ	Földgázszállító
FRSU	floating regasification, storage and unloading vessel
Fidesz	Alliance of Young Democrats (Hungary)
FKgP	Independent Smallholders, Agrarian Workers and Civic Party (Hungary)
GECF	Gas-Exporting Countries Forum
GFU	Gas Negotiating Committee (Norway)
GOG	gas-on-gas
H	hypothesis
IEA	International Energy Agency
IGA	intergovernmental agreement
IGU	International Gas Union
IV	independent variable
JCC	Japanese Customs Cleared
KDH	Christian Democratic Movement (Slovakia)
KDNP	Christian Democratic People's Party
KDU–ČSL	Christian and Democratic Union–Czechoslovak People's Party
ĽS-HZDS	People's Party–Movement for a Democratic Slovakia
LTC	long-term contract
LNG	liquefied natural gas

mcm	thousand cubic metres
MDF	Hungarian Democratic Forum
MMBtu	dollars per million British thermal units
MMcm	million cubic metres
MND	Moravské naftové doly
MOL	Magyar Olaj-és Gázipari Nyilvánosan működő Részvénytársaság
MSZP	Hungarian Socialist Party
mtoe	million tonnes of oil equivalent
NiK	Supreme Audit Office (Poland)
NBP	National Balancing Point
ODS	Civic Democratic Party (Czech Republic)
OPE	oil-price escalation
OTC	over the counter
PGNiG	Polskie Górnictwo Naftowe i Gazownictwo
PiS	Law and Justice Party (Poland)
PO	Civic Platform Party (Poland)
PSL	Polish People's Party
PSzAF	National Financial Supervisory Agency (Hungary)
RUE	RosUkrEnergo
SDK	Slovak Democratic Coalition
SDKÚ-DS	Slovak Democratic and Christian Union–Democratic Party
SDL	Party of the Democratic Left (Slovakia)
SLD	Democratic Left Alliance (Poland)
SMER-SD	Direction–Social Democracy (Slovakia)
SMK	Party of the Hungarian Community (Slovakia)
SNS	Slovak National Party
SPP	Slovensky plynarensky priemysel
SZ	Green Party (Czech Republic)
SZDSZ	Alliance of Free Democrats (Hungary)
TAP	Trans-Adriatic Pipeline
TPES	total primary energy supply
TTF	Dutch Title Transfer Facility
TWh	terawatt-hours
URE	Energy Regulatory Office (Poland)
URSO	Regulatory Office for Networks Industries (Slovakia)
US-DEU	Freedom Union–Democratic Union (Czech Republic)
UW	Freedom Union (Poland)
V4	Visegrad Group case study countries: Poland, Czech Republic, Slovakia, Hungary
VNG	Verbundnetz Gas
VV	Public Affairs Party (Czech Republic)
ZRS	Union of the Workers of Slovakia

List of Figures

Figure 1: Gas contract negotiation model 25
Figure 2: Process of LTC re-negotiations with Gazprom (2009–2014) 29
Figure 3: Importer/supplier LTC process-tracing mechanism 41
Figure 4: Case studies political timeline 54
Figure 5: Yafimava's Eurasian gas network flows conceptual framework27 62
Figure 6: A Soviet stamp commemorating pipeline projects in 1983 80
Figure 7: Map of mainline pipeline export projects 82
Figure 8: Poland market snapshot 99
Figure 9: Diversification projects considered by Poland (1989–2014) 111
Figure 10: Poland political timeline with gas LTC milestones (1989–2014) 133
Figure 11: Sector breakdown of Czech Republic's gas demand (2008) 138
Figure 12: Czech Republic market snapshot 141
Figure 13: Czech political timeline with gas LTC milestones (1989–2014) 167
Figure 14: Slovakia's total primary energy supply in 2009 172
Figure 15: Slovakia market snapshot 174
Figure 16: Slovakia's planned pipeline interconnector projects in 2014 189
Figure 17: Slovak political timeline with gas LTC milestones (1989–2014) 195
Figure 18: Hungary market snapshot 202
Figure 19: Hungary political timeline with gas LTC milestones (1989–2014) 230

List of Graphs

Graph 1: Dependence on Russian gas as % of annual consumption in 2013 5
Graph 2: Average wholesale price of Gazprom imports per country (2010) 6
Graph 3: EU gas imports by source in % of total (2009–2014) 7
Graph 4: Physical flows into the EU by source (2011–2014) 8
Graph 5: Oil price, German border and UK NBP gas prices (2005–2014) 11
Graph 6: Range of Gazprom export prices to Europe $/mcm (2010–2014) 27
Graph 7: Gross domestic product (1990-2014) 47
Graph 8: Gross domestic product annual % change (1990–2014) 48
Graph 9: Gas consumption in bcm (1965–2014) 49
Graph 10: Gas consumption by sector (2013) 51
Graph 11: Gross inland consumption by fuel as % in total mix (2013) 51
Graph 12: Net imports as % of energy use 1970–2012 52
Graph 13: Annual gas exports obligation for USSR in bcm (1970–1980)* 77
Graph 14: International comparison of wholesale gas prices (2011-2014) 84
Graph 15: Price formation of world gas imports by kind in 2014 85
Graph 16: Price formation of European gas imports by kind in 2014 85
Graph 17: Share of oil-indexed gas in EU imports from third party (2014) 86
Graph 18: Brent crude oil price in $ per barrel with V4 LTC milestones 88
Graph 19: Evolution of key global gas price benchmarks (2007–2018) 93
Graph 20: Poland consumption, production and imports (1990–2013) 125
Graph 21: Poland's actual contracted gas (1989–2014) 126
Graph 22: Poland's contracted gas under Nordic scenario (1989–2014) 126
Graph 23: Quantity of Yamal-LTC gas as share of imports (2008–2014) 129
Graph 24: Price of Poland's wholesale Russian gas imports (2010–2014) 130
Graph 25: Share of supplier in annual Czech imports (2008–2009) 159
Graph 26: Czech Republic's consumption and imports (1970–2013) 162
Graph 27: Czech Republic's actual contracted gas (1989–2014) 163
Graph 28: Price of Czech wholesale Russian gas imports (2010–2014) 164
Graph 29: Slovakia's consumption and imports (1970–2013) 191
Graph 30: Slovakia's actual contracted gas (1989–2014) 192
Graph 31: Price of Slovakia's wholesale Russian gas imports (2010–2014) 193
Graph 32: Hungary gas supply by source (2009) 217
Graph 33: Hungary's actual contracted gas (1989–2014) 225
Graph 34: Hungary consumption, production and imports (1970–2013) 226
Graph 35: Price of Hungary wholesale Russian gas imports (2010–2014) 227
Graph 36: Share of right/left-wing in 25-year review period (months) 235
Graph 37: Total yearly contracted volume by right/left (bcm) 237
Graph 38: Dependence on Gazprom and wholesale price (2012) 238
Graph 39: LTC volume in annual demand for case studies scenario 240

List of Tables

Table 1: Gazprom negotiations, discounts and arbitration (2009–2014) 12
Table 2: Wholesale price for Gazprom imports in $/mcm (2010–2014) 26
Table 3: Comparative case studies snapshot (2013) 46
Table 4: Domestic gas market snapshot (2013) 50
Table 5: Gas export volumes from the Soviet Union in bcm (1970–1980) 77
Table 6: Gas supply contracts effective in Poland (1989–2014) 131
Table 7: Gas supply contracts effective in Czech Republic (1989–2014) 165
Table 8: Gas supply contracts effective in Slovakia (1989–2014) 194
Table 9: Gas supply contracts effective in Hungary (1989–2014) 228
Table 10: Aggregated gas supply arrangements/arbitration results 234
Table 11: Supply contracts agreed by time period 236
Table 12: Entry point with capacity of >10% annual demand by time period 239
Table 13: Instances of political influence on gas supply in CE (1989-2015) 243

1 Introduction

Gas makes or breaks economies. This is clear from the consequences of disruption in supply in 2009 within the patchwork of European markets that rely on Russian imports to meet demand. Yet, despite its importance, the trade in natural gas between producers and consumers remained, to a large extent, a black box up until the mid-2010s. Contracts are closely guarded industry secrets and by 2019 there has been no single global benchmark price against which to measure its value based on international supply and demand fundamentals. Unlike their fossil fuel competitors, coal and oil, gaseous fuels also differ in that they cannot easily be loaded onto tankers or trucks. Proximity and infrastructure matter – left undirected, uncooled and uncompressed, natural gas simply disperses. These characteristics have made its trade especially prone to natural monopolies, island markets and captive consumers. This work deals with these concepts in the context of a rapidly changing European gas market up to 2014.

Focusing on four European Union (EU) member state case studies, each from the 2004 intake of former Soviet satellite states and historically dependent on external gas supply from Russia, this text draws a causal link between domestic political structure and levels of import dependence, which is taken as a proxy for price. In short, it looks at how successive governments across the left/right spectrum in each case study have pursued varying import arrangements and determined the level of contractual dependence on Russia, the incumbent dominant supplier, over the 25-year period from 1989 to 2014. In doing so it seeks to explain the differential in the average wholesale price of gas charged by Russia's export monopoly Gazprom to neighbouring import-dependent countries under comparable conditions, using a dataset for the years 2010 to 2014. The arguments included herein aim to open up the gas trade black box, illustrating the link between the input of state-level structures and output in the terms of transnational contracts.

J. Posaner, *Held Captive by Gas*, Energiepolitik und Klimaschutz. Energy Policy and Climate Protection, https://doi.org/10.1007/978-3-658-27518-1_1

It is argued that domestic political factors – chiefly the composition of parties in government and their policy drivers – had a determining influence on the level of dependence on a single gas supplier, and that this in turn relates to the price paid for those imports. This text makes its point by positing a simple explanatory model of how governments tend to prioritise different objectives in gas contract negotiations. Furthermore, the argument goes on to test these assumptions with a process tracing analysis of the four case studies under review: the Czech Republic, Hungary, Poland and Slovakia. The degree of state-ownership of the utility that operates the import contracts is a key conditional variable, intensifying the effect of the independent variable (government in office) on the dependent variable (level of dependence on single contracted gas supplier).

In dealing with domestic structure, and in recognising the institutional economics approach to the bargaining process through which gas supply contracts are configured, these findings also bolster work in the broader energy security canon by examining the background of a period of structural change in some European gas markets where the interests of consumers pursuing liberalisation agendas clash with often state-owned producers seeking to meet what they argue are necessarily long-term fixed costs associated with exploration, production and distribution. The results of an unprecedented period of contract re-negotiations from 2010 to 2014 represent a secondary process for analysis, feeding back into the findings on how different governments, and private actors, relate to a dominant supplier through ownership of the importing agency, or utility, that executes the contract.

Examining the relationship between politics and energy is not a new undertaking, nor is identifying the monopolistic practices of Russia's gas export giant Gazprom and its business arrangements in the former Soviet sphere of influence. However, existing coverage tends to emphasise the role of global or institutional factors over domestic structures, placing the process of contract negotiation in the realm of international relations. From this perspective, foreign policy analysis provides the toolbox of choice for analysing a unitary state actor in a global system. This work takes a different approach. Here, it is argued that political cleavages within national political party systems trace fault lines along which government approaches to energy security can be determined as policy drivers. This shapes ties between importer and exporter, and has played a formative role in fixing contract terms in an already politicised gas trade.

The case of the EU and its diverse set of gas markets, which have various levels of dependence on external suppliers, provides fertile background conditions against which to test these assumptions. Suppliers to EU markets have typically delivered gas via pipeline under long-term contracts. Over the last few decades this trade has taken place against a backdrop of regulatory, geopolitical and economic change, yet its fundamental characteristics – those of indexation to oil, adherence to take-or-pay and destination clauses, and usage of infrastructure dating from the 1960s and 1970s pipeline construction boom – remained largely static until recently. For EU member states, dwindling indigenous resources and infrastructure constraints have conditioned a system of diverging path dependencies among the present 28 members. This has nowhere been more starkly illustrated than in Central and Eastern Europe (CEE), the region with which this analysis is concerned.

Since independence in 1989, the CEE states remained largely locked into pipeline systems built during the Soviet era, paid more for gas than their western neighbours and did so at varying rates over the first 25 years of post-communism. The pursuit of diversification measures, contract re-negotiations and fuel-switching away from gas have varied between states, depending on the government in charge and its policy agenda, as have relations with the dominant supplier. The Czech Republic, Hungary, Poland and Slovakia – the case study countries, collectively described as the Visegrad Group after the loose institutional forum inaugurated during the early post-communist years at a summit on the banks of the Danube in 1991[1] – provide the testing ground for how domestic structures determine transnational energy relations.

Although this analysis is anchored in the dynamic through which these consuming countries, and by association their national utilities, are variously dependent on Russian gas supplied under long-term contract (LTC) by state- controlled Gazprom, it also has a broader contemporary contextual frame. Calls for an EU-wide Energy Union initiative, which transitioned from Warsaw to Brussels via the editorial pages of the *Financial Times* in April 2014, could be interpreted as a reaction to historical dependence on Russia against a backdrop of renewed crisis

1 The Visegrad Group "reflects the efforts of the countries of the Central European region to work together in a number of fields of common interest within the [sic] all-European integration" and has at times sought to foster greater integration on energy policy. See: <http://www.visegrad-group.eu/>

in Ukraine and Moscow's annexation of Crimea.[2] The European Commission's 2015 investigation into Gazprom practices in eight CEE markets, including the four under investigation here, provides additional relevance for this work.[3] What has followed has been a rapid process of legislating in Brussels and conflict over whether an expansion to the controversial Nord Stream gas pipeline linking Russia with Germany should be allowed. The result has been a greater focus on energy security across the EU, in response to a mosaic of different market places all variously dependent on gas imports at varying prices. Europe's "Energy Union" is not yet complete at the time of this publication in 2019, but the market dynamics up to 2014 tackled here explain the reasons for the policy push.

1.1 The puzzle

Why do some states under comparable conditions pay more for their gas imports than others, and which factors determine how equitable the terms under which the gas is priced and supplied are? These questions became key pillars of the European energy security debate in the 2000s, especially in the context of the EU and its member states' asymmetrical reliance on Russian gas supply. Varying levels of dependence on Gazprom are one explanatory factor that helps answer the first part of the question. On average, European consumers relied on Russia for 30.2% of total consumption in 2014.[4] But for the EU countries that are former Soviet satellites behind the iron curtain, this figure was 58% of annual consumption, flattered by recent Czech moves away from Russian gas and Romania's autarky.[5] In Poland

2 The Energy Union concept taken on by the EU dates back to an editorial by Polish Prime Minister Donald Tusk in the *FT* shortly after Russia's annexation of Crimea and before he took up the position of President of the European Council in December 2014. The text includes recognition that "excessive dependence on Russian energy makes Europe weak," while also making clear that "Russia does not sell its resources cheap – at least, not to everyone." Donald Tusk, 'A United Europe Can End Russia's Energy Stranglehold', *Financial Times*, 21 April 2014 <http://www.ft.com/intl/cms/s/0/91508464-c661-11e3-ba0e-00144feabdc0.html#axzz3ZwW0NY2m> [accessed 12 May 2015].

3 This is explored in further detail later in each of the case study chapters. European Commission, 'Antitrust: Commission Sends Statement of Objections to Gazprom for Alleged Abuse of Dominance on Central and Eastern European Gas Supply Markets', 2015 <http://europa.eu/rapid/press-release_IP-15-4828_en.htm> [accessed 12 May 2015].

4 Europe includes Turkey, but excludes Baltic States, according to Gazprom's statistics, which classify the Europe region as those continental countries beyond the boundaries of the former Soviet Union. Gazprom, 'Gazprom Expanding in European Market', 2015 <http://www.gazprom.com/-press/news/2015/june/article229268/> [accessed 12 January 2016].

5 Gazprom Export statistics and BP annual consumption figures combined. Percentages include figures for the three Baltic states, which Gazprom itself includes in the 'Gas supplies to the CIS' category.

and Hungary, for example, Russian gas held around a 70% market share in the early 2010s and in Bulgaria, Slovakia and the Baltics, nearly 100%. Statistics for 2013 included in Graph 1 illustrate the disparity.

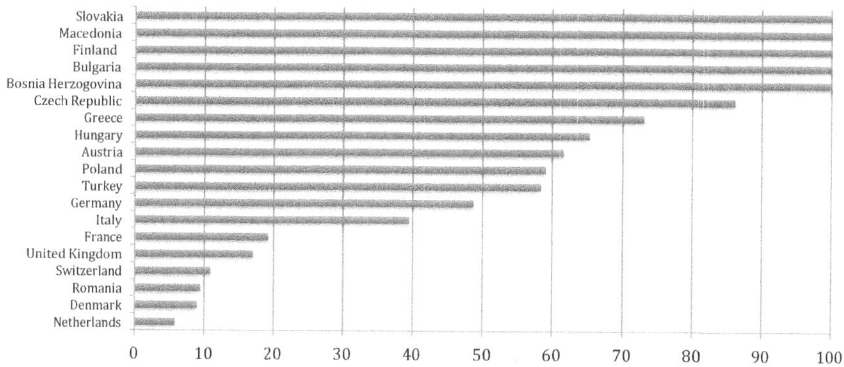

Graph 1: Dependence on Russian gas as % of annual consumption in 2013[6]

The differential in the price charged by Gazprom for its gas delivered under LTC to various EU importers is expansive. In 2010, each of the EU member states east of Germany paid above the average European wholesale price of $305 per thousand cubic metres (mcm). Austrian importers paid the average, $51 cheaper per mcm than their Slovak counterparts, $45 cheaper than Hungarians, $26 cheaper than Poles and $21 cheaper than Czechs. Despite shorter transit distances and often larger wholesale volumes bought in bulk, the cost of gas has remained more expensive for CEE consumers than for their counterparts in the west. This dynamic of varying degrees of dependence on Gazprom supply, and the price paid for its gas, is part of a broader EU supply picture that includes two further external pipeline gas suppliers and the potential for delivery of liquefied natural gas (LNG).

Taken as a whole, in 2010 the then 27 EU member states' gas consumption reached 536 billion cubic metres (bcm) according to official statistics from Eurostat. Of this, 366 bcm came via the three pipeline 'corridors' from Russia, Norway

6 Author's graph. Gazprom Export statistics set against annual consumption estimates from BP.

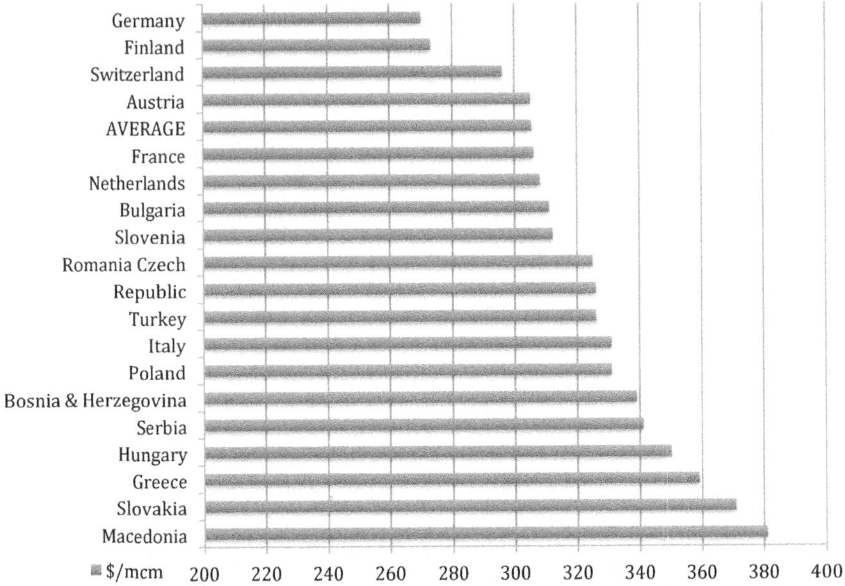

Graph 2: Average wholesale price of Gazprom imports per country (2010)[7]

and North African producers.[8] The case study countries considered here received no gas under contract from Libya and Algeria, which constitute the North African option and which historically trade with Mediterranean states, while non-'swap' Norwegian gas only flowed east of Germany in limited volumes up to 2014. LNG cargoes from production points from the Caribbean to the Gulf into receiving terminals across Europe's Atlantic seaboard also help make up the EU supply balance. So-called regasification import terminals are located at ports in Spain, the UK, France, Italy, Belgium, Portugal, Greece and the Netherlands.

Although Lithuania and Poland have also endeavoured to build terminal infrastructure at Baltic ports in Klaipėda and Świnoujście, respectively, neither site had received a cargo by the end of 2014, when this enquiry ends.

---

7 Author's graph using *Interfax* data on average wholesale gas prices. Further details on the data are provided in the second chapter.

8 Eurostat statistics. The pipeline corridors refer to three different geographic sources, but actual flows enter the EU through various entry points. The Russian corridor has three different mainline pipeline entry points: via the traditional Ukraine route developed in the 1960s and 1970s, via the Yamal pipeline from Belarus, built in the 1990s, and via the subsea Nord Stream pipeline opened in 2011.

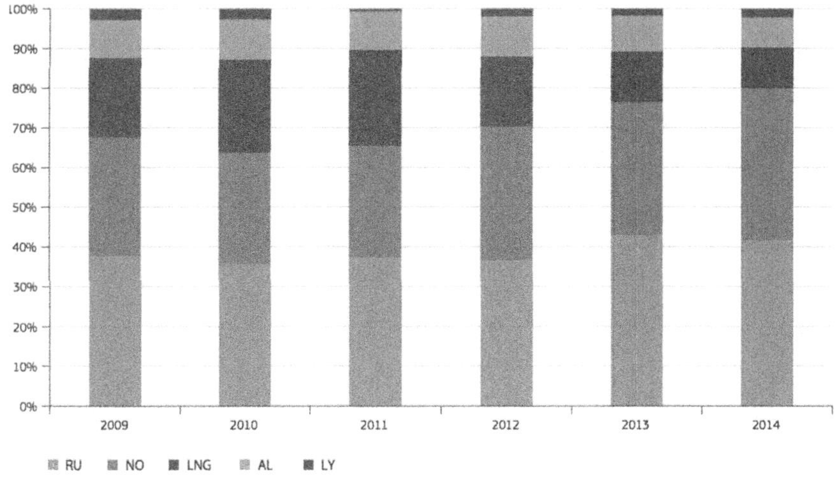

Graph 3: EU gas imports by source in % of total (2009–2014)[9]

The Russian 'corridor' is consequently the key supply line for CEE and has usually, although not always (see Graph 4), seen the largest flow rates of the three pipeline options into Europe. Supply from the east also pre-dates each of the alternative options and, during the period of the Soviet Union – with dominion over Ukrainian production and with the concurrent exception of competing Dutch output – was the first major source for Europe's burgeoning consumption in the 1960s. As will be discussed, contracts were often signed on a barter basis in return for loans and steel pipes. Countries subsumed into the Soviet system gave assistance in building out the early mainline pipeline routes west in return for deliveries from the central planners. After 1989 governments were tasked with converting these comrade-like intergovernmental agreements of the 1970s and 1980s into commercial contracts that would guarantee supply decades ahead. As will be shown, decisions taken by early post-communist governments in transition often perpetuated the ties of the Soviet era.

However, in January 2009 this web of interdependencies built since the 1960s to link producer with consumer unravelled in Europe's core. The cut to deliveries of

9 European Commission (DG Energy), *Quarterly Report on European Gas Markets (Fourth Quarter of 2014)*, 2015, p. 8. <https://ec.europa.eu/energy/sites/ener/files/documents/quarterly_report_on_european_gas_markets_2014_q4.pdf> [accessed 28 July 2015]. Data is sourced from ENTSO-G Transparency Platform. RU = Russia, NO = Norway, LNG = liquefied natural gas, AL = Algeria and LY = Libya.

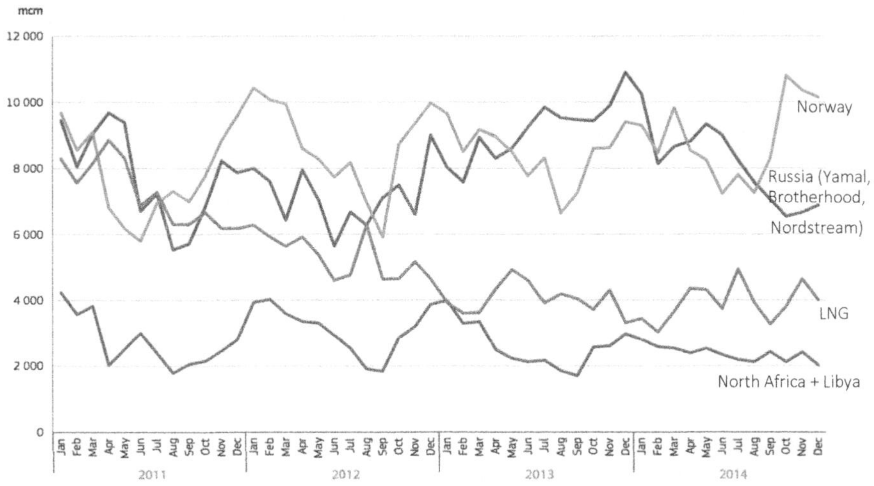

Graph 4: Physical flows into the EU by source (2011–2014)[10]

Russian gas through Ukraine was not without precedent, but the impact the three-week shutdown would have on some CEE economies exposed fundamental vulnerabilities. An earlier disruption in January 2006 had left Ukraine without gas imports for three days, with notable consequences further downstream.[11] However, the impact the 2009 'Gas War'[12] would have in the region marked the consequence of energy policy choices taken by governments in the early years of

---

10 European Commission (DG Energy), *Quarterly Report on European Gas Markets (Fourth Quarter of 2014)*, 2015, p. 7. <https://ec.europa.eu/energy/sites/ener/files/documents/quarterly_report-_on_european_gas_markets_2014_q4.pdf> [accessed 28 July 2015]. Data is sourced from Bentek/ Platts, Thomson-Reuters Waterborne.

11 A comprehensive analysis of the Ukrainian gas market and the background to the 2006 dispute can be found here: Simon Pirani, 'Ukraine's Gas Sector', *Oxford Institute for Energy Studies* <http://www.oxfordenergy.org/2007/06/ukraine%e2%80%99s-gas-sector/> [accessed 12 March 2015]. Meanwhile, a broader analysis of the 2009 crisis is here: Jonathan Stern, Simon Pirani, and Katja Yafimava, 'The Russo-Ukrainian Gas Dispute of January 2009: A Comprehensive Assessment', *Oxford Institute for Energy Studies* <http://www.oxfordenergy.org/2009/02/the-russo-ukrainian-gas-dispute-of-january-2009-a-comprehensive-assessment/> [accessed 27 July 2015].

12 A hyperbolic term most often used in reference to the 2006 and 2009 supply disputes between Russia and Ukraine. Although also used by journalists to describe 1980s petrol price cuts in provincial North America, the term can most often be found in reference to the relationship between Gazprom and its CIS transit states.

transition to market economics. From Warsaw to Sofia, dependence on external gas supply now translated into economic risk.

Slovakia is estimated to have lost €100 million per day throughout the 2009 disruption, with overall losses equal to between 1-1.5% of annual gross domestic product.[13] Approximately 1,000 local enterprises were closed,[14] according to the Slovak government of the time, with emergency caps on consumption put in place across the region. Bulgaria was forced to restart dormant coal-fired power stations and negotiated some new gas supply from an already decommissioned offshore reserve. In addition, the government in Sofia sought to agree small-scale imports via Greece in a bid to meet demand.[15] Elsewhere, consumers in Hungary and the Czech Republic looked west to Germany and north to distant Norway forreplacement supplies. Storage facilities took on an emergency strategic role, rather than just being for seasonal arbitrage, and consumers sought portable heating solutions during a cold weather period.

According to EU statistics, during January 2009 supplies to Bulgaria and Slovakia – both ordinarily nearly totally dependent on Russian gas – were cut by 100% and 97% respectively, with delivery to the Czech Republic (71%), Hungary (45%) and Poland (33%) also, albeit less critically, affected.[16] But despite their sitting side-by-side throughough Europe's interior, and with roughly comparable demand profiles, the impact on each market was markedly different. Consumer experience in Bratislava was incomparable to that in Vienna – just 80 km west along the Danube, where gas flowed fine. This disparity owed something to geography and the uneven distribution of natural resources; it also owed something to the east/west divide during the key period of system building. But it also depended on the different policy approaches taken by governments since the ripple of

---

13 Alexander Duleba, *Poučenia Z Plynovej Krízy v Januári 2009 Analýza Príčin Vzniku, Pravdepodobnosti Opakovania a Návrhy Opatrení Na Zvýšenie Energetickej Bezpečnosti SR v Oblasti Dodávok Zemného Plynu'* (Slovak Foreign Policy Association, October 2009) <http://www.old.-sfpa.sk/dokumenty/publikacie/281> [accessed 20 June 2015], p.4.

14 Ministry of Economy of the Slovak Republic, 'Government Responses to the Impact of the Financial Crisis on Energy Industries and Energy Security of the Slovak Republic', 2009 <http://www.-unece.org/fileadmin/DAM/energy/se/pp/EnComm18_Nov09/18Nov/12_Jurasek.pdf> [accessed 27 July 2015].

15 Aleksandar Kovacevic, 'The Impact of the Russia–Ukraine Gas Crisis in South Eastern Europe', *Oxford Institute for Energy Studies* <http://www.oxfordenergy.org/2009/03/the-impact-of-the-russia%e2%80%93ukraine-gas-crisis-in-south-eastern-europe/> [accessed 5 March 2015], p.12.

16 European Commission, 'Member State General Situation According the Significance of Impact' (2009) <http://europa.eu/rapid/press-release_MEMO-09-3_en.htm> [accessed 27 July 2015].

revolutions saw a 'return to Europe' for those countries previously locked into the Soviet system of five-year plans and command economies.[17]

The decision by Hungary's first democratically elected government under centre- right Prime Minister József Antall to push ahead with building a pipeline connection to Austria in the early 1990s provided a valuable alternative route for imports from the west. Likewise, Czech import arrangements with Norwegian suppliers signed in 1997 by the centre-right Václav Klaus government meant extreme cuts to Russian supply 12 years later were mitigated. The failure of Slovak officials to push ahead with the country's own alternatives explains its vulnerability years later. After January 2009, utilities reviewed portfolios of supply arrangements and LTC agreements came up for re-negotiation at anunprecedented pace, while utility ownership became a greater political issue in countries already sensitive to Russian business ties.

Gazprom recognised the challenge it faced as a monopoly supplier in some of its European markets, and that its long-standing clients were actively seeking alternatives, as illustrated by major new infrastructure initiatives like the ill- fated Nabucco pipeline and regasification terminals along the Baltic coast.[18] Gazprom's foreign sales unit, Gazprom Export, wrote in its 2010 corporate brochure:

> The Central European natural gas market is especially important due to its geographical proximity to Russia. In recent years our relations have been developing against a background of serious geopolitical changes and the desire of these countries to diversify their sources of energy product supplies.[19]

Structural contractual features of gas trade relationships helped drive the search for alternatives. One particularly contentious characteristic of the contracts under which the Russian monopoly, and many other external suppliers, had sold gas was

---

17 The Czech writer Milan Kundera articulated Central Europe's predicament in 1984 as being cut adrift from a Western Europe, with which it identified by history. Milan Kundera, 'The Tragedy of Central Europe', *The New York Review of Books*, 26 April 1984, p. 33. The collapse of the Soviet system subsequently allowed a return to Europe for Poles, Czechs, Slovaks and Hungarians through the membership of supranational institutions like the EU and NATO. Elsa Tulmets, *East Central European Foreign Policy Identity in Perspective: Back to Europe and the EU's Neighbourhood* (Palgrave Macmillan, 2014).

18 The Nabucco pipeline concept was launched in 2002 in Vienna by Austria's OMV and a consortium of European companies. This was part of a strategy to link Iranian production with EU consumers via Turkey and Central Europe as part of a new 'fourth corridor.' The scheme was finally scrapped after the consortium failed to secure a 10 bcm/y volume of Azerbaijani gas in competition with a rival project.

19 Gazprom Export, *Annual Corporate Brochure 2009*, 2010, p.16 <http://www.gazprom.com/f/posts/97/618699/layout_eng_02.06.pdf> [accessed 28 July 2015].

the preference for indexation to oil products in the pricing formula. As oil prices rose to a sustained level above $100 per barrel in the post-2009 era, the price of gas was higher than 'hub-based' rates pegged to supply and demand signals available at national platforms like the UK's National Balancing Point (NBP) in parts of Western Europe, as shown in Graph 5. Destination clauses also restricted the circulation of gas, forbidding importers from re-exporting excess stocks and acting, according to the European Commission, as "provisions that stipulate that the customer must use the purchased gas in its own country or can only sell it to certain customers within its country."[20]

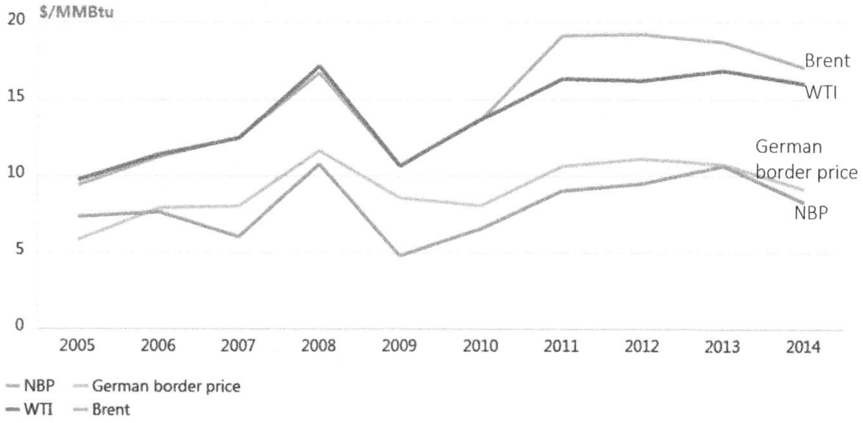

Graph 5: Oil price, German border and UK NBP gas prices (2005–2014)[21]

So-called take-or-pay clauses – which oblige consumers to receive, or offtake, a minimum percentage of the contracted volume, whether it is needed or not – also spurred consumers to trigger re-negotiation clauses in contracts as demand declined under pressure from high wholesale prices and reduced industrial intake after the financial crisis. Table 1 lists those European companies, both state-owned and private, that began re-negotiation proceedings in the period leading up to 2014, while also highlighting which companies received discounts and which pressed

20 European Commission, 'Antitrust: Commission Sends Statement of Objections to Gazprom - Factsheet' <http://europa.eu/rapid/press-release_MEMO-15-4829_en.htm> [accessed 7 April 2016].

21 IEA statistics, including data from German border agency BAFA, which is approximately comparable to the average contracted gas price. UK NBP price reflects level of hub-based pricing in Western Europe. Y-axis measured in $ per million British thermal units for comparison.

for arbitration court proceedings. It also distinguishes between state-owned utilities and those that are privately owned, a key feature applicable in the later investigation into how utility ownership patterns have determined the direction of action taken in a re-negotiation process. It is argued here that utilities under private ownership have been more likely to press for a legal contest, while state-controlled agencies can be observed as preferring compromise and settlement in return for temporary price reduction or associated infrastructure agreements. The disparity in response between different countries is stark, as illustrated in Table 1.

Table 1: Gazprom negotiations, discounts and arbitration (2009–2014)[22]

Country	Company	2009	2010	2011	2012	2013	2014
Austria	Centrex						
Austria	EconGas OMV						
Austria	Erdgas Import Salzburg						
Austria	Gazprom Austria (GWH Gashandel)						
Bulgaria	Bulgargaz						
Czech Republic	RWE Supply & Trading						
Czech Republic	Vemex						
Denmark	DONG						
Estonia	Eesti Gaas						
France	GDF Suez						
Germany	E.On						
Germany	Verbundnetz Gas						
Germany	WIEH						
Germany	Wingas						
Greece	DEPA						
Hungary	Centrex Hungary						
Hungary	Panrusgas						
Italy	Axpo Trading						
Italy	Edison						
Italy	ENI						
Italy	ERG						
Italy	PremiumGas						
Italy	Sinergie Italiane						
Latvia	Latvijas Gaze						
Lithuania	Lietuvos Dujos						
Netherlands	GasTerra						
Poland	PGNiG						
Slovakia	SPP						

Gazprom venture	**State-owned**	**Contract renegotiation**	**Discount granted**	**Arbitration case filed**
Private	**Case study**			

22 The table uses data from various press statements and corporate announcements in addition to information harvested from Gazprom financial statements in a presentation given by Anna Galkina, 'European energy security and Russian export strategy' in Budapest, 15 September 2015.

Under private ownership, Slovak importer SPP filed an arbitration case against Gazprom in 2009 before withdrawing it in return for reduced take-or-pay volumes. This was followed by a further two out-of-court re-negotiations in 2011 and 2014. Czech importer RWE Transgas, under the ownership of Germany's RWE, opted for arbitration proceedings over a two-year period from 2010 before announcing substantial re-negotiations in 2013 and 2014 following the court judgement. Hungary's two intermediaries only carried out one re-negotiation, in 2013, reflecting Gazprom-ownership in both Panrusgas and Centrex. The only constantly state-owned utility under case study analysis – Poland's PGNiG – went to arbitration in 2014. Each of these instances is explored in the case study chapters later, but they give an early indication of the findings and direction of research.

The puzzle this analysis will address is how various gas-consuming countries under comparable conditions took such divergent paths in relation to the dominant supplier post–2009 crisis, as illustrated in Table 1, and how energy policies during the initial 20-year period of democratic governance post-1989 shaped patterns of contractual dependence. After the collapse of the Soviet Union, Francis Fukuyama argued that the contest of great ideas would reach a closing settlement, or liberal consensus, at what he termed the 'end of history.'[23] This was tempered by realists like John Mearsheimer who saw Europe heading 'back to the future,' with primacy returned to competing nation states unaligned to either side of the ideological divide that separated fading state structures.[24] Samuel Huntington's 'Clash of Civilisations' proposed a Europe split along religious lines, poised for confrontation.[25] But these approaches centred on an international system determined by state actors, drawing attention away from what Kenneth Waltz termed the 'second image level' – that of states and their internal composition[26] – and by the new realm of geo-economics, which emphasises trading markets and the replacement of militarism with mercantilism.[27] Seen through this lens, the marketplace of political parties divided across cleavages of electoral agendas must manage a complex cast of

---

23 Francis Fukuyama, *The End of History and the Last Man*, (London: Penguin, 2012 [1992]).

24 John J Mearsheimer, 'Back to the Future: Instability in Europe after the Cold War', *International Security*, 15 (1990), 5–56.

25 Samuel P Huntington, *The Clash of Civilizations and the Remaking of World Order* (New York: Simon & Schuster, 1996).

26 Kenneth Neal Waltz, *Man, the State and War: A Theoretical Analysis* (New York: Columbia University Press, 1959).

27 Best summarised and promoted in Edward N Luttwak, 'From Geopolitics to Geo-Economics: Logic of Conflict, Grammar of Commerce', *The National Interest*, 1990, 17–23.

monopolies, corporations, oligarchs, regulators, technocrats and those opaque figures that exist in-between in their pursuit of the energy security ideal. Those countries that must import raw materials and fuels to keep their economies growing face a further complication: how best to deal not only with their internal actor interests, but also how to manage relations on the transnational level at which contracts are formulated.

1.2 State of research

This work seeks to bridge an analytical gap between domestic structure (party politics and electoral agendas) and its suspected determinate influence on the process of transnational contract formation between consumers and external suppliers of natural gas. It does so by tracing the energy policy of four case studies, each historically reliant on natural gas imports from Russia's Gazprom. Energy security discourse provides a broad umbrella under which these findings sit, however, whilst much work in this field engages in definition building and a compartmentalisation of the stages of achieving energy security,[28] this analysis deals with varying types of energy policies at a national level within a comparable group of countries. Another aim of this work is to address the institutional economics approach to gas contract features and how these are structured to manage risk between exporter and importer.

Much of the literature on domestic politics and the international system has focused on how the latter defines the former.[29] Waltz developed the notion of an international system conditioned by the domestic systems of states into his three

[28] Energy security definitions and the field's conceptual background are dealt with in-depth in Chapter 3. Introductions to contemporary research can be found here: B. Kruyt, D. P.van Vuuren, H. J. M. de Vries and H. Groenenberg, 'Indicators for energy security', *Energy Policy*, 37 (2009), 2166–88; Aleh Cherp and Jessica Jewell, 'The Three Perspectives on Energy Security: Intellectual History, Disciplinary Roots and the Potential for Integration', *Current Opinion in Environmental Sustainability*, 3 (2011), 202–12 and Daniel Yergin, 'Energy Security in the 1990s', *Foreign Affairs* <https://www.foreignaffairs.com/articles/united-states/1988-09-01/energy-security-1990s> [accessed 21 July 2015]. Meanwhile, a historical narrative on oil and gas can be found here: Daniel Yergin, *The Prize: The Epic Quest for Oil, Money & Power*, (New York: Free Press, 2008 [1991]).

[29] As Henry Kissinger suggests: "In the traditional concept foreign policy begins where domestic policy ends." 'Domestic Structure and Foreign Policy', *Daedalus*, 95 (1966), p. 503.

image levels of analysis.[30] However, as Gourevitch argued, reversing Waltz's paradigm, the international system can be seen as an explanatory variable for the domestic structure.[31] In proposing a third way of understanding the end of communism, distinct from realism and liberalism, Risse-Kappen sought a new course that "integrates international and domestic politics" and also recognises domestic structure as an intervening variable "between structural conditions and the definition of actors' interests and preference[s]."[32] Further presentation of domestic structure literature is made in the second chapter, but the recognition of what Putman terms the 'two-level' game, in which governments seek to deal with domestic interests while pursuing what is available at the international level, has relevance to this investigation and is useful in its analysis.[33]

Transfer these theoretical ideas from the abstract to the case conditions at hand and avenues for inquiry present themselves. One illustration of how national structures are vulnerable to external pressure from the international system is through 'meddling' from a former hegemon, and it is this element that Orbán alludes to as the lever of Russia's "energy-centred foreign policy" in CEE.[34] But, as Gourevitch notes, meddling is "less clear empirically but equally obvious conceptually."[35] Where the state and the LTC are black boxes within which we cannot clearly determine function, the inputs of government policy and output of contract terms and

---

30 Waltz, *Man, the State and War.* Realism encourages us to triangulate states' intentions and interests based on fixed assumptions of balance of power, polarity and the pursuit of power. Several threads have emerged in this theory since it was posited in its 'classic' form by Hans Morgenthau in the post- war era, with Mearsheimer's brand of offensive realism contrasting with other neorealist theorists like the 1979 'defensive' version outlined by Waltz, which assumes that great powers will seek to maximise their share of power to an infinite extent, "even though their ultimate motive is simply to survive." Classic realism is outlined here: Hans Joachim Morgenthau, *Politics among Nations* (New York: Knopf, 1967); Kenneth N. Waltz, *Theory of International Politics* (Boston: McGraw-Hill, 1979); John J. Mearsheimer, 'Back to the Future: Instability in Europe after the Cold War', *International Security*, 15 (1990), 5–56.

31 Peter Gourevitch, 'The Second Image Reversed: The International Sources of Domestic Politics', *International Organization*, 32 (1978), 881-912, p. 881.

32 Thomas Risse-Kappen, 'Ideas Do Not Float Freely: Transnational Coalitions, Domestic Structures, and the End of the Cold War', *International Organization*, 48 (1994), p. 208 and *Bringing Transnational Relations Back in: Non-State Actors, Domestic Structures and International Institutions* (Cambridge University Press, 1995).

33 Robert D. Putnam, 'Diplomacy and Domestic Politics: The Logic of Two-Level Games', *International Organization*, 42 (1988), 427–60.

34 Anita Orbán, *Power, Energy, and the New Russian Imperialism*, PSI Reports (Westport, Conn: Praeger Security International, 2008) p. 177.

35 Gourevitch, 'The Second Image Reversed', p. 883.

pricing provide helpful indicators with which to establish the affect of intervening variables such as 'meddling' in the bargaining process.

In order to do so we must first understand the various outputs that determine price, and also the other related structural features of the trade in gas, such as take-or-pay and destination clauses, as briefly presented in the previous section. There is comparatively little literature on the gas markets of Central Europe and their contractual histories compared to that covering the Commonwealth of Independent States (CIS) countries or Russia,[36] or the development of Western European gas markets and the continental system more broadly.[37] Those that focus on CEE either cover energy security and the relationship with Russia at a transnational level or deal purely with domestic market structures.[38]

This gap provides space for a detailed analysis of policy direction in the countries under investigation here, as markets distinct from the CIS, through which Russia transits large amounts of its gas, and the high-consuming markets of Western Europe, which receive the bulk of it. In effect, and as will be further described later in Chapter 3, this let us think of the four case studies as representing a secondary transit space, often transiting more gas than they consume, and key in the era before Gazprom's subsea Nord Stream pipeline bridged the Baltic to serve the highly industrialised markets of Germany, France and Italy.

---

36 See: Katja Yafimava, *The Transit Dimension of EU Energy Security: Russian Gas Transit Across Ukraine, Belarus, and Moldova* (Oxford & New York: Oxford Institute for Energy Studies, 2011); Simon Pirani, Jonathan P.Stern, Katja Yafimava and Oxford Institute for Energy Studies, *The Russo- Ukrainian Gas Dispute of January 2009: A Comprehensive Assessment* (Oxford Institute for Energy Studies, 2009); James Henderson and Simon Pirani, eds., *The Russian Gas Matrix: How Markets Are Driving Change* (Oxford: Oxford Institute for Energy Studies, 2014); Thane Gustafson, *Wheel of Fortune: The Battle for Oil and Power in Russia* (Cambridge, Mass: Belknap Press of Harvard University Press, 2012).

37 See: Jean-Michel Glachant, Michelle Hallac and Miguel Vazquez, *Building Competitive Gas Markets in the EU* (Edward Elgar Publishing, 2013); M. Arentsen and R. Kunneke, *National Reforms in European Gas* (Gulf Professional Publishing, 2003); Sandu-Daniel Kopp, *Politics, Markets and EU Gas Supply Security: Case Studies of the UK and Germany* (Springer, 2015); Anna Cretì, *The Economics of Natural Gas Storage: A European Perspective* (Springer Science & Business Media, 2009).

38 See: Anita Orbán, *Power, Energy, and the New Russian Imperialism*, PSI Reports (Westport, Conn: Praeger Security International, 2008); Joanna Agnieszka Gorska, *Dealing with a Juggernaut: Analyzing Poland's Policy towards Russia ; 1989 - 2009* (Lanham: Rowman & Littlefield, 2010); Andrej Nosko, *Energy Security in Transition: Coping with Energy Import Dependence in the Czech Republic, Slovakia and Hungary*, CEU Political Science Department PhD Theses, 2013/2 (Budapest: CEU, Budapest College, 2013); and András Deák, 'Diversification in Hungarian Manner: The Gyurcsány Government's Energy Policy', *International Issues & Slovak Foreign Policy Affairs*, 15 (2006), 44-55.

In her work on the Polish-Russia relationship, including the energy vector, Gorska outlines the potential to expand analysis to include a Central European context, looking at how different states respond to a former hegemon.[39] In arguing how states prioritise energy security in CEE, Nosko identifies the need to look at state capture in the energy sector of transitional economies, examining three out of the four countries under review here.[40] Though this investigation maintains a distance from the machinations of elites within state structures, and though it chooses as its analytical lens the work of domestic structure and energy security theorists, rather than traditional foreign policy analysis deployed by other academics working on issues of energy security, this analysis seeks to occupy the space for further research recognised by both Gorska and Nosko in their own recent analyses.

Finally, literature on the contractual relationships between major suppliers and European consumers has been a relatively recent development with Stern's 2012-edited volume, which is understood to be the first comprehensive review of global gas pricing systems,[41] helping to spark further debate on the terms under which gas is sold in different markets areas. Since the rise of oil prices the debate over oil indexation and accompanying contract terms has been sharply polarised between major suppliers like Gazprom, which favour keeping oil- linkage in place, and consumers, who argue that the system is now defunct.[42] This debate is

---

39 Joanna Agnieszka Gorska, *Dealing with a Juggernaut: Analyzing Poland's Policy towards Russia; 1989 - 2009* (Lanham: Rowman & Littlefield, 2010), p. 187.

40 Andrej Nosko, *Energy Security in Transition: Coping with Energy Import Dependence in the Czech Republic, Slovakia and Hungary*, CEU Political Science Department PhD Theses, 2013/2 (Budapest: CEU, Budapest College, 2013), p. 226.

41 Jonathan Stern, ed., *The Pricing of Internationally Traded Gas* (Oxford & New York: Oxford Institute for Energy Studies, 2012).

42 The following papers help to outline the reasons for hub-indexation in LTCs. Jonathan Stern, 'Is There a Rationale for the Continuing Link to Oil Product Prices in Continental European Long Term Gas Contracts?', *Oxford Institute for Energy Studies*, 2007 <http://www.oxfordenergy.org/2007/04/is-there-a-rationale-for-the-continuing-link-to-oil-product-prices-in-continental-european-long-term-gas-contracts/> [accessed 5 August 2015]; Jonathan Stern and Howard Rogers, 'The Transition to Hub-Based Pricing in Continental Europe - A Response to Sergei Komlev of Gazprom Export', *Oxford Institute for Energy Studies* <http://www.oxfordenergy.org/2013/02/the-transition-to-hub-based-pricing-in-continental-europe-a-response-to-sergei-komlev-of-gazprom-export/> [accessed 28 August 2015; and Luca Franza, *Long-Term Gas Import Contracts in Europe: The Evolution in Pricing Mechanisms* (Clingendael International Energy Programme). Gazprom's position can best be inferred from the following two papers: Sergei Komlev, 'Pricing the "Invisible" Commodity' (Moscow, Contracts Structuring and Pricing Directorate, Gazprom Export, 2013) and A. A. Konoplyanik, 'Evolution of Gas Pricing in Continental Europe: A View From Russia - Modernization of Indexation Formulas versus Gas-to-Gas Competition', *Oil, Gas & Energy Law Journal (OGEL)*, 9 (2011) <https://www.ogel.org/article.asp?key=3077> [accessed 24 August 2015].

expanded upon in the third chapter of this investigation as it supplies a major contextual frame for this research and is a key explanatory factor in the divergence of policy on contract re-negotiations post-2009.

Theoretically, Neumann et al. outline an institutional economics approach to understanding gas contracts that interprets them "as a device to avoid the risk of opportunistic behaviour in transactions that involve high sunk investments," such as pipelines and upstream projects.[43] This illustrates that LTCs have been signed in the gas industry to avoid what Williamson and others have conceptualised since the 1970s as the 'hold-up' problem, whereby one party is forced to make investments in advance without being certain of returns, which in turn incentivises opportunistic behaviour from the counterparty.[44] In short, the Russian government's expense in exploiting its resources and providing the transportation infrastructure to reach the consumer cannot be recouped without the provision of contracts structured to ensure it enough profit and certainty in volumes. But, as Neumann et al. have noted, early discussions of gas contracts were based on the assumption of a regulated monopolistic industry, with contracts used to maintain "secure monopolistic rents."[45] New market realities question these assumptions, with competition now considered the best way to drive innovation and lower consumer costs. Additionally, the expense of Soviet-era infrastructure has now been largely recouped, calling into question the need for volume enshrining contracts pitched decades in advance.

Additionally, this work seeks to enforce a broader point about the 'energy weapon' thesis in the region, as defined with its component parts compartmentalised by Stegen.[46] Orttung and Overland argue that analysis of energy disputes suggests "that Russia has not sought to use the energy weapon against these [European] countries in a consistent manner over time," in part owing to a declining

---

43 Anne Neumann, Sophia Rüster and Christian von Hirschhausen, *Long-Term Contracts in the Natural Gas Industry – Literature Survey and Data on 426 Contracts (1965-2014)*, Data Documentation (Berlin: Deutsches Institut für Wirtschaftsforschung, 2015), p. 7.

44 Oliver E. Williamson, 'Transaction-Cost Economics: The Governance of Contractual Relations', *Journal of Law and Economics*, 22 (1979), 233–61.

45 Neumann, Rüster and von Hirschhausen, *Long-Term Contracts in the Natural Gas Industry*, p. 9. Gas pipelines themselves have been examined as infrastructure constituting a natural monopoly for the owner: Jeff D. Makholm, *The Political Economy of Pipelines: A Century of Comparative Institutional Development* (University of Chicago Press, 2012).

46 Analysed here: Karen Smith Stegen, 'Deconstructing the "Energy Weapon": Russia's Threat to Europe as Case Study', *Energy Policy*, Sustainability of Biofuels, 39 (2011), 6505–13.

toolbox with which it can act.[47] Yafimava has argued that only CIS markets have been affected by Russia's use of energy as leverage, further suggesting that an energy weapon threat to Europe is hollow.[48] However, it is necessary to formulate a broader definition of what an 'energy weapon' can be, beyond the simple ability of a supplier to use resources as political leverage through threats, price hikes or direct disruptions. This must take into account market-based aspects of the gas trade and how they might also be also used as instruments of leverage. Much of the debate on the 'energy weapon' is based on "perception rather than objective reality," according to Högselius,[49] which serves to neglect more nuanced measures such as 'gas dumping' and how the use of hydrocarbon exports divided the capitalist world during the Cold War era. These factors are returned to in Chapter 3.

In sum, the work addresses the puzzle of how a persistent differential in the price charged by Russia's state export monopoly Gazprom to different consumers of natural gas under comparable conditions has been determined by the arrangement of parties of in power in importer markets. It does this by looking at the composition of parties in power in each case study between the years 1989 and 2014 then links that with projected contractual volumes of gas from an original dataset to measure levels of dependence, using this as proxy for price.

The observed divergence in importer state policy is especially striking because EU membership and the assumed interdependence of globalised economies could lead observers to expect a convergence on gas policy as means to ensure open, universal access to a key industrial fuel. Yet, despite shared objectives, policy convergence between EU members on gas has been limited. The Energy Union initiative developed by the European Commission provides no joint gas purchasing body. This work recognises the conflicts at the heart of the gas trade: between price and security, between flexibility and reliability, and between the interests of consumers and of producers. It also recognises the position of Central Europe as caught 'between' the hub-based trading of Western Europe and the traditional oil-indexed LTC market structures of the once-captive East.

---

47 Robert W. Orttung and Indra Overland, 'A Limited Toolbox: Explaining the Constraints on Russia's Foreign Energy Policy', *Journal of Eurasian Studies*, 2 (2011), p. 81.

48 Katja Yafimava, 'European Energy Security and the Role of Russian Gas', *IAI Istituto Affari Internazionali*, 2016 <http://www.iai.it/en/pubblicazioni/european-energy-security-and-role-russian-gas> [accessed 27 January 2016].

49 Per Högselius, *Red Gas: Russia and the Origins of European Energy Dependence* (New York: Palgrave, 2013), p. 221.

1.3 Structure

This book is split across eight chapters. The first – of which this segment is a part – serves to outline the central tenants of the argument, its rationale and its line of investigation, while briefly reviewing the literature within which it is anchored and identifying the research gap. Chapter two presents the model that makes clear the processes and hypotheses that will be identified and tested in each case study chapter later on. It also explores the theoretical base of this thesis in literature on domestic structure and party politics. A methodology is also presented, employing process tracing, while definitions are set and the data used in this analysis is introduced. Importantly, this second chapter also includes an exploration of the four case studies under analysis, justifying why they were chosen and why they are prime candidates for analysis.

Chapter three presents the energy specific background conditions, helping to set their antecedent conditions in context while constructing a top-down portrait of the Soviet system-building exercises of the 1960s and 1970s that created what Yafimava appropriated from Castells to term the 'space of flows.'[50] It also includes a review of the international gas market, and, in so far as it exists as a unitary environment, its structure and dominant features, as well as the factors that have "prepared the grounds for a fundamental change in the European gas market and for incumbent pricing models," according to Goldthau.[51] The European market and its key characteristics are also discussed in detail. This chapter closes by reviewing the development of gas contracts and the major argument between those who wish to see oil-indexation maintained and those who believe that increasing gas-on-gas competition in price formation is inevitable.

Chapters four, five, six and seven are empirical analyses devoted to each of the case studies: Poland, the Czech Republic, Slovakia and Hungary. Each begins with an introduction to the market structure during the final years of the period of

---

50 Katja Yafimava, *The Transit Dimension of EU Energy Security: Russian Gas Transit Across Ukraine, Belarus, and Moldova* (Oxford & New York: Oxford Institute for Energy Studies, 2011), p. 32. Castells's original concept dealt with new digital forms of spatial arrangement created by the development of technology in the late 1980s and early 1990s. Manuel Castells, *The Informational City: Information Technology, Economic Restructuring, and the Urban-Regional Process* (Oxford: Blackwell Publishers, 1989).

51 Andreas Goldthau, *The Politics of Natural Gas Development in the European Union* (Harvard University's Belfer Center, October 2013) <http://belfercenter.ksg.harvard.edu/files/MO-CES-pub-GeoGasEU-102513.pdf> [accessed 12 May 2015], p. 8.

investigation, 1989 – 2014. They continue as a chronological narrative, elucidating the development of gas contracts from the early Yamburg and Orenburg intergovernmental agreements reached during the Soviet era through to the commercialisation of the gas trade in the 1990s and onwards into the 2000s, up to 2014. These chapters form an integrated portrait of each national gas market and the major changes that brought about negotiation of gas supply arrangements either with the dominant supplier or with new players. Each chapter concludes with a review of the process tracing employed and a discussion of the data collected on gas contracts, total contracted volumes year-by-year, and how this data fits into the broader demand picture.

Chapter eight deals with the analysis. It tests the hypotheses based on the model presented in the second chapter and the data set forth in the case study chapters, using the theory, variables and methodology laid out earlier. It also seeks to make broader conclusions about the structure of the gas market in each case study country, and how this has affected the relationship with the dominant supplier.

Finally, chapter nine concludes with a review of the findings, while suggesting routes for further research and briefly discussing policy developments and proposals in the period following the conclusion of the period of analysis in 2014.

The central argument is that left-wing governments prioritise cooperation with the dominant supplier over the pursuit of diversification measures, and that right-wing governments seek energy security–boosting measures like multiple supply options. This helps explain the price differential. Additionally, it is argued here that state-owned utilities tend to favour short- term price discounts over long-term contract re-structuring while re-negotiating existing LTC arrangements with the dominant supplier. An important distinction is also made between the behaviour of state-run utilities and their privately- owned counterparts in the bargaining process through which gas contracts are agreed and re-negotiated. An explanation of the theoretical framework, methodological process and explanatory structure of this work is included in the following chapter.

2 Research design

The central hypothesis is that, whilst import-dependent states under left-wing governments seek to cooperate with the already dominant supplier (Gazprom), right-wing governments are more likely to prioritise energy security–boosting measures, such as new contracts and infrastructure initiatives undertaken with non-Russian suppliers. Because of this, right-wing governments can be shown to have pursued diversification measures in contracts with new suppliers, and also to have proceeded with infrastructure development plans linking their markets with new production centres. Left-wing governments can likewise be shown to have pursued new contracts with Gazprom instead of new suppliers.

This argument is presented while drawing on literature on domestic structure and energy security discourse, and institutional economics also helps us to unpack the LTC black box and explain the bargaining process through which contracts are structured. A model is deployed overleaf to illustrate the units and level of analysis, with the intention of acting as a prism through which the relationship between parties in government (independent variable) and dependence on a single supplier (dependent variable) can be understood.

A general theoretical explanation for the phenomenon of persistent price differentials between neighbouring markets in CEE is that gas exporters, who sell at different rates to different countries, seeking to maximise profits, engender dependency structures that incentivise governments to intervene in contractual negotiations as a means of achieving price reductions and formula amendments. This transfers the issue of commodity trade to the political sphere and produces issue-linkage (pipeline deals, trade concessions, support in international negotiations etc.). Over time, the specific conditions of each country's bilateral supply arrangements diverge, which perpetuates the cycle of differential pricing and allows the supplier to 'divide-and-rule' in neighbouring markets.

A specific explanation for the phenomenon is as follows:

J. Posaner, *Held Captive by Gas*, Energiepolitik und Klimaschutz. Energy Policy and Climate Protection, https://doi.org/10.1007/978-3-658-27518-1_2

(i) Gazprom sells gas to consumers that rely on imports to meet annual demand and have little or no access to alternatives. It seeks to maximise its profits, and hence sells at different prices to different countries.
(ii) Dependency structures develop between supplier and consumer, conditioned by the physical nature of gas and its transport restrictions, in addition to the take-or-pay commitments embedded in contracts.
(iii) Consumer countries often respond to dependency by seeking to maximise their agency through the importing utility that executes the LTC. They seek (mostly temporary) discounts, often linked to other political objectives, such as infrastructure developments, trade concessions, extension of importing obligation, etc.
(iv) Over time, the specific conditions of each country's bilateral supply arrangements diverge, which perpetuates the cycle of differential pricing and allows the supplier to 'divide-and-rule' in neighbouring markets.

Figure 1 presents the central argument and the variables, using the final 'dependence on a single supplier' scale as a proxy for price: the more dependent, the higher the price, it is argued.

The government of the gas-importing state is the independent variable (IV), establishing the policy drivers of the incumbent executive by their right/left position along the political spectrum, as defined from electoral agendas. A sub- process of privatisation subverts the chain by restricting the impact of government policy drivers on utility behaviour. A state-owed gas importer under various types of government ownership and a privately-owned utility are assumed to behave under different motives in the bargaining process through which a contract with a supplier of gas is negotiated. The output is that each of the different forms of ownership leads to various patterns of dependence on the existing dominant supplier as the dependent variable (DV). A utility under a left- wing government tends toward dependence on the dominant supplier, under a right-wing government less, and under private ownership to a marginal extent.

The first conditional variable (CV1) in this model is the level of state control over the utility. This determines to what extent the state can use the gas-importing agency to pursue its interests, and whether it exercises authority over its decision-making process. The beginning of each case study chapter presents a detailed overview of the market and ownership structure of key gas companies, including the

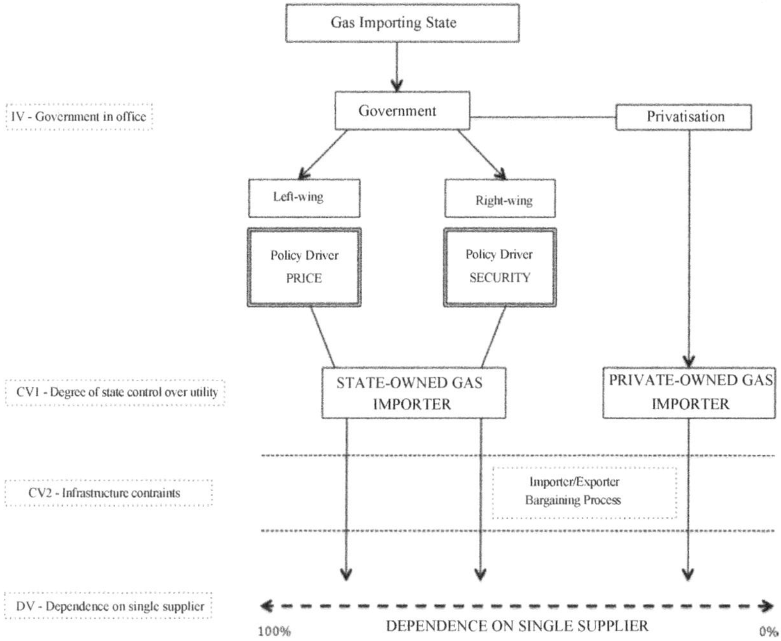

Figure 1: Gas contract negotiation model

level of state management of the importing agency. The second conditional variable (CV2) is infrastructure constraints. These restrict the ability of an importer to negotiate with suppliers, leaving available only existing supply routes or the construction of new delivery systems. Each case study chapter also provides a review of the available infrastructure in each case study country, including volumes of cross-border pipeline capacity and storage inventories as a means of holding gas.

In conclusion, it is argued that dependence on the dominant supplier is related to the price charged to the importer. As shown in Table 2, the higher the dependence, the higher the cost of gas imports, with some of Europe's most Gazprom LTC–dependent countries paying the most for their gas stocks in the explanatory period 2010 to 2014, post-2009 crisis. In this table each of the case study countries is highlighted in yellow and the highest and lowest–charged countries per year are underscored. Only in 2011 and 2014 do the rates for two countries from the case studies under analysis fall beneath the average charged to European importers, with explanatory reasons provided later in the case study chapters. The range between the cheapest and highest over the five-year period widened from $111 in 2010 to $225 in 2012, as shown in Graph 6, as the already disparately structured pricing mechanisms in contracts were variously amended during the period of re-negotiations illustrated in Table 1.

Table 2: Wholesale price for Gazprom imports in $/mcm (2010–2014)[1]

Country	2010	2011	2012	2013	2014
Slovakia	371	333	428	438	308
Germany	270	379	353	366	323
Austria	305	387	394	402	329
Switzerland	296	400	333	378	333
Hungary	350	383	416	418	338
France	306	399	398	404	338
Italy	331	410	438	399	341
Denmark	-	480	394	382	341
Finland	273	358	373	367	354
Netherlands	308	366	346	400	362
Turkey	326	381	416	382	366
Bosnia & Herzegovina	339	429	500	421	375
Czech Republik	326	419	500	400	378
Poland	331	420	433	429	379
Serbia	341	432	405	386	382
Bulgaria	311	356	435	394	388
Romania	325	390	424	387	394
Slovenia	312	377	400	396	395
Greece	359	414	475	469	400
Macedonia	381	462	558	493	483
AVERAGE	305.33	383.38	401.74	386.67	345.88

1 Alexey Novikov, *TABLE: How Prices Fell for Russian Gas* (Interfax, 6 March 2015). In this table both the most expensive and cheapest paying countries are underlined, and the case studies highlighted. The Baltic states are not included, as Gazprom publishes results for those countries separately. The figures are sourced from *Interfax* reporting in Moscow, from analysis of Gazprom financial reports and earning statements. Gazprom itself does not comment on the veracity of pricing intelligence, yet the figures published by *Interfax* are widely cited by the industry and resemble the findings of Russian newspaper *Investia* for the first half of 2012. 'Больше всех в Европе «Газпрому» платят македонцы и поляки', *Известия* <http://izvestia.ru/news/544100> [accessed 20 July 2015]. The five-year sample period used is the only available comparable data on gas pricing between different European importers.

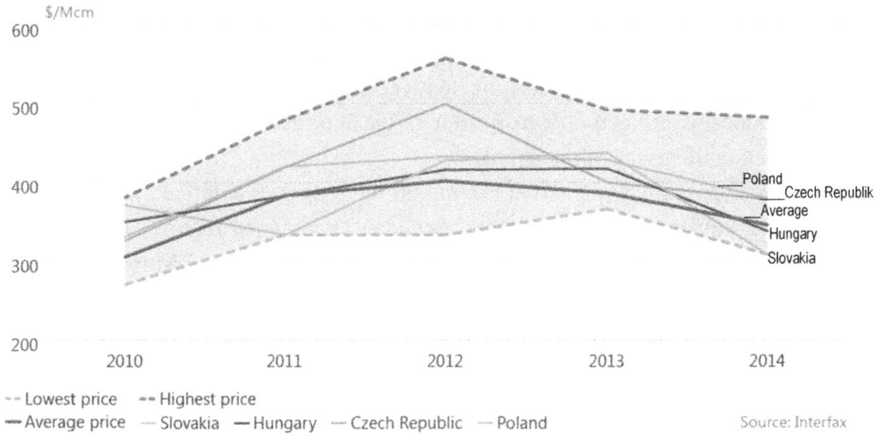

Graph 6: Range of Gazprom export prices to Europe $/mcm (2010–2014)[2]

2.1 Potential explanations

Before embarking on a full exposition of the research structure, it is also important to address alternative possible explanations for the phenomena by which governments seek further dependence on the already dominant supplier, despite relative losses in energy security and price. Though none provide a more convincing case for explaining differing policy approaches than domestic structure, they do exist. One alternative argument is that government policy is limited by transnational factors, which sideline the domestic structure element. Such an argument would rely on the assumption that external pressures force government decisions over whom to sign new contracts with and under what terms. As of yet, EU member states have been unwilling to cede responsibility for dealing with energy imports to a supranational entity, although previous talk of the Caspian Development Corporation (CDC) and more contemporary plans for a joint purchasing body as part of

2 *ibid.* The green average line running so low within the range indicates how ballooning prices in 2012 were unusual within the 20 states for which data is available. The Czech Republic and Poland were in the club of importers that saw their rate rise by more than $100 in the two-year period.

the Energy Union initiative have hinted at such a prospect.[3] Likewise, the dominant supplier has as of yet been unable to enforce purchases of its gas beyond contracted terms agreed to in advance with consumers bilaterally under LTC. Nor have producers yet been able to form a cartel like 'gas OPEC' that could effectively dictate the terms of the supply.[4]

Another possible explanation relying on internal over external considerations is that the Soviet legacy meant that descendant communist regime elites in each case study country had an incentive to pursue new contracts with Moscow for personal gain. Although the continued presence of communist-era politicians within the power structures of post-communist countries in the 1990s potentially played a part in different approaches to gas supply, the phenomena is ill-defined and would regardless likely feed into the policy behaviour of left-wing governments who, in general, acted as legacy parties in the transition period. Processes of lustration, and lack of, have also been used to determine how former elites were able to influence energy policy formation during the 1990s.[5]

One additional domestic structure–based explanation is that the length of LTC agreements – often 20 years – limits the potential for a change of government to determine the terms of its imports. Proponents of this argument would posit that dependence levels are in effect pre-programmed under the government that agrees

---

3 The CDC was designed as a means of enabling the export of gas from Turkmenistan to Europe under a joint purchasing framework. World Bank, *Caspian Development Corporation: Final Implementation Report* (The World Bank, 1 December 2010), pp. 1–155. <http://documents.worldbank.org/curated/en/2010/12/16286570/caspian-development-corporation-final-implementation-report> [accessed 1 February 2016]. Under early proposals for the EU's Energy Union concept, member states would jointly purchase gas as a means of ensuring equal pricing and security for all. Although it received support from some states led by Poland, the proposal was scrapped after objections from larger member states like Germany.

4 The Gas-Exporting Countries Forum (GECF) described itself as an "an international governmental organization which provides the framework for exchanging experience and information among [...] the world's leading gas producers." It was for a time discussed as the 'gas OPEC' but has not taken on such a prominent role in global trade. <https://www.gecf.org/about/overview.aspx> [accessed 8 June 2016].

5 An account of the process of lustration in each CEE country, and how Bulgaria opted against, is given here: Anders Aslund and Simeon Djankov, *The Great Rebirth: Lessons from the Victory of Capitalism over Communism* (Washington DC: Peterson Institute for International Economics, 2014), pp. 144 - 145. Nosko deals with the process of lustration in some of these countries and its determining role in the prioritisation of energy security: Andrej Nosko, *Energy Security in Transition: Coping with Energy Import Dependence in the Czech Republic, Slovakia and Hungary*, CEU Political Science Department PhD Theses, 2013/2 (Budapest: CEU, Budapest College, 2013).

the LTC and subsequently, through successive election cycles, until the contract expires, often 20 years later. This argument relies on the assumption that a change in government is ineffectual in determining gas contract arrangements unless they come up for renewal during its administration. However, the ability to re-negotiate contracts at regular intervals, as will be discussed later, along with procedures for transferring disputes to arbitration courts, if not resolved within six-month windows, provides the means through which government policy can translate into contractual amendments and at least some material change to levels of dependence during typical multi-year electoral cycles. Furthermore, demonstrable and constructive support for infrastructure initiatives that provide a route for non-Russian gas can also be interpreted as a commitment to amending the level of dependence in favour of alternative suppliers.

Dealing more comprehensively with the issue of gas contract re-negotiations, Figure 2 illustrates the secondary process through which contract revisions are made using the 2009-2014 data shown in Table 1. Each of the three lower boxes represents a stage of the re-negotiation process and a point at which a settlement can be reached. The first is a simple supplier discount offered to a consumer on a temporary basis, the second is an arbitration case usually ending before a ruling through an out-of-court-settlement, and the third result is a full court ruling. This process once again suggests a difference in importer behaviour along utility ownership lines between the case study countries in the region. Hungarian and Czech gas companies partly or wholly owned by Gazprom chose to accept a supplier discount during the 2010 to 2014 period, while state-owned enterprises from Poland and Slovakia applied for full arbitration proceedings before settling out of court. Only privately-held Czech importer RWE Supply & Trading pushed arbitration to a ruling, with significant results, as will be discussed in the Czech Republic case study chapter.

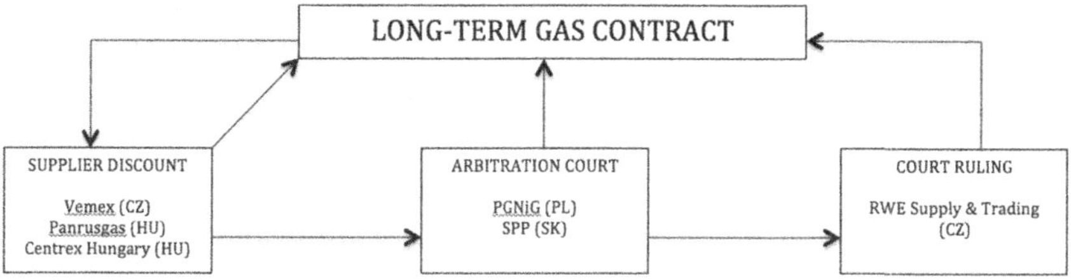

Figure 2: Process of LTC re-negotiations with Gazprom (2009–2014)

Both the analysis of a primary process of initial contract negotiation, as shown in Figure 1, and this secondary follow-up re-negotiation process for the post-2009 period under review point to a trend through which different government policies feed into varying responses to the dominant supplier in the process of gas contract formation. Though alternative explanations exist for the phenomenon of price differentials, they do not adequately account for the role of *internal political factors*, with which this work concerns itself. However, to deal with the behaviour of the importing agency, rather than the exporter, some assumptions need to be made about the behaviour of the latter – in this case Gazprom – that allow us to calibrate the transnational contextual conditions.

Here, Russia's export monopoly is conceptualised as a utility maximiser, seeking to fulfil its organisational purpose as a profit-seeking state-administered company that exports gas for revenue, which serves to swell the Russian state budget. Therefore, in this inquiry, we assume that Gazprom wished to maximise its sales into each case-study market and also maintain the highest possible profit margins for doing so over the course of the period under investigation. Such a strategy required Gazprom to act to maintain an already dominant market share and also seek to structure contracts in such a way as to guarantee it could "secure monopolistic rents," as discussed above in reference to Neumann et al.[6] Also relevant is that Gazprom is assumed to seek to maintain the current status quo in contract formation. State-ownership and the geopolitical premium attached to the supply of gas to former Soviet satellite states further complicate the trading relationship, but each of the assumptions still holds – only the levers the exporting party uses to achieve its utility are augmented, feeding back into discussions on political 'meddling' that will be returned to in Chapter 3.

CEE importers, despite an incentive to use aggregated market power to force better terms from the supplier, took diverging policy directions on gas between 1989 and 2014. Shared experiences of transition to democracy, joint accessions to institutions like the EU and NATO, and broadly equally allocated risk in the 'secondary gas transit space' have not precipitated policy convergence on gas. Neither have they encouraged cooperation between capitals on a scale necessary to effect change in the norms of LTC supply arrangements. Instead, the case studies

6 Anne Neumann, Sophia Rüster and Christian von Hirschhausen, *Long-Term Contracts in the Natural Gas Industry – Literature Survey and Data on 426 Contracts (1965-2014)*, Data Documentation (Deutsches Institut für Wirtschaftsforschung, 2015) p. 9.

remained divided in 2014 as Russia annexed the Crimean peninsula and security of gas supply again returned to the top of policymakers' agendas the following winter. Some governments opted to push ahead with new westward pipeline links, while others chose to strengthen ties with the dominant supplier. It is this regionalised puzzle that requires attention in order to draw conclusions as to why a price differential has persisted both within these markets and between the case study countries and their EU neighbours. This work aims to find out why some states, under comparable conditions, pay more for their imports, and to ask whether the terms under which gas is supplied are equitable. Answers are to be found not only in the policies of the post-2009 era, where divergence can most clearly be observed, but also in the transition to commercial contracts in the early 1990s.

2.2 Theoretical framework

This investigation deploys a theoretical framework related to the understanding of domestic structure and its causal effect on the international system and the trade in gas between countries. Here, a number of literature strands are relevant: firstly, work dealing with how domestic structure comes to shape practices at the transnational level where gas contracts are formalised; secondly, literature on party cleavages within the region under investigation, which is relevant to understanding how right and left–leaning governments behave and can be defined. This section deals with these two areas of literature briefly in the following sub-sections, with further investigation of energy security and gas market–specific texts to be found in later chapters.

This analysis seeks to add to the literature on energy security and how governments approach the thorny issue of contract formation with external suppliers of resources. Over recent decades, this strand of sector-specific literature has transitioned from a focus on the trade in oil products to risk evaluation strategies that have taken a holistic view of the energy system. Energy security discourse and institutional economics approaches to contract formation specifically are dealt with in the following chapter as part of the presentation of background conditions related to this research.

Bridging the divide between theory and reality is the constant struggle of the social scientist. As Kenneth Waltz has argued, "explanation, not prediction, is the ultimate criterion of good theory." He has argued that theory's role is to illuminate strands of independence and interdependence, which this analysis aims to do in showing how domestic political systems shape energy security policy- making. "Theory," Waltz writes, "rather than being a mirror in which reality is reflected, is an instrument to be used in attempting to explain a circumscribed part of a reality of whose true dimensions we can never be sure."[7] This investigation seeks to determine to what extent political parties' prioritisation of security in the energy sector comes to determine the price a country pays for its gas.

2.2.1 Domestic structure

Literature covering the flow of influence between the domestic structure and the international system identifies a reflexive relationship in which the internal composition of the state comes to define, and be defined by, the global community within which it sits. Waltz's presentation of a 'second image level' in his 1959 text *Man, the State and War* looks at how the ideological nature of a state's internal composition defines its behaviour as a foreign policy actor.[8] Early investigation into domestic structure in international politics often sought to locate an internal source for foreign policy actions that could help explain what factors caused states to engage in war. Otto Hintze argued in the early twentieth century that "throughout the ages pressure from without has been a determining influence on internal structure" – a pre–World War iteration of the open door between state policy and systemic international pressures.[9]

Henry Kissinger also recognised how the internal characteristics of a state apparatus helped define the landscape externally, writing in 1966 that "the domestic structure crucially affects the way the actions of other states are interpreted."[10] However, reversing Waltz's lens in a landmark 1978 paper, Gourevitch proposed the international system as an intervening variable helping to shape domestic structures within the state. His work pitched the international system as "not only a consequence of domestic politics and structures but a cause of them."[11] Two principle aspects of the international system could affect the character of domestic

---

7 Kenneth N. Waltz, 'Evaluating Theories', *The American Political Science Review*, 91 (1997) 913-917, p. 913.

8 Kenneth N. Waltz, *Man, the State and War: A Theoretical Analysis* (New York: Columbia University Press, 1959).

9 Otto Hintze, *The Historical Essays of Otto Hintze* (Oxford: Oxford University Press, 1975), p. 183.

10 Henry A. Kissinger, 'Domestic Structure and Foreign Policy', *Daedalus*, 95 (1966), p. 504.

11 Peter Gourevitch, 'The Second Image Reversed: The International Sources of Domestic Politics', *International Organization*, 32 (1978), 881-912, p. 911.

regimes, Gourevitch argued: the distribution of power amongst states and the distribution of economic activity and wealth.[12]

An uneven distribution of natural resources effectively defines the case study countries under review here as import dependent, tying their economic success to their ability to source imports from resource-rich countries at a reasonable price. During the 1970s, work to boost understanding of domestic structure in international relations and trade policy moved forward. In a 1977 paper, Katzenstein found differences between various states' foreign economic strategies to be a product of two factors – domestic structures and the international context – while articulating the central problem that "the main purpose of all strategies of foreign economic policy is to make domestic politics compatible with the international political economy."[13] He included energy policy in an earlier analysis, noting that "the consistency and the content of foreign economic policies result at least as much from the constraints of domestic structures as from the functional logic inherent in international effects."[14] Thus, government policy is not directly moulded in response to the character of the issue at stake, but rather by the constraints present in the domestic structure itself.

Both Katzenstein and Krasner, in his own work, also recognised that policy makers had to be constantly addressing two constituencies: the internal and external. Krasner identifies that "some catalytic external event seems necessary to move states to dramatic policy initiatives in line with state interests," rather than day-to-day political routine internally providing its own impetus for great change.[15] Putman's fluid interpretation of the interaction between the international and the domestic structures argues that addressing either the second image level or its reversal in isolation can only lead to "partial equilibrium" and "would miss an important part of the story, namely, how the domestic politics of several countries became entangled via an international negotiation."[16] Putman's 1988 'two-level game'

---

12 *ibid.*, p. 883.

13 Peter J. Katzenstein, 'Introduction: Domestic and International Forces and Strategies of Foreign Economic Policy', *International Organization*, 31 (1977), 587-606, p. 587.

14 Peter J. Katzenstein, 'International Relations and Domestic Structures: Foreign Economic Policies of Advanced Industrial States', *International Organization*, 30 (1976), 1-45, p. 2.

15 Stephen D. Krasner, 'State Power and the Structure of International Trade', *World Politics*, 28 (1976), 317-347, p. 341.

16 Robert D. Putnam, 'Diplomacy and Domestic Politics: The Logic of Two-Level Games', *International Organization*, 42 (1988), 427–460, p. 430.

recognised that politicians seek power by building coalitions of domestic groups that in turn seek to ensure their interests are met in the international system.

In this theory, each political leader sits "at both game boards." At the international board they sit across from their foreign counterpart flanked by diplomats and advisers, while at the domestic board they are surrounded by parliamentarians, regulators, agency chiefs, and interest groups, each promoting their own interests against a backdrop of public opinion.[17] Institutions can also play a role in this process, and more recently Risse-Kappen has proposed an approach that seeks to measure how external actors can mould policy on a given issue in a particular 'target state' through institutional structures. The more the policy area is regulated by transnational institutions, his theory claims, the more porous state boundaries become and the more 'foreign' actors become indistinguishable from 'domestic' players.[18] Though this analysis does not deal with regulatory regimes, this theory provides a useful way of understanding how domestic structure can be prone to outside influence.

While the second image level and Gourevitch's reversal are useful analytical tools taken on here, it was Putman who provided a way of understanding the dynamic interchange between each image level. Though challenging for policymakers to handle their interests at home and abroad, he noted that strategic opportunities also abound for leaders adept at balancing their internal and external audiences.[19] This too points to a greater plurality within the domestic structure. Earlier research used as its central domestic structure variable predominantly the concentration of power within a state, i.e. the executive. This put analytic weight on a static instrument not prone to regular changes. Hence, if the 'state' is going to be used to ascribe policy making power, it should instead be used as a plural noun, as Lipson and Cohen point out.[20] The myriad and constantly evolving environment of parties, interest groups and advisers is a better explanation for the nature of the state structure than its relative consolidation of power at the top.

---

17 *ibid.*, p. 434.

18 Thomas Risse-Kappen, *Bringing Transnational Relations Back In: Non-State Actors, Domestic Structures and International Institutions* (Cambridge University Press, 1995) p. 32.

19 Putnam, 'Diplomacy and Domestic Politics', p. 460.

20 Charles Lipson and Benjamin J. Cohen, *Theory and Structure in International Political Economy: An International Organization Reader* (MIT Press, 1999) p. 352.

2.2.2 *Party cleavages*

Within the vision of a plural domestic structure explained above exist various political parties split across cleavages of electoral agendas. Cleavages should be recognised as "lines of salient social and ideological division at a mass level" that through differences in society translate into "political competition and party choice," according to Whitefield's definition.[21] Once a government is in office, these differences should manifest themselves in various policy approaches, whether they are motivated by conservative, liberal, religious, or other ideologies. Some scholars have argued that cleavages have not been present in the former Soviet space, and that Central European systems of competitive party politics have been inherently unstable, undermining efforts to plot clear delineated cleavages over the relatively short incubation period from 1989 to 2014.

Concerns have centred on whether parties in the region have become institutionalised enough to support fixed cleavages, and whether new emergent parties have had the time to consolidate and stabilise quickly enough to create a so-called 'freezing point' that crystallises into a political system from which such divides can be observed over a period of time.[22] Lipset and Rokkan argued that, while in Western Europe 1920 cleavages still resembled those found in the 1960s,[23] the period of socialist dominion over the countries of CEE up to 1989 allows us no such historical depth of reference. As Sitter discussed in his attempt to transfer Lipset and Rokkan's model to CEE, cleavages relevant to the study of the region have been hard to establish.[24] This is despite many shared characteristics having been noticeable in the countries' concurrent transitions to democracy, including the experience of each major party participating in a coalition government at some point in the 1990s and of a tendency for voters to kick out rather than re-elect incumbents at polling time.[25]

---

21 Stephen Whitefield, 'Political Cleavages and Post-Communist Politics', *Annual Review of Political Science*, 5 (2002), 181–200, p. 187.

22 On Poland and its electoral cleavages in the immediate post-Soviet era, see: P.G. Lewis, 'Political Institutionalisation and Party Development in Post-Communist Poland', in *Europe-Asia Studies*, 46(5), 1994, 779-799.

23 As reported in Peter Mair, *Party System Change: Approaches and Interpretations* (Oxford: Clarendon Press, 1997), p. 57.

24 Nick Sitter, 'Cleavages, Party Strategy and Party System Change in Europe, East and West', *Perspectives on European Politics and Society*, 2002, p. 433

25 In the period 1990 to 2000 there were no less than nine governments in Poland, five in the Czech Republic, including one caretaker administration, five in Hungary and, from its independence in 1992, four in Slovakia.

As Whitefield noted about Central Europe specifically, "political cleavages have emerged in each state across the region that reflect the country's historical inheritances as well as its post-communist economic and social experiences."[26] Grzymala-Busse wrote in her own analysis of regional party political structures shortly after the millennium that coalitions in the countries under investigation here are "as diverse as they are puzzling" largely owing to the idiosyncrasies of post-authoritarian transitions.[27] She noted a regime divide between former communist legacy parties and those representing the opposition, with it being unlikely that an anti-communist party thrust into government in the 1990s would enter into coalition with the former dominant rulers for fear of losing electoral favour. In effect, this removed some coalition building blocks from the potential possibilities, distinguishing the region's politics from its western neighbours'.

Nevertheless, Whitefield saw Central Europe's cleavage structure as more closely resembling Germany or Austria than those observed in Russia and Ukraine and has discussed political competition in the region as being a contest across an axis "of support for and opposition to liberalism."[28] Kitschelt proposed that the division between economic populism and market liberalism is paramount in his 1995 analysis, though he has also remarked that the formation of clear left/right cleavages would also depend on the use of national identity–related factors deployed by some parties.[29] Sitter's study found that the development of "competitive multi-party systems in East Central Europe has been driven by the contest between parties to define the postcommunist 'right'." Specifically, this entailed competition between liberal free market parties and Christian nationalists challenging each other, while the 'left' was more easily defined as a continuation of the regime/opposition division of the transition period.[30]

---

26 Whitefield, 'Political Cleavages and Post-Communist Politics', 183.

27 Anna Grzymala-Busse, 'Coalition Formation and the Regime Divide in New Democracies: East Central Europe', *Comparative Politics*, 34 (2001), 85-104, p. 85 "At a time when ideological and policy stances were often either vague or contradictory, the most easily identifiable parliamentary cleavage was between parties of the opposition and parties stemming from the former regime," p. 87.

28 Whitefield, 'Political Cleavages and Post-Communist Politics', p. 185. Elsewhere, Whitefield also writes that the "countries of Central Europe resemble France, Austria, or Germany in the character of their political divisions much more than they resemble Russia or Ukraine." p. 197

29 Herbert Kitschelt, 'Formation of Party Cleavages in Post-Communist Democracies Theoretical Propositions', *Party Politics*, 1 (1995), 447-472.

30 Sitter, 'Cleavages, Party Strategy and Party System Change in Europe, East and West', p. 447.

Sitter's system for differentiating political ideologies of parties in CEE is taken up later as a guide in addressing party positions. However, it is also necessary to recognise the rapid development of new parties on both the right and the left as "a combination of personality politics and weakly institutionalised parties"[31] – this led to shifts in numbers of competitive parties, especially on the right.[32] This makes the representative party of most prominence on either side of the cleavage fluid across the 25-year period of inquiry. Also, periphery parties that drew on niche interests pitched against the administrative core, though largely only fleetingly successful, have also played a role as regular junior coalition partners. Such is the case with the Polish Peasants' Party.

Beyond party politics, it is also important to recognise the role played by the government in managing its institutions and agencies. Rittberger's analysis of German foreign policy since 1991 looks to a concept of administrative interest intermediation that links policymakers and the interests of private companies. This argues that private actors will be able to influence the policymaking process if they are able to provide resources in return – for example, legitimacy – to incumbent governments. The less the private entity is needed to fulfil a policymaker's organisational purpose, however, the less access it will have to the policy making process.[33] If it can be assumed that a government seeks to ensure its own survival and re-election, then it is also likely to seek to use a utility that it owns to assist it in that function and to provide lower retail prices to consumers.

The divide in behaviour between how right and left wing governments approach foreign trade relations is more difficult to define. Though considerable coverage in the field of political economy addresses trade policy generally, the role of domestic structure and its influence on transnational trade in energy products is only partially covered. Literature on the relative power of states within the international economic system leads us to conclude that trade policy should be determined by whether a state is a 'small-power' or 'a hegemon,' according to Katzenstein. He recognizes that the main aim of a state's foreign economic policy is "to make domestic policy compatible with the international political economy,"[34] and

31 *ibid.*, p. 446.
32 *ibid.* Sitter notes this had a greater effect in the Polish and Slovak political systems.
33 Volker Rittberger, *German Foreign Policy since Unification: Theories and Case Studies*, Issues in German Politics (Manchester: Manchester University Press, 2001), p. 93.
34 Peter J. Katzenstein, *Between Power and Plenty: Foreign Economic Policies of Advanced Industrial States* (University of Wisconsin Press, 1977), p. 4.

in looking at how advanced economies diverged in their responses to the OPEC supply cut, Katzenstein posed an important question: "why, in the face of a common threat, did the strategies of advanced industrial states differ so much?"[35] His answer is to point to the stresses and strains within the domestic structure, and to assess the interplay between state and industrial interests. Milner provides a way of understanding the interaction between a distribution of interests and decision-making power in presenting how international cooperation agreements function.[36] However, this still does not tackle the thorny issue of coalition-building and bargaining within parliamentary republics, or how a former vassal reacts to its old hegemon in trade.

Right-wing governments have been illustrated to have consistently taken more free trade stances than left-wing parties in power, according to Milner and Judkins, and they recognise a general differentiation that "left-wing parties prefer policies that increase government spending and induce growth, while right ones favor policies that induce lower spending, balanced budgets, and lower inflation."[37] This more general understanding of right and left gives this analysis a framework through which to judge general trade behaviour between left and right parties.

Political alignments here along the right-left spectrum are made based on the centre of gravity in each distinct case study, rather than as calibrated on a comparative basis between the four. For the left it is relatively straight forward, with each case study's political arena containing a reformed communist legacy party on the left in the period of transition, whether that be MSZP in Hungary, SDL in Slovakia, SLD in Poland or ČSSD in the Czech Republic. Set against that, Sitter's distinction of a divide within the right, between those embracing free markets and those of a traditional Christian conservative inclination, provides the basis for a split in this work's representation of the right along the cleavage scale.[38] Therefore, the reformist parties of the centre right are incorporated into a centrist-conservative category based on their relative openness to reforms and to free markets in comparison

[35] Peter J. Katzenstein, 'Conclusion: Domestic Structures and Strategies of Foreign Economic Policy', *International Organization*, 31 (1977), 879–920, p. 880.

[36] Helen V. Milner, *Interests, Institutions, and Information: Domestic Politics and International Relations* (Princeton, NJ: Princeton University Press, 1997). In Chapter 3 a model is presented that seeks to explain the domestic structure in relation to bargaining in the international system.

[37] Helen V. Milner and Benjamin Judkins, 'Partisanship, Trade Policy, and Globalization: Is There a Left-Right Divide on Trade Policy?', *International Studies Quarterly*, 48 (2004), p. 95.

[38] Nick Sitter, 'Cleavages, Party Strategy and Party System Change in Europe, East and West', *Perspectives on European Politics and Society*, 2002, 425–51, p. 437.

to the incumbent right-wing within their own party systems – for example, Civic Platform can be seen as a liberal alternative to Law and Justice in Poland, and the SDKÚ-DS as a similarly reformist yet still conservative alternative to the preceding HZDS government's in Slovakia.

In sum, this work deploys a heuristic theoretical framework that seeks to explain case-specific causal mechanisms for a persistent price differential in gas import costs not found in existing theoretical literature. By examining the way in which countries along the right/left political spectrum are observed to have pursued new gas supply LTCs with external suppliers over the 1989 to 2014 period, a relationship between politics and the trade in energy goods is proposed. How the two-tier game presents political leaders with opportunities in trade and how the domestic structure comes to project itself on the transnational system provide a useful framework for analysis. Through this lens, the domestic structure is a key explanatory variable in how states manage their relations with the states, and their agencies, on whom they depend for energy resources.

2.3 Methodology

This inquiry follows John Stuart Mill's 'method of difference': it employs four case studies with similar background characteristics but diverging studied variables to allow for identification of causal factors for why each pays different rates for their wholesale gas imports.[39] It selects the cases on the basis of the dependent variable (level of dependence on a single gas supplier) and the disparity in price paid by each country, and deploys a process-tracing technique in later chapters to find a causal mechanism for how different governments behave in regards to the dominant supplier. The hypotheses that this work seeks to test are as follows:

- H1: Left-wing governments tend to prioritise cooperation with already dominant suppliers of natural gas through LTCs, while right-wing governments seek security-boosting diversification measures (see Figure 1).
- H2: Left-wing governments are motivated to maintain downward pressure on retail prices for consumers, making lower wholesale costs a strategic priority. Right-wing governments seek greater supply security (see Figure 1).

---

[39] See John Stuart Mill, *A System of Logic, Ratiocinative and Inductive: Being a Connected View of the Principles of Evidence and the Methods of Scientific Investigation, Book II* (John W. Parker, 1843) p. 222.

- H3: In LTC re-negotiation processes, state-owned utilities under left-wing governments prioritise short-term price discounts over the structural change that right-wing governments and private utilities seek (see Figure 2).

If tested and proved, these hypotheses lead us to conclude that the domestic structures (parties and their policy programmes) come to determine the level of dependence on a single supplier as shown in Figure 1. As the inner workings of each LTC and its pricing formula are a persistent unknown, the dependent variable of level of dependence is used as a proxy for price. It is assumed, and illustrated further later in this manuscript, that in general the more dependent an importing country is, the higher the price it will pay for its imports. As shown in Graph 1 and Table 2, those states with dependence on Russian gas supply in excess of 50% of annual demand tend to pay prices higher than the European average. Furthermore, the secondary process of contract re-negotiations, as shown in Figure 2 and referenced in H3, illustrates how importing agencies under different governments in effect serve to prolong these dependency structures.

Methodologically, the case study approach undertaken here is as outlined by Van Evera and allows for a deeper study of a few cases rather than the superficial analysis of many.[40] Although it has been described as "barely better than journalism" by sociologists like Stoecker,[41] this method allows for the use of process tracing on selected cases chosen for their resemblance to the "background conditions of current policy problems."[42] As Lijphart has noted, "the intensive comparative analysis of a few cases may be more promising than a more superficial statistical analysis of many cases."[43] The specific context of the Central European gas markets relative to the general European, or even global, gas-trading system makes neighbouring countries in this region good candidates for analysis, as will be explored in section 2.4.

The process-tracing method set forth herein seeks to illustrate a path through which we can ascertain how government-owned utilities behave in relation to the

40 Stephen Van Evera, *Guide to Methods for Students of Political Science*, Reprint edition (Ithaca: Cornell University Press, 1997), p. 30.

41 Randy Stoecker, 'Evaluating and Rethinking the Case Study', *The Sociological Review*, 39 (1991), 88-112, p. 87

42 Van Evera, *Guide to Methods for Students of Political Science*, p. 77.

43 Arend Lijphart, 'Comparative Politics and the Comparative Method', *The American Political Science Review*, 65 (1971), 682-693, p. 685.

formation of new contracts that determine the level of dependence on an external supplier of gas, using this as a proxy for price. "The standard approach to comparative analysis is to take a problem confronting several nations and analyze how each nation responds," according to Hoberg.[44] As Bennett has noted in a review of how and why state policies converge, it is not always correct to assert that "comparable conditions produce comparable problems which produce comparable policies."[45] Instead, responses diverge based on unseen variables it is not always possible to identify and measure. To guide analysis in the case study chapters later, the causal mechanism is identified in Figure 3 with the aim that it be explanatory to the way government policy influences the LTC bargaining process between importer and exporter, depending on state ownership structures in the case studies under review.

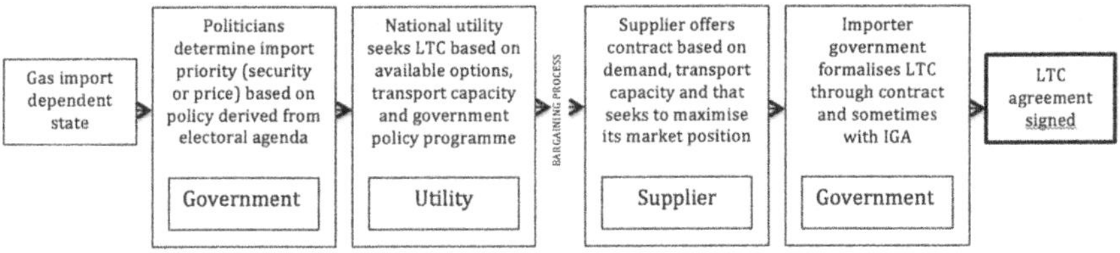

Figure 3: Importer/supplier LTC process-tracing mechanism

This process elucidates the sequence of events that lead an import dependent state through the process of identifying, selecting and executing an LTC with a gas exporter, based on the theory posited here. Assuming state ownership of both the importing agency and central exporter, as is the case in the region under review, the casual mechanism sees politicians as the decision makers of gas policy, working through a national utility that in turn negotiates based on its constraints in transport capacity to bargain out an LTC with a supplier seeking to maximise its own market share and price potential. The LTC is then formalised at the governmental level, often through an intergovernmental agreement (IGA).

44 George Hoberg Jr., 'Technology, Political Structure, and Social Regulation: A Cross-National Analysis', *Comparative Politics*, 18 (1986), 357-376, p. 358.

45 Colin J. Bennett, 'What Is Policy Convergence and What Causes It?', *British Journal of Political Science*, 21 (1991), 215-233, p. 217. As societies industrialise, so the policy convergence argument goes, so too do they begin to move through processes of staged economic development that assist in determining and correlating political and economic outcomes over time.

This analysis bases its investigation on figures from two datasets. The first is a list of 47 gas import arrangements governing the terms of supply from a range of external suppliers into the selected markets over the period 1989 to 2014. Broken down, this list includes 18 separate arrangements for Poland, 11 for Slovakia, 10 for the Czech Republic and 8 for Hungary. These start with the 1974 Orenburg IGAs signed between the Soviet Union and each respective satellite government, all the way up to the LNG import contract agreed between Poland's PGNiG and Qatargas in 2009, as well as later short-term contingency contracts agreed by Slovak utility SPP. Categories of information retrieved by the author include: the supplier, contracting party, date the agreement was signed, date deliveries began, date deliveries ceased, total combined volume of gas contracted, and annual volumes of gas scheduled to be delivered. Additional information is also provided on the terms of delivery where available. Each contract is also sub-divided by colour to distinguish between contracted gas with a Russian exporter agreed directly (red), contracted gas with a non-Russian supplier marking diversification (yellow), and contracted gas through a Russian intermediary company or through barter trading (green) (see Tables 6-9 in the case study chapters).

Where broken-down statistics for year-on-year volumes imported under each supply contract are unavailable, the volumes have been equally split across the period of validity. For example, in the event that a contract is identified with a seven-year tenure for the import of 7 bcm of gas, but a detailed annual breakdown is not found in the literature or through government statistics, then it is assumed that 1 bcm is imported each year over the length of the contract. Because of dips and peaks in demand over certain periods it may have been the case that volumes moved up and down within a range allowed under take-or-pay clauses. However, without documented proof it is clearer and more consistent to assume a stable annual supply. In cases where detailed contract volume–specific data is available – for example, in the event of volumes supplied under the Yamal LTC between Gazprom and Poland's PGNiG being published, in this instance by the national regulator – then these are taken into account in later modelling.

The author does not claim that these lists exactly resemble the portfolio of gas import options open to utilities in Bratislava, Budapest, Prague and Warsaw. The notorious lack of transparency in the European natural gas markets and the insistence by suppliers (principally Gazprom) and (most) importers that the terms of contracts are corporate secrets makes the review of actual contractual documentation impossible. The only available document is the 2009 contract and annex agreed with Ukraine, not covered here, and at the time of writing being contested in the Stockholm arbitration court. Instead, the data used here is harvested from a number of public sources, cross-referenced and expanded by analysis of news reports and official government statements. Where possible, the author has also gleaned further information from legal documentation and financial reporting. First, company press releases were consulted for information, secondly government statements were cross-referenced and, thirdly, news coverage from both mainstream print media and trade publications was checked. The dataset for each case study can be found in full at the end of each respective chapter, with detailed footnotes referencing individual articles and statements throughout. The second dataset this analysis bases its findings on is a list of a gas wholesale prices in US dollars per thousand cubic metres charged by Gazprom to European consumers over the five-year period 2010- 2014. The list covers 20 different European countries, including non–EU member states Switzerland, Bosnia-Herzegovina, Serbia, Macedonia and Turkey. It does not include the Baltic states or Ukraine, as Gazprom data includes those countries in its former Soviet Union statistics. The list does include each of the four case studies and allows a wide enough sample of data to extract a European average for further comparison. This data is presented in Table 2.

It is also useful briefly to discuss definitions in reference to the title of this work. *Held Captive by Gas* defines the sustained dependence structure built up between Gazprom (and its subsidiary Gazprom Export) as supplier and Central Europe's mirage markets as consumers. The 'price' element of the sub-title refers literally to the cost of gas imports on a wholesale basis as outlined in the second dataset, while also alluding to a presumed premium as paid by importers on account of their own political structures. As Gazprom acts as the Russian state's gas export monopoly, its contracts with European consumers are the *de facto* Russian export price, though opaque intermediary companies and offshore ownership structures have at times managed the delivery of some gas through to Poland and Hungary, as will be discussed in the respective case study chapters later.[46] The reference to Gazprom in the subtitle therefore specifically deals with the price of Russian natural gas exports. This is linked to 'politics' through the application of

---

46 See here for an investigation into some of the practices impacting supply in Central and Eastern Europe: Global Witness, *It's a Gas: Funny Business in the Turkmen-Ukraine Gas Trade*, April 2006

how a political actor – here, the state, as defined as the central policymaking power in government – works through its ownership of utility companies to affect the price of its wholesale imports. This, the work argues, is dependent on which government is in power.

2.4 Case selection

The four case studies under consideration are Poland, the Czech Republic, Slovakia and Hungary. Together they will collectively be identified as the case studies, or V4 after the Visegrad Group, of which each is a member. Each shares fundamental similarities in its experience of transition from the Soviet system to democracy and free markets, while physical geography pins these countries in between the great continental powers in what can be described today as Central Europe.[47] In his expansive history of the region, Lonnie Johnson points to historical factors such as religion, empire building and missed economic revolution cycles that distinguish Central Europe from its eastern and western counterparts.[48] Theoretically, the case studies are best described as small powers, limited in the extent to which they can project power by their size.

In 1969 Keohane defined a small state as one "whose leaders consider that it can never, acting alone or in a small group, make a significant impact on the system."[49] Poland, with a population that far outweighs its Slavic neighbours, is perhaps the only case study that fits more readily into the middle power category in

---

47 Defining the borders of Central Europe has been a challenge for geographers for decades. This issue is taken up again later but an introduction to the broader debate can be found here: Karl A., Sinnhuber, 'Central Europe, Mitteleuropa, Europe Centrale: An Analysis of a Geographical Term', *Transactions and Papers (Institute of British Geographers)*, 1954, pp. 15–39. To be clear, Jean George Affholder of the French National Geographic Institute calculated in 1989 that the centre of Europe was just outside Vilnius in Lithuania.

48 According to Johnson, the states of Central Europe never embraced eastern orthodoxy like their Slavic neighbours, instead orienting towards Roman Catholicism. This led to "fundamentally different societies and institutions" emerging. The frontiers of the medieval kingdoms of Poland-Lithuania and Hungary provide a second criterion. Multi-ethnicity and imperial subjugation are therefore essential characteristics of the "Central European historical experience." Occupation by the Ottoman Empire also helps to distinguish the area from south-eastern Europe. Finally, Johnson notes that Central Europe missed the industrial revolutions and the mushrooming of industry along the Rhine River in Germany. Subsequently, "retarded development" became structural. See Lonnie Johnson: *Central Europe: Enemies, Neighbors, Friends*, 3rd ed (New York: Oxford University Press, 2011) pp. 3-5.

49 Robert O. Keohane, 'Lilliputians' Dilemmas: Small States in International Politics', *International Organization*, 23 (1969), p. 296.

today's Central Europe, a state "whose leaders consider that it cannot act alone effectively but may be able to have a systemic impact in a small group or through an international institution."[50] Nevertheless, each case study country has historically faced a stark choice, according to Mitchell: either balance or bandwagon with the great powers: "Too weak to play opponents off against one another like Bismarck, and too exposed to ignore them like Britain, the [Central Europeans] had little choice but to pick a side and hope for the best."[51] This centuries-old choice has played out in the energy sphere over recent years, with some CEE countries choosing to balance their gas-exporting neighbour and former hegemon Russia with the pursuit of supply diversification measures and new energy partnerships; others have opted for bandwagoning by supporting Moscow's infrastructure projects and agreeing to new joint ventures.

In Table 3, each country identified as a potential component state of Central Europe, and therefore eligible for inclusion in this study, is listed. Germany is excluded because its sheer market size that would distort a comparative analysis of this kind, while Switzerland, Belarus, Ukraine, Moldova, Serbia, Macedonia and Bosnia Herzegovina are left out as they have not experienced the same benchmarks imposed by EU membership in 2004. From this table three groups of countries emerge. Firstly, landlocked states dependent on Russian gas: Austria, Slovakia, the Czech Republic and Hungary. The second group is of coastal states wholly dependent on Russian gas imports: Bulgaria, Estonia, Latvia and Lithuania. The third group is of coastal countries with alternative import options or indigenous production: Croatia, Poland, Romania and Slovenia. In terms of fixed fundamentals – factors that cannot be changed immediately and unilaterally by government policy such as population and geography – Poland stands out from the case studies with a larger populace and access to the Baltic Sea. However, with no LNG regasification terminal for gas deliveries brought on- stream by December 2014, the coastal aspect has provided no strategic bonus during the 25-year period of inquiry.[52] Poland's replacement of Austria

50 *ibid.*, p. 296.

51 Wess Mitchell, 'The Mice That Roared: How Central Europe Is Reshaping Global Politics' <http://www.cepa.org/content/report-no-16-mice-roared-how-central-europe-reshaping-global-politics> [accessed 6 August 2015], p. 4

52 The arrival of Lithuania's so-called 'Independence' floating production storage and unloading vessel under lease from Norwegian company Hoegh LNG in December 2014 provided the region with its first non-pipeline entry point at the port of Klaipeda. Commercial operations started in 2015. Poland's LNG terminal at Świnoujście was not completed by the end of the period of inquiry.

is justified by its status as a former COMECOM (Council for Mutual Economic Assistance) member and its shared experience with the rest of the V4 of being wholly reliant on Russian gas imports in 1989.

Table 3: Comparative case studies snapshot (2013)[53]

	Landlocked	Population	Share of gas by % in TPES	Self-sufficiency in %	Russian gas % of imports	Number of system entry points	Transit state*
Austria	Yes	8,479,375	22.4	16.5	63	3	Yes
Bulgaria	No	7,265,115	13.4	10	100	3	Yes
Czech Republic	Yes	10,514,272	16.1	3.5	99	4	Yes
Croatia	No	4,255,700	30.5	70.4	0	2	No
Estonia	No	1,317,997	9.9	0	100	2	No
Hungary	Yes	9,893,082	35.4	20.7	95	4	Yes
Latvia	No	2,012,647	27.4	0	100	2	No
Lithuania	No	2,957,689	36	0	100	2	No
Poland	No	38,040,196	13.9	34.1	82	7	Yes
Romania	No	19,983,693	31	84.1	92	3	Yes
Slovakia	Yes	5,413,393	26.2	1.7	99	3	Yes
Slovenia	No	2,059,953	10.1	0	58	2	No

* 'Transit state' refers not only to the ability of a country to further transmit gas imported to a neighbour. Here it refers to the use of the system as a part of the export infrastructure of a major exporter such as Gazprom. For example, Slovenia may be able to deliver gas onwards to Italy but it is not used as a major transit state.

Post-1945, the region east of the Neisse-Oder river line was assimilated into the communist bloc until 1989 – beyond the western frontier of the Soviet Union proper, but tied economically and politically to the centralised Red Empire through COMECOM and the Warsaw Pact. Not only has this served to create certain path dependencies in terms of gas supply for the case studies, as will be explored in later chapters, but it also supplies a useful benchmark for evaluating policies. The 1989–2014 period of study allows for the inclusion of the formation of the Visegrad Group by the banks of the Danube in northern Hungary in 1991 as a means to assist in the formation of the "political, economic and cultural cooperation of

53 Author's own table using BP, IEA, World Bank and Eurostat data.

these countries in the altered situation in the [sic] Central Europe."[54] Subsequent membership of NATO for all but Slovakia in 1999 (Slovakia entered the security alliance in 2004) further presents an interesting point of similarity – especially for noting how different case studies felt security pressures in the gas sector from their major external supplier during the period preceding membership in the 1990s.

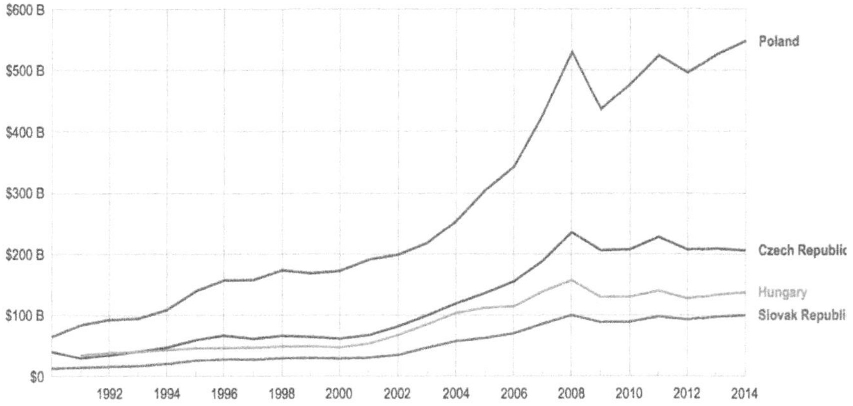

Graph 7: Gross domestic product (1990-2014)[55]

Accession to the EU for all in 2004 forced standardisation of energy market rules as the case studies entered the common market system, which sought to promote liberalised markets and, later, the erosion of models of vertical state- owned utility companies.[56] Privatisation waves in the early years of the millennium, coupled

---

[54] Presidents of Poland, Hungary and Czechoslovakia, *Visegrad Declaration 1991: Declaration on Cooperation between the Czech and Slovak Federal Republic, the Republic of Poland and the Republic of Hungary in Striving for European Integration*, 15 February 1991. Although the initiative has not undertaken the role many in Warsaw, Budapest, Prague and Bratislava hoped it might, the opportunity regularly to benchmark national policy in the region – including on gas supply security – supplies another point of similarity, even if at times those policies have diverged.

[55] World Bank statistics in US dollars not adjusted for inflation. Graph generated using Google Public Data.

[56] Each case study had to have its market participants aligned with the second energy market directives agreed in 2003 and brought in to force in 2004. These measures included legal unbundling of each unit of the supply – transmission from production, for example. They also included opening the market for consumers to access alternative suppliers. European Parliament, 'Directive 2003/55/EC of the European Parliament and of the Council of 26 June 2003 Concerning Common Rules for the Internal Market in Natural Gas and Repealing Directive 98/30/EC', 2003 <http://eur-lex.europa.eu/legal-content/EN/TXT/?uri=celex:32003L0055> [accessed 15 July 2015].

with the development of major new transit infrastructure, has also had an effect on the gas market position of each country as it moved towards EU membership. Economic growth patterns have also been broadly comparable, despite Poland not falling into recession during the 2009 financial crisis, as shown in Graph 8. The Czech Republic and Hungary share similar population sizes, while the Slovak Republic joins them as a landlocked state, with its pipeline system linked to that of the Czech Republic, with which it was one until the Velvet Divorce of 1993 and the subsequent construction of a border gas terminal at Lanžhot in the following year.

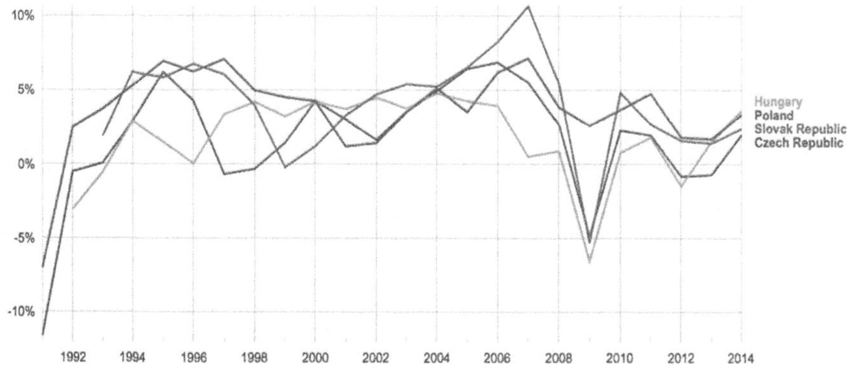

Graph 8: Gross domestic product annual % change (1990–2014)[57]

Importantly, each country also acts a transit state through which gas from the major external supplier, Gazprom, is sent to markets further west. Hungary, the Czech Republic and Slovakia use Soviet-era pipelines and Poland transits gas to Germany through the Yamal pipeline, built in the 1990s. The countries also each receive gas transited from the supplier through a third-party non–EU member state: Ukraine and/or Belarus. Russia supplied 100% of imported gas to each in 1989 and has remained the dominant external supplier despite the development of alternative options. Consumption patterns for each of the case studies show steady growth from the 1960s until the early 1990s, as illustrated in Graph 9, when demand either plateaued or dropped owing to the decline in industrial output, no longer supported by demand from the east. A brief period of renewed growth was followed by years

57 World Bank statistics in US dollars with % change of real GDP adjusted for inflation compared to the previous year. Graph generated using Google Public Data.

of broadly stable consumption until the financial crisis in 2009 for both Slovakia and the Czech Republic. Continued growth after the millennium for both Hungary and Poland diverged around 2004, with the latter continuing its ascent to over 16 bcm/y and the former to 8 bcm/y by 2014. Forecasts for the period after 2014 predict further growth in Poland,[58] though the development of nuclear power projects may dampen demand elsewhere.

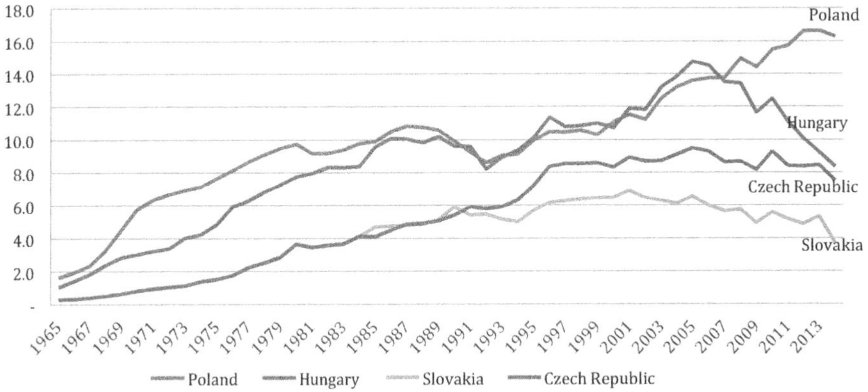

Graph 9: Gas consumption in bcm (1965–2014)[59]

One important way in which the case studies diverge is the shape in which the gas industries have come to be structured. State ownership of all modes of supply – from local production and overseas procurement to transmission, storage and retail distribution – has been reformed in markedly different ways over the 25-year period of study, helping to outline a key conditional variable on which this thesis bases its enquiry: the degree of government ownership. This provides an interesting variable factor for each case study within the group as shown in Table 4.

For example, as of 2013 the Czech Republic has completely privatised its import and transmission operators, and no third-party company operates between

---

[58] According to reported projections by Poland's Economics Ministry, by 2020 national demand will reach 17.1 bcm, by 2025 19 bcm, and by 2030 20 bcm. 'Ministry of the Economy: Gas Consumption Will Rise in Poland | Info Shale: Shale Gas & Oil from Shale', Issued by Polish Geological Institute' <http://infolupki.pgi.gov.pl/en/economy/news/ministry-economy-gas-consumption-will-rise-poland> [accessed 14 June 2016].

[59] BP, *Statistical Review of World Energy 2015* <http://www.bp.com/en/global/corporate/about-bp/energy-economics/statistical-review-of-world-energy.html>. [accessed 12 June 2016].

them and their external suppliers, or manages infrastructure through which gas imports flow. Poland, meanwhile, has retained ownership of its transporter and importer, while also co-owning the operating company for the Yamal gas pipeline – EuRoPol Gaz – with Gazprom. Slovakia and Hungary are mixed cases, with instances of privatisation and effective re-nationalisation, and also the appearance of gas supply intermediaries part-owned by the supplier, Gazprom.

Table 4: Domestic gas market snapshot (2013)[60]

	Czech Republic	Hungary	Poland	Slovakia
State-owned importer	No	No	Yes	Yes
State-owned transmission system operator	No	Yes	Yes	Yes
Third-party intermediary in gas supply/transmission	No	Yes	Yes	No
Alternative source option for 25%> import volume	Yes	Yes	Yes	No
Annual consumption (2013)	8.4 bcm	8.6 bcm	16.7 bcm	5.4 bcm
Share of gas by % in TPES (2013)	16.10%	35.40%	13.90%	26.20%
Dependence on Russian gas supplies as % of consumption (2013)	94%	70%	59%	100%
Storage capacity as percentage of conumption	35%	63%	17%	69%
Gazprom long-term contract expiry date	2035	2015	2022	2028

Of course, gas market structure also owes something to the position of rival fuels. Nuclear and especially coal present two major competitors in Central Europe. Poland and the Czech Republic have readily available coal reserves, which for the former constitute over 90% of electricity produced.[61] Both the Czech Republic and Slovakia have embraced nuclear technology, maintaining reactors and planning new units at the time of this research.[62] Graph 10 breaks down consumption in each case study market by sector according to IEA statistics for the year 2013, showing a clear disparity in which area gas is consumed. In Hungary, around 30% of gas demand, or 2.6 bcm in 2013, accounted for electricity or heating production, while a comparatively smaller stake of around 15% was used by industry. Conversely, Poland's demand pattern leans far more heavily towards industrial consumption, with only a small volume dedicated to power and heating. Hungary is

---

60 Author's own table using statistics from BP, IEA and Gazprom Export.

61 According to the IEA, in 2011 coal accounted for 55% of primary energy supply and 92% of power generation. IEA, *Energy Policies of IEA Countries: Poland 2011* (Paris: Organisation for Economic Co-operation and Development, 2011) <http://www.oecd-ilibrary.org/content/book/9789264098190-en> [accessed 17 January 2015].

62 A useful review of nuclear energy policies in each of the case studies and Bulgaria can be found here: *Energy of the Future? Nuclear Energy in Central and Eastern Europe* (Heinrich-Böll-Stiftung Praha, February 2011) <http://cz.boell.org/sites/default/files/energy_of_the_future.pdf> [accessed 12 August 2015].

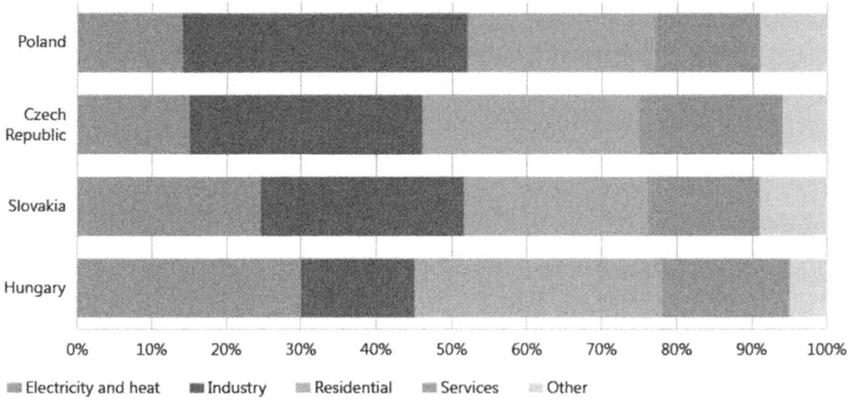

Graph 10: Gas consumption by sector (2013)[63]

the only case study country to generate as much as a third of its power from natural gas, as shown in Graph 11, although it too has nuclear generating capacity and plans further, Russian-built projects.

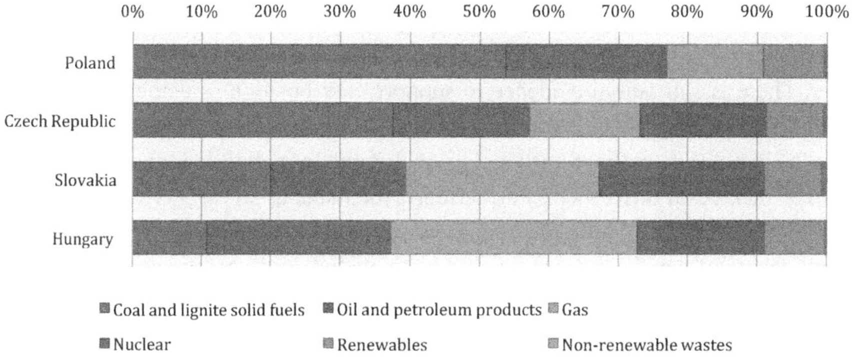

Graph 11: Gross inland consumption by fuel as % in total mix (2013)[64]

Statistics shown in Graph 11 illustrate a wide range of fuel-mix configurations between the four case studies, with the only commonality being a marginal

63 IEA statistics.

64 Eurostat statistics. Eurostat Statistical Books, *Energy Balance Sheets: 2013 Data* (Eurostat, 2015) <http://ec.europa.eu/eurostat/documents/3217494/6898731/KS-EN-15-001-EN-N.pdf/e5851c73-9259-462e-befc-6d037dc8216a> [accessed 11 August 2015].

utilisation of renewables in the mix. Graph 12 shows how each country has differed in respect to dependence on imports for total energy consumption over the period stretching from 1970 to 2012. This illustrates a trend of convergence, with the range tightening over the period. The big coal-producing countries, Poland and Czech Republic, were only around 25% dependent in 2012.

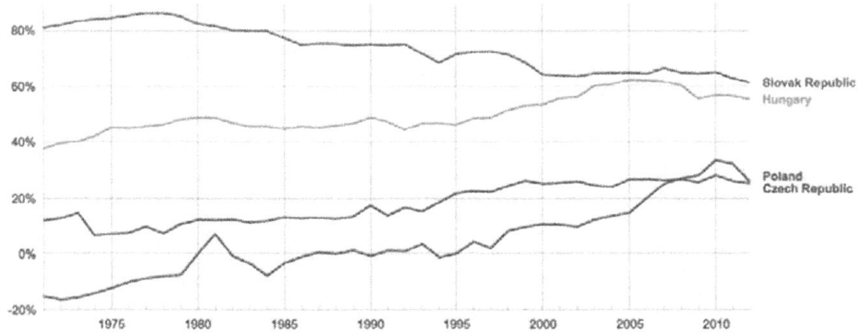

Graph 12: Net imports as % of energy use 1970–2012[65]

The factors presented above, covering geographic, economic and energy sector-specific criteria, make the four countries under review perfect candidates for analysis. There is substantial evidence to support their position as comparable states with similar background characteristics but diverging variables through which to test the hypothesis outlined earlier. This makes the four eligible for analysis under Mill's 'method of difference.' Furthermore, the make up of the gas sector of each state gives a different perspective on how varying ownership structures work. To exclude one of the chosen cases would be to exclude one specific combination of ownership structures.

A final point of interest for the comparison of these case studies is the composition of the countries' political systems, relevant for analysing domestic structures as outlined earlier. The institutional structure of the political systems under analysis is important to define. Each country is a parliamentary republic, holding elections at regular intervals, with the Prime Minister being the head of the executive.

[65] Net energy imports estimated total primary energy consumption subtracting national production. Minus illustrates that country is a net exporter. World Bank statistics generated using Google Public Data.

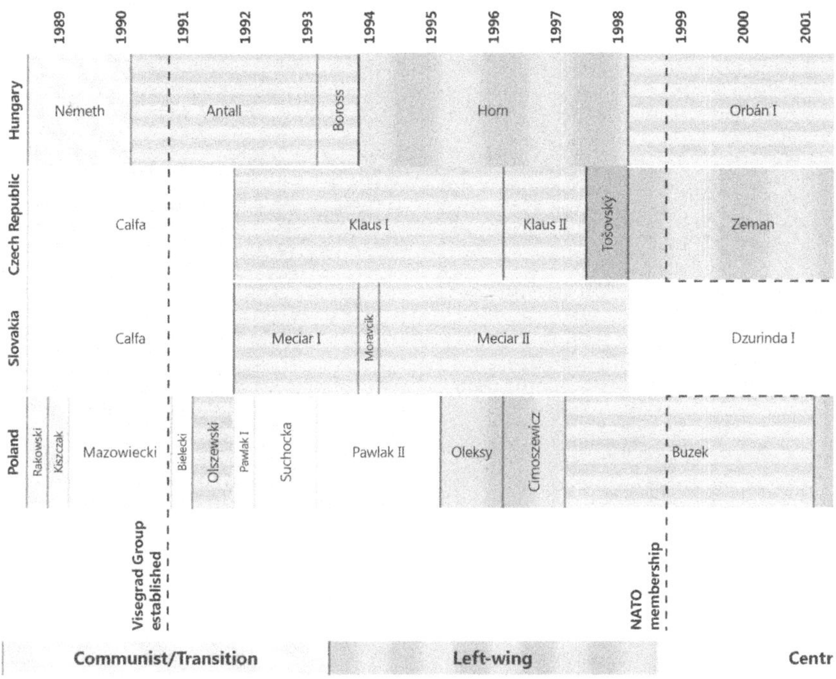

Poland

Government name	Prime Minister	In office from	In office until	Governing parties
Mazowiecki	Tadeusz Mazowiecki	24 Aug 1989	4 Jan 1991	KO'S', ZSL, PZPR, SD
Bielecki	Jan Krzysztof Bielecki	4 Jan 1991	6 Dec 1991	KLD, ZChN, PC, SD
Olszewski	Jan Olszewski	6 Dec 1991	5 Jun 1992	PC, ZChN, PSL.PL
Pawlak I	Waldemar Pawlak	5 Jun 1992	11 Jul 1992	PSL
Suchocka	Hanna Suchocka	11 Jul 1992	26 Oct 1993	UD, KLD, ZChN, PChD, PPPP, PSL.PL
Pawlak II	Waldemar Pawlak	26 Oct 1993	7 Mar 1995	SLD, PSL, BBWR
Oleksy	Józef Oleksy	7 Mar 1995	7 Feb 1996	SLD, PSL
Cimoszewicz	Włodzimierz Cimoszewicz	7 Feb 1996	31 Oct 1997	SLD, PSL
Buzek	Jerzy Buzek	31 Oct 1997	19 Oct 2001	AWS, UW
Miller	Leszek Miller	19 Oct 2001	2 May 2004	SLD, UP, PSL
Belka I	Marek Belka	2 May 2004	11 Jun 2004	SLD, UP
Belka II	Marek Belka	11 Jun 2004	31 Oct 2005	SLD, UP
Marcinkiewicz	Kazimierz Marcinkiewicz	31 Oct 2005	14 Jul 2006	PiS, SRP, LPR
Kaczynski	Jaroslaw Kaczynski	14 Jul 2006	16 Nov 2007	PiS, SRP, LPR
Tusk I	Donald Tusk	16 Nov 2007	18 Nov 2011	PO, PSL
Tusk II	Donald Tusk	18 Nov 2011	22 Sep 2014	PO, PSL
Kopacz	Ewa Kopacz	22 Sep 2014	–	PO, PSL

Slovakia

Government name	Prime Minister	In office from	In office until	Governing parties
Meciar I	Vladimír Meciar	24 Jun 1992	15 Mar 1994	HZDS, later joined by SNS
Moravcík	Jozef Moravcík	15 Mar 1994	13 Dec 1994	DEÚS, KDH, SDL, NDS
Meciar II	Vladimír Meciar	13 Dec 1994	30 Oct 1998	HZDS, ZRS, SNS, RSS
Dzurinda I	Mikuláš Dzurinda	30 Oct 1998	15 Oct 2002	SDK (later SDKÚ), SDL, SMK, SOP
Dzurinda II	Mikuláš Dzurinda	16 Oct 2002	4 Jul 2006	SDKÚ, SMK, KDH, ANO
Fico I	Robert Fico	4 Jul 2006	8 Jul 2010	SMER-SD, SNS, LS-HZDS
Radicová	Iveta Radicová	8 Jul 2010	4 Apr 2012	SDKÚ-DS, SaS, KDH, M-H
Fico II	Robert Fico	4 Apr 2012	-	SMER-SD

Cze

Go
Cal Slo Re
Kla Re
Kla
Toš (Ca
Ze
Špi
Gr
Pa
To
To
Fis
Ne
Ru
Sol

Figure 4 presents the various governments in office along the political spectrum during the period of enquiry, using Sitter's analysis on cleavages to distinguish

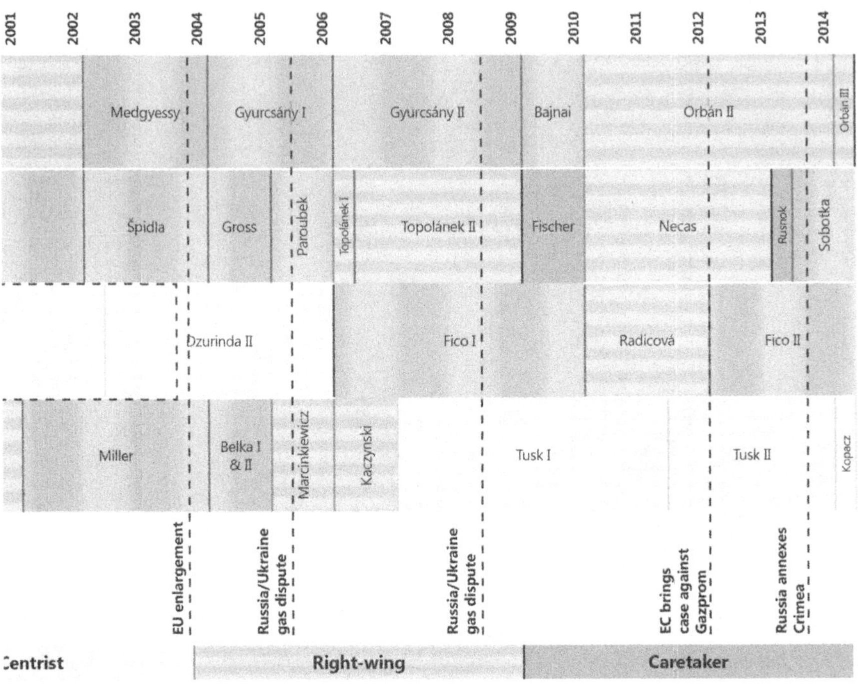

Czech Republic

Government name	Prime Minister	In office from	In office until	Governing parties
Calfa (Czech and Slovak Federative Republic)	Marián Calfa	10 Dec 1989	2 Jul 1992	OF, HSD-SMS, CSL
Klaus I (Czech Republic)	Václav Klaus	2 Jul 1992	4 Jul 1996	ODS, KDU-CSL, ODA, KDS
Klaus II	Václav Klaus	4 Jul 1996	2 Jan 1998	ODS, KDU-CSL, ODA
Tošovský (Caretaker)	Josef Tošovský	2 Jan 1998	22 Jul 1998	–
Zeman	Miloš Zeman	22 Jul 1998	15 Jul 2002	CSSD
Špidla	Vladimír Špidla	15 Jul 2002	4 Aug 2004	CSSD, KDU-CSL, US-DEU
Gross	Stanislav Gross	4 Aug 2004	25 Apr 2005	CSSD, KDU-CSL, US-DEU
Paroubek	Jiří Paroubek	25 Apr 2005	4 Sep 2006	CSSD, KDU-CSL, US-DEU
Topolánek I	Mirek Topolánek	4 Sep 2006	9 Jan 2007	ODS
Topolánek II	Mirek Topolánek	9 Jan 2007	8 May 2009	ODS, KDU-CSL, SZ
Fischer (Caretaker)	Jan Fischer	8 May 2009	13 Jul 2010	–
Necas	Petr Necas	13 Jul 2010	10 Jul 2013	ODS, TOP 09, VV (replaced by LIDEM)
Rusnok (Caretaker)	Jiří Rusnok	10 Jul 2013	29 Jan 2014	
Sobotka	Bohuslav Sobotka	29 Jan 2014		CSSD, ANO 2011, KDU-CSL

Hungary

Government name	Prime Minister	In office from	In office until	Governing parties
Németh	Miklós Németh (Provisional)	23 Oct 1989	23 May 1990	MSZP
Antall	József Antall	23 May 1990	12 Dec 1993	MDF, FKGP, KDNP
Boross	Péter Boross	12 Dec 1993	15 Jul 1994	MDF, EKGP, KDNP
Horn	Gyula Horn	15 Jul 1994	8 Jul 1998	MSZP, SZDSZ
Orbán I	Viktor Orbán	8 Jul 1998	27 May 2002	Fidesz, FKGP, MDF
Medgyessy	Péter Medgyessy	27 May 2002	29 Sep 2004	MSZP, SZDSZ
Gyurcsány I	Ferenc Gyurcsány	29 Sep 2004	9 Jun 2006	MSZP, SZDSZ
Gyurcsány II	Ferenc Gyurcsány	9 Jun 2006	14 Apr 2009	MSZP, SZDSZ
Bajnai	Gordon Bajnai	14 Apr 2009	29 May 2010	MSZP
Orbán II	Viktor Orbán	29 May 2010	6 Jun 2014	Fidesz, KDNP
Orbán III	Viktor Orbán	6 Jun 2014	–	Fidesz, KDNP

Figure 4: Case studies political timeline

between right and left leaning. Caretaker administrations and centrist governments are also illustrated with coalition make-up beneath.

3 Energy security

This chapter locates the analysis in the broader energy security debate and to outline the background conditions within which the case studies sit as part of a Eurasian gas supply conundrum. Energy security discourse is marked by the occasions on which the circuitry of interdependencies between producers and consumers has tripped – the events of 1973, 2006, and 2009 provide examples. An uneven distribution of hydrocarbon deposits connected to a patchwork of consumer markets through largely static transit systems establishes a chessboard of entrenched interests that need to be balanced between importers, exporters, policymakers and industry. This complexity means that "problems can no longer be effectively studied or resolved in isolation from each other" according to Cherp and Jewell,[1] warranting an integrated understanding of the energy security challenge.

The 1973 oil crisis is the most oft-cited example of this breakdown in the energy supply circuitry.[2] However, the concept of energy security itself goes back further. With World War I looming in summer 1913, Winston Churchill, at the time First Lord of the Admiralty in the British navy, announced in the House of Commons that the fleet would shift its feedstock from domestic coal to foreign oil

---

1 Aleh Cherp and Jessica Jewell, 'The Three Perspectives on Energy Security: Intellectual History, Disciplinary Roots and the Potential for Integration', *Current Opinion in Environmental Sustainability*, 3 (2011), 202–212, p. 202.

2 A detailed narrative of the events surrounding 1973 can be found here: Daniel Yergin, *The Prize: The Epic Quest for Oil, Money & Power*, Reissue edition (New York: Free Press, 2008) In brief, the crisis saw Arab producers hike the export price of oil and restrict sales to the US and the Netherlands in response to their support for Israel during the Yom Kippur War.

J. Posaner, *Held Captive by Gas*, Energiepolitik und Klimaschutz. Energy Policy and Climate Protection, https://doi.org/10.1007/978-3-658-27518-1_3

in a bid to increase manoeuvrability and outpace rivals.[3] In a speech justifying the decision, Churchill told the House that "on no one quality, on no one process, on no one country, on no one company, and no one route, and on no one oil field must we be dependent. Safety and certainty in oil lie in variety, and in variety alone."[4] Proponents of diversification in gas supply security start here.

Since 1913, global political flashpoints have consistently threatened the stable trade of energy resources. The race for control of Romanian oil fields in World War II, the Suez crisis in 1956, OPEC and 1973, Germany's Cold War *Ostpolitik*, Chinese moves into the South China Sea and the Ukraine gas transit crises of 2006 and 2009 are all examples of the nexus where politics has overrun into the technical arena of energy and its safe supply. This analysis bears down on one specific dynamic of global energy security: the relationship between Russia and its former communist vassals in the trade of gas. However, this is just one string in an ever more complicated and interconnected energy system matrix.

3.1 Securitising energy

As argued by Buzan et al, the politicisation process that has surrounded the trade in energy products means problems in the sector are often only interpreted in the form of an 'emergency' mode, which has served to justify actions "outside the bounds of normal political procedure" by actors in the area.[5] This in turn transfers the provision of energy resources from supplier to consumer outside the bounds of 'normal politics' and from the civilian to the military sphere.[6] This process has aided in the construction of a new vocabulary to govern energy supply, colouring

---

3 Even then, Churchill's opponents in the House of Commons demanded answers regarding the costs of transformation and evidence of the contracts to supply oil. "We are, or soon shall, be able to draw oil from Burmah [sic]., California, Persia, Texas, Roumania [sic]., Borneo, Egypt, Mexico, and Trinidad," Churchill told the Commons before adding later "we must become the owners, or at any rate, the controllers at the source of at least a proportion of the supply of natural oil which we require." *Debate on SHIPBUILDING, REPAIRS, MAINTENANCE, ETC. —PERSONNEL.— (VOTE 8, SECTION 1.)*, 55 ols. (House of Commons: Hansard, 1913) <http://hansard.millbanksystems.com/commons/1913/jul/17/shipbuilding-repairs-maintenance-etc> [accessed 21 July 2015].

4 Daniel Yergin, *The Prize: The Epic Quest for Oil, Money & Power*, Reissue edition (New York: Free Press, 2008), p. 160.

5 The key text for the so-called 'Copenhagen school' of securitisation theorists can be found here: Barry Buzan, Ole Wæver and Jaap de Wilde, *Security: A New Framework for Analysis* (Boulder, Lynne Rienner Publishers, 1998), p. 23.

6 Katja Yafimava, *The Transit Dimension of EU Energy Security: Russian Gas Transit Across Ukraine, Belarus, and Moldova* (Oxford/New York: Oxford Institute for Energy Studies, 2011) p. 12

risks and vulnerabilities in commodity trade with the language of conflict. Subsequently, 'energy diplomacy' becomes “the use of foreign policy to secure access to energy supplies abroad and to promote (mostly bilateral, that is, government to government) cooperation” according to Goldthau and Witte.[7]

Additionally, as has already been discussed, an ‘energy weapon’ can also be deployed by suppliers to try and extort political or economic benefits and gain leverage over captive consumers. Stegen argues that its deployment is contingent on the ability of a government to exercise full control over the stages of resource extraction, transmission and ultimately delivery assets; there is hence some debate over the relevance of the term ‘energy weapon’ and its usefulness in interpreting how resources are deployed by producers.[8] As mentioned in the Introduction, Högselius broadens the understanding to include ‘gas dumping’ techniques to undermine other fuels in the national mix and the overall balance of national economies, or the use of fuel deliveries for ‘divide- and-rule’ or prestige purposes. Essentially, Högselius sees any way in which a country can use energy to “deliberately hurt or weaken another country or region, directly or indirectly” as evidence of an energy weapon, giving us a far more holistic way of understanding the ways in which resource trade and politics can merge.[9]

In this vocabulary, gas supply disruption quickly becomes a ‘gas supply crisis’, and conflict over gas contract terms becomes a ‘gas war.’ Although European perspectives on the security of energy have been more subdued compared to US views traditionally, the 2006 NATO summit in Riga saw an agreement reached that would bring the subject under the remit of the security alliance’s discussions.[10]

---

[7] Andreas Goldthau, ‘Energy diplomacy in trade and investment of oil and gas’, in Andreas Goldthau and Jan Martin Witte, eds., *Global Energy Governance: The New Rules of the Game* (Berlin, Germany: Washington, D.C: Brookings Institution Press and Global Public Policy Institute, 2010), pp. 25-46, p. 28.

[8] There remain questions over how effective this argument really is. This work attempts to add a nuance to the debate. Further analysis can be found here: Karen Smith Stegen, ‘Deconstructing the “Energy Weapon”: Russia’s Threat to Europe as Case Study’, *Energy Policy*, Sustainability of biofuels, 39 (2011). 6505-6513. Cherp and Jewell note that the first time an ‘oil weapon’ was referred to was by the League of Nations while considering sanctions against Italy in 1935. See: Aleh Cherp and Jessica Jewell, ‘The Three Perspectives on Energy Security: Intellectual History, Disciplinary Roots and the Potential for Integration’, *Current Opinion in Environmental Sustainability*, 3 (2011), 202–212, p. 203.

[9] Per Högselius, *Red Gas: Russia and the Origins of European Energy Dependence* (New York: Palgrave, 2013), p. 222.

[10] Richard Youngs, *Energy Security: Europe’s New Foreign Policy Challenge* (Routledge, 2009), p. 44.

The Riga summit declaration included the recognition that "security interests can also be affected by the disruption of the flow of vital resources."[11] In the context of states dependent on a former hegemon, as is the case in the post-Soviet realm, the primarily economic boons of exploitation of domestic shale gas reserves or the acquisition of a new LNG receiving terminal come to be understood as supplying 'independence' from outside interests and freedom from the 'energy weapon' in the period following the Ukraine/Russia supply disruptions of 2006 and 2009.[12] Over these years, energy and security had become inseparable concepts in minds of electorates already sensitive to reliance on Russian resources.

Nonetheless, despite much focus on its meaning, energy security as a concept still has an uncertain definition. Its boundaries shift depending on where the reader is in the world. The Paris-based International Energy Agency (IEA) describes it as the "uninterrupted availability of energy sources at an affordable price."[13] US author Daniel Yergin sees it as the need to "assure adequate, reliable supplies of energy at reasonable prices and in ways that do not jeopardize major national values and objectives."[14] Meanwhile, the Asia Pacific Energy Research Centre (APERC) in Japan chooses to define it as "the ability of an economy to guarantee the availability of energy resource supply in a sustainable and timely manner with the energy price being at a level that will not adversely affect the economic performance of the economy."[15] Larsson has also argued that the Russian concept of energy security differs too, prioritising access to consumer markets for its oil and gas and seeking to "ensure that vital infrastructure is developed and kept under state control."[16]

---

11 NATO, 'Riga Summit Declaration', 2006 <http://www.nato.int/docu/pr/2006/p06-150e.htm> [accessed 15 June 2016].

12 A reference to the politicised development of shale gas in Poland and the arrival of the floating LNG regasification terminal into Klaipeda port in Lithuania last December – literally called the 'Independence' vessel. Both projects can be interpreted as motivated at least partly by supply security fears and over dependence on Russian gas.

13 IEA, *Energy Security* <http://www.iea.org/topics/energysecurity/> [accessed 21 July].

14 Daniel Yergin, 'Energy Security in the 1990s', *Foreign Affairs* <https://www.foreignaffairs.com/articles/united-states/1988-09-01/energy-security-1990s> [accessed 21 July 2015].

15 Asia Pacific Energy Research Centre, *A Quest for Energy Security in the 21st Century: Resources and Constraints*, 2007 <http://aperc.ieej.or.jp/file/2010/9/26/APERC_2007_A_Quest_for_Energy_Security.pdf> [accessed 30 July 2015], p. 6.

16 Robert L. Larson, *Nord Stream, Sweden and Baltic Sea Security* (Swedish Defence Research Agency, 2007), p. 81.

Each of these definitions illustrates the often-conflicting interests at play between Tokyo, Washington DC, Moscow and Paris. In Japan, APERC references clearly the need to ensure supplies for a heavily industrialised island nation with few indigenous natural resources of its own to draw from. Yergin's definition gives way to broader security considerations often associated with US foreign policy endeavours. The IEA interpretation is the most open, reflecting the membership of 29 states since its creation in the aftermath of the 1973 oil crisis. It is the most readily applicable to this analysis, in addition to the concept set forth by Kruyt et al., which suggests four dimensions of energy security - availability, accessibility, affordability and acceptability[17] - giving broader reign to interpretation depending on the fuel and location under consideration.

Put simply, where you are the in world governs how you conceptualise energy security. Besides the very few countries that do not fit into the 'consumer dependent on foreign imports', or 'exporter dependent on sales revenues' puzzle, the rest remain caught in a web of interdependencies governed by the international system of institutions and trade dynamic between the two groups. Although sceptical that the system of geo-economics has outstripped geopolitics as the arena for power politics in the twenty-first century, neoliberal scholar Joseph Nye has recognised that "international economic systems rest upon international political order."[18] In the modern age of Yergin's ever-consuming 'hydrocarbon man,'[19] both systems rely on each element of Kruyt's four As and the maintenance of a functioning marketplace where supply and demand can meet at a mutually acceptable price, under mutually acceptable terms.

In Europe, contemporary energy security discourse relies on the need to 'keep the lights on' by balancing dependencies on external suppliers, the roll-out of intermittent renewable energy sources like wind and solar, and the need to maintain performance across what Sovacool and Mukherjee determine as their five policy dimensions of energy security: "availability, affordability, technology development and efficiency, environmental and social sustainability, and regulation and

---

17 B. Kruyt, D. P.van Vuuren, H. J. M. de Vries and H. Groenenberg, 'Indicators for Energy Security', *Energy Policy*, 37 (2009), 2166–88.

18 Joseph Nye, 'East Asian Security: The Case for Deep Engagement', *Foreign Affairs* <https://www.foreignaffairs.com/articles/asia/1995-07-01/east-asian-security-case-deep-engagement> [accessed 1 August 2015].

19 Chapter 27 in Yergin, *The Prize*.

governance."[20] Though the first waves of energy security literature were concerned with risks to oil supply, later generations in the post- 1989 era have focused more on how to quantify risk, and on the relationship between gas supplier and gas consumer in Europe and the former Soviet space.

As Churchill's speech in 1913 put forward, import dependent states have seen their relative security defined by the balance between long-term fixed price arrangements and the opportunity to react to demand and changes in the market environment. Churchill said in the June 1913 address to the House of Commons:

> The future of the oil market is so uncertain, the subject is so specialised, and present prices are so unfavourable, that a balance has to be struck on the one hand between the relative advantages and disadvantages of making forward contracts at fixed prices, and of providing for rapid periodical revisions of price on the other hand.[21]

Change the date to a century later in 2013 and the fuel from 'oil' to 'gas' and the same could be applied to Central Europe.

3.1.1 The Eurasian gas system

The security of supply to the European gas market is inextricably linked to that of the broader Eurasian network. As discussed, Europe's principle external supplier is Russia's Gazprom and its transport network is programmed into European markets through a pipeline system built from the 1960s onwards. Suppliers from the Central Asian 'heartland' of Eurasia must supply via the Russian system, which acts as a transcontinental pivot point for gas flows to Europe.[22] As Baev has argued, "Russia is set to remain locked in the European gas market, but it is very

---

[20] This is then broken down into a further twenty components and an eventual list of 320 simple indicators and 52 complex indicators that "policymakers and scholars can use to analyze, measure, track, and compare national performance on energy security." Benjamin K. Sovacool and Ishani Mukherjee, 'Conceptualizing and Measuring Energy Security: A Synthesized Approach', *Energy*, PRES 2010, 36 (2011), 5343–55.

[21] *Debate on SHIPBUILDING, REPAIRS, MAINTENANCE, ETC. —PERSONNEL,—(VOTE 8, SECTION 1.)*, 55 vols. (House of Commons: Hansard, 1913) <http://hansard.millbanksystems.com/commons/1913/jul/17/shipbuilding-repairs-maintenance-etc> [accessed 21 July 2015].

[22] British geographer Halford Mackinder first described Central Asia as the 'heartland' in a 1904 speech, a concept that would eventually be replaced by the US academic, and so-called 'godfather of containment,' Nicholas Spykman, who championed the 'rimland' concept instead. Both laid the foundations for modern geopolitics. Nicholas John Spykman, *America's Strategy in World Politics: The United States and the Balance of Power* (Piscataway, Transaction Publishers, 1942).

slow in adjusting to the irreversible changes."[23] These changes come through the parallel processes of market integration and liberalisation.

In terms of the trade in gas across Eurasia, Yafimava suggests that it is helpful to think of this web as a "circuitry of flows" between various public and private actors engaged in "relationships of interdependence."[24] These are conducted in spaces where commercial contracts, bilateral and multilateral agreements, international treaties and political relations coalesce.[25] Currency and energy resources run through this 'space of flows' with disruption to any of its component parts leading to tripped circuitry and potential disruption to supply. This work frames its argument within Yafimava's conceptual framework of transit regimes, energy legislation and industry norms enshrined in platforms like the Energy Charter Treaty (ECT) and EU energy market liberalisation directives.[26] It makes only one addition to this framework: the inclusion of the Central European countries collectively identified in Figure 5 as the V4, or the Visegrad Group, which includes the case studies under review here.

Although the V4 functions as a sub-regional structure at a sub-institutional level under the EU, it has made attempts to converge national policies on gas market liberalisation through a 2012 'Gas Roadmap' document.[27] Although, as the work will go on to illustrate, it remains uncertain as to whether the V4 platform will encourage policy convergence between the four signatories or provide a barometer

---

23 Pavel K. Baev, 'From European to Eurasian Energy Security: Russia Needs and Energy Perestroika', *Journal of Eurasian Studies*, 3 (2012), 177-184, p. 183.

24 Yafimava, *The Transit Dimension of EU Energy Security*, p. 32.

25 A **contractual space** covers the business relationship between producer and consumers and allows for quantities, payment and transit to be formalised. This space provides the primary arena for a circuitry of flows. A **regulatory space** accounts for legislation governing the gas sector, whether at a state level or imposed by a multilateral institution such as the EU. A **political space** accounts for the relationship between states often at opposite ends of the circuitry of gas and cash. These include intergovernmental agreements for the development of pipeline projects, or the signing of a Memorandum of Understanding for new gas supply contracts. Finally, a **geographical space** covers technical factors for the transit of gas, including pipeline infrastructure in place, local terrain and jurisdictional factors that determine the physical transport of the commodity.

26 The Energy Charter Treaty (ECT) is an international agreement setting out a multilateral framework for cooperation in the energy sector, and was initially focused on integrating the post-Soviet space into the global energy system. Entering into force in 1998 after being signed in Lisbon in 1994, it includes binding rules seeking to encourage market transparency and investment. The ECT currently has 54 signatories: 52 states, the European Commission and the EU's joint nuclear fuel purchasing body, Euratom.

27 Visegrad Group, *Road Map towards the Regional Gas Market among Visegrad 4 Countries*, 16 June 2013.

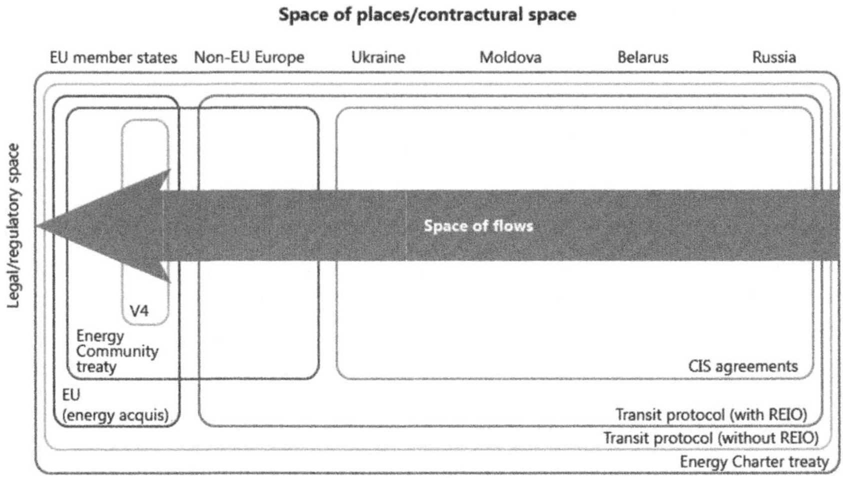

Figure 5: Yafimava's Eurasian gas network flows conceptual framework[28]

against which policy divergence can be measured, it provides a useful means of distinguishing the case studies as a distinct 'secondary transit space' within the Eurasian 'space of flows.'

One definitive way in which state policies towards external actors are divided in Eurasia, in addition to along the institutional lines, is through ideational factors. Each of the four case studies can count on some degree of subjective influence in its foreign policy formation when presented with Russia as a trading partner. In the case of Poland, Sanford has argued that "both Polish national identity and the ideological basis of the country's foreign policy are heavily permeated and conditioned by the historical inheritance."[29] The significant 'Other' for Central European countries wishing to build up European integration is Russia, as Iver Neumann argued in the early years of independence in 1993.[30] Though these perspectives are not immediately relevant to an investigation of domestic structures, they are important in understanding the specific nature of the bilateral relationships at play in the region.

---

[28] Yafimava, *The Transit Dimension of EU Energy Security*, p. 36.

[29] George Sanford, 'Overcoming the Burden of History in Polish Foreign Policy', *Journal of Communist Studies and Transition Politics*, 19 (2003), 178-203, p. 178.

[30] Iver B Neumann, 'Russia as Central Europe's Constituting Other', *East European Politics & Societies*, 7 (1993), 349-369, p. 369.

Historical patterns of dependence have left the countries of CEE sensitive to the way in which Western European countries have consented to and, in some cases, actively supported, Russian gas infrastructure projects that would circumnavigate the regional overland transit space. These projects, like Nord Stream, have been seen as tantamount to "crimes against European solidarity" according to Noël. He has argued that the "gas supply insecurity syndrome" in CEE has been perceived as anti-Russian propaganda by elites in bigger consumers like Germany, France and Italy.[31] However, a Swedish Defence Research Agency report commissioned to review Russian energy policy, as Gazprom pressed ahead with work on the first two lines of its subsea Nord Stream gas pipeline in 2007, identified a "coercive" energy policy from the Russian supplier in at least 55 instances since 1991, whereby cuts, threats or new pricing policy were deployed in the energy sector with "strategic underpinnings in almost every case."[32] This points to the use of an 'energy weapon' and suggests that what is seen as paranoia in CEE should not be dismissed.

Most of the recorded disruptions occurred in the former Soviet countries and helped deepen a split through Europe's core on gas policy over the 25-year period from 1989 to 2014. As Mez has noted, the varying paces of market liberalisation pushed forward by the EU since the late 1990s served to accentuate this split further.[33] This process of easing competition into national markets is just one of a number of factors that have helped determine the demand profile and domestic supply patterns of natural gas in Europe, according to Goldthau. He has argued that "the EU's liberalization efforts, the EU's decarbonisation agenda, supply security and environmental policies on national and EU levels, and the economic crisis" all affect the current and future position of gas as a fuel in the European energy mix.[34] It is oft

31 Pierre Noël, *EU Gas Supply Security: Unfinished Business* (EPRG, Faculty of Economics, University of Cambridge, 1 April 2013) <https://www.repository.cam.ac.uk/handle/1810/244756> [accessed 30 June 2016], p. 3.

32 In total, forty of those had come against the Baltic states or former CIS countries, while twenty had occurred under the Presidency of Vladimir Putin by the time of the reports' publication in 2007. See: Robert L. Larson, *Nord Stream, Sweden and Baltic Sea Security* (Swedish Defence Research Agency, 2007), p. 80.

33 Lutz Mez, 'Germany's Merger of Energy and Climate Change Policy', *Bulletin of the Atomic Scientists*, 68 (2012), p. 24, Lutz Mez, 'The Transformation of the German Gas Supply Industry', in *National Reforms in European Gas*, ed. Maarten J. Arentsen and Rolf W. Künneke, Elsevier Global Energy Policy and Economics Series (Oxford: Elsevier Science, 2003), pp. 213-43, p. 223.

34 Andreas Goldthau, *The Politics of Natural Gas Development in the European Union* (Harvard University's Belfer Center, October 2013) <http://belfercenter.ksg.harvard.edu/files/MO-CES-pub-GeoGasEU-102513.pdf> [accessed 12 May 2015], p. 33.

cited as the 'bridge-fuel' to a low-carbon future as the subsidised roll out of inconsistently producing renewables continues. Though this book does not address regulation and liberalisation directly, it is an important determining factor in the varying importer ownership structures in each case study country, as discussed later.

In a paper entitled 'A New EU Gas Security of Supply Architecture?', a number of cross-institutional authors concluded that "the prerequisite to solidarity is transparency" in the continental gas sector,[35] often missing in the areas of LTCs and infrastructure development agreements. They called for long-term security scenarios, arguing that "security of demand is a prerequisite for security of supply and vice versa" in the gas market area of Europe.[36] These long-term concerns, focusing on geographical, geopolitical, economic and environmental factors, must be understood as distinct from the processes needed for short-term energy security, such as consumption patterns, pipeline flows and storage inventories. A short-term approach to energy security considers the impact of supply disruptions over weeks and months, rather than those factors that have a longer-term impact, such as regulation or production forecasts.

How observers and policy makers in Europe and beyond go about evaluating these risks is covered in work that aims to provide a method for quantifying energy security risks and levels of resilience in a national system. Jewell's model of short-term energy security, or MOSES, published by the IEA, takes an energy systems approach to assessing "vulnerabilities of primary energy sources and assessing how these affect the security of secondary fuels."[37] Though MOSES is useful, a more relevant tool for this LTC-focused investigation is Stern's gas supply security framework, which takes a long-term view and defines gas supply security as "threats of supply and price disruptions arising from risks associated with the sources of gas supplies, the transit of gas supplies and the facilities through which gas is delivered."[38]

---

35 Jacques de Jong, Jean-Michel Glachant, Manfred Hafner, Nicole Ahner and Simone Tagliapietra, 'A New EU Gas Security of Supply Architecture?', *European Energy Journal*, 2 (2012) <http://www.clingendaelenergy.com/inc/upload/files/A_new_EU_gas_SoS_architecture_2_1.pdf> [accessed 4 August 2015], p. 40.

36 *ibid.*, p. 33.

37 Jessica Jewell, *The IEA Model of Short-Term Energy Security (MOSES) Primary Energy Sources and Secondary Fuels* (IEA, 2011) <https://www.iea.org/publications/freepublications/publication/moses_paper.pdf> [accessed 22 July 2015], p. 7.

38 Jonathan Stern, *Security of European Natural Gas Supplies: The Impact of Import Dependence and Liberalization* (London: The Royal Institute of International Affairs, July 2002), p. 6.

Stern goes on to outline the two dimensions through which risks can be approached in the gas sector. According to Stern these are between "the short- term supply availability versus long-term adequacy of supply and the infrastructure for delivering this supply to markets" and the "operational security of gas markets, i.e. daily and seasonal stresses and strains of extreme weather and other operational problems versus strategic security, i.e. catastrophic failure of major supply sources and facilities."[39] This 'traditional' approach looks firstly at reserves and reserve-to-production ratios as a means of assessing upstream security, then long-term supply arrangement in the form of LTCs and major infrastructure investments, before assessing the downstream issues of import dependence.

This work looks at the second and third aspects of the traditional gas security framework, aiming to provide a review of the LTC agreements in the four case studies that gives an explanation for the causes of import dependence that are related to domestic structures and party politics. In building this argument, the work looks at importer policy for the formation of long-term energy security– providing frameworks – the supply and delivery of gas over years, rather than weeks – as the structure of a contract is usually aimed at resolving a trade arrangement for multi-year periods. But in dealing with LTCs, we must also turn to the available literature on institutional economics that helps provide theoretical reasoning for the terms and clauses embedded within these agreements. Such structural features of LTCs are one of the unseen associated aspects of the trade in gas that allow producers to deploy their notional energy weapon "even without 'firing it'," as Cherp and Jewell have recognised.[40]

3.1.2 *Institutional economics*

Beyond energy security, economic theory that covers trade relationships and transaction costs in commodity exchange is also relevant to this study's exploration of contractual terms, in what Cherp and Jewell term the 'resilience' perspective of energy security.[41] Institutional economics emphasises the key role of institutions in shaping economic systems and setting the rules of the game. From this perspective, the economy is "an open and evolving system, situated in a natural environ-

39 *ibid.*, p. 6.
40 Cherp and Jewell, 'The Three Perspectives on Energy Security', p. 206.
41 *ibid.*, p. 207.

ment, effected by technological changes, and embedded in a broader set of social, cultural, political, and power relationships," according to Hodgson.[42] As has been shown, in the Eurasian gas system the key power relationship exists between a dominant supplier and the consumers that are dependent upon it. The LTC is the formalised tool in which that structural relationship plays out over a fixed period of time.

Neumann et al. outline an institutional economics approach to gas supply that "interprets long-term contracts as a device to avoid the risk of opportunistic behaviour in transactions that involve high sunk investments," such as pipelines and major upstream projects.[43] This carries well in a market environment where high investment costs still need to be met, such as the development of new production centres and pipelines necessary to carry output to consumers. This argument states that LTCs have been signed in the gas industry to avoid what has been conceptualised as the 'hold-up' problem, through which one party is forced to make investments in advance without being certain of returns, which in turn incentivises opportunistic behaviour from the counterparty.[44] A secondary objective, related to the element of the research question that addresses whether contract terms are equitable, is to ask whether the 'hold-up' problem, and the subsequent need for contractual certainty through take-or-pay conditions, still applies in the context of the Central European consumers and Russian supply. Or, does it instead reverse the opportunity for opportunistic behaviour, allowing the exporter to maximise its revenue stream once it has paid down the costs of production and transport?

Research in the 1980s first applied institutional economics theory to the trade in natural gas as a case study. In two separate papers – Masten and Crocker in 1985, and then Crocker and Masten in 1988 – sought to apply a theoretical structure to the need for LTCs in a business with high initial production costs, where producers needed security that they would recoup early investment. They argued that take-or-pay "obligations contained in contracts written in unregulated environments provide for efficient adaptation to changing circumstances in long-term

---

42 Geoffrey M. Hodgson, 'What Is the Essence of Institutional Economics?', *Journal of Economic Issues*, 34 (2000), 317-329, p. 318.

43 Anne Neumann, Sophia Rüster and Christian von Hirschhausen, *Long-Term Contracts in the Natural Gas Industry – Literature Survey and Data on 426 Contracts (1965-2014)*, Data Documentation (Berlin, Deutsches Institut für Wirtschaftsforschung, 2015), p. 7.

44 Oliver E. Williamson, 'Transaction-Cost Economics: The Governance of Contractual Relations', *Journal of Law and Economics*, 22 (1979), 233–61.

contractual relationships."[45] The clause obliges the buyer to offtake a certain percentage of the gas contracted annually (typically 80% to 90% of the total) across the full length of the contract (traditionally 15 to 25 years).[46] The European Commission defined take-or-pay in 2002 as a contract between a buyer and a seller, whereby the former agrees to purchase from the latter a fixed quantity of a product for a given price over a certain period of time. Irrespective of the quantity which is finally needed and transferred, the buyer is bound by its commitments and is required to pay for the whole volume of sales at the contractual terms agreed upon.[47]

In a notoriously fluctuating demand environment – often based year-to-year on changing winter temperatures, the position of competing fuels and industrial demand patterns connected to economic activity – such minimum thresholds agreed years in advance provide worrying dilemmas for importers.

Inflexibility in dealing with supply security over long-term scenarios is mitigated in LTCs with the imposition of these specific clauses, according to Creti and Villeneuve. Take-or-pay "requires that gas has to be paid [for] whether taken or not, and specifies an obligation for the seller to make available defined volumes of gas."[48] The provision of take-or-pay clauses stopped "ex post bargaining opportunities created by the features of natural gas," according to Mulherin.[49] This at least partially supports the argument of Gazprom's European export- wing, Gazprom Export, which has claimed that the physical characteristics of gas and its pricing indexation to oil make it a "unique case" in the array of natural resource commodities.[50]

The frequency of repeat transactions in the gas trade and uncertain forecasts for demand also provide the rationale for complex contractual clauses layered into

---

45 Scott E. Masten and Keith J. Crocker, 'Efficient Adaptation in Long-Term Contracts: Take-or-Pay Provisions for Natural Gas', *The American Economic Review*, 75 (1985), 327-343, p. 1091. A second article on the design and duration of contracts can be found here: Keith J. Crocker and Scott E. Masten, 'Mitigating Contractual Hazards: Unilateral Options and Contract Length', *The RAND Journal of Economics*, 19 (1988), 327–43.

46 Stern, *Security of European Natural Gas Supplies*, p. 9.

47 European Commission, *Glossary of Terms Used in EU Competition Policy Antitrust and Control of Concentrations*, 2002, p. 45.

48 Anna Creti and Bertrand Villeneuve, 'Longterm Contracts and Take-or-Pay Clauses in Natural Gas Markets', *Energy Studies Review*, 13 (2004), 75-94, p. 1.

49 J. Harold Mulherin, 'Complexity in Long-Term Contracts: An Analysis of Natural Gas Contractual Provisions', *Journal of Law, Economics, and Organization*, 2 (1986), 105-117, p. 109.

50 "Natural gas presents a unique case because it is the only commodity in the world that, in many cases, is indexed to another commodity," Gazprom Export's head of contract structuring wrote in a 2013 research paper. See: Sergei Komlev, 'Pricing the "Invisible" Commodity' (Contracts Structuring and Pricing Directorate, Gazprom Export, 2013), p. 9.

LTCs. These include 'make-up' clauses allowing importers to postpone deliveries until a later date, or 'carry-forward' options that allow future quantities to be reduced if excess stocks are consumed one year. They augment 'swing' clauses that allow take-or-pay contract holders to make daily nominations within defined minimum and maximum boundaries on a seasonal or yearly basis. In addition to supplying valuable flexibility within the constraints imposed by an LTC, these clauses allow importers to postpone deliveries of expensive gas under contract when market rates are cheaper.[51] In essence, historically, take-or-pay clauses aimed to even out the risk between the contracting parties, while price indexation to oil in the formula stopped the cost of gas from rocketing above its competitor fuels.

Traditionally, oil-indexation was utilised in contracts to maintain a competitive price of gas against alternative fuels available to the end consumer. This so- called 'netback market value' approach did not necessarily primarily focus on meeting the costs of gas production, or sustaining parity with global oil prices, but sought to make sure consumers who had switched from oil to gas in the 1970s, following the sharp rise in oil price post-1973, did not have a price incentive to revert once the price per barrel dropped again.[52] As Neumann has explained, the deployment of these two clauses meant that "the price risk was transferred to the seller, and the buyer took on the full quantity risk."[53] This way, the price would be set against a globally traded alternative fuel to gas, with clear cost benchmarks in Brent and WTI, but future demand fluctuations would need to be mitigated by the importer, which would be tied to a volume agreed and enshrined in the take-or-pay clause.

Mulherin has argued that gas contracts "often include complex quantity and price provisions", seeking to explain these phenomenon either as a manifestation of market power, a bargaining design to allocate risk evenly between producer and consumer, or as part of the transaction cost.[54] Mulherin concluded that complexity in contracts was an attempt to find a bargaining structure between buyer and seller. As Neumann et al. have noted, early discussion of gas contracts was based on the

---

51 Enrico Edoli, Stefano Fiorenzani, Samuele Ravelli, and Tiziano Vargiolu, 'Modeling and Valuing Make-up Clauses in Gas Swing Contracts', *Energy Economics*, Quantitative Analysis of Energy Markets, 35 (2013), 58-73, p. 63.

52 Jonathan Stern, 'Is There a Rationale for the Continuing Link to Oil Product Prices in Continental European Long Term Gas Contracts?', *Oxford Institute for Energy Studies* <http://www.oxfordenergy.org/2007/04/is-there-a-rationale-for-the-continuing-link-to-oil-product-prices-in-continental-european-long-term-gas-contracts/> [accessed 5 August 2015], pp. 1-3.

53 Neumann, Rüster and von Hirschhausen, *Long-Term Contracts in the Natural Gas Industry*, p. 8.

54 Mulherin, 'Complexity in Long-Term Contracts', p. 105.

assumption of a regulated monopolistic industry, with contracts not only acting as a risk allocation instrument but also as means of maintaining "secure monopolistic rents" for the exporter and the transmission company that secured revenue for transporting the fuel.[55]

Gas pipelines themselves have also been examined as infrastructure constituting a natural monopoly for the owner.[56] In 1989, scholars from Norway's Central Bureau of Statistics echoed earlier complaints that high-end prices for consumers had "severely limited the expansion of the market and resulted in underutilization of transmission capacity." They concluded that "transmission companies have exploited monopoly power, and thus restricted gas consumption" in Norway.[57] Despite the presence of multiple suppliers, the static layout of the gas transmission system encourages a system of imperfect competition whereby some producers are able to hold some parts of their market captive, a symptom of geographic concentration of production relative to consumption and the physical nature of gas.

The direction of change in the European gas market makes necessary a reevaluation of old assumptions. With costs already sunk into pipeline systems and production facilities, are fixed LTCs that index the price of gas to oil really still justifiable in the European market context? Also, do the terms of historical gas contracts serve to undermine the position of gas in relation to its competitor fuels now? Both these questions point to inherent conflicts in the contemporary gas trade environment: between price and security, between flexibility and reliability, between the interests of consumers and producers, and between monopolies and oligopolies. Central Europe here is a region caught 'between' the two market realities in which Europe as a whole buys and sells its gas.

3.2 Historical context: 1945–1989

Gas use in Central Europe dates back to the discovery of hydrocarbons in territory formally controlled by Hungary (now contemporary Romania) and around the Car-

55 Neumann, Rüster and von Hirschhausen, *Long-Term Contracts in the Natural Gas Industry*, p. 9.

56 Jeff D. Makholm, *The Political Economy of Pipelines: A Century of Comparative Institutional Development* (University of Chicago Press, 2012).

57 Olav Bjerkholt, Eystein Gjelsvik and Øystein Olsen, 'Gas Trade Demand in Northwest Europe: Regulation, Bargaining and Competition', *Norwegian Central Bureau of Statistics*, 1989, <http://www.ssb.no/a/publikasjoner/pdf/DP/dp_045.pdf> [accessed 29 June 2016], p. 8.

pathian mountains in the nineteenth and early twentieth centuries.[58] The first gas pipeline in Hungary was not built until 1938, to connect production sites with facilities south of Lake Balaton. The country's first cross- border pipeline was not opened until 1958, when a connection between Tiszapalkonya and Csenger on the Romanian border was built.[59] Poland received its first gas imports from the Soviet Union along a line built by Nazi engineers in 1943 to ship gas approximately 200 km from Galician production sites in today's Ukraine to the industrial town of Stalowa Wola.[60] Gas extraction had taken place around the Carpathian Mountains since the 1910s,[61] but the pipeline to Stalowa Wola became the first dedicated 'export' line for Soviet Ukraine, making it a 'born' gas exporter following World War II.

3.2.1 'Brotherhood' corridor

It would take another 20 years until Soviet gas deliveries beyond the iron curtain became a possibility. In early 1964, with gas reserve estimates rising across the USSR, Soviet planners agreed to begin work on the Bratsvo (Brotherhood) pipeline that would send gas to Czechoslovakia at the frontier of the communist bloc. Under a contract agreed in December 1964, exports to Czechoslovakia were to start at 270 MMcm/y in 1967 before ramping up to 1 bcm/y three years later in 1970.[62] Through the new pipeline gas would reach Bratislava, just kilometres from the Austrian border. The Soviet leadership considered exports to the capitalist world as a means of enabling the reciprocal import of steel pipelines to build out a swiftly expanding internal transport system that could link disparate production

---

58 Janos Toth, 'A SHORT REVIEW OF THE HUNGARIAN PETROLEUM AND NATURAL GAS INDUSTRY FROM THE BEGINNINGS UP TO THE PRESENT DAY' (Museum of the Hungarian Petroleum Industry: Museum of the Hungarian Petroleum Industry, 1988) <https://pp.bme.hu/ch/article/view/2748/1853> [accessed 18 June 2016], p. 78.

59 FGSZ, *CÉGISMERTETŐ* <https://fgsz.hu/content/cegismerteto> [accessed 18 August 2015].

60 Högselius, *Red Gas*, p. 14. Stalowa Wola was built from scratch in the 1930s to host a steel mill and its workers. The city has remained a key industrial site, with a gas-fired power station built in the area during 2014. Stern remarks that deliveries did not exceed 350 million cubic metres (MMcm/y) and no details on the pricing are available. The Stryi field located near the city of Lviv had previously been under Polish jurisdiction. Jonathan Stern, 'Pricing of Gas in International Trade: An Historical Survey', in Jonathan Stern, ed., *The Pricing of Internationally Traded Gas* (Oxford/New York: Oxford Institute for Energy Studies, 2012), pp. 40-84, p. 40f.

61 Jan Golonka and Frank J. Picha, *The Carpathians and Their Foreland: Geology and Hydrocarbon Resources, AAPG Memoir 84* (Boulder, American Association of Petroleum Geologists, 2006), p. 833.

62 Högselius, *Red Gas*, p. 35.

sites across red empire in Ukraine, Siberia and the Central Asian republics with consumption centres in the socialist bloc and beyond. The need for foreign currency earnings was another rationale. Italy was the original target for gas exports, with a transit route through Hungary and Yugoslavia mooted.[63] But with the Brotherhood pipeline already taking gas to the Austrian border from 1967, and Czechoslovakia trading 'virtually' with Austrian companies by negotiating ratios of production from the Zwerndorf gas field straddling the border, it was decided that discussions would start with Vienna-based importers.

The picturesque lakeside retreat at Schloss Hernstein-Berndorf south of Vienna provided the venue for talks between Austrian officials and a Soviet delegation in August 1967.[64] Vienna sought Soviet gas to meet rising demand and mitigate declining production, but initial negotiations stalled on three issues: price, volume and timing. Further discussions forced progress and the eventual signing of an LTC between the Soviet Union and Austria's OMV in June 1968 marked Moscow's first gas export arrangement with a capitalist country. Under the terms of the arrangement, OMV would receive 30 bcm over a 23-year period starting in 1968.[65] A concurrent deal was signed through via which the Austrian Control Bank would supply the USSR's Foreign Trade Bank with an $81 million credit facility with which to part-purchase large-diameter steel pipes.[66]

The supply contract included a number of key clauses now fundamental to the gas trade in Europe. A re-negotiation option for pricing was incorporated from 1975, with deadlines for annual and quarterly nominations also set in place, allowing the importer some flexibility in what it could order on a daily basis within a range of minimum and maximum volumes. An arbitration court in the Swedish capital Stockholm was chosen as the independent arbiter in case of any contractual dispute.[67] Even the arrival of Warsaw Pact tanks into Prague during August 1968, putting an end to the reforms of Alexander Dubček and attracting condemnation from the west, did not disrupt the start-up of deliveries. At a ceremony held at the Baumgarten compressor station in Austria in September 1968, the architect of the Soviet Union's

---

63 *ibid.*, p. 43.

64 *ibid.*, p. 59f.

65 *ibid.*, p. 63.

66 The total cost of the deal reached in Vienna on 1 June 1968 for pipe exports was $115 million. See: George Ginsburg and Robert Melville Slusser, *A Calendar of Soviet Treaties: 1958-1973* (Leiden, BRILL, 1981), p. 442.

67 Högselius, *Red Gas*, p. 64.

export strategy, the Gas Industry Minister of the USSR, Alexey Kortunov, joined Austrian officials in turning the valve to begin flows across the iron curtain.[68] With the Austria deal done, importers further west looked to Soviet gas as an increasingly viable option. A contract was soon signed with Italy's Eni while Germany and France began to consider seriously their own imports as demand for 'blue gold' rose.[69] Although deliveries to Austria experienced a number of early disruptions owing to infrastructure failures, by 1972 exports west had stabilised.[70]

A deal was reached between West German utility Ruhrgas and the Soviet Union on deliveries amounting to an initial 3 bcm/y in February 1970.[71] The Bavarian town of Waidhaus just across from the Czechoslovak town of Rozvadov and around 400 km northeast of Baumgarten in Austria was selected as the initial entry point for Soviet gas into West Germany. The 'gas-for-pipes' deal also included the delivery of German large-diameter pipelines to the Soviet Union and marked a definitive development in Chancellor Willy Brandt's '*Ostpolitik'* strategy aimed at easing tensions between Bonn and Moscow.[72] In July 1972, French company Gaz de France agreed to import Soviet gas through a swap system that would see Italian energy company Eni import the physical gas and then forward on its contracted volume from Dutch production to France.[73] Red gas was slowly but surely securing market share.

---

68 Gazprom Export, *Blue Fuel: Gazprom Export Global Newsletter*, April 2013, p. 5.

69 The agreement with Italy was to last 20 years and stipulated natural gas supply in the amount of 6 bcm/y, with the Soviet Union also given a loan of $200 million with which to purchase equipment from local companies. The first Soviet gas would reach Italy on 1 May 1974. Gazprom, *40th Anniversary of Russian Gas Supplies to Italy*, 10 December 2009 <http://www.gazprom.com/about/history/events/italy40/> [accessed 26 August 2015].

70 Högselius reports a total of eight instances of supply disruption in deliveries to Austria in 1969, each lasting between 10 and 72 hours. See: *Red Gas*, pp. 94–102.

71 Three agreements were signed on 1 February at the Hotel Kaiserhof in Essen. One covered the delivery of gas following up on an earlier deal from November 1969, the second and third catered to the delivery of pipes to the Soviet Union and an associated credit facility. See: George Ginsburg and Robert Melville Slusser, *A Calendar of Soviet Treaties: 1958-1973* (Leiden, BRILL, 1981) p. 799. The contract stipulated a possible expansion to 5 bcm/y in deliveries. See: Högselius, *Red Gas*, p. 129.

72 Jonathan Stern, *Gas Pipeline Co-Operation between Political Adversaries: Examples from Europe* (Royal Institute of International Affairs (Chatham House), January 2005) <https://www.chathamhouse.org/sites/files/chathamhouse/public/Research/Energy,%20Environment%20and%20Development/jsjan05.pdf> [accessed 22 August 2015]. p. 2. Further agreements on expanding the quantity of gas to be delivered to Germany were reached over the following decade in 1972, 1974 and 1979.

73 Högselius, *Red Gas*, p. 132.

3.2.2 *Sands, steppes and lowlands*

Soviet reserves were not the only source of gas to emerge during the 1960s as European demand increased by 208% between 1965 and 1975, driven by a rapid increase in consumption in West Germany, Italy, the UK and the Netherlands.[74] Algerian gas first reached British shores as LNG in October 1964 and arrived in France a year later following the discovery of the massive the Hassi R'Mel gas field in 1956.[75] The discovery of the giant Groningen field in the Netherlands in 1959 created prospects for large-scale production within continental Europe and, by 1974 the Dutch had annual export commitments equal to domestic consumption of over 40 bcm/y.[76] Groningen gas flowed to consumers in neighbouring markets like Germany and Belgium, but also further south to France, Switzerland and Italy, where Soviet planners sought market share. Further reserve discoveries in Norwegian and British waters also helped shape demand continentally, with the giant Troll field in Norway, tapped during the 1980s, supplying gas directly to northeast Europe via the subsea Norpipe system that reached Emden in Germany and was first brought on-stream in 1977.[77]

Some hoped in the 1960s that the arrival of Soviet and Algerian gas to continental Europe would help create a competitive market against which gas could be priced. Gerard de Corval, research director at the French agency Société Commerciale du Méthane Saharien, looked to a future market in which "gas from the sands and gas from the steppes" would meet in the middle of Europe and create a point of price parity: to the east it would be more economical to look to the Soviet Union and to the west southward across the Mediterranean for gas.[78] However, it would take until the 2000s for Russian gas to penetrate continental Europe's far western

[74] According to BP statistics, demand grew in Germany from 2.9 bcm/y in 1965 to 43.7 bcm/y in 1975, and in Italy from 8.1 bcm/y in 1965 to 20 bcm/y in 1975. Both were key destination markets for deliveries of red gas west. BP, *Statistical Review of World Energy 2015* <http://www.bp.com/en/global/corporate/about-bp/energy-economics/statistical-review-of-world-energy.html>.

[75] Glenda G. Rosenthal, *The Mediterranean Basin: Its Political Economy and Changing International Relations* (Netherlands: Elsevier, 2013), p. 78. A number of other export arrangements were agreed for Algerian gas throughout the 1970s.

[76] A. Correlje, C. Van der Linde and T. Westerwoudt, *Natural Gas in the Netherlands. From Cooperation to Competition?* (Oranje-Nassau Groep, 2003), p. 67f. The Groningen field is also referred to as the Slochteren gas field after the town closest to the field.

[77] Jonathan P. Stern, 'Norwegian Troll Gas: The Consequences for Britain, Continental Europe and Energy Security', *The World Today*, 43 (1987), 1–4.

[78] As reported by Högselius in *Red Gas*, p. 28.

reaches and, despite several attempts dating back to the 1960s, Algerian gas never moved northeast of the Alps in large volumes.[79] Instead, Dutch gas would act as the initial market maker, with all other importers "strongly influenced by the commercial [...] framework created for Dutch imports," according to Stern.[80]

The 'net-back market' concept for pricing Groningen gas exports devised in 1962 by the Netherlands' Minister of Economic Affairs and Aalsmeer-native, Jan Willem de Pous, would provide a template for future continental contract formation. The formula would set aside a simple 'cost-plus' calculation[81] and price gas in reference to the fuels it was competing against on a sector-by-sector basis, rather than on a calculation of its own inherent value.[82] Put simply, this system based the export price at the border on the maximum a consumer was willing to pay referenced to the cost of an alternative fuel – in most cases, oil. In the 1960s, state-owned regulated utilities would need to be incentivised to switch fuels and invest in new infrastructure like pipelines and power stations to facilitate the build-out of gas-burning turbines. Additionally, the interesting factor in favour of the Dutch in securing the market-making position was their proximity to buyers and subsequent ability to be more flexible in delivery at shorter notice. A key feature of the sale of Groningen gas was that more distant suppliers like Algeria, Russia and Norway could not imitate "the provision of daily and annual supply flexibility sufficient to cover seasonal and other market fluctuations" for the consumer, according to Melling.[83]

79 Plans for the delivery of Algerian gas to Central and South-Eastern Europe date back to the 1970s with proposals for pipeline deliveries to Yugoslavia via Italy mooted and an LNG terminal project on Croatia's Adriatic coast considered by a consortium of companies that included Czechoslovak foreign trade group Metalimex, Austria's OMV and local company INA. German regional gas supplier Bayerngas also sought to arrange its own shipments of North African gas to avoid dependence on Ruhrgas and north German states. None of the planned projects ever proceeded, with a plan for an LNG import terminal on the Adriatic island of Krk still in development as of 2014, but no longer specifically designed of Algerian gas.

80 Jonathan Stern, 'Pricing of Gas in International Trade', p. 55.

81 Cost-plus simply calculated the price against the cost of production with transportation, any business overheads and a profit margin added in.

82 Konoplyanik outlines the pricing formula in early net-back contracts as having included a 60% indexation to light fuel oil in the case of households and a 40% reference to heavy fuel oil where gas would compete with industrial consumers. See: Andrey A. Konoplyanik, 'Evolution of Gas Pricing in Continental Europe: Modernization of Indexation Formulas Versus Gas to Gas Competition', International Energy Law and Policy Research Paper Series, 2010/01 (2010) p. 8.

83 Anthony J. Melling, *Natural Gas Pricing and Its Future: Europe as a Battleground* (Washington, D.C.: Carnegie Endowment for International Peace, 2010) p. 26.

Destination clauses were also a feature of these early contracts as a means of ensuring that cheaper gas leaving the Dutch border and destined for far away markets such as Italy "could not be used to undercut higher priced gas sales in, for example, the German market," according to Correlje et al.[84] Separately, Algerian exporter Sonatrach insisted on a full oil-indexation pricing formula leading to conflict with its principle buyers and suspended deliveries during the late 1970s as part of what became an early 'gas battle.'[85] In Western Europe's adolescent gas markets, contracts and rules of trade were yet to be established but these early systems of price reference and risk allocation in the export of Dutch gas would soon become structural features.

For Soviet gas deliveries to the economic alliance of the Council for Mutual Economic Assistance (COMECOM) countries the so-called Bucharest formula devised in 1958 was applied. This methodology calculated rates set against 'world market prices,' initially over each five-year plan period.[86] This helped to shield the countries of CEE against volatile price fluctuations in the international market until the system was revised in 1975 to better follow the sharp increase in oil-prices internationally post-1973. Cofala argued that the prices paid for imports by the COMECOM countries were below the cost of production, playing an important role in the Soviet system where "a complicated system of central allocation of energy to industrial and household consumers was in operation."[87]

As Soviet planners negotiated exports west of the iron curtain in the late 1960s they faced the struggle of reconciling the net-back system used for Groningen with their own Bucharest formula. For example, the price agreed for Soviet exports to Austria in 1968 was $15.13 per mcm,[88] but negotiations over the delivery of Soviet gas to West Germany in 1969 struggled to establish a price that would compete

---

84 A. Correlje, C. Van der Linde and T. Westerwoudt, *Natural Gas in the Netherlands. From Cooperation to Competition?* (Oranje-Nassau Groep, 2003) p. 69.

85 A full analysis of the dispute between Algeria and its clients can be found in Chapter 3 of this text: David G. Victor, Amy M. Jaffe, and Mark H. Hayes, *Natural Gas and Geopolitics From 1970 to 2040* (Cambridge: Cambridge University Press, 2006).

86 Before 1975 these prices were calculated as an average of the prices for the combined preceding Soviet five-year plan. After 1975 this system switched to a shifting average of the previous five years, meaning a different annual rate. This is also known as the 'Moscow formula.' See: Stern, 'Pricing of Gas in International Trade', p. 63.

87 Janusz Cofala, 'Energy Reform in Central and Eastern Europe', *Energy Policy*, 22 (1994), 486-498, p. 488.

88 Högselius, *Red Gas*, p. 63.

with Dutch gas that was being offered that year at an approximate rate of just \$12.71 per mcm.[89]

Flexibility also dogged the 1969 negotiations, with Ruhrgas agreeing a minimal take-or-pay delivery level of 70% with its Dutch supplier, but the Soviets were not prepared to settle for less than 90% of their total contracted volume.[90] As has already been discussed, this gave the Dutch negotiators an advantage over their competitors owing to the close proximity of the Netherlands' production sites to its key export markets, which meant it could offer greater flexibility in offtake levels, as it needed a lower pipeline utilisation rate.[91]

3.2.3 Golden age of gas

Following the resolution of the pricing negotiations and the subsequent signing of the first round of LTCs by Moscow, in 1976 the Soviet Union's total export obligations reached over 25 bcm, which would more than double to 52 bcm by 1980, as the contemporary estimates in Table 5 show.[92] By 1975, COMECOM members such as Poland were receiving 2.5 bcm/y, Czechoslovakia 2.7 bcm/y, East Germany 3.3 bcm/y, and Hungary 600 MMcm (million cubic metres)/y, with deliveries having begun to the last only that year.[93] Just a decade after 1970, Soviet exports would rise by over 1500%, illustrating the rapid development of gas demand in Europe and the feverish pace at which new reserves and infrastructure would need to be laid out by planners.

Such a sharply increasing obligation as is shown in Graph 13 necessitated the fast development of pipeline infrastructure both internally – like the Northern Lights transport system, which began development in 1967 to link production around the Ural Mountains with consumers in Moscow and Belarus – and externally. A transport corridor through the Soviet republic of Ukraine and Czechoslovakia was chosen as the key export route for Soviet gas, with new lines to be laid along the route of the Brotherhood pipeline. In October 1970, the Czechoslovak pipeline

---

89 The \$12.71 per mcm figure is a calculation by the author based on the 0.56 Pfennig per megacalorie rate quoted by Högselius in *Red Gas,* p. 114. The calculation used a full-year average exchange rate of 3.9230 Deutsche marks to the dollar for 1969.

90 Högselius, *Red Gas* p. 117.

91 Stern, 'Pricing of Gas in International Trade', p. 57.

92 Högselius, *Red Gas,* p. 135.

93 Robert G. Jensen, Theodore Shabad and Arthur W. Wright, *Soviet Natural Resources in the World Economy* (University of Chicago Press, 1983), p. 373.

Table 5: Gas export volumes from the Soviet Union in bcm (1970–1980)[94]

Country	1970	1973	1974	1975	1976	1980*
Austria	1	1.6	2.1	1.9	2.8	2.9
Bulgaria	-	-	0.3	1.2	2.2	4.6
Czechoslovakia	1.4	2.4	3.2	2.7	4.3	7.3
East Germany	-	-	2.9	3.3	3.4	5.7
Finland	-	-	0.4	0.7	0.8	1
France	-	-	-		1	4
Hungary	-	-	-	0.6	1	3.5
Italy	-	-	0.8	2.3	3.7	7
Poland	1	1.7	2.1	2.5	2.5	5.9
Romania	-	-	-	-	-	1
West Germany	-	-	2.2	3.1	4	10.7
Yugoslavia	-	-	-	-	-	2
TOTAL	3.4	5.7	13.8	18.3	25.7	55.6

* = Statistics are estimates from Western countries. Preceding yearly statistics came from Vneshnyaya torgovlya SSSR official trade figures, which ceased reporting individual quantities in 1977.

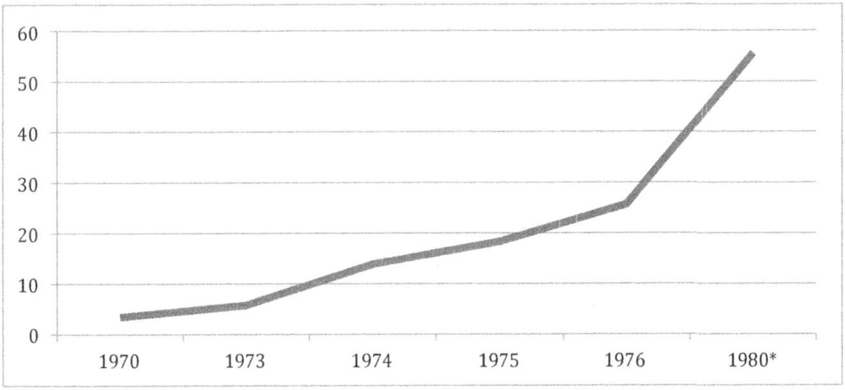

* = Statistics are estimates from Western countries, see footnote 94.

*Graph 13: Annual gas exports obligation for USSR in bcm (1970–1980)**[95]

94 Table using statistics from Jonathan Stern, 'Soviet Natural Gas in the World Economy', in *Soviet Natural Resources in the World Economy*, 1983 (University of Chicago Press, 1983), p. 373.

95 Jonathan Stern, 'Soviet Natural Gas in the World Economy', in *Soviet Natural Resources in the World Economy*, 1983 (University of Chicago Press, 1983), p. 373.

operator agreed to begin work on a new 28 bcm/y pipeline system that would transport Soviet gas to western markets. In 1971, Tranzitní plynovod Praha, or Transgas, was set up to manage the scheme and construction started in March that year.[96]

The development of the Czechoslovak transit system alone was the largest project during the country's five-year plan from 1970-1975, with 600,000 tonnes of pipeline scheduled to be laid during construction.[97] A number of technical challenges would disrupt operations as Soviet engineers rushed to build out a network that need to cross perma-frosted ground in Siberia and the Carpathian Mountains in Ukraine all the way into Czechoslovakia.[98] Nevertheless, at an event heavy on symbolism, Soviet Minister for the Gas Industry, Sabit Orudzhev, was at the Waidhaus border crossing on 1 October 1973 to commemorate the launch of gas exports to West Germany and remarked that hydrocarbons were travelling without "passport and visa."[99] However, as Brandt's *Ostpolitik* bore its first results, behind the iron curtain Soviet planners in Moscow struggled to meet the rapid surge in both internal and external demand. Ukraine was the notable victim and saw gas production from its Galicia region pumped abroad as priority that meant local supplies were heavily reduced. The Ukrainian cities of Kharkiv, Lviv and Kiev were particularly badly hit as the Soviet leadership chose export stability and foreign currency over reliable supply to its own republics.[100]

3.2.4 Plotting pipelines

In June 1974 at the COMECOM summit in Sofia, the Soviet satellite states also agreed to work on a major new gas pipeline project that would link the riches of the Orenburg field with Uzhogorod in Ukraine, over 2,750 km away. In return for labour and construction services from East Germany, Bulgaria, Czechoslovakia, Poland, Hungary and (later) Romania, each country would receive 2.8 bcm/y

---

96 Net4Gas, *40 Years of Natural Gas Transit through the Czech Republic*, 24 March 2015 <http://www.net4gas.cz/en/media/brozury/N4G_40_year_history_brochure_EN.pdf?jis=20150324133252> [accessed 21 May 2015], p. 2.

97 Högselius, *Red Gas*, p. 152.

98 For example, floods in Czechoslovakia during the autumn of 1974 caused the collapse of pipeline supports and a complete cut to gas supplies for a six-day period. An explosion in February 1975 disrupted the same weak link in the transport system. See: Högselius, *Red Gas*, p. 164.

99 *ibid.*, p. 159.

100 *ibid.*, p. 162.

through the so-called Soyuz (Union) export pipeline once it slowly ramped up to full capacity between 1978 and 1980.[101]

A follow-up project in the 1980s saw the same countries agree to assist in the construction of another export pipeline in return for gas deliveries starting in 1989. Work and equipment would be provided for the development of the Yamburg, or Progress Pipeline, project that, in addition to the previous Orenburg deal, created the two supply arrangements under which the case study countries were to receive gas in the immediate post-Soviet era under discounted terms referenced to the Bucharest formula. These are further discussed in the case study chapters.

Meanwhile, in the 1980s, infrastructure development elsewhere also gathered pace, with the Norwegian export system being expanded and the first phase of the Trans-Mediterranean Pipeline providing the first direct connection between Italy and North African production being commissioned in 1983.[102] As the continental network expanded, trade lines and relationships became entrenched. Output from the Maghreb region limited demand for alternative gas supplies from some Mediterranean importers for Russian gas and Atlantic seaboard countries in Western Europe were satisfied with domestic production and did not need to seek LTC agreements with distant suppliers across the iron curtain divide.

The rapid build-out of pipeline infrastructure and the subsequent associated dependence on new exporters gave rise in European capitals to concerns over security of supply throughout the 1970s. The 1973 oil crisis had been one of the key drivers behind an increase in the use of gas, as available reserves around Europe were seen as viable alternatives to Middle Eastern oil. As early as 1964, the then-six member states of the European Community agreed a Protocol on Energy Problems that outlined a commitment to market integration, as coal was increasingly being replaced by oil in the members' energy mix.[103] However, levels of commitment to joint action within the group were mixed: France advocated the inclusion of European Community officials in talks over the formation of a single market,

---

[101] Robert G. Jensen, Theodore Shabad and Arthur W. Wright, *Soviet Natural Resources in the World Economy* (University of Chicago Press, 1983) p. 373.

[102] Rosenthal, *The Mediterranean Basin*, p. 86.

[103] European Community, Protocole d'accord relatif aux problèmes énergétiques intervenu entre les gouvernements des États membres des Communautés européennes, à l'occasion de la 94e session du Conseil spécial de ministres de la Communauté européenne du charbon et de l'acier tenue le 21 avril 1964 à Luxembourg, 1964 <http://eur-lex.europa.eu/legal-content/EN/TXT/?qid=1440423481217&uri=CELEX:41964A0430(01)> [accessed 24 August 2015].

Figure 6: A Soviet stamp commemorating pipeline projects in 1983[104]

while German officials, worried about Dutch attempts to limit the entry of new suppliers and ensure their own captive market, were less enthused about closer cooperation in the energy sector.[105] Brussels would not find a role in bilateral gas contract talks until the 2000s, but the debate on how to integrate and harmonise national markets can be shown here to date back over 50 years.

In the 1980s, politically motivated disruption to Soviet gas supplies was not the only concern for importers in capitalist Europe. With his country targeted directly alongside the US during the 1973 oil crisis, Dutch Prime Minister Joop den Uyl threatened to turn off the gas taps to neighbouring markets if their governments did not agree to re-sell oil imports further on to the Netherlands.[106] Algerian exporter Sonatrach also restricted LNG exports temporarily during the crisis, with politicians explicitly linking the Arab–Israeli conflict to stable gas supplies.[107] In 1981, strikes at Norwegian production sites around the Frigg and Ekofisk reserves also disrupted deliveries to Germany.[108] The Soviets were the least of the problems for continental supply security.

---

104 *A USSR Stamp, 1983. Gas Main Urengoy–Uzhhorod.*, 5 December 2007, uploaded to Wikimedia by Mariluna, <https://commons.wikimedia.org/wiki/File:1983_CPA_5445.jpg> [accessed 22 August 2015].

105 Högselius, *Red Gas*, p. 127.

106 Per Högselius, 'The European Natural Gas Industry and the Oil Crisis of 1973/74', 2013 <https://networks.h-net.org/system/files/contributed-files/henergy-p-hogselius-natural-gas-and-oil-crisis-1973.pdf> [accessed 16 December 2015].

107 Högselius, *Red Gas*, p. 170.

108 *ibid.*, p. 192.

Moscow had not linked the outcome of the conflict in the Middle East to gas supply and under a command economy strikes were deemed unlikely. Plans to begin deliveries of Iranian gas through the Soviet system to Europe from 1981 also appeared to illustrate a vote of confidence from European capitals in Moscow's ability to reliably transport gas[109] This was despite the US administration under President Ronald Reagan sharply opposing the continued development of Soviet gas exports to Europe, warning of critical dependence levels. Plans for the North Star LNG terminal, mooted in the 1970s, which would have sent liquefied gas from a facility near Murmansk in the Arctic Sea to the US east coast were scrapped under Reagan and sanctions were imposed on the sale of vital hardware for compressor station infrastructure to companies wishing to help the Soviet system-building venture.[110] The European Community responded to the sanctions in 1982 by claiming that the Soviet share of gas would be minimal in the total energy mix and not pose a risk:

> Gas from the Soviet Union will help to conserve the Community's own stock of gas, oil and other fuels, and will reduce the Community's own reliance on other foreign sources. Use of Siberian gas will not create a dangerous dependence on that source. Even when gas is flowing at the maximum rate, in 1990, it will represent less than 4% of the Community's total energy consumption.[111]

With the dissolution of the Soviet Union, the countries of CEE were among the most energy intensive in the world in the early 1990s, with intensity levels at up to four times those of developed market economies.[112] A drop in gross energy consumption across the region from 326 million tonnes of oil equivalent (mtoe) in 1989 to 243 mtoe in 1992 was driven by the collapse of import markets to the east that had sustained the manufacturing and industrial sectors. Industrial output in Poland, Hungary and Czechoslovakia dropped by a fifth over the three- year period.[113] Additionally, payments for energy imports now needed to be made in hard currency rather than 'soft ruble' or barter, as had previously been the case. However, the Orenburg and Yamburg agreements would help soften the transition from

---

109 *ibid.*, p. 183.

110 Jonathan P. Stern, 'Specters and Pipe Dreams', *Foreign Policy*, 1982, 21–36.

111 Reuters, 'TEXT OF COMMON MARKET STATEMENT ON EMBARGO', *The New York Times*, 13 August 1982, section Business <http://www.nytimes.com/1982/08/13/business/text-of-common-market-statement-on-embargo.html> [accessed 24 August 2015].

112 Cofala attributes this to a focus on basic industry, low import prices for fuel and a dirtier fuel mix. Janusz Cofala, 'Energy Reform in Central and Eastern Europe', *Energy Policy*, 22 (1994), 486-498, p. 487.

113 Broken down, this included a 26% decline in gas consumption over the period. See: *ibid.*, p. 489f.

the Bucharest formula gas pricing to net-back market rates, ensuring gas would continue to flow.

By 1990, Gerard de Corval's vision of distant gas sources meeting at the heart of Europe was not yet realised. Instead, a patchwork of national markets still relied on bilateral contracts with various pipeline suppliers and a cocktail of indigenous production and/or LNG. Over the next 25 years, new export infrastructure to feed Russian gas through to Europe would be developed. The Yamal–Europe pipeline was built during the 1990s to expand capacity to Germany and Western Europe through a new transit corridor that would cross Belarus and Poland. The first two Nord Stream lines would send gas under the Baltic Sea directly to the German town of Greifswald from 2011 as part of a Gazprom strategy for easing its reliance on gas transit via Ukraine following the disputes of 2006 and 2009, which saw the Russian export monopoly shut down gas supplies to its neighbour.

As of 2016, two new pipelines that would double the capacity of Nord Stream are planned, in addition to a new export route that would run through southeastern Europe. Figure 7 shows the operational mainline pipelines. The scale of Gaz prom's

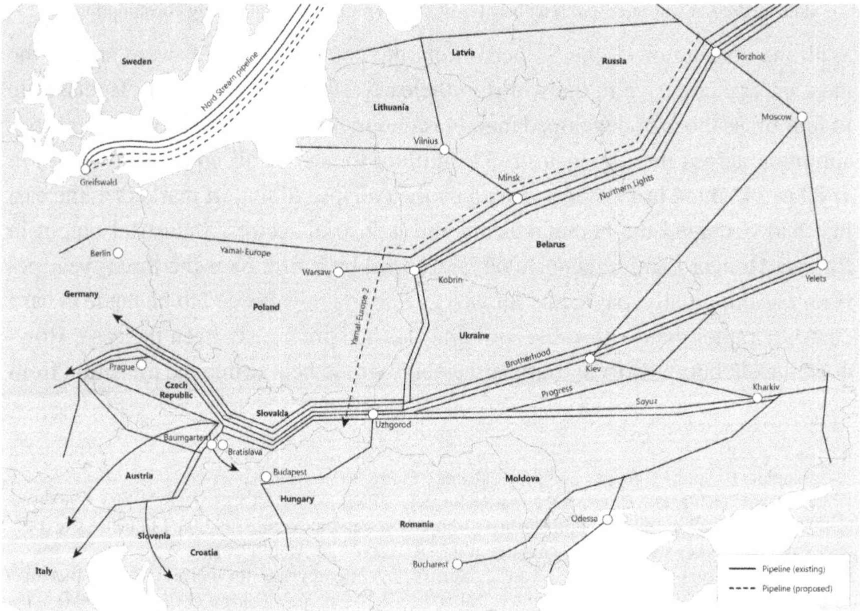

Figure 7: Map of mainline pipeline export projects

control of each transportation route it had into the European market – measured from field to sales point – between 1989 and 2014 has come into question. EU efforts to unbundle ownership structures forced Gazprom to cede control of transmission companies it supplies, for example. At the end of the time period under review, the Ukrainian route (along Soyuz and Progress) stretched 4,700 km and was controlled 66% by Gazprom; the Yamal route through Poland was 4060 km and controlled 83% by Gazprom through its ownership of the Belarusian transmission system operator; Nord-Stream's entire delivery route is 4240 km and is owned 100% by Gazprom.[114] There were several factors supporting the Russian company's monopoly on supply to the region under investigation, but infrastructure constraints remain central. Gas flows in the direction pipelines allow it to, and Gazprom's system was built one-way.

3.3 European market context

The global gas trade is heavily regionalised, with market areas localised according to proximity to production centres and infrastructure. This has led to the emergence of various forms of pricing and contract structures in each distinct area. Three major market areas exist: the US, Europe and Asia. The US, with gas priced mostly against the Henry Hub reference point in Louisiana, is often the cheapest, with a 'porous' border for exports north to Canada and south to Mexico helping to influence those neighbouring markets too.[115] The European market area is mixed between the hubs of the west and the pipeline-supply dependent markets of CEE. In Asia, LNG is king and importers typically pay the highest price to attract cargoes.[116] Although LNG is building bridges between these major global market areas, and to smaller isolated markets like Australia, no clear price had emerged by 2014 that could be taken as a representation of global supply and demand.

As discussed earlier, the use of netback pricing and Bucharest formula mechanisms were historically two separate pricing systems used on either side of the

---

114 Tomáš Mareček, Chairman of the Board of Directors, 'Usual Questions, Unusual Answers' (presented at the Central European Energy Conference, Bratislava, Slovakia, 2014) <http://ceec.sk/wp-content/uploads/2014/12/Mare%C4%8Dek-OK.pdf> [accessed 25 August 2015].

115 Howard Rogers, 'The Interaction of LNG and Pipeline Gas Pricing: Does Greater Connectivity Equal Globalisation' in Jonathan Stern, ed., *The Pricing of Internationally Traded Gas* (Oxford/New York: Oxford Institute for Energy Studies, 2012), pp. 375–423, p. 377.

116 LTCs for LNG supply to Asia are often priced against Japanese Customs Cleared (JCC), a cocktail of oil products. Although unlike the European system, these contracts have rarely been modified, creating various difference prices that reflect snapshots of when the contracts were originally signed. See: *ibid.*, p. 378.

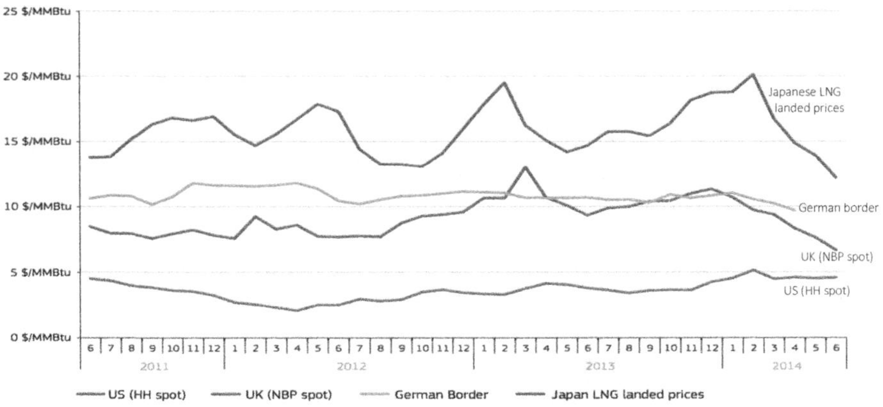

Graph 14: International comparison of wholesale gas prices (2011-2014)[117]

iron curtain. After 1989, consensus settled on the former, originally developed to price exports from the Dutch Groningen field in the 1960s, as a way of calculating the rate on new commercial contracts. The first LTCs agreed between Russia's state-owned vehicle for gas production and export, Gazprom, with consumers in CEE during the 1990s were priced using an indexation to oil products, just as the existing commercial contracts used by Western buyers were. However, by 2005 gas prices in Western Europe were increasingly pegged to another reference, defined not against a substitute fuel in oil, but against forces of supply and demand for gas determined at 'hubs.' In a survey of global wholesale gas prices from 2005 to 2014, the International Gas Union (IGU) provided a summary of pricing formulae and their use in market areas worldwide. The various forms applicable for imports into Europe are defined as follows:[118]

---

117 Measured in dollars per million British thermal units, or MMBtu. Data is sourced from Reuters and BAFA and reproduced from: European Commission, *Quarterly Report on European Gas Markets (volumes 6 and 7)*, 2014 <https://ec.europa.eu/energy/sites/ener/files/documents/201410_q3-4_quaterly_report_gas_market.pdf> [accessed 28 August 2015], p. 18.

118 When looking at the pricing of total consumption instead of total imports, the array of pricing mechanisms expands to include various forms of regulated rates granted by producing countries' governments to heavy industry and households. International Gas Union, *Wholesale Gas Price Survey - 2015 Edition: A Global Review of Price Formation Mechanisms 2005 - 2014*, May 2015 <http://www.igu.org/sites/default/files/node-page-field_file/IGU%20Whole%20Sale%20Gas%20Price%20Survey%20Report%20%202015%20Edition.pdf> [accessed 27 July 2015], p. 13.

- Oil-price escalation (OPE) links the price of gas to a competing fuel, typically a basket of oil products or sometimes coal or electricity prices. In this thesis, this formula is commonly described as oil-indexation.
- Gas-on-gas (GOG) prices gas against supply and demand fundamentals over daily, monthly or annual time periods at exchange platforms such as Henry Hub, National Balancing Point in the UK or the Dutch Title-Trade Transfer system. This also includes the LNG spot market.
- Bilateral Monopoly (BIM) refers to the price being determined between two parties – often a large seller and large buyer – who fix a price for a certain period of trading time, usually a year. For example, this form of pricing can often be used between large industrial consumers and state-owned producers.

Global gas imports in 2014 were priced according to Graph 15. OPE, or oil- indexation, represents the formula for the majority of gas imported – 51% in 2014. In Europe, where the IGU reported "the most significant changes in price formation mechanisms" since 2005, gas-on-gas competition clearly represented the majority by 2014, with a 59% share according to the IGU statistics used in Graph 16. In 2005, GOG had taken just a 15% share of total European price formation, which included

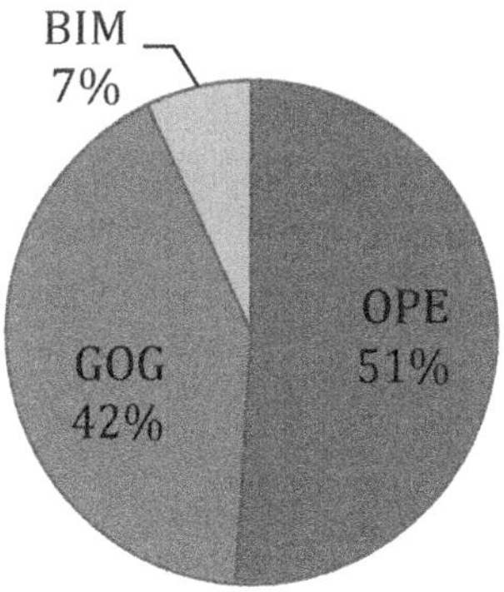

Graph 15: Price formation of world gas imports by kind in 2014[119]

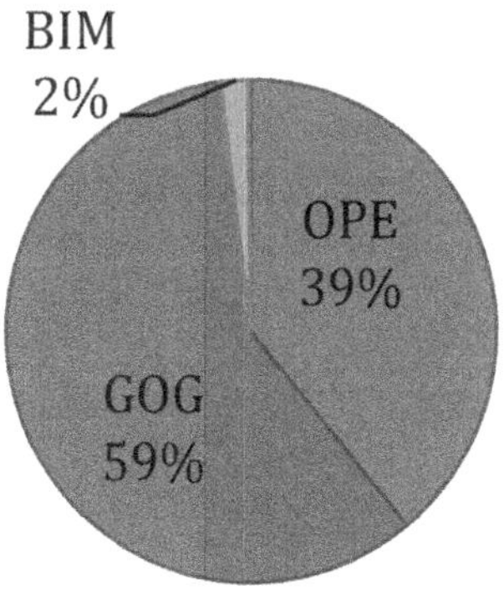

Graph 16: Price formation of European gas imports by kind in 2014[120]

[119] *ibid.*, p. 16.
[120] *ibid.*

domestic production sold locally, in addition to imports. In Central Europe, the swing from oil-indexation to hub pricing has been stark. according to the statistics. OPE dropped from 85% in 2005 in Central Europe to 32% in 2014 and gas-on-gas rose from 0% to 53% in the same period.[121] These figures are key to understanding the repeated reference in coverage on the European gas market to a structural revolution in how the fuel is being supplied and priced.

Gazprom statistics, however, argue that oil-indexation and quasi oil-indexed gas remained key to pricing imports into the EU from third countries in 2014. The growth of hybrid pricing models that incorporate reference both to oil products and hubs became an increasing feature of the European gas market after 2000 as consumers sought revisions not only to their pricing but also to the structural formula from suppliers like Gazprom, Norway's Statoil and Algeria's Sonatrach. According to Gazprom statistics re-produced in Graph 17, 69.9% of 2014 imports into the EU

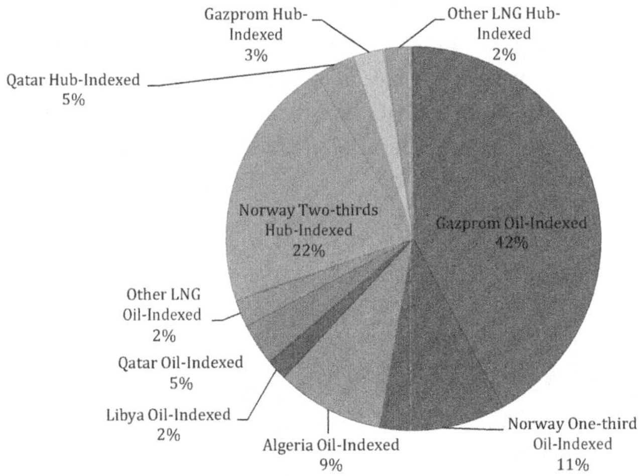

Graph 17: Share of oil-indexed gas in EU imports from third party (2014)[122]

[121] Central Europe includes Austria, Czech Republic, Hungary, Poland, Slovakia and Switzerland. International Gas Union, *Wholesale Gas Price Survey - 2015 Edition: A Global Review of Price Formation Mechanisms 2005 - 2014*, May 2015 <http://www.igu.org/sites/default/files/node-page-field_file/IGU%20Whole%20Sale%20Gas%20Price%20Survey%20Report%20%202015%20Edition.pdf> [accessed 27 July 2015], p. 27.

[122] As presented by Sergei Komlev, 'European Gas Market State and Prospects: View from Gazprom Export' (presented at the Flame Conference, Amsterdam, 2015).

included some reference to oil products in the formula, giving the pricing method a dominant position. However, whichever statistics are accepted as most representative, a declining role for oil-indexation is evident. Gazprom statistics show a drop from 71.1% for the price formation method year-on-year from 2013.

The importing countries under investigation here carry much of the exposure to Gazprom's 42% share of oil-indexed gas. Also, much of the sharp increase in GOG-traded gas in Central Europe reported by the IGU came in Austria and Switzerland, where hub trading has quickly developed over recent years. Analysis of the data collected for this research illustrates that around 80% of the contracted gas for the four case study countries' import portfolios combined was under oil-indexed LTC with Gazprom in 2014.[123] This came at the end of a period of steeply rising oil prices that took per barrel prices – via a brief boom and bust in 2008/2009 – to above $100 for most of the 2010 to 2014 period before the price collapse in late 2014 (which falls outside the period of inquiry here). This almost uninterrupted oil price environment of $100-plus per barrel from February 2010 to October 2014 conditioned a rising gas price for European consumers as the lagged contract indexation mechanism of 6-9 months passed into LTC prices, causing consumers to push for discounts and price revisions, as shown earlier in Table 1. This period of price-ratcheting came after an escalation of geopolitical strife in the European market, with disruptions to Gazprom supply via Ukraine in 2006 and 2009. The high prices post-2009 also reflected a market reality not envisaged when the gas LTCs for each case study under review here were signed with Gazprom.

The European Commission's Directorate General for Energy conceded in 2014 that there are "pronounced differences in the [gas market] dynamics across different member states," but added that "the pace of price convergence on major European gas hubs is a success of an ever growing integration of European gas markets."[124] As illustrated earlier in Graph 14, there had been a notable correlation in prices between NBP and the official German border price from summer 2013, il-

---

[123] Calculation based on data to be presented in the following chapter. Considers 38.55 bcm of total contracted gas for the four countries in 2014, of which 30.75 bcm was Gazprom LTC gas. This includes an assumption that the Qatar LNG contract between PGNiG and Qatargas was active and that an extension of the terms of the Vemex contract for imports into the Czech Republic was undertaken.

[124] European Commission, *Quarterly Report on European Gas Markets (volumes 6 and 7)*, 2014 <https://ec.europa.eu/energy/sites/ener/files/documents/201410_q3-4_quaterly_report_gas_market.pdf> [accessed 28 August 2015], p. 1.

Graph 18: Brent crude oil price in $ per barrel with V4 LTC milestones[125]

lustrating a potential linkage between the pipeline-supplied rate attributed to Gaz prom gas and its openly traded hub-priced counterpart in the UK. "Improving transport capacity access has allowed price signals from larger and more liquid hubs in Northwest Europe to increasingly be transmitted to hubs in Southern Europe," the Commission said.[126] Though the reason for the price convergence is under debate, the position of hub-priced gas is expanding through Europe.

It is assumed that infrastructure developments integrating CEE with its western neighbours will assist in bringing regional prices down to levels comparable not only with bigger importers such as Germany, but also to hub rates possibly linked to a price set at the Central European Gas Hub (CEGH) based around the Baumgarten storage centre in Austria. However, over the course of the 1989–2014 period studied here, relatively little infrastructure development took place that reversed the east-to-west pipeline flows presented in the preceding section. Much of what has been developed took place in the final fifth of the studied period, following 2009. For example, full reverse-flow capacity on the Yamal– Europe pipeline between Poland and Germany was only brought onstream in 2014, and no LNG terminal was operational beyond the Danish Straits. The rapid growth in trading at the CEGH at Baumgarten provides one potential avenue for price reference in the region, but a lack of physical capacity and high network access costs in neighbouring markets have stymied

[125] US Energy Information Administration using Thomson Reuters data. Arrows denote when Gazprom agreed LTCs still valid in 2014 with each of the case studies.

[126] *ibid.*, p. 22.

progress.[127] A notable exception was the development of the HAG Pipeline between Austria and Hungary in the 1990s, as will be discussed later in Chapter 7.

3.3.1 Oil-indexation vs. hub-based pricing

As infrastructure investments are made, debate over the future of gas pricing in the European market area has continued to rage. Should hub-based pricing be embraced as the benchmark for new contracts or should oil-indexation be maintained? On one side, Gazprom officials such as Sergei Komlev, head of the contract structuring and price formation directorate at Gazprom Export, and energy economist and Gazprom adviser, Andrey Konoplyanik, provide the case for the 'producer:' oil-indexation should be maintained and it plays an important role in underpinning hubs that give the appearance of inherent gas price.[128] On the other side, the rate of re-negotiation requests between 2010 and 2014 from the 'consumer' camp, as illustrated in Table 1, suggests importer preferences for revised terms and new LTC structures, as supported by academics such as Stern and Rogers from the Oxford Institute for Energy Studies.[129] Analysis of how gas contracts are formed

---

[127] The CEGH operates the Austrian virtual trading point and supplies a variety of trading products for companies wishing to buy or sell gas either over the counter (OTC) or on futures contracts. In 2015, CEGH reported a total trading volume of 478.3 TWh of natural gas at the OTC Market, a 9% rise on 2014, and 26.5 TWh at the CEGH Gas Exchange, a 25% rise on the year before. Though a Prague trading platform has also now been launched, a lack of physical infrastructure to disburse gas through Central Europe and high grid access costs in Slovakia have hindered progress towards regional integration.

[128] Gazprom's position can be best inferred from the following two papers by the authors mentioned: Sergei Komlev, 'Pricing the "Invisible" Commodity' (Contracts Structuring and Pricing Directorate, Gazprom Export, 2013) and A. A. Konoplyanik, 'Evolution of Gas Pricing in Continental Europe: A View From Russia - Modernization of Indexation Formulas versus Gas-to-Gas Competition', *Oil, Gas & Energy Law Journal (OGEL)*, 9 (2011) <https://www.ogel.org/article.asp?key=3077> [accessed 24 August 2015].

[129] Their arguments have been supported by Alan Riley from City University in London and Luca Franza from the Clingendael International Energy Programme based in the Netherlands. The following papers help to outline the reasons for hub-indexation in LTCs: Jonathan Stern, 'Is There a Rationale for the Continuing Link to Oil Product Prices in Continental European Long Term Gas Contracts?', *Oxford Institute for Energy Studies*, 2007 <http://www.oxfordenergy.org/2007/04/is-there-a-rationale-for-the-continuing-link-to-oil-product-prices-in-continental-european-long-term-gas-contracts/> [accessed 5 August 2015], Jonathan Stern and Howard Rogers, 'The Transition to Hub-Based Pricing in Continental Europe - A Response to Sergei Komlev of Gazprom Export', *Oxford Institute for Energy Studies* <http://www.oxfordenergy.org/2013/02/the-transition-to-hub-based-pricing-in-continental-europe-a-response-to-sergei-komlev-of-gazprom-export/> [accessed 28 August 2015], and Luca Franza, *Long-Term Gas Import Contracts in Europe: The Evolution in Pricing Mechanisms* (Clingendael International Energy Programme) <http://www.clingendaelenergy.com/publications/publication/long-term-gas-import-contracts-in-europe> [accessed 12 November 2015].

and priced in contemporary Europe during the post-2009 period requires an understanding of this debate.

Komlev asserts that oil-indexation should be maintained as part of a hybrid-pricing mechanism because it provides the only reasonable benchmark for gas, protecting consumers and producers against price volatility and fairly apportioning risk between the contracting parties. Komlev's argument takes issue with the representation of "unfair and burdensome oil-indexed contract prices versus fair, transparent and cheaper hub prices," prevalent in discourse.[130] Following his argument, hub prices are not reflective of supply and demand, but derivative from the rates of oil-indexed contracts from suppliers like Gazprom.

NBP and the Dutch Title Transfer Facility (TTF) hubs are therefore double derivatives, based on LTC prices, which are themselves derived from oil prices. The argument continues that in the post-2009 period, rising oil prices provided a signal to which gas hubs responded, whilst importers who had over-contracted gas supplies pre-financial crisis rushed to dump excess volumes on the open market. Gas hub prices then "settle at a discount to contract prices, only occasionally equalling the contract price," Komlev posited.[131] Konoplyanik has argued that a natural evolution of gas contracts could lead to an increase in the types of commodity prices included in the basket of oil-indexation beyond only oil products, such as 'must-run' power prices, but he argued in 2010 that the "European gas market is not prepared [...] to switch over to gas-to-gas competition as the key pricing mechanism,"[132] even as the volume of gas traded on hubs was continuing to rise:

> The Groningen model of LTCEC [long-term gas export contract] has been the constantly adapted instrument of organization of international trade in gas. At the same time, this model maintains its major characteristic features. Moreover, Groningen LTGEC model, including modifications of its pricing mechanisms, has been the fundamental basis of the international trade in gas and thus the guaranty of the stable and secure international gas supply.[133]

Furthermore, Komlev argued that although oil and gas have not been directly substitutable fuels in over 20 years, a physical connection between them as alternatives will soon be re-established as the result of the increasing use of natural gas–

130 Sergei Komlev, 'Pricing the "Invisible" Commodity' (Contracts Structuring and Pricing Directorate, Gazprom Export, 2013), p. 51.

131 *ibid.*, p. 50.

132 Andrey A. Konoplyanik, 'Evolution of Gas Pricing in Continental Europe: Modernization of Indexation Formulas Versus Gas to Gas Competition', International Energy Law and Policy Research Paper Series, 2010/01 (2010), p. 29.

133 *ibid.*, p. 17.

fuelled vehicles and vessels in the transportation sector. On this point his adversaries tentatively agree, but note that rates of market penetration for gas in transport remain minimal.[134] Gazprom's position in favour of oil- indexation in a high-price environment between 2010 and 2014, even as other suppliers like Norway's Statoil accepted the greater incorporation of hub pricing into their supply portfolios,[135] posed a further question regarding whether the Russian state supplier was seeking a 'high price-low volume' or 'low price-high volume' export strategy in the European market. It appeared to be the former.

Consultancy firm Timera Energy has argued that oil-indexed prices act as a "magnetic ceiling" that pulls spot prices back in line as the market balances out:
Oil-indexation has a particularly important influence on spot prices in Asia and Europe because of its influence on the exercise of contract volume flexibility. The ability to vary swing contract take is optimised based on the differential between oil-indexed contract prices and spot gas prices. When spot gas is cheaper than oil-indexed contract prices, contract volume take is reduced and incremental hub gas purchased (and vice versa). This means that oil-indexed contract prices act as an important longer term anchor for gas prices.[136]

The authors also note, however, that this relationship is eroding as LTCs expire, and as new deals are signed, the role of hub pricing will be defined by the decisions taken by suppliers like Gazprom.

The argument against continued oil-indexation in LTCs, posited most prominently by Stern and Rogers, is that the move to gas-on-gas competition in price formation is inevitable. According to them, the concept of fuel-substitution dating back to Groningen and the 1960s is out of date and no longer provides an adequate rationale for isolating gas from its own supply and demand fundamentals. Stern and Rogers argue that proponents of oil-indexation seek to retain the mechanism as it provides the highest revenues for the producer as part of a one-sided notion

---

134 Komlev, 'Pricing the "Invisible" Commodity', p. 36.

135 For example, by winter 2013 all of Statoil's contracts for supply to Germany were indexed to hub prices. See: Ajay Makan, 'Statoil Breaks Oil-Linked Gas Pricing', *Financial Times*, 19 November 2013 <http://www.ft.com/intl/cms/s/0/aad942d6-4e25-11e3-b15d-00144feabdc0.html#axzz3kaFh8ghK> [accessed 2 September 2015].

136 Timera Energy, 'Hub Pricing in a Converging Global Gas Market', 2015 <http://www.timera-energy.com/a-converging-gas-price-world/> [accessed 17 June 2016].

of fairness in the bargaining process.[137] Liquidity concerns in European hubs is a receding issue, they argue, with TTF and NBP both mature and stable enough to be reliable price discovery points by 2011. Additionally, they argue that traded volumes on other hubs in France, Belgium, Germany and Austria are rising and have followed price signals from their more established counterparts, which are helping to form an inherent gas price:

> New long-term contracts will be shorter, much more flexible than their predecessors and with hub-based prices", Stern and Rogers argued in 2011, before warning that there was a "possibility that these events may be accompanied by a significant deterioration of relations between buyers and sellers of gas, which may have much larger consequences for the future of gas in Europe.[138]

Total European gas demand fell dramatically between 2010 and 2014 and, according to IEA statistics, the 32 markets it considers as the region saw their demand fall from 585 bcm in 2010 to 476 bcm in 2014.[139] By February 2013, with the oil-indexed LTCs priced high, the Oxford academics warned that "unless gas prices are rapidly adjusted to hub prices, European gas demand will continue to fall, with the effect that gas will become a 'sunset industry' in Europe."[140]

Graph 19 gives an impression of the overall instability in the various proxies for gas prices as represented by Timera Energy. Ultimately, the oil/hub rates argument centres on disagreement over what constitutes the fairest means of pricing gas. The 'producer' argument in favour of oil-indexation claims that spot prices do not provide a balanced market that takes into account the costs levied on the developer for exploration and transmission. The 'consumer' argument is for a pricing system that bases itself on the inherent supply and demand signals of the commodity in question, and which should not guarantee the producer a profit. As will be discussed in later chapters, the Czech national importer's success in arbitration proceedings against Gazprom forced concessions on price, formula calculation and take-or-pay volume in a 2013 landmark case for the European gas market. Hun-

---

137 Jonathan Stern and Howard Rogers, 'The Transition to Hub-Based Pricing in Continental Europe - A Response to Sergei Komlev of Gazprom Export', *Oxford Institute for Energy Studies* <http://www.oxfordenergy.org/2013/02/the-transition-to-hub-based-pricing-in-continental-europe-a-response-to-sergei-komlev-of-gazprom-export/> [accessed 28 August 2015], p. 4.

138 Jonathan Stern and Howard Rogers, 'The Transition to Hub-Based Gas Pricing in Continental Europe', in Jonathan Stern, ed., *The Pricing of Internationally Traded Gas* (Oxford ; New York: Oxford Institute for Energy Studies, 2012), pp. 145–177, p. 172.

139 As reported here: Timera Energy, 'European Gas Demand, LNG Flow & Hub Prices', 2015 <http://www.timera-energy.com/european-gas-demand-lng-flow-hub-prices/> [accessed 12 December 2015].

140 Stern and Rogers, 'The Transition to Hub-Based Pricing in Continental Europe', p. 6.

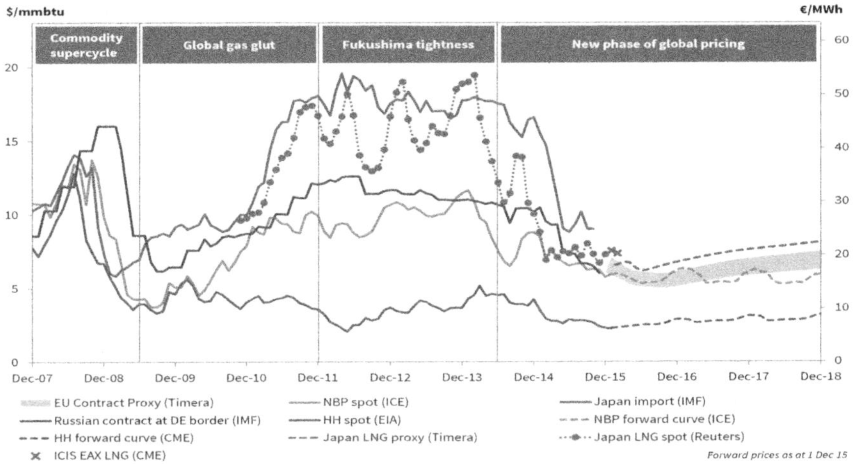

Graph 19: Evolution of key global gas price benchmarks (2007–2018)[141]

gary's importer – co-owned by Gazprom – agreed a contract extension that effectively annulled its take-or-pay provision in 2015 as its LTC expired. Slovak and Polish importers continue to make their case for change at the end of the studied period. This work illustrates the conditions that have led to this dramatic period of change in the European gas market.

3.3.2 EU regulatory landscape

The key regulatory actor in the European gas market environment is the EU. Since becoming members in 2004, each of the four case studies has been required to transpose EU legislation on the energy market generally, and on the gas sector more specifically. From its first inception as the European Coal and Steel Community (ECSC) in 1951, the EU as a continent-wide supranational structure has been concerned with managing resources, but the foundation of a legislative toolbox with which to act out a long-term energy strategy has been a relatively recent development and remains a work in progress. The ECSC's common market

141 As published in Timera Energy, 'Hub Pricing in a Converging Global Gas Market', 2015 <http://www.timera-energy.com/a-converging-gas-price-world/> [accessed 17 June 2016]. Graph 19 shows how NBP hub prices largely undercut Russian contract prices into Germany throughout the global gas glut, and the tightness in demand following the Fukushima nuclear accident in Japan that saw LNG sought to plug the generation gap.

for coal and steel originally sought to bind France and West Germany closer and neutralise any potential risk of further conflict. A new set of institutions and intergovernmental structures emerged in the 1950s.[142]

The European Atomic Energy Community, or Euratom, was launched in 1957 to manage the nascent nuclear energy sector,[143] but even by the 1992 Maastricht Treaty "measures significantly affecting a Member State's choice between different energy sources and the general structure of its energy supply" were still exempted from EU policymaking power.[144] However, by 1995, measures were put in place to increase transparency in the oil sector and create a system whereby crude oil imports into the community and between its member states would be registered, and costs reported.[145] In April 1996, the EU also set new rules for reporting on investment projects across the energy sector, obligating member states to provide information on new gas schemes that included "transfrontier gas pipelines and projects of common interest," in addition to LNG import terminals and storage facilities with a capacity of more than 150 million cubic metres, for which construction was to start up to five-years ahead.[146]

Later, the First Gas Directive of 1998 dealt with the internal market, setting forth a system of common rules that would be the first legislative move towards liberalisation.[147] A second directive in 2003, which repealed both the first directive and another out-dated gas transit directive from 1991, sought to create non-discriminatory access to infrastructure, but by the 2003 EU Nice Treaty, there

---

142 The Netherlands, Luxembourg, Italy and Belgium were the other first signatories to the ECSC, with the European Economic Community launched in 1957 through the Treaty of Rome.

143 Euratom holds the same membership as the EU but is in effect a separate structure. EU, 'Consolidated Version of the Treaty Establishing the European Atomic Energy Community', 1957.

144 European Council, '"Maastricht Treaty" on European Union', 1992 <http://europa.eu/eu-law/decision-making/treaties/pdf/treaty_on_european_union/treaty_on_european_union_en.pdf> [accessed 12 June 2016], p. 59.

145 European Council, '1999/280/EC: Council Decision of 22 April 1999 Regarding a Community Procedure for Information and Consultation on Crude Oil Supply Costs and the Consumer Prices of Petroleum Products', 1999 <http://eur-lex.europa.eu/legal-content/EN/TXT/?uri=CELEX%3A31999D0280> [accessed 17 June 2016].

146 European Council, 'Council Regulation (EC) No 736/96 of 22 April 1996 on Notifying the Commission of Investment Projects of Interest to the Community in the Petroleum, Natural Gas and Electricity Sectors', 1996 <http://eur-lex.europa.eu/legal-content/EN/TXT/?uri=celex%3A31996R0736> [accessed 17 June 2016].

147 European Union, 'Directive 98/30/EC of the European Parliament and of the Council of 22 June 1998 Concerning Common Rules for the Internal Market in Natural Gas', 1998 <http://eur-lex.europa.eu/legal-content/EN/TXT/?uri=celex%3A31998L0030> [accessed 17 June 2016].

remained no continent-wide energy strategy.[148] A comprehensive energy policy document was only approved during the 2005 EU Council summit in the UK, with the European Commission recognising shortly afterwards that the "most important persisting shortcoming is the lack of integration between national markets. Key indicators in this respect are the absence of price convergence across the EU and the low level of cross-border trade."[149] An earlier EU Green Paper on security of energy supply made clear that a "worrying level of dependence on gas imports" was emerging,[150] while the 2004 European Council directive put in place further measures for defining a common framework for the gas sector, while also proposing that member states report on "long-term gas supply contracts concluded by companies established and registered on their territory, and in particular their remaining duration".[151] Aspects of security were beginning to mix with questions of energy market design and how to harmonise regimes in a widening club of countries as the former communist states joined in 2004.

The EU institutions would focus on market liberalisation, intensifying unbundling efforts that would require energy companies to be split between trading, infrastructure managers and distributors. The 2009 third energy package – which included provisions on both the gas and electricity sectors, repealing the second gas directive – sought to reinforce regulator powers while setting forth three ways in which utilities could be separated. The first, called 'ownership unbundling' would mean that "no supply or production company is allowed to hold a majority share or interfere in the work of a transmission system operator." The other two models would allow ownership by a parent company as long as it hived off

---

148 European Union, 'Directive 2003/55/EC of the European Parliament and of the Council of 26 June 2003 Concerning Common Rules for the Internal Market in Natural Gas and Repealing Directive 98/30/EC', 2003 <http://eur-lex.europa.eu/legal-content/GA/ALL/?uri=CELEX:32003L0055> [accessed 17 June 2016].

149 European Commission, 'COMMUNICATION FROM THE COMMISSION TO THE COUNCIL AND THE EUROPEAN PARLIAMENT Report on Progress in Creating the Internal Gas and Electricity Market', 2005 <http://ec.europa.eu/transparency/regdoc/rep/1/2005/EN/1-2005-568-EN-F1-1.Pdf> [accessed 12 June 2016], p. 2.

150 EU, 'Green Paper on the Security of Energy Supply. Towards a European Strategy for the Security of Energy Supply', 2000 <http://eur-lex.europa.eu/legal-content/EN/TXT/?uri=uriserv:l27037> [accessed 17 June 2016].

151 European Council, 'Council Directive 2004/67/EC of 26 April 2004 Concerning Measures to Safeguard Security of Natural Gas Supply (Text with EEA Relevance)', 2004 <http://eur-lex.europa.eu/legal-content/EN/TXT/?uri=CELEX%3A32004L0067> [accessed 17 June 2016].

management to either a subsidiary or another company.[152] Such provisions were designed to prevent companies from restricting access to their network, while also significantly challenging the position of incumbent suppliers like Gazprom that had had ownership over utilities it supplied. Competition was king in the new market design.

The 2010 gas security supply regulation, coming shortly after the highly disruptive cut-off to Russian supplies running through Ukraine in 2009, made reference to crisis prevention measures and included the condition that "supply from third countries [...] not distort competition and [be] in accordance with internal market rules."[153] Since then, the position of the EU as an actor in the energy sector has intensified, but consensus on the role it can play in determining and intervening in gas LTCs was unresolved by the end of this period of investigation in 2014, despite policy suggestions for a joint gas purchaser and both price and IGA–reporting obligations from member states. A European Commission anti-trust case launched in 2014 also shone a light on Gazprom's market practices in eight CEE member states, including the four included in this analysis, with the first external accusation of unfair business practices against a gas supplier.[154] The result remained pending at the end of the period of this analysis in 2014, but much of its explanation can be found in how Poland, Slovakia, Hungary and the Czech Republic first turned their comrade supply deals into commercial LTCs in the early transition.

---

152 European Commission, 'DG Energy: Market Legislation' <https://ec.europa.eu/energy/en/topics/markets-and-consumers/market-legislation> [accessed 10 January 2016].

153 European Union, 'Regulation (EU) No 994/2010 of the European Parliament and of the Council of 20 October 2010 Concerning Measures to Safeguard Security of Gas Supply and Repealing Council Directive 2004/67/EC Text with EEA Relevance', 2010 <http://eur-lex.europa.eu/legal-content/EN/ALL/?uri=CELEX%3A32010R0994> [accessed 17 June 2016].

154 European Commission, 'Antitrust: Commission Sends Statement of Objections to Gazprom - Factsheet' <http://europa.eu/rapid/press-release_MEMO-15-4829_en.htm> [accessed 7 April 2016].

4 Poland

Poland has been an importer of gas from the east since 1944, according to Gazprom Export, making it one of Russia's oldest hydrocarbon customers.[1] Annual demand has trended upwards since 1989 – sitting at 16.7 bcm in 2013[2] – and imports constitute roughly two-thirds of this total. Domestic production covers the remaining share and output began in the interwar period, notably around the Krosno Jasło field in the Galicia region, which is today near the Slovak border. Gas production peaked initially in 1943 at 932 MMcm, but despite post-war discoveries in the Silesia region, a steady increase in demand necessitated raising imports throughout the 1950s and 1960s.[3] After falling to a low of 2.6 bcm in the early period of transition, production rose to a peak of 4.4 bcm in 2004, with levels stabilising just below that for the following decade.[4] According to BP figures, Poland had conventional gas reserves of 115 bcm as of the end of 2013.[5]

Planned unconventional gas development has so far been unsuccessful, although reserves have been estimated at a likely minimum 346 bcm.[6] Poland's dependence on imports for at least around two-thirds of its annual demand throughout the period of investigation has thus so far been maintained. Gas made up 13.9% of total primary energy supply in Poland in 2013, a slight increase on the 13%

---

1 Gazprom Export, 'Poland' <http://www.gazpromexport.ru/en/partners/poland/> [accessed 29 April 2015].

2 BP, *Statistical Review of World Energy 2014* <http://www.bp.com/en/global/corporate/about-bp/energy-economics/statistical-review-of-world-energy.html> [accessed 29 April 2015].

3 Robert F. Byrnes and Oscar Halecki, *East-Central Europe Under the Communists: Poland* (London: Atlantic Books, 1957), p. 333.

4 BP, *Statistical Review of World Energy 2014* <http://www.bp.com/en/global/corporate/about-bp/energy-economics/statistical-review-of-world-energy.html> [accessed 29 April 2015].

5 *ibid.*

6 Polish Geological Institute, *Zasoby Gazu Z Łupków W Polsce – Gwarancja Z Zapasem*, 21 March 2012 <http://www.pgi.gov.pl/pl/instytut-geologiczny-informacje-prasowe/4109-zasoby-gazu-z-lupkow-w-polsce> [accessed 13 May 2015].

J. Posaner, *Held Captive by Gas*, Energiepolitik und Klimaschutz. Energy Policy and Climate Protection, https://doi.org/10.1007/978-3-658-27518-1_4

level in 2009, with coal the dominant fuel for power generation.[7] Industry is the major gas consumer, constituting 35% of demand in 2012, with the residential sector consuming 26%.[8] Polskie Górnictwo Naftowe i Gazownictwo (PGNiG) is the national gas utility, owning all storage assets and holding a dominant market share in the retail sector. Gaz-System is the transmission system operator. Both are state-owned, with the former founded in 1982 and latter spun off in 2004, in line with the EU's Third Energy Package rules on separation of network ownership. The two companies both effectively operate as state entities, with the Polish government in control of PGNiG's management, and therefore of the company that manages the country's LTCs with Gazprom and other suppliers. According to CV1 as shown in Figure 1, this gives the state control and influence over the importing entity in its decision-making processes.

As of 2014, Poland has five notable gas network entry points: two with Belarus (Wysokoje and the entry point for the Yamal–Europe Pipeline at Kondratki), one with Ukraine (Drozdowicze), one with Germany (Lasów) and a single interconnection with the Czech network (Cieszyn), opened in 2011. A number of smaller-capacity entry points exist with negligible supply volumes. Total import capacity as of 2014 was 137.33 MMcm per day, with Russian supply routes via Belarus and Ukraine accounting for 123.75 MMcm/d of that. The remaining 13.58 MMcm/y had largely been developed over the few years leading up to 2014, giving Polish importers limited physical capacity with which to arrange alternative supply contracts with western exporters, as outlined under CV2 in Figure 1.

By December 2014, total gas storage capacity in Poland was 1.83 bcm across eight facilities, equivalent to 45 days of average gas demand in 2011, as shown in Figure 8.[9] Interconnectors with both Slovakia and Lithuania are planned and an LNG import terminal with an initial regasification capacity of 5 bcm/y came onstream in winter 2015 at the Baltic Sea port of at Świnoujście, but did not receive its maiden cargo until June 2016. The centre-right government elected shortly after the period of this investigation ends in 2014 has sought to ramp up alternative options for gas supply, proposing a revival of a Scandinavian pipeline project and

---

7 IEA, *Energy Policies of IEA Countries: Poland 2011* (Paris: Organisation for Economic Co-operation and Development, 2011) [accessed 17 January 2015], p. 98 and IEA statistics.

8 IEA, *Gas Trade Flows in Europe*, 2015 <http://www.iea.org/gtf/index.asp> [accessed 8 June 2015].

9 PGNiG, 'Storage' <http://en.pgnig.pl/segments-of-activity/trade-and-storage/storage> [accessed 12 June 2015].

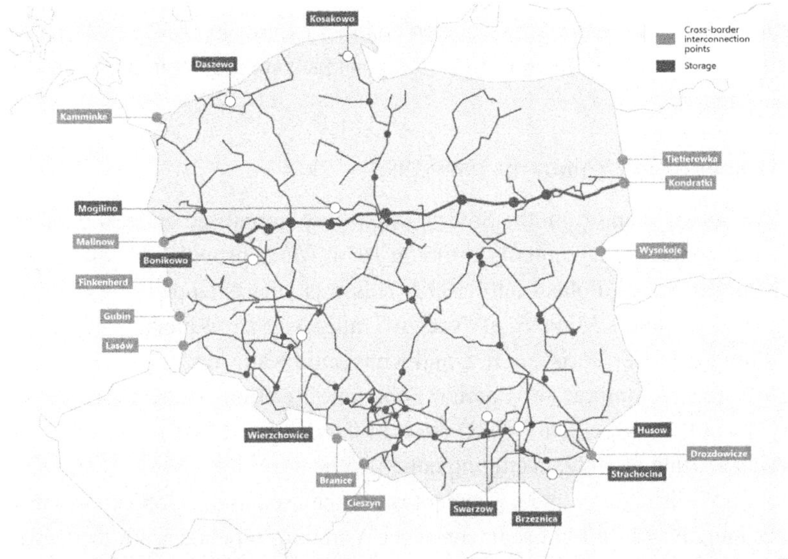

PGNiG's storage capacity, existing

	Working capacity in 2013	Target capacity	Year construction/extension expected to be complete
Strachocina	330 MMcm	360 MMcm	2014
Swarzów	90 MMcm	90 MMcm	-
Wierzchowice	575 MMcm	1.2 bcm	2014
Bonikowo	200 MMcm	200 MMcm	-
Daszewo	30 MMcm	30 MMcm	-
Brzeznica	65 MMcm	100 MMcm	2015
Husow	350 MMcm	500 MMcm	2014
Kosakowo	51.2 MMcm	250 MMcm	2021
Mogilno	407.9 MMcm	800 MMcm	2027
Total	2.10 bcm	3.53 bcm	

Source: PGNiG

Mainline pipeline entry points

Location	Operators	Capacity	Flow
Lasow (from Germany)	Ontras	4.48 MMcm/d	Firm one way with virtual in the other
	Gaz-System		Firm one way
Drozdowicze (from Ukraine)	Ukrtransgaz Gaz-System	12.60 MMcm/d	Firm one way
Wysokoje (from Belarus)	Gazprom Transgaz Belarus Gaz-System	15.71 MMcm/d	Firm one way
Kondratki (from Belarus)	Gazprom Transgaz Belarus Gaz-System	94.76 MMcm/d	Firm one way
Tietierowka (from Belarus)	Gazprom Transgaz Belarus Gaz-System	0.68 MMcm/d	Firm one way
Cieszyn (from Czech Republic)	Net4Gas Gaz-System	2.60 MMcm/d	Firm one way
Mallnow (from Germany)	Gascade Gaz-System	6.50 MMcm/d	Firm one way

*All data for April 2014. Source: ENTSO-G

Poland's annual consumption and production

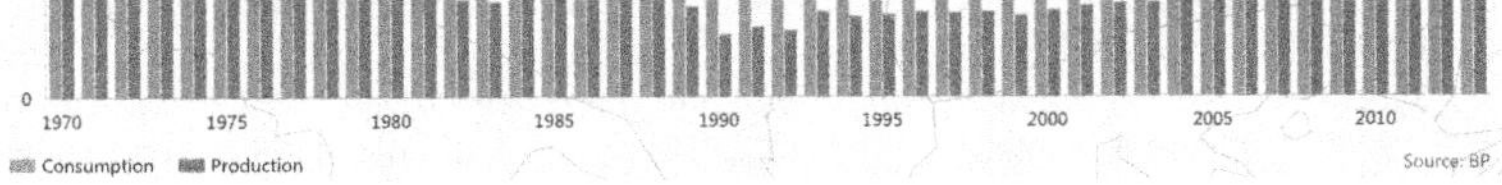

Figure 8: Poland market snapshot[10]

---

[10] Data taken from ENTSO-G, PGNiG, Gaz-System, BP Statistical Review of World Energy and IEA, *Energy Policies of IEA Countries: Poland 2011* (Paris: Organisation for Economic Co-operation and Development, 2011).

suggesting that after the current Gazprom contract expires in 2022 it will not be renewed. PGNiG also has an ambitious storage expansion project in place, as also shown in Figure 8.

4.1 Orenburg and Yamburg: 1989–1993

Gas deliveries to Poland from the Soviet Union were formalised under the framework of the Orenburg Agreement starting in 1974, which provided for the supply of 2.6 bcm/y of gas to Poland until 1998. This was later extended to 1999.[11] In January 1987, Poland's Minister of Foreign Trade, Andrzej Wojcik, Soviet Minister of Foreign Trade, Boris Aristov, and Konstantin Katushev, the Chairman of the USSR State Committee for Foreign Economic Relations, signed the supplementary Yamburg Agreement, which covered the delivery of 45 bcm over a 20-year period starting in 1989, averaging out at 2.5 bcm/y.[12]

In return, Polish labour and equipment would be used to develop export infrastructure, including a 360 km segment of the Yamburg pipeline, with the Soviet Union to repay Poland with gas deliveries over the following 20-year period.[13] Hanna Suchocka, Poland's Prime Minister from 1992 to 1993 in a multi- party centrist coalition, estimated Polish contributions to the Yamburg project to have been $700 million in total.[14] However, stagnation in the Soviet economy, Russia's requirement for hard-currency payments, coupled with increasing demand for imports from Poland, led to almost immediate pressure on the labour-for-gas system following the collapse of the Soviet Union and subsequent uncertainty over whether the communist era supply deals could be maintained.

For Poland's first post-communist government under Prime Minister Tadeusz Mazowiecki, stability of gas supply was one of many concerns requiring clarity on the terms of the Yamburg and Orenburg deals. Polish Foreign Trade Minister Marcin Święcicki claimed in March 1990 that the Soviet Union should supply 10

---

11 Aleksander Zawisza, *Gaz dla Polski. Zarys historii sektora gazu ziemnego w ostatnich dwóch dekadach w Polsce* (Instytut Sobieskiego) <http://sobieski.org.pl/wp-content/uploads/Zawisza-Aleksander-Gaz-dla-Polski-IS.pdf> [accessed 5 May 2015], p. 14.

12 Joanna Agnieszka Gorska, *Dealing with a Juggernaut: Analyzing Poland's Policy towards Russia;1989 - 2009* (Lanham: Rowman & Littlefield, 2010) p. 106, and 'Poland to Help on Pipeline', *The Globe and Mail*, 3 February 1987, section ROB, p. B2. Reports of the annual volumes vary between 2.3-2.5 bcm/y, but averaged out over the full contract tenor quantities would be 2.5 bcm/y.

13 'AGREEMENT ON POLISH PARTICIPATION IN PROGRESS GAS PIPELINE PROJECT', *BBC Monitoring Service: Central Europe & Balkans*, 5 February 1987.

14 Gorska, *Dealing with a Juggernaut*, p. 106.

bcm more than it was prepared to over the following five-year period under the terms of Poland's assistance in the development of the Yamburg project.[15] A re-negotiation of the terms of the Yamburg deal in July 1991, during the administration of centrist conservative Prime Minister Jan Bielecki's Liberal Democratic Congress (KLD) coalition, agreed that Poland would receive a total of 13 bcm, split across 1.2 bcm in 1991, 1.65 bcm in 1992 and 2.5 bcm/y thereafter from Russia.[16] However, the method of payment continued to be the subject of conflict as late as 1993.[17] Transit payments for each mcm of Russian gas delivered through Poland per 100 km in 1993 were approximately $1.50.[18]

Just days after the dissolution of the Soviet Union in December 1991, Poland agreed a part-barter deal with Russia worth a reported $2.8 billion that would see five million tonnes of oil and 8.1 bcm of gas delivered in 1992 in return for food-stuff, pharmaceuticals, sulphur and coal.[19] The deal came shortly after Prime Minister Jan Olszewski's Catholic conservative Centre Agreement-led governemnt took office for what would be a five-month term, and just in time for an emerging gas supply crisis. In January 1992 supplies from Russia were cut by 40% in apparent error, with Polish officials not notified in advance of the reduction.[20] "They were busy dismantling the Soviet Union and failed to send the information down in time," an official from the trade ministry said at the time.[21]

With heavy industry and chemical production suspended in Poland,[22] Foreign Trade Minister Adam Glapiński reached a new gas supply deal set to begin on 1 February during an emergency visit to Moscow in late January that ostensibly

15 'Poland, Soviet Union wrangle over natural gas', *Reuters News*, 25 March 1990. Under the communist system quantities of gas supplies had been arranged in five-year packages, with 1990 beginning a new cycle.

16 Soviet Gas Pipeline Project Renegotiated', *Rzeczpospolita*, 20 July 1991, p. 1.

17 'Poland Still Negotiating Purchasing Methods with Russia for 1993', *East European Energy Report*, 17 March 1993, p. 17.

18 Gorska, *Dealing with a Juggernaut*, p. 112.

19 'Polish-Russian Trade Agreement Signed', *Rzeczpospolita*, 27 December 1991, p. 1.

20 Another explanation is that Yeltsin vetoed the deal and instead instructed suppliers to focus on hard- currency deals. Polish representatives were not informed of the planned reduction in supply in advance. The level of reduction was in line with plans to export 4.5 bcm to Poland in 1992 before the December barter deal was reached.

21 'RUSSIA CUTS POLISH NATURAL GAS SUPPLIES IN ERROR', *Reuters News*, 9 January 1992.

22 Michael Simmons, 'Industry Faces Disaster Unless Russia Turns the Gas Back On', *The Guardian*, 31 January 1992, p. 24.

guaranteed deliveries of 6.6 bcm in 1992.[23] Initial volume increases in line with the new Moscow agreement did not take place, but warmer weather allowed industry to return to normal during February, and a follow-up agreement increased planned deliveries to 7.1 bcm in 1992.[24]

Barter trading had also allowed for deliveries in excess of the combined 5-5.5 bcm ensured by the Yamburg and Orenburg deals, with a 'Gas for Food' (gaz za żywność) exchange system in place.[25] Private company Bartimpex – owned by one of Poland's richest men, Aleksander Gudzowaty – delivered foodstuff worth a combined $141 million between 1991 and 1993 in exchange for gas and would continue to play a role in Russia–Poland gas trade over the following decade. The company claims to have made arrangements for deliveries of 12 bcm between 1992 and 2005, but the figure is likely to be far higher.[26]

In 1994 – after the left-wing Democratic Left Alliance (SLD) and Polish People's Party (PSL), had won elections in late 1993 and formed a supermajority government with PSL leader Waldemar Pawlak, appointed to his second term as Prime Minister after an earlier 33-day stint – Bartimpex reached a deal with the Moscow city authorities to receive 2 bcm: 400 MMcm to come that year, and the remaining 1.6 bcm in 1994. In return, dairy products, meat and canned food were among the goods sent to Russia.[27] Meanwhile, Poland had also traded small quantities with Germany under deals between PGNiG and trader Verbundnetz Gas (VNG). Gas deliveries began in June 1993, with annual quantities of 37 MMcm.[28] Supplies into Poland were

---

23 'POLAND, RUSSIA SEAL NEW DEAL ON RUSSIAN GAS SUPPLIES', *Reuters News*, 27 January 1992.

24 A March 1992 meeting in Warsaw between the deputy ministers for economic cooperation set out a financial framework for a 1992 trade deal. Deliveries of oil would be increased to 7-8 million tonnes, with Poland in return supplying 2 million tonnes of coking coal, 2 million tonnes of coke, 100,000 tonnes of sulphur, pharmaceuticals worth $134 million and transportation tanks for liquefied natural gas. 'Russian Oil and Gas Supplies Assured', *Rzeczpospolita*, 12 March 1992, p. 1.

25 Aleksander Zawisza, *Gaz dla Polski. Zarys historii sektora gazu ziemnego w ostatnich dwóch dekadach w Polsce* (Instytut Sobieskiego) <http://www.sobieski.org.pl/gaz-dla-polski/> [accessed 5 May 2015] p.14.

26 Bartimpex, 'Współpraca Z Rosją' <http://www.bartimpex.pl/index.php/index.php?lang=pl&id=3&d=2> [accessed 1 June 2015].

27 'Russia: Moscow Government Barter Gas to Poland for Food. Signs Contract with Russian Govt to Barter 2 Bil Cu Meters of Natural Gas to Poland for Food', *Kommersant*, 20 October 1994, p. 10.

28 PGNiG, '10 Lat Wymiany Gazu Ziemnego Między VNG I PGNiG', 2003 <http://zielonagora.pgnig.pl/aktualnosci/-/news-list/changeYear/2003?_newslistportlet_WAR_newslistportlet_urlTitle=10-lat-wymiany-gazu-ziemnego-miedzy-vng-i-pgnig&_newslistportlet_WAR_newslistportlet_newsGroupId=10184&_newslistportlet_WAR_newslistportlet_action=newsDetails&_newslistportlet_WAR_newslistportlet_currentPage=3> [accessed 13 May 2015].

channelled over the Oder-Neisse line via Görlitz/Zgorzelec and later also between the border towns of Guben/Gubin. Gas was returned to Germany through the Kamminke delivery point on the island of Usedom, the eastern end of which includes the port of Świnoujście, which had been granted to Poland following World War II and would later prove important as the prospective site for an LNG import terminal.

4.2 Yamal and the Contract of the Century: 1994–1999

As early as May 1992, under Olszewski's conservative Centre Agreement government, and with continued uncertainty over Russia's ability to maintain long-term supply stability without a clear commercial contract, a bilateral treaty on neighbourly cooperation signed by Poland's Solidarity movement leader President Lech Wałęsa and Russian President Boris Yeltsin referenced the development of a new pipeline system for the export of Russian gas from Siberian fields to European markets.[29] Although controversial, a new Russian export route was justified in Poland by a subsequent report from the national Economic Committee of the Council of Ministers in December 1992, which suggested annual demand would reach 27-35 bcm/y by 2010, far in excess of actual demand that year.[30] Fears over the stability of supplies through aging Soviet infrastructure helped support the rationale for a new import route and LTC, as did fears that the decision by Moscow in the 1960s to route its key export lines through the Czech Republic would isolate Poland and leave it open to supply disruption.

In August 1993, an IGA on the construction of a new 67 bcm/y high-capacity pipeline through Poland was signed in Warsaw during the final weeks of the Suchocka seven-party coalition government.[31] Financing would come through foreign loans for the $3 billion segment running through Poland, of which Warsaw

---

29 The *Treaty of Friendly and Neighbourly Cooperation (Traktat o przyjaznej i dobrosąsiedzkiej współpracy)* was signed in Moscow on 22 May 1992. <dziennikustaw.gov.pl/D1993061029101.pdf> [accessed 15 May 2015].

30 Szurlej, 'The State Policy for Natural Gas Sector / Sektor Gazu Ziemnego W Polityce Państwa', *Archives of Mining Sciences*, 58 (2013), p. 928 and Peter Zeniewski, 'Poland's Energy Security and the Origins of the Yamal Contract with Russia', *The Polish Quarterly of International Affairs*, 925–40, p. 40.

31 The *Agreement between the government of the Republic of Poland and the government of the Russian Federation on construction of a transit gas pipeline system for transportation of Russian natural gas through the territory of the Republic of Poland and on deliveries of Russian gas to the Republic of Poland* was signed in Warsaw by Poland's Deputy Prime Minister, Henryk Goryszewski, and Russia's Deputy Prime Minister, Oleg Łobow, in the presence of Yeltsin and Suchcocka. See: Szurlej, 'The State Policy for Natural Gas Sector / Sektor Gazu Ziemnego W Polityce Państwa'.

would be responsible for arranging 15% of the total cost.[32] The Yamal gas supply framework initially agreed in 1993 under Suchocka's government covered deliveries of 14 bcm/y, including 'take-or-pay' and 'destination clause' provisions, which were absent from both the Yamburg and Orenburg agreements.[33] The EuRoPol Gaz joint-venture special purpose vehicle, created to build and manage the Polish segment of the pipeline, was established in September and registered in Poland in December 1993 under Pawlak's second term as Prime Minister.[34] PGNiG and Gazprom each held 48% of the shares in EuRoPol Gaz, with the decisive 4% being held by private company Polish Gas- Trading (itself co-owned by PGNiG) and Gazprom subsidiary Gazexport, plus Bartimpex.[35]

EuRoPol Gaz's only source of income was to be the transit fees paid by Gazprom for deliveries to Germany across Polish territory. As co-owner of the consortium, Gazprom would therefore receive part of the fess it paid to EuRoPol Gaz, while the operator would have to raise loans to fund construction itself. By 1995 it had become clear that Polish gas demand would not rise at the level expected in 1992 and a trade minister's protocol of February that year – negotiated by Poland's Minister for Industry and Trade under the SLD left-wing alliance government of Prime Minister Jan Oleksy, Marek Pol – outlined a more detailed timetable for the Yamal pipeline construction leading up to 2010 and sought to reduce the expected offtake to a more manageable level.[36] This protocol outlined the construction of five compressor stations across 665 km of pipeline that would be built in two phases, the first 32 bcm/y line being due on-stream in 1997 and the second 35 bcm/y line in 2001.[37] Contracted gas via Yamal would from then on also replace the existing Soviet era deals, as opposed to being supplied in addition to them.[38]

---

32 Timothy Heritage, 'Russia, Poland Sign Deal on Gas Pipeline to West', *Reuters News*, 25 August 1993.

33 Gorska, *Dealing with a Juggernaut*, p. 112.

34 EuRoPol GAZ, 'History' <http://www.europolgaz.com/en/o_firmie/geneza_powstania/> [accessed 5 November 2015].

35 Polish Gas-Trading's ownership structure remains unclear, but although it remains a Poland-registered company, with PGNiG and local coal exporter Węglokoks as co-shareholders, Gazprom also owns a stake, in addition to Bartimpex and Germany's Wintershall BASF. See: Szurlej, 'The State Policy for Natural Gas Sector / Sektor Gazu Ziemnego W Polityce Państwa', p.928.

36 Anita Orbán, *Power, Energy, and the New Russian Imperialism*, PSI Reports (Westport, Conn: Praeger Security International, 2008) p. 44.

37 Peter Zeniewski, 'Poland's Energy Security and the Origins of the Yamal Contract with Russia', *The Polish Quarterly of International Affairs*, 38-62, p. 41.

38 Orbán, *Power, Energy, and the New Russian Imperialism*, p. 25.

Under the successive SLD left-wing government of Prime Minister Włodzimierz Cimoszewicz, in September 1996 Gazprom and PGNiG agreed a detailed gas supply contract for 250 bcm to be delivered over a 25-year period. First gas deliveries were scheduled for 1997.[39] Annual offtake under the Yamal contract was reduced to 12.5 bcm/y, rather than the 14 bcm/y agreed in 1993. The contract also included a flexibility option, allowing Poland to import its minimum requirement from Gazprom each year according to take-or-pay rules – 85% of the contracted amount – and seek the rest on the Ukrainian market if needed. If unsuccessful there, PGNiG could always fall back on the flexible portion of the Yamal contract to meet demand, thus supplying a valuable back-up option.[40] A 'make-up' clause also meant that any amount of gas that PGNiG was obliged to import under the LTC fixed segment would be delayed over the following 10-year period and would also have to be paid for eventually.[41] For example, according to the LTC terms, in the event that PGNiG took on less than 85% of the gas it was contracted to that year, then it would be obliged to pay for that quantum under take-or-pay rules and still import the remaining 15% at some point over the next 10 years.[42]

In the development phase of Yamal, and with both the Yamburg and Orenburg deals almost concluded, Polish consumption had been met through a series of *ad hoc* barter deals, such as a further one struck through Bartimpex in 1998 that saw payment for the 7.6 bcm imported partially made in goods and construction services on the Yamal pipeline.[43] In December 1999, during the centre-right government of Jerzy Buzek, which had taken office shortly after the Yamal supply contract was signed in 1997, the first string of the Yamal pipeline was brought onstream, with a capacity of 20 bcm/y. Poland was to receive 2.88 bcm/y of its imports via this first stretch.[44]

39 'Poland, Russia to Sign Gas Deal despite Criticism. [CORRECTED 15:45 GMT]', *Reuters News*, 24 September 1996.

40 Orbán, *Power, Energy, and the New Russian Imperialism*, p. 41.

41 Zeniewski, 'Poland's Energy Security and the Origins of the Yamal Contract with Russia', p. 43.

42 Aleksander Zawisza, *Gaz dla Polski. Zarys historii sektora gazu ziemnego w ostatnich dwóch dekadach w Polsce* (Instytut Sobieskiego) <http://sobieski.org.pl/wp-content/uploads/Zawisza-Aleksander-Gaz-dla-Polski-IS.pdf> [accessed 5 May 2015], p. 35.

43 'RUSSIA'S GAZPROM SEALS GAS BARTER DEAL WITH POLAND', *Reuters News*, 19 January 1998.

44 Orbán, *Power, Energy, and the New Russian Imperialism*, p. 70.

Yamal-1 would not reach its intended capacity of 32.9 bcm/y until March 2006, with the completion of compressor station infrastructure.[45] By then, Gazprom had already hinted at putting off the second phase development of Yamal, which would have seen capacity greatly expanded. Once operational, it had become clear that the agreed transit fees for Yamal-1 were not enough for EuRoPol Gaz to repay the loans it had taken out to finance construction of the first line, leading to disputes between the shareholders and near bankruptcy for the operator.[46] Instead of Yamal-2, Gazprom looked at plans for an inter-system connector (Peremychka) that would link Yamal with the Brotherhood pipeline running through Ukraine and into Slovakia.[47] Plans for an alternative sub-sea pipeline also first appeared in 1997, which would link Russia with Germany through the Baltic Sea, bypassing transit countries – especially Ukraine. This concept gathered pace following the millennium, eventually becoming Nord Stream.[48]

4.3 'Little' and 'big' Nordic contracts: 2000–2004

As early as 1992, with momentum gathering for a new Russian pipeline, Polish officials had also mooted plans to bring North Sea gas production to Poland via Denmark under what was initially dubbed the Polpipe project.[49] PGNiG and Norway's Statoil had also begun talks in 1996 that would eventually lead to the signing of the so-called 'little' and then 'big' supply contracts later.[50] Under Jerzy Buzek's

---

45 'Gazprom Launches Zambrow Station on Yamal-Europe Pipe', *Interfax Energy News Service*, 1 March 2006.

46 'Gazprom Official Says No Change in Transit Rates for Poland', *BBC Monitoring European*, 8 December 2007.

47 Orbán, *Power, Energy, and the New Russian Imperialism*, p. 59. This project would have arced from Kobrin in Belarus to Veľké Kapušany in eastern Slovakia through Polish territory.

48 Nord Stream started as a Finnish–Russian joint venture in 1997 but, by 2001, Gazprom, Finnish energy company Forum and German utilities Ruhrgas and Wintershall agreed to begin work on a feasibility study. By 2005, Fortum had sold its share in the project company and Gazprom, Wintershall's new owner BASF and Ruhrgas's new owner, E.On, signed a deal on the development of the North European Gas Pipeline. In 2006 the project was officially re-christened Nord Stream, with company headquarters set-up in the Swiss town of Zug just before the end of 2005. Dutch company Gasunie joined in 2007 and French utility GDF in 2010. Construction was completed on the first line in 2010 and the second in 2011, allowing a combined capacity of 55 bcm/y to flow.

49 Szurlej, 'The State Policy for Natural Gas Sector / Sektor Gazu Ziemnego W Polityce Państwa', p. 928. The plans were based on PGNiG becoming one of the operators of the Britannia field in the North Sea - 'POLAND ON SHORT LIST OF BRITANNIA GAS FIELD OPERATORS', *Rzeczpospolita*, 29 April 1993, p. 1.

50 Statoil, 'Polish Talks Continue', 1999 <http://www.statoil.com/en/NewsAndMedia/News/1999/Pages/PolishTalksContinue.aspx> [accessed 16 May 2015].

conservative government from 1997 to 2001, attempts to create a new, non-Russian infrastructure route for gas imports gained further impetus and, during the Prime Minister's visit to Oslo in May 1999, the 'little' contract for the export to Poland of 500 MMcm/y of Norwegian gas for five years, starting in 2001, was signed.[51] Buzek's government made gas supply security a policy priority, agreeing a further 'big' Statoil contract worth $11.3 billion just before leaving office in 2001.[52]

PGNiG had signed the 'big' contract with Norwegian companies under the exporting country's Gas Negotiating Committee (GFU) system to import 74 bcm over a 16-year period starting in 2008.[53] Another deal, signed in July 2001, saw PGNiG agree a contract with Denmark's DONG Energy for 2 bcm/y in imports over an eight-year period starting in 2003. The gas would have been sent via the planned BalticPipe system that replaced early plans for Polpipe and was being considered by investors as recently as 2009.[54] Unlike the contracts with Gazprom, neither the Danish nor Norwegian agreements included destination clauses allowing the re-sale of surplus quantities without penalty.[55] However, without a physical supply route open through which to send the gas, both the DONG and GFU contracts were only hypothetical options.

With security pressures from Russia mounting in response to Poland's NATO membership in 1999, attempts to secure diversification of gas supply options gathered pace. Flows from Germany, although expensive compared to those from the east, were expanded to 400 MMcm/y in a larger deal with VNG and E.On Ruhrgas starting in 1998.[56] The offer of a 'swap' deal from Nederlandse Gasunie, whereby Dutch gas would have been sent to Germany as a substitute for Russian gas, was rejected as another potential option for delivery from the west.[57] Instead, the Buzek

---

51 According to Statoil, the delivery point was Emden in north-west Germany, with PGNiG responsible for onward transit to Poland. Statoil, 'Poland Buys Norwegian Gas', 1999 <http://www.statoil.com/en/NewsAndMedia/News/1999/Pages/PolandBuysNorwegianGas.aspx> [accessed 15 May 2015].

52 Norway, Poland Seal $11.3b Gas Deal' <http://gulfnews.com/business/norway-poland-seal-11-3b-gas-deal-1.424146> [accessed 27 April 2015].

53 Statoil, 'Agreement with Poland Signed' <http://www.statoil.com/en/NewsAndMedia/News/2001/Pages/AgreementWithPolandSigned.aspx> [accessed 5 May 2015].

54 'Projekt budowy Baltic Pipe bardziej realny', *Parkiet*, 16 November 2007.

55 Paweł Reszka, 'Kontrakt Norweski Podpisany', *Rzeczpospolita*, 4 September 2001 <http://archiwum.rp.pl/artykul/351593-Kontrakt-norweski-podpisany.html> [accessed 5 November 2015].

56 A.Ła, 'Po niższej cenie, ale więcej', *Rzeczpospolita*, 16 September 2004.

57 'Polish-Dutch Gas Supply Agreement in Store', *Polish News Bulletin*, 28 December 1998.

government preferred to pursue options for direct physical interconnections with Scandinavia that would guarantee new gas could flow into Poland. Controversy also mounted in 2000 when a company co-owned by EuRoPol Gaz, Bartimpex and Gazprom laid a telecommunications cable along the route of the Yamal pipeline, apparently without official government permission.[58]

The SLD, under the leadership of Leszhek Miller, threatened to annul the Norway import contracts before winning the election of September 2001 and taking office the next month, arguing that the cost of Scandinavian gas would far exceed that of existing Russian supplies.[59] Progress slowed on the BalticPipe infrastructure scheme under the Miller administration and by 2007 the Danish deal was off, replaced with a general protocol on cooperation. The Miller government's focus on price discounting over new supply options, coupled with oversupply on the Polish gas market by 2002, led PGNiG to seek instead to re- negotiate its contract with Russia, rather than open up new import routes. A total of 12 meetings took place that year between the Polish importer and Russian gas supplier Gazexport, with the financial management of the EuRoPol Gaz joint venture also becoming a key point of dispute as the transit deficit continued.[60]

Meanwhile, having already been involved in private barter trading with Gazprom throughout the 1990s, and as a shareholder in EuRoPol Gaz's key minority shareholder Polish Gas-Trading, Bartimpex had by 1999 set up a consortium with Germany's Ruhrgas to manage the development of a 5 bcm/y pipeline between the town of Bernau on the northern outskirts of Berlin and the Polish city of Szczecin as a means of opening up its own alternative entry point from the west that could potentially have been used to send large quantities of Scandinavian gas into Poland.[61] The pipeline was envisaged as a physical conduit for the Norwegian gas arranged under the 1999 contract, lacking a clear route to Poland other than through possible 'swap trading' in Germany or via the low-capacity import points used in the 1990s for trade with VNG. However, fearful that the Bernau–Szczecin project would perpetuate reliance on Russia by channelling only Russian gas back into Poland from Germany, the Polish government gave the scheme no clear

58 'Poland Questions Yamal Fibre Optic Line for Commercial Data Transmission', *BBC Monitoring European - Political*, 27 November 2000.

59 'Polish Government Defends Gas Deal with Denmark', *Reuters News*, 5 July 2001.

60 Gorska, *Dealing with a Juggernaut,* p. 125.

61 A. Morka, 'Mały Kontrakt - Nie, Duży - Tak', *Rzeczpospolita*, 27 May 2000 <http://archiwum.rp.pl/artykul/277949-Maly-kontrakt---nie-duzy---tak.html> [accessed 16 May 2015].

backing, and instead PGNiG and VNG investigated a similar pipeline concept of their own, rather than back Bartimpex's scheme.[62]

Under Miller's SLD-led left-wing coalition, Poland sought a 10-year extension to the Yamal supply contract with Gazprom that would retain the existing quantities, allowing it to reduce its annual offtake burden by a third year-by- year, but perpetuating the dependence on Russian gas for a further decade.[63] However, in February 2003, the deputy prime ministers of Poland and Russia agreed a protocol to their gas contracts concluded in the 1990s. Contracted exports to Poland under the Yamal contract were cut by 35%, meaning Poland would now receive 143 bcm between 2003 and 2020, instead of the planned 218 bcm.[64] Broken down, the new agreement reached during the visit of Poland's Deputy Prime Minister Marek Pol – who had signed the February 1995 Yamal protocol as trade minister – to Moscow meant that Poland would import up to 6.5 bcm/y until 2009, then 8 bcm/y from 2010 and 9 bcm/y between 2020 and 2022.[65] The contract was also extended by a further two-years to 2022. Polish officials estimated budget savings to be $5 billion.[66] A transit deal was also reached to boost the rate EuRoPol Gaz would receive from $1.35 for every mcm of Russian gas transported over 100 km to $2.74 as part of efforts to guarantee the liquidity of pipeline operator. However, the transit fee payment would taper down to $1 for very mcm by 2019.[67] A deal was also signed on EuRoPol Gaz's outstanding debt, staving off bankruptcy for the company.

Also during the SLD Miller administration, PGNiG sought to open another import line from the east, agreeing a tripartite gas supply deal with Naftogaz Ukrainy and Eural Transgas (an opaque intermediary with uncertain ownership structures) in October 2003 that would see 2 bcm/y of Central Asian gas delivered through Ukraine and Russia.[68] In 2004 PGNiG received 2.67 bcm under this con-

62 Andrzej Kublik, 'PGNiG potajemnie zawiesiło umowę o połączeniu z niemieckimi gazociągami', *Gazeta Wyborcza*, 6 April 2006.

63 Orbán, *Power, Energy, and the New Russian Imperialism*, p. 71.

64 Gorska, *Dealing with a Juggernaut*, p. 125.

65 'RUSSIAN GAS SUPPLIES TO POLAND BEGIN AT 6-6.5 BLN CUBIC METERS TO 2009', *Interfax: Petroleum Report*, 12 February 2003.

66 Gorska, *Dealing with a Juggernaut*, p. 125.

67 'POLISH REVENUE FROM GAS TRANSIT TO FALL BY USD 1.4 BLN TO 2019 DUE TO REVISED RUSSIAN GAS DEAL', *Interfax Poland Business News Service*, 20 March 2003.

68 The curious case of Eural Trans Gas is tackled here: Global Witness, *It's a Gas: Funny Business in the Turkmen-Ukraine Gas Trade*, April 2006.

tract alone, with a clause in place to ensure increased deliveries from 2006.[69] However, by March 2005 the contract would be transferred to new Swiss-based intermediary RosUkrEnergo, set up in 2004 by Gazprom and Centragas Holdings to handle the gas trade between Russia and Ukraine.[70] A day after Poland joined the EU on 1 May 2004, Miller quit as Poland's Prime Minister, to be replaced by Marek Belka, also from the SLD. As part of plans aimed at increasing gasification in the "blank spot" Hrubieszów region of southeast Poland, PGNiG agreed a low-quantity supply contract directly with Ukraine's state gas company Naftogaz Ukrainy in October 2004. Deliveries would be made along a new pipeline connecting the Ukrainian town of Ustiług with Hrubieszów. After beginning in July 2005, supplies would reach 17.5 MMcm/y by the end of 2007, but from 2008 total deliveries would be expanded to 200 MMcm/y.[71] The contract was scheduled to run until 2020 but was cancelled in November 2013 after the Ukrainian government ruled to retain domestic production for inland consumption only.[72]

Russia's Gazexport had demanded further re-negotiations of the Yamal contract with PGNiG by 2005, during Belka's troubled second administration as the Prime Minister struggled to gain backing from the Sejm lower house of parliament

69 Gas under this contract was to be of Kazakh, Turkmen and Uzbek origin, with Naftogaz responsible for ensuring transit through Ukraine. PGNiG, 'Zmiana Partnera W Kontrakcie Trójstronnym', 2005 <http://www.pgnig.pl/aktualnosci/-/news-list/changeYear/2005?_newslistportlet_WAR_newslistportlet_urlTitle=zmiana-partnera-w-kontrakcie-trojstronnym&_newslistportlet_WAR_newslistportlet_newsGroupId=10184&_newslistportlet_WAR_newslistportlet_action=newsDetails& _newslistportlet_WAR_newslistportlet_currentPage=6> [accessed 2 June 2015].

70 Centragas Holdings is based in Vienna and majority owned by Dmytro Firtash. A Mystery Player in Russia-Ukraine Gas Row', *Reuters*, 3 January 2009 <http://www.reuters.com/article/2009/01/03/us-russia-ukraine-gas-rosukrenergo-sb-idUSTRE5021BN20090103> [accessed 2 June 2015].

71 Both Ukrainian production and Central Asian gas supplies transited through Russia would compose the deliveries according to PGNiG. A.Ła, 'Z Ukrainy dla Hrubieszowa', *Rzeczpospolita*, 27 October 2004; PGNiG, 'Umowa Na Dostawy Gazu Do Hrubieszowa', 2004 <http://www. pgnig.pl/aktualnosci/-/news-list/changeYear/2004?_newslistportlet_WAR_newslistportlet_urlTitle=umowa-na-dostawy-gazu-do-hrubieszowa&_newslistportlet_WAR_newslistportlet_newsGroupId=10184&_newslistportlet_WAR_newslistportlet_action=newsDetails&_newslistportlet_WAR_newslistportlet_currentPage=1> [accessed 12 May 2015].

72 'POLSKIE GÓRNICTWO NAFTOWE I GAZOWNICTWO SA rozwiązanie Umowy na', *PAP - EMITENT*, 6 November 2013, section BIZ. The reason for the cancellation had been changes to Ukrainian law from 2010, "according to which the entire quantity of natural gas from domestic production should be directed exclusively to the needs of Ukraine," the Polish energy regulator said in its 2011 report. URE, *Przedstawiamy Charakterystykę Polskiego Rynku Gazu* <http://www.ure.gov.pl/pl/liberalizacja-rynku-ga/4589,Przedstawiamy-charakterystyke-polskiego-rynku-gazu.print> [accessed 1 June 2015].

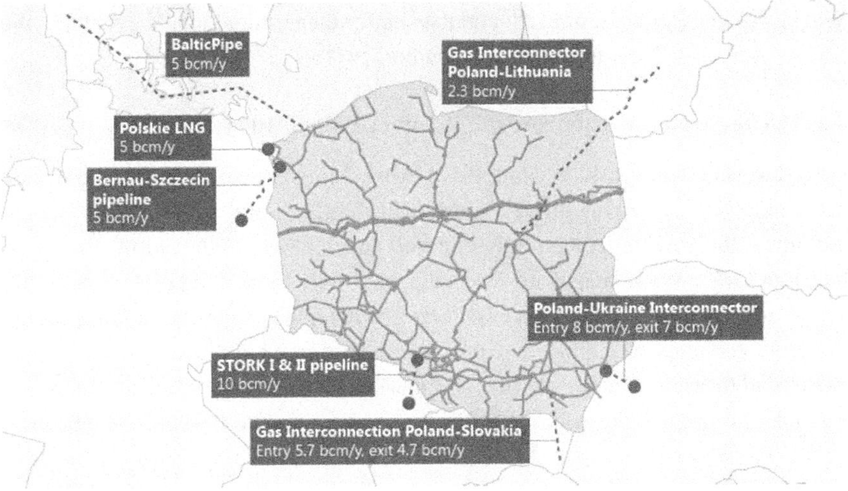

Figure 9: Diversification projects considered by Poland (1989–2014)

and Polish gas prices were at around a reported $140-$150/mcm.[73] However, under the newly elected right-wing Prime Minister Kazimierz Marcinkiewicz of the Law and Justice (PiS) party, following elections in 2005, the Polish government and PGNiG refused to re-negotiate, arguing there was no basis to do so in November that year.[74] Work on the second phase of the Yamal pipeline was also suspended, just as the first leg was brought to full capacity by 2006. Plans for an LNG terminal on Poland's Baltic Sea coast also began to progress in 2005,[75] with the Polskie LNG project company registered by PGNiG in 2007.[76] A 2006 offer of cheap LNG in return for pipeline financing from Algeria was also considered in

73 'Gazexport Wants More from Poland's PGNiG', *International Gas Report*, 18 November 2005, section NEWS HIGHLIGHTS, p. 10. Belka's troubles are summarised here: Stratfor, 'Little Room to Maneuver for Poland's Belka', *Stratfor*, 2004 <https://www.stratfor.com/analysis/little-room-maneuver-polands-belka> [accessed 22 June 2016].

74 "We do not agree with the arguments of the Russian company. We believe that there are no grounds to renegotiate gas prices and the answer will pass," PGNiG's President Marek Kossowski said. A. Ła, 'Nie zgadzamy się na podwyżkę', *Rzeczpospolita*, 4 November 2005, section Ekonomia, p. Ekonomia i rynek.

75 Judy Dempsey, 'Poland Intends to Cut Reliance on Russian Gas', *International Herald Tribune*, 18 November 2005, 3 edition, section FINANCE/BUSINESS, p. 13.

76 In August 2008 ownership of Polskie LNG was transferred to Gaz-System. Polskie LNG, 'Informacje O Spółce' <http://www.polskielng.pl/the-company/information-about-the-company/> [accessed 5 November 2015].

Warsaw by the PiS government[77] and the site for the terminal would eventually be Świnoujście, just 2 km from the German border.[78]

4.4 The 'Molotov–Ribbentrop' pipeline: 2006-2010

After Jarosław Kaczyński became PiS's Prime Minister in July 2006 – replacing Marcinkiewicz and taking office alongside his brother Lech, who was President at the time – the government strongly opposed development of the North- European Gas Pipeline project, later Nord Stream, as part of a suspected policy that would allow Gazprom to circumnavigate Ukraine and the transit states of Central Europe, therefore endangering supply. The project was portrayed in Polish discourse as an existential threat to energy security, and in May 2006 Defence Minister Radosław Sikorski compared the German–Russian project to the Molotov–Ribbentrop pact.[79] Piotr Naimski, deputy Minister of the Economy in the PiS government of the mid-2000s and a key architect of national energy policy, wrote in 2007 that "while the official strategy of the Russian Federation provides for the use of energy resources to obtain political goals, the biggest European countries remain silent, and the concern grows bigger." Naimski added in the paper that Nord Stream was a "vivid example" of that point.[80] Gazprom's continued requests for a price re-negotiation on the Yamal contract, which had been refused in 2005, continued to be rebuffed in 2006, although Nord Stream and the Ukraine–Russia dispute over payment for gas increasingly politicised energy relations across the region. Furthermore, the entrance of intermediary companies such as RosUkrEnergo in the mid-2000s further complicated trade.

On 1 January 2006, supplies of Russian gas to Poland dropped 14% through the Drozdowicze border import point with Ukraine as a result of the price and

77 'Polish Gas Monopolist PGNiG Studying USD 4 Bln African Pipeline Project for Cheap LNG Source', *Interfax Poland Business News Service*, 24 February 2006.

78 Gdansk was initially considered as the best location for a gas-receiving terminal during the 1990s. However, Świnoujście was eventually chosen as the primary option as it could receive larger ships and large gas consumers were in the vicinity.

79 Hans Michael Kloth, 'Indirect Hitler Comparison: Polish Minister Attacks Schröder and Merkel', *Spiegel Online*, 1 May 2006, <http://www.spiegel.de/international/indirect-hitler-comparison-polish-minister-attacks-schroeder-and-merkel-a-413969.html> [accessed 5 May 2015]

80 Piotr Naimski, 'Energy Diversification Strategy for Poland' (Secretary of State at the Ministry of Economy Republic of Poland / Colombia University, 2007) <http://www.columbia.edu/cu/ece/academics/regional/conf/Piotr_Naimski_at_Columbia%20University070917_.pdf> [accessed 12 June 2016] p. 16.

transit conflict between Kiev and Moscow.[81] Household demand was met in Poland, but supplies to industrial consumers did not return to normal until 7 February, according to PGNiG, with daily nomination volumes from Naftogaz Ukrainy only then confirmed as being at a normal level.[82] In agreeing a deal to renew imports of Central Asian gas via Ukraine through the intermediary RosUkrEnergo contract in 2006, before the existing deal had expired in December that year, PGNiG also agreed to a 10% increase in the price it paid for Yamal gas with Gazprom.[83] Concurrently, RosUkrEnergo had restricted supplies to Poland in October 2006, just before a new contract was signed, raising fears that Gazprom was using a subsidiary to enforce changes to its own contract with PGNiG.[84] "RosUkrEnergo made the signing of the contract for gas supplies in 2007–2010 dependent on Warsaw's consent to raise the prices of gas Gazprom supplied under the long-term contract," analysts Agata Łoskot-Strachota and Katarzyna Pełczyńska-Nałęcz argued in April 2008.[85]

However, as bilateral relations with Russia continued to decline on gas issues, the Polish government and PGNiG focused on developing the existing small-scale import options from the west. A 10-year agreement with Germany's VNG was

---

81 PGNiG, 'Komunikat Dotyczący Skutków Ograniczenia Dostaw Gazu Przez Gazprom Dla Ukrainy', 2006 <http://www.pgnig.pl/aktualnosci/-/news-list/changeYear/2006?_newslistportlet_WAR_newslistportlet_urlTitle=komunikat-dotyczacy-skutkow-ograniczenia-dostaw-gazu-przez-gazprom-dla-ukrainy&_newslistportlet_WAR_newslistportlet_newsGroupId=10184&_newslistportlet_WAR_newslistportlet_action=newsDetails&_newslistportlet_WAR_newslistportlet_currentPage=9> [accessed 12 May 2015].

82 PGNiG, 'Przywrócenie Pełnych Dostaw Gazu Największym Odbiorcom Przemysłowym', 2006 <http://www.pgnig.pl/aktualnosci/-/news-list/changeYear/2006?_newslistportlet_WAR_newslistportlet_urlTitle=przywrocenie-pelnych-dostaw-gazu-najwiekszym-odbiorcom-przemyslowym&_newslistportlet_WAR_newslistportlet_newsGroupId=10184&_newslistportlet_WAR_newslistportlet_action=newsDetails&_newslistportlet_WAR_newslistportlet_currentPage=8> [accessed 12 May 2015].

83 PGNiG, *PGNiG Zawarło Kontrakt Na Dostawy Gazu Od Stycznia 2007 Roku*, 18 November 2006 <http://www.pgnig.pl/aktualnosci/-/news-list/changeYear/2006?_newslistportlet_WAR_newslistportlet_urlTitle=pgnig-zawarlo-kontrakt-na-dostawy-gazu-od-stycznia-2007-roku&_newslistportlet_WAR_newslistportlet_newsGroupId=10184&_newslistportlet_WAR_newslistportlet_action=newsDetails&_newslistportlet_WAR_newslistportlet_currentPage=2> [accessed 20 May 2015].

84 'Gas Trader Ends Supply to Poland | News', *The Moscow Times* <http://www.themoscowtimes.com/sitemap/free/2006/10/article/gas-trader-ends-supply-to-poland/201825.html> [accessed 8 June 2015].

85 Agata Łoskot-Strachota and Katarzyna Pełczyńska-Nałęcz, *Gazprom's Expansion in the EU – Co-Operation or Domination?*, April 2008 <http://aei.pitt.edu/57997/1/gp_eu_en_.pdf> [accessed 20 May 2015], p. 14.

signed in 2006, which allowed for 400 MMcm/y to flow into Poland via the Lasów border point. A later 2008 deal, after the right-wing PiS administration had given way to a more centrist Civic Platform–led government under Prime Minister Donald Tusk, provided for deliveries of 500 MMcm for three years and replaced the earlier VNG contract launched alongside E.On Ruhrgas in 1998, but last re-negotiated in 2004.[86] These deals aimed to shore up some alternative supply options from the west as rancour between Russia and its major transit country Ukraine continued through 2007 and 2008.

On 7 January 2009, Gaz-System – which had been spun off from PGNiG to manage the Polish transmission system days before EU membership in 2004 – again reported the suspension of transit via the Drozdowicze station on the Polish–Ukrainian border. Increased imports via the Wysokoje border station with Belarus meant supplies to Poland were only reduced by 16% during the early part of the second major crisis over Russian gas supplies to Ukraine.[87] However, an EU memo on the impact the disruption was having on 9 January 2006 estimated cuts of 33% to Polish supply, while also reporting that deliveries through Yamal and gas storage withdrawal were covering the shortfall.[88] Supplies resumed via Drozdowicze on 21 January, two weeks after the disruption had initially begun.[89]

RosUkrEnergo was removed as the intermediary for the supply of Central Asian gas to Ukraine and Poland following the 2009 Russia/Ukraine dispute, and PGNiG faced an approximately 2.5 bcm/y deficit in its annual imports, owing to the collapse of its contract with the seller. With fears over a shortfall ahead of the following winter season mounting in Warsaw, PGNiG sought approval from the government to negotiate a 1.024 bcm replacement contract directly with Gazprom for supplies that could be sent straight into gas storage leading up to the end of September 2009. The deal was approved in June by the Civic Platform (PO)

---

86 'PGNiG Signs Est. PLN 1.85 Bln Deal with VNG for 500 Mln m3 Annual', *PAP Market Insider*, 29 September 2008.

87 Gaz-System, 'CAŁKOWITE WSTRZYMANIE DOSTAW GAZU W PUNKCIE DROZDOWICZE NA GRANICY POLSKO-UKRAIŃSKIEJ', 2009 <http://www.gaz-system.pl/press-centre/news/information-for-the-media/artykul/1070/> [accessed 12 May 2015].

88 European Commission, 'Member State General Situation According the Significance of Impact', 2009 <http://europa.eu/rapid/press-release_MEMO-09-3_en.htm> [accessed 25 June 2015].

89 Gaz-System, *WZNOWIENIE DOSTAW GAZU PRZEZ UKRAINĘ*, 21 January 2009 <http://www.gaz-system.pl/centrum-prasowe/aktualnosci/informacja/artykul/1392/> [accessed 16 May 2015].

government at a reported cost of approximately $300 million according to Poland's Ministry of the Treasury.[90]

Meanwhile, with construction of the LNG terminal at Świnoujście also finally underway, PGNiG signed off on a 20-year Heads of Agreement contract with Qatargas for LNG imports starting in 2014 during April 2009. The annual quantity of prospective LNG imports was set at 1 million tonnes per annum (1.5 bcm/y).[91] PGNiG also agreed another small-scale supply contract with Swiss trader Vitol in September 2009 that ensured 140 MMcm/y in annual deliveries to the Lasów border crossing with Germany and which added to the volumes agreed earlier.[92]

Despite the ramp-up of alternatives to Russian gas by PGNiG and the development of the so-called Polskie LNG terminal by Gaz-System, the bilateral dispute over the Yamal LTC between PGNiG and Gazprom continued. The eventual annex to the Yamal contract, agreed with the European Commission as broker, for the first time in LTC negotiations in October 2010 saw the removal of destination clauses, which had prevented the re-sale of surplus gas, and calibrated a new import schedule.[93] The deal also set yearly quantities that PGNiG would import directly from Russia at 9.7 bcm in 2010, 10.5 bcm in 2011 and 11 bcm between 2012 and 2022. The pricing formula remained unchanged, with a focus on oil-indexation

---

90 Ministry of Treasury Republic of Poland, 'Umowa Na Dostawy Gazu Do Polski Podpisana', 2009 <http://msp.gov.pl/pl/media/aktualnosci/6565,Umowa-na-dostawy-gazu-do-Polski-podpisana.html?search=71873492> [accessed 20 May 2015]. "The contract with Gazprom will enable Poland to fill its underground gas storage tanks for the upcoming winter season. It would otherwise be impossible due to the failure of RosUkrEnergo to execute the contract," Poland's Ministry of the Treasury said in its statement. It added that PGNiG could use both the Drozdowicze border point with Ukraine and Wysokoje crossing with Belarus if necessary.

91 Qatargas, 'Qatargas Signs New Agreement with PGNiG', 2009 <https://www.qatargas.com/English/MediaCenter/news/Pages/Article_131.aspx> [accessed 5 May 2015].

92 The contract was not announced at the time of signing, but referenced during the announcement of a later supply contract with Vitol in 2011. PGNiG, *PGNiG SA Podpisało Dwie Umowy Na Dostawy Gazu*, 13 May 2011 <http://www.pgnig.pl/aktualnosci/-/news-list/changeYear/2011?_newslistportlet_WAR_newslistportlet_urlTitle=pgnig-sa-podpisalo-dwie-umowy-na-dostawy-gazu&_newslistportlet_WAR_newslistportlet_newsGroupId=10184&_newslistportlet_WAR_newslistportlet_action=newsDetails&_newslistportlet_WAR_newslistportlet_currentPage=6> [accessed 2 June 2015].

93 "We managed to ensure that the Intergovernmental agreement between Russia and Poland was brought into line with EU law. This means in particular that Gaz-System as pipeline operator will be responsible for concluding transmission contracts on a non-discriminatory basis and that Poland can re-export Russian gas delivered in Poland," EU Commissioner for Energy, Günther Oettinger, said in Warsaw on 4 November. EU Commissioner for Energy, 'Statement on the Yamal-Pipeline and the Gas Agreement between Poland and Russia' (European Commission, 2010) <http://europa.eu/rapid/press-release_SPEECH-10-620_en.htm> [accessed 2 June 2015].

retained, but PGNiG reported savings of between $200 and $250 million, achieved through a discount price mechanism that would last until 2015.[94] Although the details were not officially announced, the discount is understood to have comprised a 15% reduction on 1.5 bcm/y of the contracted volume per year between 2011 and 2014.[95]

An earlier negotiating session at Gazprom headquarters in January 2010 had also led to Russia agreeing to extend the use of the Yamal pipeline for transit until 2045, with Poland agreeing a deal that could potentially have seen its own offtake from the project extended beyond 2022 to 2037.[96] In line with the EU's Third Energy Package, aimed at securing third-party access for all overland infrastructure, Gaz-System became the full transmission system operator on the Polish stretch of the Yamal pipeline as of 17 November 2010, shortly after the Gazprom LTC agreement was resolved.[97] Meanwhile, Nord Stream's project company sealed a multi-billion debt financing from banks and export credit agencies in March 2011 that paved the way for its completion later that year. The first phase of 22.5 bcm/y was augmented with a second line the following year.[98]

4.5 Towards an Energy Union: 2011–2014

While financing closed on Nord Stream in March 2011, PGNiG and Gazprom signed a new annex to the Yamal contract that increased the maximum daily nomination through the Wysokoje border crossing with Belarus until the end of 2011 at a reported cost of 3.5% above the existing fee. The annex was due to low storage

94 PGNiG, *PGNiG SA Signs an Annex to the Yamal Contract for Natural Gas Supplies*, 11 February 2010 <http://norway.pgnig.pl/news/-/news-list/changeYear/2010?_newslistportlet_WAR_newslistportlet_urlTitle=pgnig-sa-signs-an-annex-to-the-yamal-contract-for-natural-gas-supplies&_newslistportlet_WAR_newslistportlet_newsGroupId=18252&_newslistportlet_WAR_newslistportlet_action=newsDetails&_newslistportlet_WAR_newslistportlet_currentPage=1> [accessed 12 June 2015]

95 Gorska, *Dealing with a Juggernaut*, p. 133.

96 Gazprom, 'Gazprom, PGNiG and EuRoPol GAZ Sign Long-Term Agreement of Cooperation in Gas Sector', 2010 <http://www.gazprom.com/press/news/2010/january/article75614/> [accessed 2 June 2015].

97 Gaz-System took over management of the pipeline system to ensure third party access on non-contracted capacity, in line with EU rules. Gaz-System, 'GAZ-SYSTEM S.A. OPERATOREM POLSKIEGO ODCINKA GAZOCIĄGU JAMALSKIEGO' <http://www.gaz-system.pl/press-centre/news/information-for-the-media/artykul/201120/> [accessed 5 September 2015].

98 Nord Stream, '"Nord Stream Completes Phase II Financing" - Press Releases', *Nord Stream AG* <http://www.nord-stream.com/press-info/press-releases/nord-stream-completes-phase-ii-financing-305/> [accessed 23 June 2016].

inventories in Poland following a cold winter, PGNiG said.[99] However, by the end of that month, the state-owned importer had begun the re-negotiation process with Gazprom Export over the pricing in its LTCs as energy security continued to be positioned high on the agenda of the PO-led government.[100]

In May 2011 PGNiG announced the signing of two new supply contracts, with gas to be transported through the Cieszyn and Lasów crossing points with the Czech Republic and Germany, respectively. Vitol agreed to supply 550 MMcm/y through Cieszyn in a deal worth €550 million and due to run from 1 October 2011 to 1 October 2014 after the STORK interconnector with the Czech Republic was inaugurated in September that year.[101] A further short-term deal with VNG allowed for an extra 50 MMcm to flow through Lasów between 15 May and 30 June that year. The deal was worth €13 million and was later extended until 30 September. Both the Vitol and VNG contracts were to be priced against the NetConnect Germany hub price rather than oil-indexation, PGNiG said.[102]

A month after the PO party under Prime Minister Donald Tusk won election for a second term. once more in coalition with PSL, in October 2011, PGNiG filed a case against Gazprom with the Arbitration Institute of the Stockholm Chamber of Commerce after the six-month period under which bilateral negotiations were required to take place on price had expired. The re-negotiation process that had begun in March 2011 had not resulted in a deal and PGNiG was convinced of its case for a better price, saying in a 7 November 2011 statement that it hoped "to reach an agreement allowing for the purchase of gas at prices that reflect the con-

---

99 The annex did not change the yearly contracted volume, but instead appears to have served to redirect flows to certain storage facilities in Poland. PGNiG, 'PGNiG SA Podpisało Aneks Do Kontraktu Jamalskiego Na Dostawy Gazu Ziemnego', 2011 <http://www.pgnig.pl/aktualnosci/-/news-list/changeYear/2011?_newslistportlet_WAR_newslistportlet_urlTitle=pgnig-sa-podpisalo-aneks-do-kontraktu-jamalskiego-na-dostawy-gazu-ziemnego&_newslistportlet_WAR_newslistportlet_newsGroupId=10184&_newslistportlet_WAR_newslistportlet_action=newsDetails&_newslistportlet_WAR_newslistportlet_currentPage=8> [accessed 2 June 2015].

100 Poland's Energy Regulatory Office (URE), *National Report*, July 2012, p. 15.

101 Net4Gas, *ZAHÁJENÍ PROVOZU ČESKO-POLSKÉHO PROPOJE*, 14 September 2011.

102 PGNiG, *PGNiG SA Podpisało Dwie Umowy Na Dostawy Gazu*, 13 May 2011 <http://www. pgnig.pl/aktualnosci/-/news-list/changeYear/2011?_newslistportlet_WAR_newslistportlet_urlTitle=pgnig-sa-podpisalo-dwie-umowy-na-dostawy-gazu&_newslistportlet_WAR_newslistportlet_newsGroupId=10184&_newslistportlet_WAR_newslistportlet_action=newsDetails&_newslistportlet_WAR_newslistportlet_currentPage=6> [accessed 2 June 2015]. PGNiG said at the end of June that it had received five bids from potential suppliers but opted to select VNG for the rest of the summer.

ditions shaping the European gas market."[103] A period of cold weather late in the 2009/2010 winter season had caused a spike in demand across Europe and in February Russian domestic consumption peaked at over 2 bcm per day. A number of European consumers subsequently reported reductions in their daily flows from Gazprom compared to nominations,[104] with Poland responding to the deficit by using a swap trading mechanism along the Yamal pipeline with Germany.[105]

With the Stockholm case still pending in the courts, PGNiG and Gazprom finally reached an out of court settlement on their arbitration dispute almost two years after it was first lodged in November 2012. The Polish side was reported to have received between a 10% and 15% retroactive price cut, although its take-or-pay levels would remain as outlined in the LTC agreement at 85%.[106] Oil-indexation was also retained in the pricing structure, with a spot market component excluded from the deal. PGNiG subsequently dropped its arbitration proceedings against Gazprom.[107] An October renegotiation with VNG on its 10-year 400 MMcm contract, valid until 2016, led to the incorporation of a spot market reference, although oil-indexation remained part of the overall mechanism too.[108]

As other arbitration cases against Gazprom mounted in 2012, the European Commission opened its own investigation into the Russian monopoly, alleging market abuse by the exporter in Central European markets – including Poland – in September that year. Previously EU officials had conducted early morning unannounced inspections at the offices of a number of European energy companies,

---

103 PGNiG, *Ceny Gazu Przed Arbitrażem W Sztokholmie*, 11 July 2011 <http://www.pgnig.pl/aktualnosci/-/news-list/changeYear/2011?_newslistportlet_WAR_newslistportlet_urlTitle=ceny-gazu-przed-arbitrazem-w-sztokholmie&_newslistportlet_WAR_newslistportlet_newsGroupId=10184&_newslistportlet_WAR_newslistportlet_action=newsDetails&_newslistportlet_WAR_newslistportlet_currentPage=2> [accessed 3 June 2015]. A full claim was filed at the Stockholm court on 20 February 2012.

104 'Lessons from the February 2012 European Gas "crisis"', *Oxford Institute for Energy Studies* <http://www.oxfordenergy.org/2012/04/lessons-from-the-february-2012-european-gas-%e2%80%9ccrisis%e2%80%9d/> [accessed 12 May 2015].

105 'Price Spike Tests EU Market Liberalisation', *Interfax Global Energy* </gasdaily/article/6883/price-spike-tests-eu-market-liberalisation> [accessed 3 June 2015].

106 'Poland's PGNiG Renegotiates Natural Gas Contract with Gazprom' <http://www.icis.com/resources/news/2012/11/06/9611556/poland-s-pgnig-renegotiates-natural-gas-contract-with-gazprom/> [accessed 27 April 2015].

107 'Gazprom and PGNIG Reach Agreement on Gas Price' <http://www.gazprom.com/press/news/2012/november/article147730/> [accessed 29 April 2015].

108 'VNG Agrees to Spot Natural Gas Element in Contract with Poland's PGNiG' <http://www.icis.com/resources/news/2012/10/18/9605304/vng-agrees-to-spot-natural-gas-element-in-contract-with-poland-s-pgnig/> [accessed 13 May 2015].

seeking to investigate anti-trust practices. The companies raided included PGNiG, Gaz-System and Gazprom subsidiaries in Germany, Bulgaria and the Czech Republic.[109]

The European Commission said in its September 2012 announcement that it was

> investigating three suspected anti-competitive practices in Central and Eastern Europe. First, Gazprom may have divided gas markets by hindering the free flow of gas across Member States. Second, Gazprom may have prevented the diversification of supply of gas. Finally, Gazprom may have imposed unfair prices on its customers by linking the price of gas to oil prices. Such behaviour, if established, may constitute a restriction of competition and lead to higher prices and deterioration of security of supply. Ultimately, such behaviour would harm EU consumer.[110]

Against this backdrop, PGNiG requested above contracted daily deliveries from Gazprom during the third week of March 2013 as another late winter cold snap took hold and demand peaked.[111] Days later in April, Gazprom and EuRoPol Gaz signed a Memorandum of Understanding on the development of the long- postponed second phase of the Yamal pipeline project with a capacity of what was agreed to be no less than 15 bcm/y, which could transit Poland to serve the Slovak and Hungarian markets.[112] In effect, the project would have more closely resembled the Peremychka inter-system connector suggested by Gazprom in the late 1990s. The PO government in Warsaw was not informed in advance of the memorandum agreed by EuRoPol Gaz and the agreement, though not binding in legal terms, would have immediate consequences for PGNiG's management.

Reacting to the unplanned announcement during a period of tense bilateral relations with Russia on energy supply, Tusk dismissed Treasury Minister Mikołaj Budzanowski on 19 April, with PGNiG's chief executive Grażyna Piotrowska-Oliwa relieved of her post 10 days later.[113] Although the government accepted that

---

109 European Commission, *Antitrust: Commission Confirms Unannounced Inspections in the Natural Gas Sector*, 27 September 2011 <http://europa.eu/rapid/press-release_MEMO-11-641_en.htm?locale=en> [accessed 3 June 2015] and 'E.ON, RWE, Gazprom among Groups Raided in European Commission Natural Gas Probe' <http://www.icis.com/resources/news/2011/09/28/9496017/e-on-rwe-gazprom-among-groups-raided-in-european-commission-natural-gas-probe/> [accessed 3 June 2015].

110 European Commission, *Antitrust: Commission Opens Proceedings against Gazprom*, 4 September 2012 <http://europa.eu/rapid/press-release_IP-12-937_en.htm> [accessed 12 May 2015].

111 'Poland Asks for More Gazprom Gas', *Interfax: Russia & CIS Energy Newswire*, 29 March 2013.

112 'Gazprom and EuRoPol GAZ to Cooperate under Yamal – Europe-2 Gas Pipeline Project' <http://www.gazprom.com/press/news/2013/april/article159672/> [accessed 3 June 2015].

113 The agreement envisages a feasibility study by October 2014. 'Budzanowski zwolniony za gaz', *Rzeczpospolita*, 20 April 2013 and 'Lecą głowy w zarządzie PGNiG', *Rzeczpospolita*, 30 April 2013.

the memorandum did not harm Polish energy interests, Tusk's government launched a review of decision-making in the energy sector and was forced to deny that its previous gas price reduction deal, reached to end the arbitration gas, was contingent on infrastructure development. The key problem was a lack of state supervision of PGNiG, the government said.[114] Delays to construction on the Polskie LNG terminal also left the PO government open to criticism when the site failed to be ready for hand-over for operation by June 2014. In its later report on the project's delay Poland's Supreme Audit Office (NiK) said:

> Poland still cannot launch the gas port in Świnoujście, or receive liquefied gas supplies and transfer it to recipients because the companies responsible for key works related to that investment failed to complete some of their tasks properly.

Also the supervision over the LNG terminal construction process on part of relevant ministries proved insufficient.[115]

However, in April 2014, construction work at the Mallnow gas pumping station near Frankfurt (Oder) in Germany allowed for physical reverse-flow deliveries of 2.3 bcm/y along the Yamal pipeline back into Poland as of 1 April, with the potential to raise capacity to 5.5 bcm/y in the event of crisis or suspension of supplies from the east.[116] The spectre of new cuts to transit of Russian gas supply through Ukraine rising, the completion of Gazprom's Nord Stream pipeline allowing an alternative transport route to the German market, and increasing fears in European capitals over the Russian states use of energy a leverage meant that national energy strategy under the second Tusk PO government became assimilated with broader security policy. In an editorial also published by the *Financial Times* in April 2014, Tusk argued for a continental Energy Union based on six principles, one of which dealt directly with the transparency and pricing of gas LTCs.

---

[114] Polish Government, *Donald Tusk: There Will Be a Report on Gas Memorandum*, 4 September 2013 <https://www.premier.gov.pl/en/news/news/donald-tusk-there-will-be-a-report-on-gas-memorandum.html> [accessed 3 June 2015]. Following the scandal, the relationship between Gazprom and PGNiG officials at EuRoPol Gaz deteriorated with Polish board members resigning in November and their Russian counterparts refusing to attend the following meeting. 'Uncertainty Clouds Yamal-Europe Meetings', *Interfax Global Energy* <http://interfaxenergy.com/gasdaily/article/4683/uncertainty-clouds-yamal-europe-meetings> [accessed 3 June 2015].

[115] Supreme Audit Office of Poland, 'NIK O Budowie Terminalu LNG - Najwyższa Izba Kontroli', 2015 <https://www.nik.gov.pl/aktualnosci/nik-o-budowie-terminalu-lng.html> [accessed 23 June 2016].

[116] Gaz-System, *WIĘKSZE TECHNICZNE ZDOLNOŚCI IMPORTU GAZU DO POLSKI Z KIERUNKU ZACHODNIEGO*, 4 January 2014 <http://www.gaz-system.pl/press-centre/news/information-for-the-media/artykul/201826/> [accessed 2 June 2015].

In his editorial, Tusk set forth the key point relevant to gas:

> First, Europe should develop a mechanism for jointly negotiating energy contracts with Russia. It would be created in stages. Initially, bilateral agreements would be stripped of any secret and market-distorting clauses; then, a template contract would be created for all new gas contracts; finally, the European Commission would be required to take a role in all new negotiations.[117]

As already discussed, Poland was the first country to allow the EU in as a broker in gas contract negotiations with Russia, and had already launched arbitration proceedings once against the Russian exporter.

Then, on 8 September 2014, PGNiG and a series of other importers across Central Europe reported that Gazprom had not met daily nominations. PGNiG said that deliveries were 20% less than orders on 8 September, and 24% less on 9 September.[118] The deficit peaked on 10 September at 45% below nominations.[119] The disruption was denied by Gazprom but attributed by analysts to be an attempt to halt the deliveries of Russian gas back into Ukraine from Poland, Slovakia and Hungary that had been ramped up following the annexation of Crimea and the suspension of Russian gas deliveries to Ukraine in June 2014 after the Maidan revolution had toppled the government of President Viktor Yanukovych.[120] Gazprom's chief executive, Alexei Miller, had described the delivery of gas through

117 Donald Tusk, 'A United Europe Can End Russia's Energy Stranglehold', *Financial Times*, 21 April 2014 <http://www.ft.com/intl/cms/s/0/91508464-c661-11e3-ba0e-00144feabdc0.html#axzz3ZwW0NY2m> [accessed 12 May 2015].

118 PGNiG, 'Informacja O Zmniejszeniu Dostaw Gazu Ziemnego Z Kierunku Wschodniego', 2014 <http://www.pgnig.pl/aktualnosci/-/news-list/changeYear/2014?_newslistportlet_WAR_newslistportlet_urlTitle=informacja-o-zmniejszeniu-dostaw-gazu-ziemnego-z-kierunku-wschodniego&_newslistportlet_WAR_newslistportlet_newsGroupId=10184&_newslistportlet_WAR_newslistportlet_action=newsDetails&_newslistportlet_WAR_newslistportlet_currentPage=4> [accessed 5 May 2015].

119 PGNiG, 'Iformacja O Sytuacji Ws. Dostaw Gazu Ziemnego Z Kierunku Wschodniego', 2014 <http://www.pgnig.pl/aktualnosci/-/news-list/changeYear/2014?_newslistportlet_WAR_newslist-portlet_urlTitle=informacja-o-sytuacji-ws-dostaw-gazu-ziemnego-z-kierunku-wschodnie-1&_news-listportlet_WAR_newslistportlet_newsGroupId=10184&_newslistportlet_WAR_newslistportlet_action=newsDetails&_newslistportlet_WAR_newslistportlet_currentPage=3> [accessed 5 May 2015].

120 Although not officially confirmed by Gazprom, analysts have consistently claimed that the timing of disruption and quantity of volumes cut indicated an attempt by Gazprom to halt reverse-flow deliveries to Ukraine. Russian state media also actively pursued the line that deliveries back into Ukraine were illegal. Pasquale De Micco, *A Cold Winter to Come? The EU Seeks Alternatives to Russian Gas* (DIRECTORATE-GENERAL FOR EXTERNAL POLICIES: European Commission, October 2014) <http://www.europarl.europa.eu/RegData/etudes/STUD/2014/536413/EXPO_STU%282014%29536413_EN.pdf> [accessed 16 May 2015].

reverse-flow pipeline back into Ukraine from EU countries through Poland as a "half-fraud mechanism."[121]

In November 2014, PGNiG had requested another review of its LTC pricing mechanism with Gazprom Export as part of the initial rate agreed under the original 1996 Yamal contract. PGNiG attributed its latest move to the "significant changes that took place on the European energy market over the last few years."[122] In accordance with contract terms, if no agreement could be reached within six months, PGNiG said it would have the right to begin arbitration proceedings afresh, just a few years after closing the last arbitration case with an out of court settlement.[123] Meanwhile, Prime Minister Donald Tusk left for Brussels in late 2014, taking up the position of President of the European Council on 1 December that year and leaving the role of Prime Minister to Ewa Kopacz, who would serve as PO's leader until the 2015 elections. Without a bilateral deal over the Gazprom LTC, arbitration proceedings at the Stockholm courts subsequently began in May 2015 at the end of the six-month negotiation period.[124]

With the Polskie LNG terminal project still not yet ready by the end of the review period, PGNiG was forced to seek a deferment of LNG deliveries under the terms of the 2009 Heads of Agreement contract with Qatargas in December 2014, which would see cargoes under the 1.5 bcm/y agreed volume placed in alternative markets. PGNiG agreed to cover any difference in price offered by international importers, with the condition that if the price were too high it could opt to reserve the shipment for delivery in later years.[125] The contract would not be

---

121 'Gas Supplies from Poland, Hungary to Ukraine Contradict Contract with Gazprom - Miller', *Interfax*, 6 December 2014.

122 PGNiG, *PGNiG Rozpoczyna Negocjacje Cenowe Z Gazpromem*, 11 May 2014 <http://www.pgnig.pl/aktualnosci/-/news-list/changeYear/2014?_newslistportlet_WAR_newslistportlet_urlTitle=pgnig-rozpoczyna-negocjacje-cenowe-z-gazpromem&_newslistportlet_WAR_newslistportlet_newsGroupId=10184&_newslistportlet_WAR_newslistportlet_action=newsDetails&_newslistportlet_WAR_newslistportlet_currentPage=2> [accessed 5 May 2015].

123 *ibid.*

124 'Arbitration Cases Pile up against Gazprom', *Interfax Global Energy* <http://interfaxenergy.com/gasdaily/article/16138/arbitration-cases-pile-up-against-gazprom> [accessed 2 June 2015].

125 PGNiG, *PGNiG I Qatargas Podpisały Porozumienie Do Umowy Ws. Dostaw Skroplonego Gazu LNG*, 12 September 2014 <http://www.pgnig.pl/aktualnosci/-/news-list/changeYear/2014?_newslistportlet_WAR_newslistportlet_urlTitle=pgnig-i-qatargas-podpisaly-porozumienie-do-umowy-ws-dostaw-skroplonego-gazu-lng&_newslistportlet_WAR_newslistportlet_newsGroupId=10184&_newslistportlet_WAR_newslistportlet_action=newsDetails&_newslistportlet_WAR_newslistportlet_currentPage=1> [accessed 16 May 2015].

activated until summer 2016, when full commercial deliveries began into the terminal under the returned right-wing PiS government, elected as the first single-party government in Poland's post-communist history. The terminal would eventually be christened 'Lech Kaczynski LNG' after the former President, who had died in the 2010 Smolensk air crash, with Statoil supplying spot cargoes in addition to Qatargas.[126] Throughout the final months of the PO administration in 2015, Poland had continued to ship gas to Ukraine, with German utility RWE also delivering gas via the Gaz-System network.[127] The Polish TSO and its Ukrainian counterpart Ukrtransgaz also agreed to begin work on a feasibility study for a large-scale reverse-flow interconnector during December 2014.[128]

In its April 2015 'Statement of Objections' against Gazprom for alleged abuse of dominance in the gas supply markets of Central and Eastern Europe, the European Commission alleged that the exporter was hindering the development of competition in eight markets, including Poland. Specifically, the case argued that destination clauses had allowed Gazprom to pursue an "unfair pricing policy" in Poland, Bulgaria and the Baltic states. It also alleged that Gazprom may have used its dominant market position to make gas supplies to Bulgaria and Poland "conditional on obtaining unrelated commitments from wholesalers concerning gas transport infrastructure."[129] Gazprom denied the charges.[130]

---

126 Kancelaria Prezesa Rady Ministrów, 'Lech Kaczyński Patronem Terminala LNG W Świnoujście', 2016 <https://www.premier.gov.pl/wydarzenia/aktualnosci/lech-kaczynski-patronem-terminala-lng-w-swinoujsciu.html> [accessed 23 June 2016].

127 RWE, *RWE Beliefert Die Ukraine Mit Erdgas*, 15 April 2014 <https://www.rwe.com/web/cms/en/113648/rwe/press-news/press-release/?pmid=4010923> [accessed 3 June 2015].

128 Gaz-System and Ukrtransgaz agreed a deal to begin working on a feasibility study in December 2014, with a political agreement reached in January 2015 that could see a pipeline with a capacity of 10 bcm/y built. Ukrainian Government Web-Portal, *PM: Ukraine and Poland Inked an Agreement to Construct Gas Pipeline with the Capacity of 10 Billion Cubic Meters*, 19 January 2015 <http://www.kmu.gov.ua/control/en/publish/article?art_id=247881283&cat_id=244314975> [accessed 2 June 2015].

129 European Commission, 'Antitrust: Commission Sends Statement of Objections to Gazprom for Alleged Abuse of Dominance on Central and Eastern European Gas Supply Markets', 2015 <http://europa.eu/rapid/press-release_IP-15-4828_en.htm> [accessed 12 May 2015].

130 Gazprom, 'Statement of OAO "Gazprom" with Respect to the Adoption of "statement of Objections" by the European Commission under the Antitrust Investigation', 2015 <http://www.gazprom.com/press/news/2015/april/article224444/> [accessed 12 May 2015].

4.6 Poland policy review

Uncertainty over the stability of gas supplies in the early months and years of transition, coupled with projections of steeply rising domestic demand leading up to 2010, were key motivating factors for the Polish governments of the 1990s to pursue new LTCs with Russia. It is also clear that Moscow's decision to route its mainline export pipelines through Czechoslovakia in the 1960s had left Poland theoretically more susceptible to gas supply disruption, as its system did not transit gas to lucrative sales markets in Western Europe. Marek Pol, who negotiated the initial 1996 Yamal contract and conducted its re-negotiation in 2003, articulated this in an interview with Polish weekly *Wprost* in 1999. Pol said:

> Poland did not have a permanent contract for gas deliveries and our country was located at the end of Russian pipelines. The cutting off of gas running through them wouldn't have had any economic consequences for anyone else but Poland.[131]

The importance of the Yamal pipeline deal can be understood in this context.

The supply disruption of January 1992 further stoked fears in Warsaw that, without a new formalised LTC framework beyond the Yamburg and Orenburg agreements, it would be impossible to ensure stable supplies. The Economic Committee of the Council of Ministers in Warsaw report that year, forecasting annual demand of between 27 bcm/y and 35 bcm/y by 2010[132] – around double actual levels – helped encourage the idea that further imports from Russia would be necessary to fuel a growing economy. The 1993 agreement stipulating the 14 bcm/y figure of annual imports, with take-or-pay provisions included, immediately put Poland in a weak negotiating position from which to bargain later. Demand forecasts were quickly revised downwards, but even with a reduced annual quantity of 12.5 bcm/y under the final 1996 contract, the 85% take-or-pay clause in effect forced PGNiG to remain firmly dependent on Gazprom deliveries into the 2000s.

Successive Polish governments, and PGNiG as the state-owned importer, repeatedly faced challenges to their attempts at diversification, owing to the terms

131 'Nabici W Rurę', *Wprost.pl*, August 15 1999, p. 30.

132 Szurlej, 'The State Policy for Natural Gas Sector / Sektor Gazu Ziemnego W Polityce Państwa', p. 928.

and quantities laid down in the first 1996 Yamal contract. Plans for the BalticPipe project would have had to have been contingent on Poland first being able to re-negotiate down its commitments to import Russian gas in order to make a new project such as that economically viable. A consistent gap between total demand and contracted Russian gas in combination with domestic production did not open up until 2003/2004, providing space for new gas imports. However, this came after the government had scrapped the Scandinavian import arrangements and opted instead to re-negotiate with Gazprom.

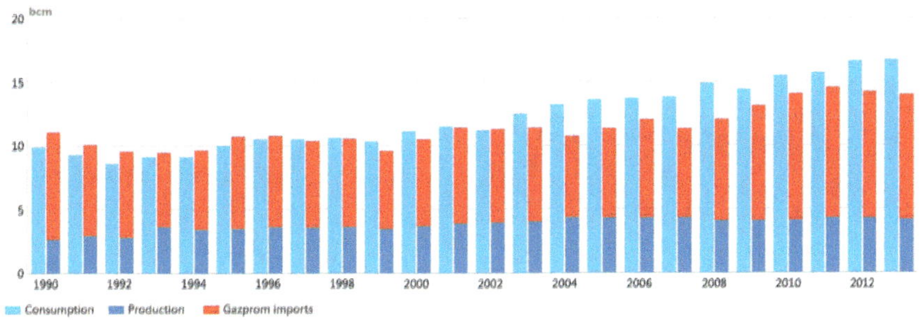

Graph 20: Poland consumption, production and imports (1990–2013)[133]

Politics also served to undermine diversification efforts around the millennium, with the progress made by the conservative Buzek government during the late 1990s towards opening up a new western supply route being undermined by the freezing of planned contracts with Norway and Denmark by the subsequent SLD left-wing administration of Lezhek Miller. Furthermore, by 2002, oversupply on the Polish market and the steady but incremental growth in domestic production gave the illusion that Gazprom supplies would be sufficient to cover demand, and that there would be no room for new gas. Instead, officials opted to re-negotiate with Gazprom and seek improved terms from the near-monopoly supplier.

Both the DONG contract for 2 bcm/y and the 'big' Statoil contract signed around the millennium would have supplied a combined volume of an initial

133 Data used from BP annual statistics and Gazprom.

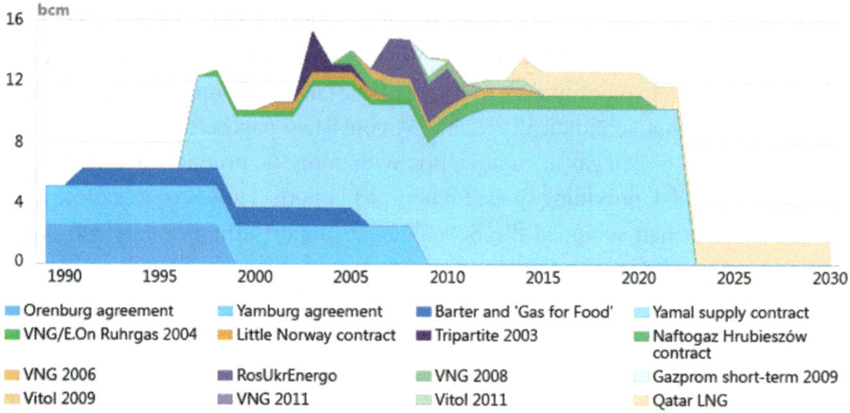

Graph 21: Poland's actual contracted gas (1989–2014)[134]

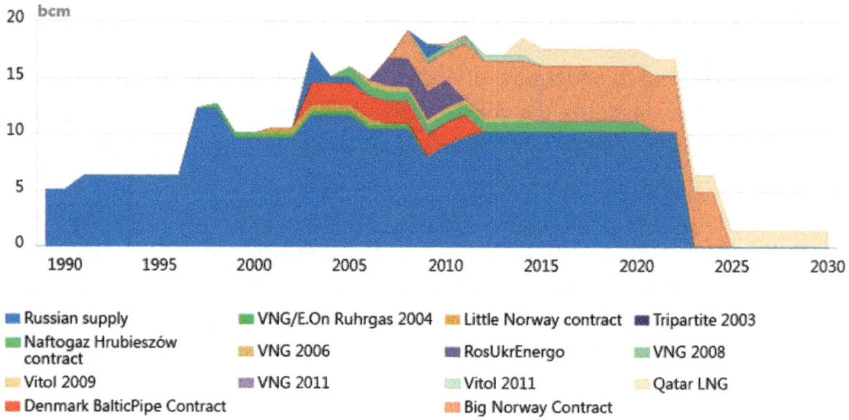

Graph 22: Poland's contracted gas under Nordic scenario (1989–2014)[135]

---

[134] Graph uses all data reported in Chapter 4 of contracts undertaken, as illustrated in Table 6.

[135] Graph uses all data reported in Chapter 4 of contracts under a scenario that also considers the fulfilment of the Scandinavian contracts, as illustrated in Table 6.

additional 4.5 bcm/y of non-Russian gas, giving Poland the option to halve its imports from Gazprom and remove destination clauses that, as noted earlier, were not present in the DONG LTC framework signed in 2001. Such measures would have brought PGNiG in line with the Polish government's report of 1992, which predicted the steady growth in demand, but also cautioned that supply diversification would be necessary to provide alternatives and avoid persisting dependence.[136]

However, the take-or-pay clause in the Yamal contract would have restricted new Nordic gas from competing with Russian stocks. The choice to re-negotiate with Gazprom led to accusations in the national media that the price of imports from the east was the highest in Europe. Responding to an article in Polish daily *Wprost* in March 2003, which claimed that the Yamal contract revision eventually reached that year meant that Poland paid the highest price for gas imports in Europe, PGNiG claimed that this was untrue and that prices were instead comparable to UK levels.[137]

The Warsaw-based company said that

> [Gazprom gas] is not the most expensive gas in Europe. Much more expensive is, for example, gas purchased by PGNiG from the western direction. Gas purchased from Denmark would be much more expensive, contrary to what is suggested by the Wprost journalists. Besides buying 2 bcm/y would not be an independence from Russian supplies.[138]

However, in a 2004 review of national gas supply, Poland's Supreme Audit Office was highly critical of the 2003 re-negotiation with Gazprom, describing the new

---

136 Szurlej, 'The State Policy for Natural Gas Sector / Sektor Gazu Ziemnego W Polityce Państwa', p. 928.

137 PGNiG, 'Komunikat PGNiG S.A. W Sprawie Artykułów We "Wprost" Opublikowanych 3.11.2003 R.' <http://www.pgnig.pl/aktualnosci/-/news-list/changeYear/2003?_newslistportlet_WAR_newslistportlet_urlTitle=komunikat-pgnig-s-a-w-sprawie-artykulow-we-wprost-opublikowanych-3-11-2003-r-&_newslistportlet_WAR_newslistportlet_newsGroupId=10184&_newslistportlet_WAR_newslistportlet_action=newsDetails&_newslistportlet_WAR_newslistportlet_currentPage=1> [accessed 2 June 2015].

138 PGNiG, 'Komunikat PGNiG S.A. W Sprawie Artykułów We "Wprost" Opublikowanych 3.11.2003 R.' <http://www.pgnig.pl/aktualnosci/-/news-list/changeYear/2003?_newslistportlet_WAR_newslistportlet_urlTitle=komunikat-pgnig-s-a-w-sprawie-artykulow-we-wprost-opublikowanych-3-11-2003-r-&_newslistportlet_WAR_newslistportlet_newsGroupId=10184&_newslistportlet_WAR_newslistportlet_action=newsDetails&_newslistportlet_WAR_newslistportlet_currentPage=1> [accessed 2 June 2015].

terms as "unfavourable" and claiming that they would "further restrict diversification possibilities."[139]

Over the following decade, PGNiG and Gazprom would consistently be in and out of negotiations on contract revision, with arbitration proceedings eventually taken to the Stockholm courts in 2011 and 2014. PGNiG wanted to reduce volumes and, later, incorporate a spot-market indexation, while Gazprom fought to retain the oil-linkage and extend the terms of the supply contract to lock-in market access. PGNiG announced occasional victories on short-term discounts, the extension of the contract length and subsequent reduction in yearly volumes, and the abolition of destination clauses after the EU-brokered deal in 2010. However, as of the end of 2014, it had been unable to force hub-indexation into the formula or reduce the take-or-pay provision beneath 85%, according to available data.

Nonetheless, after BalticPipe had effectively been sidelined, other projects to diversify gas supply to Poland gathered pace, with increased momentum and financing at the EU level available following the 2009 Russia/Ukraine crisis. EU funding helped support the development of the LNG import terminal at Świnoujście, which would handle an initial throughput capacity of 5 bcm/y, or roughly a third of annual national consumption.[140] Earlier pipeline interconnectors like STORK and Yamal reverse-flow also allowed PGNiG to expand its contracts with suppliers like VNG and Vitol, though at comparatively low levels, as illustrated in Graph 21.

Despite the reported success of the EU-brokered Yamal contract negotiations with Gazprom in 2010, an annual import obligation of 10.3 bcm/y until 2019 has meant that PGNiG has had continued difficulty in pursuing options for price optimisation through pipeline links with the Czech Republic and Germany. Furthermore, in December 2009 PGNiG's chief executive Michał Szubski said in an interview with Polish daily *Gazeta Wyborcza* that companies had refused to engage in supply deals with his importer unless Gazprom first approved the transaction. Szubski said that

139 Najwyższa Izba Kontroli, *Informacja O Wynikach Kontroli Zaopatrzenia W Gaz Ziemny*, 2004, p. 4

140 European Commission, 'New Liquefied Natural Gas Terminal Improves Energy Supply and Security in Poland', 2009 <http://ec.europa.eu/regional_policy/en/projects/poland/new-liquefied-natural-gas-terminal-improves-energy-supply-and-security-in-poland> [accessed 10 May 2015]

> Western energy firms refuse to go into business with us without Gazprom's blessing and there is nothing we can do about it. All of them are doing business with Gazprom on a much larger scale than they could with us and will not risk their negotiating position to sell Poland 1 bcm of gas.[141]

As a means of increasing domestic production to cut imports, the Polish government pursued a high-profile campaign to drill for unconventional gas between 2010 and 2014. Despite significant estimates of total reserves available, the policy push ended unsuccessfully, with no commercial production of shale gas in the period of investigation.[142] The slow development of the LNG terminal project also further undermined attempts at supply diversification, leaving Poland nearly as dependent on Russian gas in December 2014 as it was in the early years of transition, although with added small-scale capacity to deal with crisis supply disruptions via Germany and the Czech Republic.

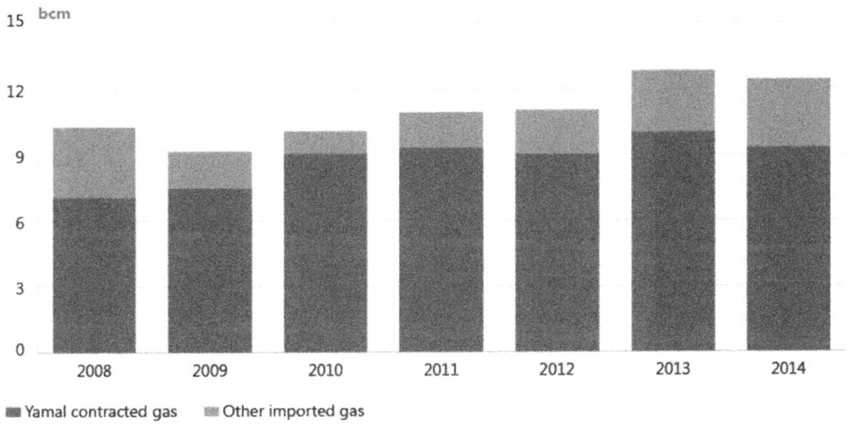

Graph 23: Quantity of Yamal-LTC gas as share of imports (2008–2014)[143]

---

[141] 'Szubski: Poland Cannot Afford to Wage War on Gazprom', *Polish News Bulletin*, 23 December 2009.

[142] Poland's state auditor once again gives a damning verdict on government policy related to the shale push here: Supreme Audit Office of Poland, *NIK O Poszukiwaniach Gazu łupkowego - Najwyższa Izba Kontroli*, 2012 <https://www.nik.gov.pl/aktualnosci/nik-o-poszukiwaniach-gazu-lupkowego.html> [accessed 23 June 2016].

[143] Data from Polish regulatory agency URE's annual reports. URE, *National Reports* (URE, 2013, 2012, 2011, 2010, 2009 2014) <http://www.ure.gov.pl/pl/urzad/informacje-ogolne/sprawozdania/2916,Sprawozdania.html> [accessed 2 June 2015].

By the end of the period of investigation in 2014, the European Commission's anti- trust investigation into Gazprom's trading practices in the eight CEE markets, including Poland, provided the best chance of structural reform to the country's LTC arrangements. This comes in addition to the on-going bilateral Stockholm arbitration case, the second such dispute since 2010. However, without any notable change to the status quo terms in the trading relationship since the Yamal contract was signed in 1996, and no major amendment to the level of dependence in that time, PGNiG continued to pay above the European average for its wholesale imports throughout the period of investigation, according to the data presented earlier in Table 2.

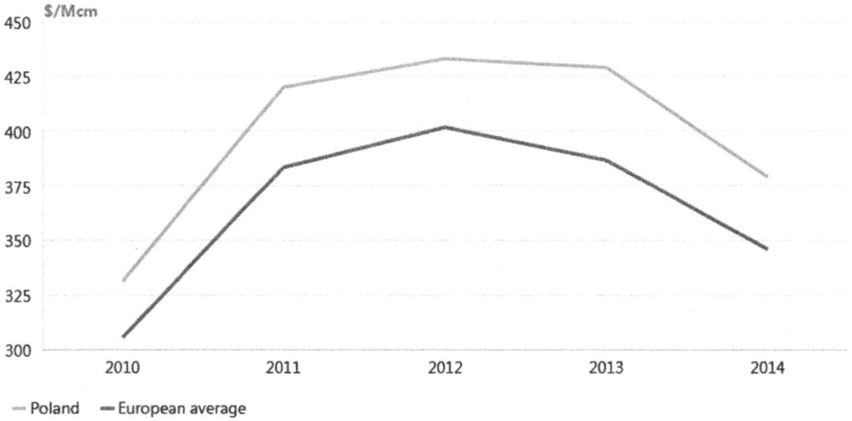

Graph 24: Price of Poland's wholesale Russian gas imports (2010–2014)[144]

[144] As cited earlier, data from: Novikov, Alexey, *TABLE: How Prices Fell for Russian Gas* (Interfax, 6 March 2015).

Table 6: Gas supply contracts effective in Poland (1989–2014)[145]

	Importer	Exporter	Contract signed	Start of deliveries	End of deliveries	Total volume	Yearly volume	Re-negotiations
Orenburg Agreement	Poland	Soviet Union	June, 1974	1978	1998 (Extended to 1999)	54.6 bcm (at rate of 2.6 bcm/y)	2.6 bcm or 2.8 bcm	
Yamburg Agreement	Poland	Soviet Union	January, 1987	1989	2008	45 bcm	2.5 bcm	July, 1991 13 bcm to be delivered split across 1.2 bcm in 1991, 1.65 bcm in 1992 and 2.5 bcm/y thereafter
Barter and 'Gas for Food'	Bartimpex/Poland	Itera/Gazprom/Moscow Authorites		January, 1991	2005	14.3 bcm	800 mcm (Kolmex 1991) 1.5 bcm (state 1991) 12 bcm in total (Bartimpex)	March 1991 (Kolmex) October 1991 (State) Bartimpex (1991)
Yamal Supply Contract	PGNiG	Gazprom	September, 1996	1997 (Pipeline not ready until 1999)	2022	250 bcm (later revised to 218 bcm)	14 bcm/y (1993 deal) 12.5 bcm/ (1996 contract) - First 6 bcm in 1997 until 2002 2003 onwards 8bcm/y After 2010 reneg 2010: 9.03 bcm/year 2011: 9.77 bcm/year 2012-2022: 10.24 bcm /year	2003, 2010, 2012 (Price and term revisions. Change in price formula in 4Q 2012 from 100% oil link to oil/spot mix)
Little Norway Contract	PGNiG	Norwegian Gas Negotiating Committee	May, 1999	2001	October, 2006	2.6 bcm	500 mcm	2006 (Extended for indefinite period but with PGNiG able to offtake the gas at multiple points inlcuding TTF)
Denmark BalticPipe Contract	PGNiG	DONG	July, 2001	2003	2011	16 bcm	2 bcm	2007 (Cancelled)
Big Norway Contract	PGNiG	Norwegian Gas Negotiating Committee	September, 2001	2008	2024	74 bcm	2.5 bcm in 2008 up to 5 bcm from 2011	2003 (Extension of ratification and ostensibly cancelled in December)
Tripartite Contract	PGNiG	NAK Naftogaz (as transit guarantor) / Eural Trans Gas	October, 2003	November, 2003	December, 2006	3 bcm	2 bcm by July 2004 (2.67 bcm was delivered). Agreement provides for additional 500 mcm deliveries from July 2004 to June 2005 and from July 2005 to December 2006.	From 1 March 2005 RosUkrEnergo replaced Eural in the contract. Terms largely unchanged but 200 mcm to be delivered per month.
VNG/E.On Ruhrgas 2004	PGNiG	VNG-Verbundnetz Gas / E.On Ruhrgas	September, 1998	September, 1998	September, 2008	4 bcm	400 mcm	Original deal only 1 year, renewing existing regional trading. Re-negotiated in 2004. Replaced by 2008 VNG deal.
Hrubieszów Region Contract	PGNiG	NAK Naftogaz	October, 2004	July, 2005	2020	53.5 mcm (combined contracted gas)	9 mcm	17.5 mcm to be delivered between 1 July 2005 and December 2007. Supply will rise from 2008. Deal terminated 6 November 2013.
VNG 2006	PGNiG	VNG-Verbundnetz Gas	August, 2006	October, 2006	October, 2016	4.2 bcm	500 mcm in 2006, 2007. 400 mcm until 2016	Re-negotiation on price formula in 2012, took effect 1 October.
RosUkrEnergo	PGNiG	RosUkrEnergo	November, 2006	January, 2007	January, 2010	5 bcm (combined contracted gas)	2.5 bcm	2006
VNG 2008	PGNiG	VNG-Verbundnetz Gas	September, 2008	September, 2008	October, 2011	1.5 bcm	500 mcm	
Qatar LNG	PGNiG	Qatargas	April, 2009	2014	2034	30 bcm	1.5 bcm	2014 (Deferrment)
Gazprom Short-Term 2009	PGNiG	Gazprom	June, 2009	June, 2009	September, 2009	1.024 bcm	1.024 bcm	
Vitol 2009	PGNiG	Vitol	September, 2009	October, 2009	October, 2011	280 mcm (combined contracted gas)	140 mcm	
VNG 2011	PGNiG	VNG-Verbundnetz Gas	May, 2011	May, 2011	September, 2011	100 mcm	100 mcm	Deal extended in July 2011.
Vitol 2011	PGNiG	Vitol	May, 2011	October, 2011	October, 2014	1.65 bcm	550 mcm	

Russia	Diversification	Barter

145 Data compiled by author from PGNiG, IEA, Statoil, Bartimpex data and various news and analyst reports. All information included herein is cited and referenced in the preceding case study chapter.

4.7 Poland policy conclusions

How does the information outlined in the preceding chapter and the data collected on Poland's gas sector between 1989 and 2014 align with the hypotheses as presented in Chapter 2? To re-cap, hypothesis 1, or H1, posits that left-wing governments – in the case of Poland those led by the communist legacy SLD party – tend to prioritise cooperation with already dominant suppliers of natural gas like Gazprom, while right-wing governments, such as the PiS administration of the mid-2000s and the earlier Buzek government, seek security-boosting diversification measures through LTCs with non-dominant suppliers. A further hypothesis posited as H2 suggests that left-wing governments are motivated to maintain downward pressure on retail prices for consumers, which in turn makes lower wholesale costs a strategic priority in LTC talks. Right-wing governments, meanwhile, seek greater supply security and are willing to pay a premium for gas from sources that re-enforces that security through diversification. Finally, H3 argues that in the LTC re-negotiation process state-owned utilities – PGNiG in the case of Poland – under left-wing governments opt for short-term price discounts over the structural change that right-wing governments and private utilities seek.

In the case of Poland, there is clear evidence that left-wing governments sought to reinforce cooperation with Russia, the dominant supplier, as shown in Figure 10. For example, under the Oleksy and Cimoszewicz SLD-led coalition governments of the 1990s, the Yamal contract and its earlier protocol agreement were signed, supporting development of the pipeline project itself and the LTC arrangement that would lock PGNiG into Gazprom supply volumes for the rest of the review period and up until the 2020s. After returning to office in 2001, the SLD Miller government opted to extend the Yamal contract by a further decade, while ostensibly cancelling alternative agreements that would have opened up a new supply route for non-Russian gas to flow from Scandinavia. Miller's successor as SLD Prime Minister, Belka, then oversaw PGNiG during a period in which it signed off on an import contract with opaque Russian intermediary company Eural Trans Gas, enhancing the share of Russia's gas supply to the national market.

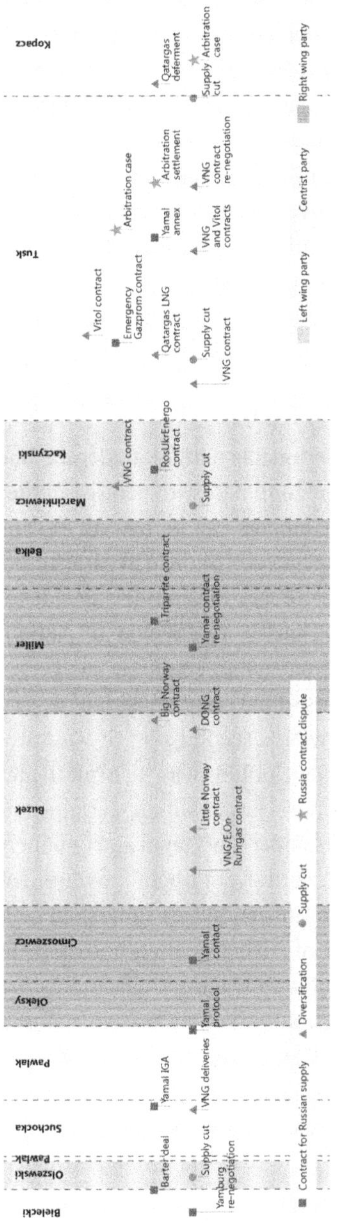

Figure 10: Poland political timeline with gas LTC milestones (1989–2014)

Dealing firstly with the traditional right-wing parties, the Buzek government under the Solidarity Electoral Action (AWS) and Freedom Union (UW) coalition, which would eventually give way to PO and PiS as the most promninent centre-right parties, can be shown to have committed significant policy energy to gas-supply security measures, agreeing two contracts with Norway's Statoil and other producers under the GFU framework and a further supply deal with Denmark's DONG Energy. Furthermore, the Buzek government had earlier signed off on a small-scale supply contract with German suppliers VNG and E.On. Under the later PiS governments that took office in 2006, impetus was given to the Polskie LNG project and PGNiG signed a further VNG import arrangement that would see small supplies coming from the west. Meanwhile, PGNiG under the PiS government refused to sanction negotiations with Gazprom after the Russian exporter had re-quested re-negotiation talks in 2005.

Dealing finally with the right-wing governments that fall under the liberal free market canopy, and which for ease are here conflated with centrist parties and/or coalitions: the behaviour of the early governments can be partially excluded because of the fluid multi-party cabinet configurations of the early transition period, as shown in Figure 4. This gave little or no time for a clear policy agenda to emerge as cleavages settled and democratic institutions were developed. Although after 1995 Poland's maximum configuration of parties in coalition has been three at once, before that, during the six governments of the early transition phase between the administrations of Mazowiecki and Pawlak's second stint, it was rare to have fewer than three. Early coalition government policy was also motivated by an overarching desire to secure gas deliveries post- haste, with uncertainty surrounding Russia's ability to meet its commitments under the Yamal and Orenburg agreements, as already discussed. The later PO centre-right liberal governments under Tusk and Kopacz from 2006 until the end of this enquiry's time-span in 2014 can be observed to have followed a tradition of diversification-boosting measures. PGNiG agreed an LNG supply arrangement with Qatargas during this period and a series of smaller import contracts that would utilise increased import capacity along the STORK interconnector with the Czech Republic, and reverse-flow capabilities on Yamal were agreed. Though PO also oversaw a period during which PGNiG gained state approval for a back-up contract with Gazprom to replace the cancelled RosUkrEnergo deal, it also brought in European Commssion negotiators to assist in the work of concluding talks on the Yamal contract structure in 2010 and was in office for the start of both arbitration cases lodged against Gazprom by PGNiG.

Assessing the applicability of H2, it is clear that Miller's SLD government sought to change policy course following the Buzek government's emphasis on diversification measures, opting instead to negotiate for cheaper gas from Gazprom. In 2002 the SLD Economy Minister Wacław Martyniuk told the Polish Sejm that "[e]verything that increases the cost, rises [sic] the price [...] should be rejected" in their contract talks with external suppliers.[146] The 2003 deal reached by PGNiG under an SLD government saw a 35% reduction in contracted volumes under the Yamal LTC. In exchange, the company agreed to extend its imports into the 2020s for relief with immediate quantities of gas needed.

On the other side of the electoral divide, the BalticPipe initiative launched under Buzek's 1997-2001 administration would surely have made Norwegian and Danish gas more expensive than existing imports when factoring in infrastructure costs, though the new LTCs could also have provided relief from some of Gazprom's favoured clauses as discussed earlier. The pursuit of an LNG import terminal on the Baltic coast under the rightist PiS, and later PO, governments was also predicated on the recognition that it would be potentially more expensive to attract LNG cargoes compared to the rate Gazprom could offer for pipeline gas, but the alternative opened up a valuable new option that made up for the 'security premium' and could perhaps bring Russian negotiators lower on price when faced with competition.

Regarding H3 and the tendency for state-owned companies to behave in different ways during re-negotiations with the dominant supplier between 2010 and 2014: the arbitration proceedings of 2011 launched by PGNiG against Gazprom in the Stockholm court just a week before the elections of November that year appear to corroborate the assumption that state companies are prone to accepting a temporary contract price discount. Though PGNiG under the PO government did eventually submit to a short-term deal based around price discounts, it failed to implement structural change in the contract, such as a reduction in take-or-pay rates or overall pricing methodology. The eventual out-of-court settlement agreed in 2012 was reported to have given PGNiG between a 10% and 15% retroactive

---

[146] Gorska, *Dealing with a Juggernaut*, p. 123.

price discount. Another arbitration case was launched in 2014, thought its result was not confirmed at the time of writing.

In sum, H1 is tentatively proved, with a clear divide between the policies of the left-wing SLD governments of 1995-1997 and 2001-2005, and the right-wing AWS coalition 1997 -2001, which was later replaced by PiS and PO, who in turn occupied government from 2005 until the period of inquiry ended in 2014. There is only assumptive evidence to prove H2, based on the policy of SLD governments in opting to re-negotiate with Gazprom in 2002, and the earlier decision to pursue Yamal in the 1990s. Regarding H3, the evidence collected appears to suggest that state-owned companies are willing to opt for price discounts, though more comparative findings are needed to draw further conclusions, and a lack of clear resolution to the second arbitration process launched by PGNiG in 2014 makes the single case open to analysis somewhat anecdotal.

5 Czech Republic

Russian gas supplies to the territory of today's Czech Republic first started in 1967 as the gas system build-out reached the frontier of the Soviet space.[1] With the completion of the Brotherhood pipeline system, direct deliveries into the country reached 1.4 bcm in 1970 and Czechoslovakia was also an important transit state for Soviet gas exports from the late 1960s onwards.[2] 'Red gas' was exported to a non- COMECOM member, Austria, through Czechoslovak territory for the first time in 1968, following a 5 km extension of the pipeline network from Bratislava to Baumgarten an der March on the western side of the iron curtain.[3] Since 1970, Czech demand has risen consistently, according to BP statistics, including a sharp rise during the early years of transition from the communist system after 1989. Consumption plateaued at between 8 bcm/y and 9 bcm/y around the millennium before rising to a peak of 9.5 bcm/y in 2005. It has since fallen back to the 8.2 bcm recorded in 2013, as shown in Figure 12.[4]

Indigenous gas production is limited to small-scale work mostly located in the Moravia region and conducted largely by Moravské naftové doly (MND). Production constituted 207 MMcm in 2013.[5] The gas is developed both conventionally and as the by-product of coal mining in northern Moravia.[6] Total recoverable

---

1 Gazprom Export, *Annual Corporate Brochure 2010*, 2011, p. 9.

2 Robert G. Jensen, Theodore Shabad and Arthur W. Wright, *Soviet Natural Resources in the World Economy* (Chicago: University of Chicago Press, 1983), p. 373.

3 Per Högselius, *Red Gas: Russia and the Origins of European Energy Dependence* (New York: Palgrave, 2013), p. 66.

4 BP, *Statistical Review of World Energy 2014* <http://www.bp.com/en/global/corporate/about-bp/energy-economics/statistical-review-of-world-energy.html> [accessed 29 April 2015].

5 Ministerstvo životního prostředí, *SUROVINOVÉ ZDROJE ČESKÉ REPUBLIKY NEROSTNÉ SUROVINY 2014 - Statistické Údaje Do Roku 2013*, 2014 <http://www.geology.cz/extranet/publikace/online/surovinove-zdroje/SUROVINOVE-ZDROJE-CESKE-REPUBLIKY-2014.pdf> [accessed 22 May 2015], p. 196.

6 IEA, *Energy Supply Security: The Emergency Response of IEA Countries - 2014 Edition* (Paris: IEA, 2014), p. 136.

J. Posaner, *Held Captive by Gas*, Energiepolitik und Klimaschutz. Energy Policy and Climate Protection, https://doi.org/10.1007/978-3-658-27518-1_5

reserves in the Czech Republic were estimated at 5.5 bcm in 2013, although slow exploitation means the country is effectively totally dependent on imports.[7]7 A mixture of coal and nuclear dominates the power generation sector in the Czech Republic, with gas holding only a 16.1% share in total primary energy consumption in 2013, around the same as the level in 2008. An IEA sector breakdown for that year is shown in Figure 11.[8] Industry constituted 31% of gas consumption, with the residential sector 29%, according to later 2012 figures.[9]

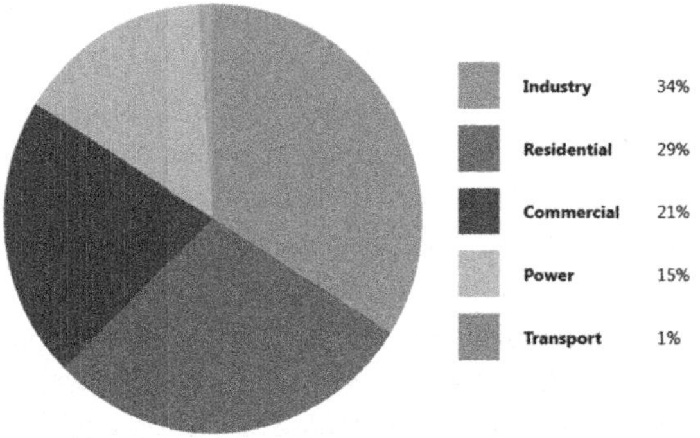

Figure 11: Sector breakdown of Czech Republic's gas demand (2008)[10]

LTC gas is imported mainly by RWE Supply & Trading CZ, which was rebranded from RWE Transgas in 2013. The company has been owned by Germany's second largest utility, RWE, since privatisation in 2002, shortly before the Czech Republic joined the EU in 2004. Trading company Vemex – in which Gazprom holds a stake – has also imported gas under contract with the Russian monopoly since 2006. The national transmission system operator is Net4Gas, having been rebranded from

7 Ministerstvo životního prostředí, *SUROVINOVÉ ZDROJE ČESKÉ REPUBLIKY NEROSTNÉ SUROVINY 2014 - Statistické Údaje Do Roku 2013*, 2014 <http://www.geology.cz/extranet/publikace/online/surovinove-zdroje/SUROVINOVE-ZDROJE-CESKE-REPUBLIKY-2014.pdf> [accessed 22 May 2015], p. 196.

8 IEA, *Energy Policies of IEA Countries: Czech Republic 2010* (Paris: Organisation for Economic Co-operation and Development, 2010) <http://www.oecd-ilibrary.org/content/book/9789264094710-en> [accessed 17 January 2015] and IEA, *Gas Trade Flows in Europe*, 2015 <http://www.iea.org/gtf/index.asp> [accessed 8 June 2015].

9 IEA, *Gas Trade Flows in Europe*, 2015 <http://www.iea.org/gtf/index.asp> [accessed 8 June 2015].

10 IEA, *Energy Policies of IEA Countries: Czech Republic 2010* (Paris: Organisation for Economic Co-operation and Development, 2010) <http://www.oecd-ilibrary.org/content/book/9789264094710-en> [accessed 17 January 2015].

RWE Transgas in March 2010. The company was unbundled from the supply side in 2007 and controls over 3,600 km of pipeline, four border points and five compressor stations.[11] It was sold by German utility RWE to private equity buyers Allianz and Borealis Infrastructure in 2013, and the state has no control. According to CV1 as shown in Figure 1, private ownership of the main importer restricts government control over the utility and its decision-making processes, which in turn limits the manifestation of domestic structures on import policy. Liberalisation of the Czech market since 2007 has also greatly increased the share of traded gas in the country, making consumers less reliant on LTCs. In 2012 a total of 25 companies are reported to have supplied gas to the Czech Republic, including German traders like Wingas and VNG.[12]

As of 2014, the Czech gas network had five major international connection points: one with Slovakia, opened in 1994 following the separation of Czechoslovakia (Lanžhot), and four with Germany (Olbernhau, Brandov, Hora Svaté Kateřiny and Waidhaus). The entry point at Brandov is where the OPAL pipeline that transits gas from Nord Stream to the Czech border meets the 30 bcm/y Gazelle pipeline, which in turn ships gas back into Germany though the Waidhaus border crossing point that meets the MEGAL system for onward dissemination through Germany and into France. Total Czech import capacity as of 2014 was 258.54 MMcm per day, with supply routes via Germany and Slovakia used for importing Russian and Norwegian stocks. The range of supply route options gives Czech importing agencies choice over how and when to contract gas when it comes to seeking new gas supply arrangements, as outlined under CV2 in Figure 1.

Gas can enter at all these system nodes, while gas exits only at Waidhaus, Olbernhau, Hora Svaté Kateřiny and, since 2009, back through the Lanžhot line into Slovakia.[13] Russian gas had traditionally been shipped through Lanžhot out into Germany at Olbernhau, where it also meets the STEGAL pipeline system running through the German regions of Saxony and Thuringia. This makes the Czech system key to circulating gas between some of the federal regions of Germany. The

---

11 Net4Gas, *40 Years of Natural Gas Transit through the Czech Republic*, 24 March 2015 <http://www.net4gas.cz/en/media/brozury/N4G_40_year_history_brochure_EN.pdf?jis=20150324133252> [accessed 21 May 2015], p. 5.

12 European Commission, *Country Report: Czech Republic*, 2014 <https://ec.europa.eu/energy/sites/ener/files/documents/2014_countryreports_czechrepublic.pdf> [accessed 24 May 2016], p. 47.

13 IEA, *Energy Supply Security: The Emergency Response of IEA Countries - 2014 Edition* (Paris: IEA, 2014), p. 138.

STORK pipeline border crossing into Poland at Cieszyn could only handle outward flows as of 2014, with plans in place to make this bi-directional and eventually increase throughput capacity beyond its current 550 MMcm/y volume.[14] The Czech Republic transits far more gas than it consumes per year – up to 50 bcm/y according to Net4Gas – approximately split across 20% for domestic use and 80% purely for transit to foreign markets.[15] In 2013, for example, 7.3 bcm of Gazprom gas was delivered to the Czech Republic – including that required for the operation of compressor stations – while 27.3 bcm of Russian gas was transited via the network.[16] As mentioned, reverse-flow capability through the Lanžhot border transfer station was initiated in 2009, allowing gas to flow back to Slovakia along a historically east-to-west transmission route. The Gazelle pipeline was brought on-stream in 2011, with a new border entry point on the German border at Brandov, as was the STORK interconnector with Poland at an opening ceremony held in September that year.[17] An interconnector with Austria is also planned.

There are currently three gas storage operators in the Czech Republic: MND, RWE Gas Storage – which was unbundled from transmission system operator RWE Trangas in 2007 – and SPP Storage, a subsidiary of Slovak utility Slovenský plynárenský priemysel. They operate eight facilities in total, with a combined capacity of 3.5 bcm – enough to cover demand for approximately 50 days in the event of supply disruption.[18] The facility at Dolní Bojanovice is located in the Czech Republic but used exclusively for the neighbouring Slovak market under its own separate long-term contract signed in 1999.[19] However, this is effectively replaced by capacity at the Láb underground gas storage facility near Bratislava,

---

14 As gas could only be delivered out of the Czech network by 2014, the STORK border crossing at Cieszyn is not considered a mainline connection. The so-called STORK II project is listed as one of the EU's Projects of Common Interest and would considerably increase bi-directional capacity but, as of December 2014, it had not made progress towards a construction phase.

15 Net4Gas, *40 Years of Natural Gas Transit through the Czech Republic*, 24 March 2015 <http://www.net4gas.cz/en/media/brozury/N4G_40_year_history_brochure_EN.pdf?jis=20150324133252> [accessed 21 May 2015], p. 3.

16 Gazprom Export, 'Czech Republic' <http://www.gazpromexport.ru/en/partners/czech/> [accessed 24 June 2015].

17 RWE, 'The Opening of the Poland - Czech Republic Gas Pipeline', 2011 <https://www.rwe.com/web/cms/de/37110/rwe/presse-news/pressemitteilungen/pressemitteilungen/?pmid=4006808> [accessed 26 June 2016].

18 IEA, *Energy Supply Security: The Emergency Response of IEA Countries - 2014 Edition* (Paris: IEA, 2014), p. 138.

19 Filip Černoch and Tomáš Vlček, *The Energy Sector and Energy Policy of the Czech Republic* (Brno: Masaryk University, 2013), p. 116.

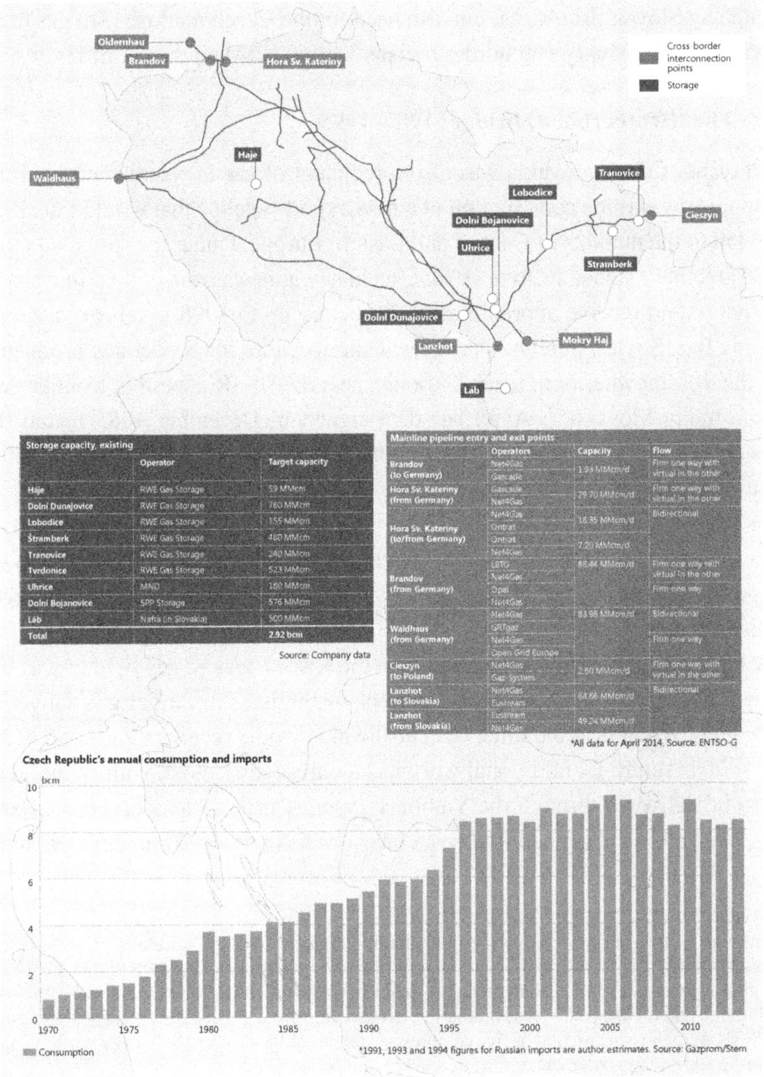

Storage capacity, existing

	Operator	Target capacity
Háje	RWE Gas Storage	59 MMcm
Dolni Dunajovice	RWE Gas Storage	760 MMcm
Lobodice	RWE Gas Storage	155 MMcm
Štramberk	RWE Gas Storage	480 MMcm
Tranovice	RWE Gas Storage	240 MMcm
Tvrdonice	RWE Gas Storage	523 MMcm
Uhrice	MND	180 MMcm
Dolni Bojanovice	SPP Storage	576 MMcm
Láb	Nafta (in Slovakia)	500 MMcm
Total		2.92 bcm

Source: Company data

Mainline pipeline entry and exit points

	Operators	Capacity	Flow
Brandov (to Germany)	Net4Gas Gascade	1.93 MMcm/d	Firm one way with virtual in the other
Hora Sv. Kateriny (from Germany)	Gascade Net4Gas	29.70 MMcm/d	Firm one way with virtual in the other
Hora Sv. Kateriny (to/from Germany)	Net4Gas Ontras	18.35 MMcm/d	Bidirectional
	Ontras Net4Gas	7.20 MMcm/d	
Brandov (from Germany)	LBTG Net4Gas	88.44 MMcm/d	Firm one way with virtual in the other
	Opal Net4Gas		Firm one way
Waidhaus (from Germany)	Net4Gas GRTgaz	83.98 MMcm/d	Bidirectional
	Net4Gas Open Grid Europe		Firm one way
Cieszyn (to Poland)	Net4Gas Gaz-System	2.60 MMcm/d	Firm one way with virtual in the other
Lanzhot (to Slovakia)	Net4Gas Eustream	64.66 MMcm/d	Bidirectional
Lanzhot (from Slovakia)	Eustream Net4Gas	49.24 MMcm/d	

*All data for April 2014. Source: ENTSO-G

Figure 12: Czech Republic market snapshot[20]

[20] Data taken from ENTSO-G, Net4Gas, BP Statistical Review of World Energy and IEA, *Energy Policies of IEA Countries: Czech Republic 2010* (Paris: Organisation for Economic Co-operation and Development, 2010) <http://www.oecd-ilibrary.org/content/book/9789264094710-en> [accessed 17 January 2015].

operated by Slovak firm Nafta, but also used for the Czech market, with gas transited via the local Mokrý Háj border transfer station between the countries.[21]

5.1 The 'Brotherhood' bridge: 1989–1995

Like Poland, Czechoslovakia was also a recipient of gas in return for labour and assistance towards the construction of a new export pipeline that would transit gas 2,750 km to the markets of Central and Eastern Europe. Under the so-called Orenburg Agreement signed in June 1974, Czechoslovakia was one of six Soviet satellites that would receive approximately 2.8 bcm/y up to 1998 in return for co-developing the 'Soyuz' pipeline that gave a supply route for Soviet gas production from the Russian interior to reach Ukraine,, near the USSR's western frontier, with what is today Slovakia.[22] A further deal signed in December 1985 meant that Czechoslovakia would receive an additional 5 bcm/y from 1990 to 2010 in return for building part of a new export pipeline from the Yamburg field, and for developing compressor station infrastructure.[23] Czechoslovak gascompany Tranzitní plynovod agreed to build 576 km of pipeline, four compressor stations and a gas storage facility in Russia leading up to 1994 as part of the so-called 'Progress' pipeline project.[24]

A further commitment to help develop the Karachaganak gas field in Kazakhstan was agreed in 1986 and was to see repayment made in further gas deliveries. According to reports at the time, Czechoslovakia would receive a further 5 bcm/y from 1995 in return for additional work its labourers carried out, with an initial 1.2 bcm to be delivered through the Yamburg pipeline in 1989 and 2.5 bcm in 1990, before the volume plateaued five years later.[25] An August 1991 amendment to the

---

21 The Láb facility is connected to the Baumgarten hub in Austria and also to the Czech network through a dedicated border crossing at Mokry Haj. The first three storage units at Láb are used by Nafta, with a fourth 620 MMcm facility owned by private company Pozagas.

22 Högselius, *Red Gas,* p. 171. According to Net4Gas, among its predecessor company's responsibilities were the construction of five compressor stations at Pallasovka, Antipovka, Frolovo, Kalininská and Sochranovka, in addition to 556 km of pipeline.

23 'OIL AND NATURAL GAS: PIPELINE DEVELOPMENTS', *BBC Monitoring Service: Former USSR*, 3 January 1986.

24 Net4Gas, *40 Years of Natural Gas Transit through the Czech Republic*, 24 March 2015 <http://www.net4gas.cz/en/media/brozury/N4G_40_year_history_brochure_EN.pdf?jis=20150324133252> [accessed 21 May 2015], p. 3.

25 'CZECHOSLOVAK PARTICIPATION IN CONSTRUCTION OF PROGRESS GAS PIPELINE', *BBC Monitoring Service: Central Europe & Balkans*, 9 January 1986.

Yamburg deal was signed in Prague after the so-called Velvet Revolution and reiterated that the Soviet Union would continue to make deliveries and ship a combined 16.35 bcm to Czechoslovakia under the terms of the deal as work continued on infrastructure projects as planned.[26] Between 1975 and 1999, Czechoslovakia – and then the Czech Republic, after the 'Velvet Divorce' separation from Slovakia, effective from 1 January 1993 – imported 40.26 bcm from Russia in return for CZK 72.8 billion of equivalent investment in the former USSR.[27]

In addition to direct deliveries, customers of Russian gas in Central and Western Europe sought to ensure secure transit through Czechoslovakia as the main transit corridor that, at the time, brought Soviet exports through the Brotherhood pipeline from the Ukrainian to the Austrian and German borders. A trilateral deal between Germany's Wintershall, Czech utility Český plynárenský podnik (CPP) and Prague-based foreign trade agency Metalimex, agreed in late February 1992 after the collapse of the Soviet Union, allowed for gas deliveries of 4.5 bcm/y from the Czech–Ukraine border station at Veľké Kapušany all the way through to the Hora Svaté Kateřiny exit point at the Czech border with Germany. Deliveries through that transit deal were planned to start in July 1992 and last for 25 years.[28] Germany's VNG also agreed a similar deal with Metalimex to receive 7 bcm/y through Czechoslovak territory, formalising the country's position as the key transit state for Russian gas deliveries into Europe's major high-volume importers.[29]

In November 1992, Metalimex – at the time the only company in Czechoslovakia importing gas – said it would receive 13 bcm from Russia that year under three separate contracts. The first was for 5 bcm carried out under the terms of the Yamburg agreement. A second contract was for a further 5 bcm/y under which Metalimex would ensure transit for Russian gas to western markets, and in return Moscow gave the company a status as "preferential supplier," paying transit fees in gas. Although officially unconfirmed, this can be taken as part of the Soviet-era

---

26 'Czechoslovakia Will Receive Soviet Natural Gas in Payment of the Debt', *USSR Economics & Foreign Trade Nova Soviet-West German JV*, 28 August 1991.

27 Net4Gas, *40 Years of Natural Gas Transit through the Czech Republic*, 24 March 2015 <http://www.net4gas.cz/en/media/brozury/N4G_40_year_history_brochure_EN.pdf?jis=20150324133252> [accessed 21 May 2015], p. 3.

28 Changes WINTERSHALL SIGNS LONG TERM CONTRACT FOR CIS GAS SUPPLY', *Platt's International Petrochemical Report*, 27 February 1992, p. 5.

29 'Agreement on Transit of Russian Gas to Germany', *BBC Monitoring Service: Central Europe & Balkans*, 5 March 1992.

contract for additional deliveries that was due to plateau at 5 bcm/y by 1995. The third Russian import contract saw gas imports paid for at market rates in US dollars.[30]

Supply contracts from Russia were being arranged on a year-by-year basis in the early 1990s, and with the added complexity of Czech transit being paid for with gas, it remains impossible to quantify accurately exactly how much gas under either the Orenburg and Yamburg agreements (or through further barter exchanges, or temporary commercial contracts) was actually delivered. Data supplied from Gazprom does show that Russia exported 12.6 bcm to Czechoslovakia in 1990, 13.7 bcm in 1991, 12.8 bcm in 1992 and 13.2 bcm in 1993 before the Velvet Divorce split the country in two and the Lanžhot border station was built to separate the national market areas of Slovakia and the Czech Republic formally. However, the Czech Republic's role as a key transit state for Russian exports to secure hard currency payment in return meant that Moscow saw it as imperative to maintain direct deliveries through the Brotherhood pipeline system and to avoid any early disruption, as occurred in Poland.

Although deliveries did continue under the Orenburg deal during the early 1990s, Moscow sought to delay some supplies under the Yamburg agreement as part of a strategy to secure hard-currency payment from importers. Russia hoped to secure direct cash payments for the 4.7 bcm scheduled to be delivered to the Czech and Slovak Republics in 1993.[31] In response to uncertainty over future supplies, Czech companies subsequently sought alternative import options. The build-out of connections with Germany was one potential option, as was creating both a physical and contractual link to Norwegian gas supply.

After the centre-right Civic Democratic Party (ODS) took office under Prime Minister Václav Klaus, heading a conservative coalition that also included the Christian and Democratic Union–Czechoslovak People's Party (KDU–ČSL) as the Czech Republic's first elected government in 1992, importers sought to take advantage of the country's position to attract new deliveries of gas from non- Russian suppliers. In summer 1993, CPP signed a deal with Germany's Ruhrgas that

---

30 'Import of 13,000 Cubic Metres Russian Gas Planned.', *CTK Business News*, 30 November 1992, p. 11.

31 Work prices at the time would have amounted to approximately $92 per MMcm, according to local reports. 'Russia Demands Hard Currency for Gas Supplies', *CTK Business News*, 26 November 1992, p. 2.

would see 200 MMcm delivered in the first quarter of 1994.[32] Commercial ties between the two companies stretched back to 1991 and to the construction of the Waidhaus–Rozvadov border interconnection through which Ruhrgas had already supplied 100 MMcm to the Czech Republic during a period of cold weather in early 1992.[33] Ruhrgas was also interested in taking a stake in CPP during the government's privatisation drive, which would eventually only happen in 2002, as Prague sought to clarify its Russian import schedule.

According to a protocol signed in September 1993, the Czech Republic alone would receive 6.7 bcm of Russian gas that year.[34] However, with its three-year contract for Russian imports linked to transit rights due to expire in December 1995, the Czech side began working on a replacement option. Negotiations with Gazprom over a new LTC with the Russian exporter dragged on through 1995, with first a September and then a December deadline for closing the deal missed as the country neared a new 1996 election that would see Klaus and the ODS re-elected for a second term. In December 1995, a deal was expected within weeks that would have seen gas deliveries over another three-year period, while the transit of Russian gas would have continued for a further 13 years. A protocol agreement would ensure deliveries continued after the original contract ended that month. Under the new supply contract 8 bcm/y would be imported in 1996 and 1997, rising to 9 bcm/y for 1998.[35]

Meanwhile, as Czechoslovakia was being broken in two, the sub-division of the Transgas pipeline system, vital for sending Russian gas into west European markets, into distinct sections along territorial lines was confirmed with a law passed in December 1992 that outlined how the single gas market area would be split. It also covered how contracts held by Metalimex would be transferred to a Slovak entity in early 1993, with that country's territory the first entry point for

[32] 'GERMAN GAS CONTRACT TO PROVIDE ONLY 3% OF CZECH NEEDS', *CTK Business News*, 15 October 1993, p. 4. The contract was described as an 'option' deal designed to cover any shortfall in the event of disruption to Russian supply.

[33] 'CESKY PLYNARENSKY PODNIK SIGNS CONTRACT WITH RUHRGAS', *Hospodarske Noviny*, 28 June 1993, p. 2.

[34] 'CZECH-RUSSIAN PROTOCOL ON MUTUAL SUPPLIES OF GOODS', *CTK Business News*, 1 September 1993, p. 17.

[35] 'TRANSGAS TO SIGN 1996 GAS DEAL IN JANUARY', *Hospodarske Noviny*, 27 December 1995, p. 1.

Russian gas along the Brotherhood pipeline after it crossed from Ukraine.[36] Under the eventual accord, the Czech Republic took gas being delivered under contract through the CIS at a 2:1 ratio, while also agreeing to pay Slovakia a transit fee of $1.30 per mcm over 100 km.[37] The separation proved controversial, with Klaus forced to deny that the Czech Republic had withheld transit fees from Slovakia in early 1993.[38] But the border metering transfer station at Lanžhot was inaugurated in January 1994, lying on the mainline rail connection between Bratislava and Prague.[39] Its completion allowed for the effective separation of the two markets that year.

5.2 Norwegian corridor: 1996–2005

Finally, in December 1996, the Czech Republic opened a new phase of negotiations with Gazprom over an LTC that would run for between 15-25 years.[40] Key to the Czech negotiating position was an objective to ensure that import obligations from Russian were beneath annual consumption, allowing room for source diversification. Under the second Klaus government, the Czech Republic pursued a strategy of energy supply diversification, aiming to open up new options for supply from the west and to ease dependence on Russia. Innuclear projects, the Czech government chose to replace Soviet designs with those of US firm Westinghouse for construction of reactors at the Temelin project, while a new oil pipeline allowing crude to flow from a refinery near the city of Ingolstadt in Germany to Kralupy outside Prague was opened in 1996.[41]

---

36 VLÁDA ČESKÉ REPUBLIKY, *K Návrhu Na Další Postup Při Transformaci a Privatizaci Státního Podniku Český Plynárenský Podnik, Odštěpný Závod Tranzitní Plynovod, v Souvislosti S Dělením České a Slovenské Federativní Republiky*, 1992 <https://racek.vlada.cz/usneseni/usneseni_webtest.nsf/0/4D35582BC2830E9BC12571B6006E7A17> [accessed 15 June 2015].

37 Robert A.. Young and Queen's University (Kingston ON) Institute of Intergovernmental Relations, *The Breakup of Czechoslovakia* (IIGR, Queen's University, 1994), p. 61. The transit fee was thought to be significantly under market rates.

38 'Fees for Natural Gas Transit Not Being Withheld, Says Klaus', *CTK Business News*, 3 March 1993, p. 4.

39 Net4Gas, 'History: Separation of Czechoslovakia' <http://www.net4gas.cz/en/history/> [accessed 10 June 2016].

40 Jan Lopatka, 'Gazprom in Long-Term Czech Supply Talks', *Reuters News*, 3 December 1996.

41 Jolyon Naegele, 'Czech Republic: Norwegian Gas Deal Final Step In Energy Independence', *RadioFreeEurope/RadioLiberty*, 9 March 1997, <http://www.rferl.org/content/article/1083931.html> [accessed 27 June 2016].

The final piece of the energy security jigsaw was gas, and Czech Minister of Industry and Trade Vladimír Dlouhý signed a contract with Norway's Gas Negotiating Committee (GFU) suppliers in September 1996, just a few months after Klaus had won re-election for a second term. The 20-year contract was approved in Prague during March 1997 and outlined deliveries of 53 bcm over the total length of the deal starting that year.[42] Norwegian gas first flowed into the Czech Republic on 1 May 1997, with the country expected to receive 700 MMcm in the first year.[43] The gas would reach Czech territory through the German network, flowing into the Emden receiving terminal on the North Sea coast and then east towards the multiple border entry points of the Czech network.

Talks on a Norway deal had begun as early as 1993, with Dlouhý's predecessor as trade minister, Vratislav Ludvík, hosting a Norwegian delegation in Prague with a view to the Scandinavian producing country supplying approximately 2 bcm/y[44] As late as April 1995, a mooted deal between Transgas and the GFU would only have seen 1 bcm/y delivered from 2000, a third of the original deal.[45] The suppliers under Norway's GFU framework would have been Norsk Hydro, Saga Petroleum and Statoil. The failure to secure a new LTC with Gazprom meant that the Czech government spent most of 1996 locked in a debate over how best to secure future gas supplies. Norway was the primary available choice other than Russia, but options for bringing in Dutch gas stocks from Nederlandse Gasunie and Wintershall were also considered.

Meanwhile, Transgas supplied record volumes of gas in 1996 as Czech consumption grew sharply. The country imported a total of 9.3 bcm that year: 8.1 bcm came from Gazprom under existing deals, 300 MMcm from Russian– Czech joint venture RCTd and 200 MMcm from Wintershall via Germany. A further 700 MMcm was also delivered by Gazprom to cover a peak in winter demand in early 1996.[46] However, by 1997 Russia was already facing competition in the Czech market, and increased security pressure on Prague from Moscow over the country's move towards NATO membership also served to expedite the conclusion of

42 Jan Lopatka, 'FOCUS - Czechs Seal Historic Gas Deal with Norway', *Reuters News*, 19 March 1997.

43 'Norská Dodávka Plynu Překročila Hranici', *Hospodářské Noviny* <http://archiv.ihned.cz/c1-914641-norska-dodavka-plynu-prekrocila-hranici> [accessed 23 May 2015].

44 'Czechs Wish to Import Norwegian Natural Gas', *Reuters News*, 20 February 1993.

45 'Norway in Gas Sales Talks with Czech Firm', *Reuters News*, 20 April 1995.

46 'Transgas Supplied Record 58 Mil Cu Mt of Gas on 29 December Natural-Gas Importer Should Import 9.3 Bil Cu Mt of Gas in 1996', *Ekonomicke Zpravodajstvi*, 31 December 1996, p. 9.

an alternative LTC to Gazprom gas. In March 1997, just days before the Norwegian contract was announced, Russia's recently appointed ambassador to Prague, Nikolai Ryabov, the former chairman of the Central Electoral Commission in Moscow, implicitly linked gas trade to NATO membership,[47] saying to Russia's NTV: "Agreements fundamental to the Czech Republic, such as gas deliveries and nuclear energy, create a basis for future problems that our countries would face."[48]

Meanwhile, the Russian and Norwegian supply contracts were supplemented by a small-scale import contract with German suppliers BEB and VNG, first agreed in November 1997, shortly before Klaus was forced to resign by the ODS and a caretaker administration under the former governor of the Czech National Bank, Josef Tošovský, was appointed by President Václav Havel. The BEB/VNG deal was later expanded in November 1998. That contract ensured up to 2 MMcm/d from BEB into the Czech system, as required, with Transgas anticipating 25 to 30 MMcm of requirements over the November to February period for which the deal was valid.[49] A second deal included Mobil Erdgas-Erdoel and outlined "stopgap" deliveries of up to 3 MMcm/d through the Hora Svaté Kateřiny system entry point.[50] The deals were aimed at shoring up Czech security of supply and granting alternative short-term import options to cover peaks in demand during cold-weather periods.

Elections in 1998 saw the left-wing Czech Social Democratic Party (ČSSD) take office in a minority single-party government, with their leader Miloš Zeman appointed Prime Minister from July that year. A full LTC was finally agreed directly with Gazprom subsidiary Gazexport in November 1998, through which Gazprom would deliver between 8 bcm/y, later rising to 9 bcm/y, starting in January 1999 and scheduled to run for 15 years, with the option to extend this for a further 10 years automatically if required.[51] Under pressure to retain its market share in the Czech Republic, by 1997 Gazprom had also appointed Gaz- Invest as

47 Jonathan P. Stern, *The Future of Russian Gas and Gazprom* (Oxford: Oxford University Press, 2005), p. 115.

48 'Russia Hints at Reprisals If Czechs Join NATO', *Reuters News*, 16 March 1997.

49 Deliveries would only be required that winter if temperatures dipped below -12C, Transgas expected. 'German Firms BEB Erdol and VNG to Supply Gas to Czech Rep.', *CTK Business News*, 21 November 1997, and 'CZECH REPUBLIC', *Platt's Oilgram News*, 25 November 1997, section NEWS BRIEFS: International, p. 6.

50 'CZECHS SIGN FOR WINTER GAS SUPPLY FROM GERMANY', *Platt's Oilgram News*, 12 November 1998, p. 2.

51 David Long, Geoff Moore and Gay Wenban-Smith, *Gas Trading Manual: A Comprehensive Guide to the Gas Markets* (Elsevier, 2001), p. 30 and Filip Černoch, and Tomáš Vlček, *The Energy Sector and Energy Policy of the Czech Republic* (Brno: Masaryk University, 2013), p. 112.

an intermediary for additional gas supplies into the country, but the company was largely restricted to small-scale trading.[52] The 1998 deal was the first long-term commercial arrangement for the supply of gas from Russia since the transition-era began and accompanied a separate transit agreement worth $10 billion and put in place to ensure Russian gas flows through Czech territory would last at least until 2008.[53]

In December 1998, during a visit to Moscow by a Czech delegation led by deputy Prime Minister Pavel Mertlík, the issue of further barter trading for gas deliveries was discussed.[54] A year later, in November 1999, Transgas agreed to import a further 100 MMcm through intermediary Gaz-Invest, with approximately 38% of the cost to be paid through the delivery of Czech goods.[55]

The deal was signed to cover an expected increase in demand and marked the first such contract with a third party intermediary in the Czech Republic. Meanwhile, an extension of the Gazprom transit deal, reached in November 1999, added a guaranteed 13 bcm/y transit flow from 2009 to 2020.[56]

Talks with Russia over gas debt, stretching back to the 1985 Soviet deal to develop the Yamburg field and pipeline project, bore results in 2001, with Moscow agreeing to make a token payment to settle the issue. Meanwhile, Kiev also recognised its obligation to pay for $79 million worth of work with 1.25 bcm, and money was set aside as part of the national budget in 2004 by the Verkhovna Rada national parliament to fulfil the commitment.[57] A similar claim for payment from Kazakhstan was also pursued by Prague, but by the end of 2014 both cases remain unresolved.[58]

Impending EU membership spurred the Czech government to privatise its state- owned assets, including Transgas, in the early 2000s as part of what became a frenzied government sell-off. Under Zeman's administration, Germany's RWE announced it had won the bidding process to take majority control of Transgas and

---

52 Stern, *The Future of Russian Gas and Gazprom*, p. 115.

53 'TRANSGAS/GAZPROM AGREE NAT. GAS SUPPLY CONTRACT', *Petroleum Review*, 9 November 1998, p. 10.

54 'Czech Delegation Discusses Barter Trade in Moscow', *CTK Business News*, 17 December 1998.

55 'TRANSGAS, GAS INVEST INK SUPPLEMENTARY IMPORT AGREEMENT', *Interfax Czech Republic & Slovakia Weekly Business*, 17 December 1999.

56 'Czech Transgas, Russian Gazexport Sign Transit Deal', *Reuters News*, 18 November 1999.

57 'UKRAINE WILL REDEEM ITS DEBT ON THE YAMBURG AGREEMENT FROM FUNDS', *Interfax Ukrainian News (Russia)*, 17 June 2004.

58 'Kazakhstan Stops Talks on Debt to CzechRep', *CTK Business News*, 13 November 2006.

the Czech Republic's various regional gas distributors in December 2001. The Essen-based company's chief executive for the gas business, Manfred Scholle, said at the time that that deal would allow his company "direct access to Europe's largest gas exporter, Gazprom."[59] The gas sector privatisation was the largest ever deal in the Czech Republic, worth approximately €4.1 billion. The deal was approved at the end of January 2002[60] and other bidders included a consortium of Ruhrgas and Gaz de France, in addition to Duke Energy and E.On.[61]

The second ČSSD government – this time under Prime Minister Vladimír Špidla at the head of a multi-party left-of-centre coalition with KDU–ČSL and the liberal Freedom Union–Democratic Union party (US-DEU) – took office in July 2002 as the privatisation process gathered pace and EU membership was bestowed on 1 May 2004. A further two ČSSD administrations would take office over the next four years, first under Prime Minister Stanislav Gross, from August 2004 to April 2005, and second under Jiří Paroubek, from April 2005 to September 2006, each with the same coalition configuration. Meanwhile, no further gas supply contracts would be publicly announced, but a brewing conflict over the terms and pricing of Russian gas supply back along the transportation chain in Ukraine would soon have disastrous effects for regional supply security.

5.3 'Gas Wars': 2006–2009

The first major cut to gas supply on account of the dispute between Russia and Ukraine in January 2006 did not have an immediate impact on Czech imports, with RWE Transgas saying on 2 January that year that deliveries were proceeding in "the context of agreed flexibility of gas supply corresponding to contractual agreements," and the that onward distribution was ensured.[62] RWE Transgas's chief executive, Martin Chalupsky, said on 3 January that his company "did not notice any trouble with the gas supplies from the East. The pressure in the pipeline is

---

59 RWE, *RWE Wins Bidding Process for Privatization of Czech Gas Industry*, 17 December 2001 <https://www.rwe.com/web/cms/en/113648/rwe/press-news/press-release/?pmid=54572> [accessed 15 June 2015]. The Czech government had invited bids for a 97% stake in Transgas and between 46% and 58% interests in each of the eight regional gas utilities. RWE gained the majority in six of the eight regional gas utilities and was reported to be only bidder for the main gas importer.

60 'Czechs Conclude Sale of Transgas to RWE Gas', *Reuters News*, 30 January 2002.

61 'Czech Privatisation Controversy', *BBC*, 17 December 2001, section BUSINESS <http://news.bbc.co.uk/2/hi/business/1716193.stm> [accessed 27 June 2016].

62 RWE Transgas, 'Zásobování České Republiky Zemním Plynem Je Aktuálně Zajištěno', 2 January 2006 <http://www.net4gas.cz/cs/archiv-556/> [accessed 24 June 2015].

absolutely normal. The Czech Republic is receiving the amount of gas stipulated by the contract."[63] However, the subsequent impetus given to the development of the Nord Stream pipeline project by Gazprom later that year as a means of avoiding transit through Ukraine would put in doubt the Czech position as a key transportation hub for Russian deliveries further west. It also threatened to reduce transit revenues for RWE Transgas, with Nord Stream's envisaged 55 bcm/y of direct throughput capacity under the Baltic Sea direct to Germany, in concert with the Yamal pipeline running through Poland, being sufficient to bypass the Brotherhood pipeline system completely.

In this context, RWE announced it would renew the terms of its 1998 Czech supply contract in December 2006 until 2035, with annual deliveries pitched at 9 bcm/y. In its announcement, the company said it was ensuring supply and creating the framework for a competitive national gas market in the future:

> The network of RWE Transgas in the Czech Republic is not only used to secure the supply of the Czech market, but may even be considered to be a key pillar of the entire European natural gas supply system. Approximately one third of all Russian natural gas supplies to Western Europe are transported through the Czech Republic. This agreement provides the basis for continuing gas transit cooperation after the completion of the Baltic Sea Pipeline [Nord Stream].[64]

Meanwhile, the Czech government sought to allay fears that it was ill prepared for another cut-off after Mirek Topolánek was installed as Prime Minister at the head of an initially temporary administration in September 2006, which eventually won an election to build a centre-right coalition in January 2007 led by the ODS with KDU-ČSL and the Green Party (SZ) as junior partners. In March 2008, the Czech Ministry of Industry and Trade posted a statement noting that a contractual reliance on Russia had been avoided, with 25% of consumption coming through the Norway contract. The ODS's Minister of Industry and Trade Martin Říman said in the statement:

> Gas is not delivered to us only from Russia, but also from Norway and thanks to a mild winter, we have a sufficient supply in the underground tanks. Long-term contracts guarantee the security of deliveries as well as the fact that we are a significant transit country, through which tens of billions of cubic meters of gas is channelled to other EU states, every year.[65]

---

63 Interfax, *Regular Gas Supplies Restored in Slovakia, No Trouble in Czech Republic*, 3 January 2006.

64 RWE, *RWE Baut Position Im Europäischen Gasmarkt Aus*, 21 December 2006 <https://www.rwe.com/web/cms/en/113648/rwe/press-news/press-release/?pmid=4001475> [accessed 24 June 2015].

65 Czech Ministry of Industry and Trade, *Securing Delivery of Natural Gas to the Czech Republic*, 3 June 2008 <http://www.mpo.cz/zprava41367.html> [accessed 10 June 2016].

Germany's Wingas, a joint venture between Wintershall BASF and Gazprom, had also made its entry into the Czech gas market in January 2006, although initially only through a single supply contract with glassmaker Vetropak Moravia Glass.[66] Gazprom, meanwhile, looked at further ways to ensure its access to the Czech market through its majority-owned gas trading operation Vemex, which had been registered in Prague since 2001. In March 2006, Vemex had signed a new gas supply contract with Gazprom that would see deliveries of 186 MMcm over the following 18 months.[67] Its customers would largely be industrial concerns, but targets were put in place for increasing the company's market penetration.[68] Ownership of Vemex was split three ways in 2014 between Gazprom subsidiary ZMB GmbH, holding 50.14%, Austria-based Centrex Europe Energy & Gas AG, with a further 33%, and Czech producer MND, which held the final 16.86%.[69]

The contract with Vemex provided the first direct large-scale contracted gas competition to RWE Transgas's position as monopoly importer. In October 2007, Gazprom signed an expanded deal with Vemex for annual deliveries of 500 MMcm between 2008 and 2012, with the possibility of a further five-year extension.[70] In April 2008, Vemex also agreed a Memorandum of Understanding with MND on the joint development of a gas storage facility in the Czech Republic.[71] This was followed by the acquisition of the Czech company's stake in Vemex

---

66 Energetický regulační úřad, *The Czech Republic's National Report on the Electricity and Gas Industries for 2005*, July 2006 <http://www.eru.cz/documents/10540/488714/NZaj2005.pdf/3531af86-926f-48b0-9930-641640f46b64> [accessed 24 June 2015], p. 7.

67 'Gazprom Signs Term Gas Deal with Czech Vemex', *Reuters News*, 11 October 2007.

68 As of 2010, Vemex supplied gas to the following major consumers across 13 of the 15 regions of the Czech Republic: Škoda Auto (carmaking), Česká rafinérská (refinery complex), Plzeňský Prazdroj (brewing), Pilsen Steel (steel), Dalkia Česká republika, ČEZ Energetické služby, Pražská plynárenská (Prague gas company), Spolana (chemical industry), ŽDB Group and Cukrovary a lihovary TTD (sugar refining and alcohol distillation). Gazprom Export, *Blue Fuel: Gazprom Export Global Newsletter*, June 2010 <http://www.gazprom-mt.com/WhatWeSay/Lists/PublicationsList/Gazprom%20export%20-%20Blue%20Fuel%20June%202010.pdf> [accessed 15 June 2015], p. 10.

69 Vemex, 'VLASTNICKÁ STRUKTURA' <http://www.vemex.cz/cs/about/structure/> [accessed 24 June 2015].

70 Gazprom, *Делегация ОАО «Газпром» Приняла Участие В Праздновании 40-Летия Поставок Российского Газа В Чехию*, 1 November 2007 <http://www.gazprom.ru/press/news/2007/november/article56380/> [accessed 23 June 2015].

71 Vemex, 'MND and VEMEX Sign a Memorandum of Cooperation', 2008 <http://www.mnd.eu/wp-content/uploads/2015/03/17042008-tz-mnd-vemex-memorandum-aj.pdf> [accessed 22 June 2015].

during 2012 by its parent company KKCG, owned by Czech billionaire Karel Komárek.[72] Ceská plynárenská also entered the gas import sector in 2008 through a deal with StatoilHydro to import what was initially reported to be around 5-10% of Czech consumption – or a minimum 475 MMcm/y, according to reports.[73] The deal was agreed to come into effect in May that year.

Russian gas supplies to the Czech Republic were cut by 75% as of 6 January 2009 after falling 9% the day before. The sudden collapse during a period of cold weather was mitigated by storage reserves in excess of 2 bcm and by Norwegian deliveries. However, onward transit to Germany was reduced and plans were drawn up for broader measures if reductions persisted and the temperature dropped beneath -10C.[74] The crisis coincided with the Czech Republic holding the rotating presidency of the EU, meaning Topolánek played a leading role in managing the stand-off and facilitating negotiations between Moscow and Kiev.[75]

Former Czech Prime Minister-turned-President, Václav Klaus, summoned Russia's ambassador to Prague Castle to discuss the cuts on 6 January.[76] In a joint statement issued on 9 January, the Czech government and European Commission said:

> Without prior warning and in clear contradiction with the reassurances given by the highest Russian and Ukrainian authorities to the European Union, gas supplies to some EU member States have been substantially cut. This is completely unacceptable. The Czech EU Presidency and the European Commission demand that gas supplies be immediately restored to the EU and that the two parties resume at once negotiations with a view to a definitive settlement of their bilateral commercial dispute.[77]

Also suffering from reduced flows to its contract, Vemex signed an agreement with VNG on 8 January for deliveries of 3 MMcm/d, effective immediately through the Hora Svaté Kateřiny border point with Germany.[78] The cut to supply

---

72 'Czech Natural Gas Storage Operator Finalises Vemex Stake Buy' <http://www.icis.com/resources/news/2012/01/19/9525417/czech-natural-gas-storage-operator-finalises-vemex-stake-buy/> [accessed 24 June 2015].

73 'Norway to Supply CeP', *Platts Energy in East Europe*, 25 April 2008, section OIL & GAS NEWS; Czech Republic, p. 94.

74 'Russian Gas Supplies to CR Cut by 75 Pct Today-Transgas', *CTK Business News*, 6 January 2009.

75 Ondřej Soukup, 'Ruský plyn stále neteče', *Hospodářské Noviny*, 12 January 2009, p. 1.

76 'Klaus to Meet Russian Ambassador over Cuts in Gas Supplies', *CTK Business News*, 6 January 2009.

77 Czech EU Presidency and European Commission, *Joint Statement by the Czech EU Presidency and the European Commission*, 6 January 2009.

78 'Vemex Ups Gas Supplies from Germany by up to 3 Million m3 a Day', *CTK Business News*, 8 January 2009.

gave RWE Transgas the impetus to begin construction work on the border transfer station at Lanžhot that would allow reverse-flow deliveries back into Slovakia in the event of supply disruption.[79] On 16 January, Topolánek offered Slovakia's Prime Minister Robert Fico 20 MMcm/d of capacity through Lanžhot that would see flows from the Yamal line into Poland looped back through Central Europe.[80] Ceská plynárenská also said on 9 January that it had sealed a deal to receive a further 1 MMcm/d from StatoilHydro, which it sold directly to RWE Trangas to cover its shortfall of Ukraine-transited gas.[81]

Welcoming the resumption of full supplies following a deal between Russia and Ukraine on 19 January, the Czech government warned that the "bilateral dispute has harmed the confidence placed into the two countries."[82] The cut-off sparked debate on the future of Russian gas supply to Europe, encouraging EU states to put support behind the Nabucco gas pipeline project at a summit held in Prague on 8 May that year. The 'Southern Gas Corridor' concept, of which Nabucco was a part, was aimed at building infrastructure that could deliver gas from the Caspian and Middle East to EU markets. A statement following the Prague summit called to address the strategy said that the strategic target was the identification of new "gas volumes available for marketing in the EU and Turkey."[83] The search for non-Russian gas would soon intensify in Europe.

With the development of Gazprom's Nord Stream well underway by 2010, the OPAL pipeline, connecting its landfall site at Greifswald in northern Germany with the Brandov point at the Czech border, was connected to the Gazelle pipeline, developed by RWE Transgas to transit Russian gas across the country between the

79 'Slovak Eustream Works on Reverse Flows to Ship Gas', *European Gas Markets*, 16 July 2009. In its 2012 report on the Slovak market, the IEA said that reverse-flow deliveries through Lanžhot would be possible within two hours of a supply crisis. IEA, *Energy Policies of IEA Countries: Slovak Republic 2012* (Paris: Organisation for Economic Co-operation and Development, 2012) <http://www.oecd-ilibrary.org/content/book/9789264173507-en> [accessed 17 January 2015], p. 77.

80 'UPDATE 2-Czechs Offer Slovakia Gas Option', *Reuters News*, 16 January 2009.

81 'Přísun Plynu Ze Západu Na Český Trh Roste', *Hospodářské Noviny*, 9 January 2009, <http://archiv.ihned.cz/c1-32483790-prisun-plynu-ze-zapadu-na-cesky-trh-roste> [accessed 18 June 2015].

82 Government of the Czech Republic, *Czech Presidency Welcomes Resumption of Russian Gas Deliveries through Ukraine*, 20 January 2009 <http://www.vlada.cz/en/media-centrum/aktualne/czech-presidency-welcomes-resumption-of-russian-gas-deliveries-through-ukraine-52486/> [accessed 25 June 2015].

83 EU and Presidents of Azerbaijan, Georgia and Turkey, 'The Declaration - Prague Summit, Southern Corridor', 2009 <https://www.consilium.europa.eu/uedocs/cms_data/docs/pressdata/en/misc/107598.pdf> [accessed 25 June 2015].

German regions of Lower Saxony and Bavaria. Although flows were principally envisaged to transit Czech territory, four interconnection points allowed for domestic offtake. More interconnections would allow the Czech Republic to take advantage of growing competition in its domestic market and act as a growing sorting house for gas supplies regionally, though to do this more physical cross-border links would be needed.

5.4 Reversing the flow: 2010–2014

While the gas crisis was playing out under a Czech EU presidency across the continent, the Topolánek government was collapsing at home owing to a vote of no-confidence launched by the opposition in parliament. A caretaker administration was brought in, with the non-partisan former head of the Czech Statistical Office, Jan Fischer, as Prime Minister. The administration took over on the day the 'Southern Corridor' conference was held in Prague, and lasted until new elections were called in early 2010. The government that followed was another centre-right coalition, with the ODS leading under Prime Minister Petr Nečas, along with the liberal Public Affairs party, or VV, which would eventually be replaced by LIDEM, and the conservative TOP 09. Nečas maintained support for the Caspian corridor and spoke of the importance of reverse-flow gas pipeline developments.[84]

Meanwhile, facing greater competition on the domestic retail market and rising costs for its oil-indexed LTC gas since 2009, privatised gas importer RWE Transgas reported losses of $300 million for the full year 2010.[85] Owing partly to the effects of the financial crisis during the earlier years, gas demand had sunk by over a billion cubic metres between 2006 and 2009. RWE Trangas's take-or- pay commitment of 90% on the 1998 contract now gave it little flexibility to maximise traded gas flows or imports under the Norwegian LTC. By August 2010, Gazprom Export had already filed an arbitration case against RWE Transgas at the International Court of Arbitration of the International Chamber of Commerce in Paris. The plaintive alleged that RWE Transgas had not met the terms of its take-or-pay agreement and sought over $500 million in compensation for unpaid fees. Separately, in December 2010, RWE sought to reduce the price of its imports with a

84 Czech Ministry of Foreign Affairs, 'CASPIAN REGION HAS SIGNIFICANT POTENTIAL WHICH MUST BE USED', 2012 <http://www.mzv.cz/file/946031/> [accessed 3 June 2016].

85 Interfax, 'RWE Loses $300 Mln in Czech Republic on Gas Price Differentials in 2010', 5 May 2011.

case lodged at the Stockholm arbitration court as part of the standard LTC terms that allowed re-negotiation to take place.[86]

The Paris lawsuit centred on Addendum #1 of the 1998 contract between RWE Transgas and Gazprom. RWE argued that it was entitled to reduce the level of its annual take-or-pay obligations in accordance with how much gas Gazprom was selling directly on the market. Through Gazprom's co-ownership of Vemex it was distributing yearly volumes of 500 MMcm in the Czech Republic, and the exporter also held an interest in German gas trader Wingas, which had expanded its initial foothold in the Czech Republic. However, Gazprom argued that this clause was invalid and sought payment for uncollected gas under take-or-pay volumes not met for 2008, 2009, 2010 and 2011.[87] Take-or-pay levels in the contract were reported to be 90%.[88] RWE Transgas sought to get this reduced to 80% and backdated to 1 January 2008.[89]

The Paris court ruled against Gazprom in the take-or-pay case in October 2012, just months before the Nečas government fell over a spying scandal and was replaced by another caretaker administration under former ČSSD minister Jiří Rusnok. The Russian export monopoly said in a statement after the judgement that, although the clause relevant to its direct sales on the Czech market was upheld to the benefit of RWE Transgas, a symmetrical arrangement allowing the Russian importer to raise the take-or-pay level pegged to the amount of gas RWE sells in markets where Gazprom is active was not. Such an arrangement was against EU law, Gazprom argued, and it had approached RWE Transgas about amending those terms previously. Gazprom Export said after the initial ruling against it in August 2012:

> The decision taken by the arbitration that allows the European company – a monopoly player on the Czech market – to retain its monopoly position in the country through the contract validity,

86 Open Joint Stock Company Gazprom, 'Programme for the Issuance of Loan Participation Notes', 2013 <http://www.ise.ie/debt_documents/Supplements_a7586c82-0984-49e7-87ab-c45a07ffc26c.PDF> [accessed 25 June 2015], p. 4.

87 Gazprom argued that this clause was made redundant following the Czech Republic's accession to EU membership in 2004 under article 101 of the Treaty on the Functioning of the European Union.

88 Interfax, *Gazprom Looking into Appealing Arbitration Court Ruling on Lawsuit against RWE (Part 2)*, 25 October 2012.

89 Interfax, 'REVIEW: Europe Rethinking Contracts with Gazprom', 9 March 2010.

> thus restricting competition in the EU market, gains additional poignancy in the context of recent inquiries of the European Commission.[90]

Seeking to overturn the earlier Paris ruling with RWE Transgas, Gazprom launched an appeal process at the Vienna Commercial Court in January 2013, arguing that the initial decision constituted a "public order" offence and contravened EU anti-monopoly rules.[91] The initial ruling was upheld during a hearing in April 2013, with Gazprom notified of the loss on 20 June that year.[92] Further appeals were heard in the high provincial court of Vienna later in 2013 and the supreme court of Austria in 2015, but Gazprom lost in all cases and failed to retrieve the $524 million it sought in unpaid take-or-pay fines.[93] With Czech politics mired in controversy through 2013, no state position on gas emerged.

In the gas pricing case heard in Stockholm, the tribunal awarded RWE a retroactive reimbursement for payments made since May 2010, while also adjusting the purchase price formula of the 1998 contract by introducing a spot- market indexation. According to RWE, this reflected the court's opinion of relevant conditions on the gas market as of May 2010.[94] Gazprom claimed partial victory, arguing that the court had not granted its now re-branded Czech counterpart RWE Supply & Trading the amendments and spot-indexation formula it had demanded:

> RWE Supply & Trading CZ had been putting forward many weakly substantiated demands on the free fall of price and radical pricing formula revision, however most of these claims were rejected

90 'Gazprom Looking into Appealing Arbitration Court Ruling on Lawsuit against RWE (Part 2)', *Interfax: Russia & CIS Business and Financial Newswire*, 25 October 2012. "In the course of our commercial negotiations, we have been repeatedly approaching RWE Transgas to annul this controversial addendum because of its non compliance to the European norms. It was the RWE's denial to do that that served as reason for arbitration," Gazprom Export also said in the statement.

91 Gazprom Export, *«Газпром Экспорт» Обратился В Торговый Суд Вены Для Отмены Решения Арбитража С «РВЕ Трансгаз»*, 18 January 2013 <http://www.gazpromexport.com/presscenter/news/809/> [accessed 6 June 2015].

92 Interfax, 'Gazprom Loses Take-or-Pay Suit vs. RWE', 14 August 2013.

93 Interfax, 'Gazprom Loses All Lawsuits to Collect $524 Mln from RWE for Take-or-Pay', 15 May 2015.

94 RWE, *Analysis of the Arbitral Award Concerning the Price Revision Proceedings Between RWE Supply & Trading CZ and Gazprom Export Completed*, 1 July 2013 <https://www.rwe.com/web/cms/mediablob/en/2402170/data/1360742/2/rwe-supply-trading/press/press-archive/Analysis-of-the-Arbitral-Award-Concerning-the-Price-Revision-Proceedings-Between-RWE-Supply-Trading-CZ-and-Gazprom-Export-Completed.pdf> [accessed 17 June 2015].

by the arbitration. As a result, the pricing formula has been adjusted in a certain way, but this adjustment is far away from the original demands made by RWE Supply & Trading CZ.[95]

Elections in late 2013 saw the ČSSD returned as the largest party, eventually taking office in January 2014 with leader Bohuslav Sobotka as Prime Minister leading a coalition with the KDU–ČSL and ANO 2011, a newly launched centre- right liberal party formed by businessman Andrej Babiš. A final settlement on the gas price dispute between RWE and Gazprom was reached out of court in February 2014, with the next window for price re-negotiation not opening until summer 2016.[96] RWE had also said in 2012 that it had agreed "structural solutions" with each of its Norwegian suppliers "such that the pricing is adapted to wholesale traded market levels, or, in one case, the contractual relationship was even terminated."[97] Statoil had earlier lost an arbitration case on its gas supply contracts to the Czech Republic in 2006.[98]

By 2011, deliveries of both Russian and Norwegian gas into the Czech Republic had sharply reduced, and a steep increase in the volume of gas sourced from neighbouring European trading market areas was recorded as wholesale purchasers optimised their imports on the cheaper hub-priced gas.[99] A planned cooperation venture on power projects in Europe between RWE and Gazprom, which would have established a larger end-market for the Russian gas in Europe, was cancelled in December 2011.[100] Gazprom deliveries to the Czech Republic dropped from 7.9 bcm in 2013 to 4.76 bcm in 2014 following the resolution of the dispute, according to Gazprom statistics. A more dramatic collapse came in the volumes received

95 Gazprom Export, *ООО «Газпром Экспорт» О Решении Арбитража С RWE Supply & Trading CZ По Пересмотру Цены*, 28 June 2013 <http://www.gazpromexport.com/presscenter/news/1000/> [accessed 23 June 2015].

96 Comment to author in personal correspondence: Martin Chalupský, RWE Česká republika Head of Corporate Affairs, 2015.

97 RWE Transgas, *Annual Report For The Period Of Six Months Ended 31 December 2012*, 2013 <https://www.rwe.cz/media/o-rwe/rwe/VZ_2012_RWE_Transgas_EN.pdf> [accessed 22 June]. The GFU was comprised of two permanent members, Statoil and Norsk Hydro, who acted together on gas exports to EU markets from around 1989.

98 Sally Bogle, 'Statoil Loses Arbitration over Long-Term Gas to Czech Market; Norwegian Gas Output Static in March', *Global Insight Daily Analysis*, 11 May 2006.

99 Ministry of Industry and Trade of the Czech Republic, *Preventative Action Plan Required for Removing or Mitigating Identified Risks for Providing Deliveries of Natural Gas in the Czech Republic*, 30 November 2012, p. 14.

100 RWE, *RWE Beendet Gespräche Mit Gazprom*, 22 December 2011 <https://www.rwe.com/web/cms/de/110504/rwe/investor-relations/news/news-ad-hoc-mitteilungen/?pmid=4007315> [accessed 25 June 2015].

from Norway, with the Ministry of Industry and Trade noting in a 2012 preventative plan for future crises that the "vast majority of contracted gas supplies for the Czech Republic from Norway was sold abroad" in 2011.[101] Relief from structural clauses in LTCs following the Gazprom arbitration cases and the apparent result of the 2006 case and the later negotiations with Norwegian suppliers gave RWE Supply & Trading the ability to balance its portfolio and seek out cheaper sources of gas on the open market. The STORK pipeline with Poland was opened in 2011, which can be used as an additional export route, while a link with Austria remains in development.[102]

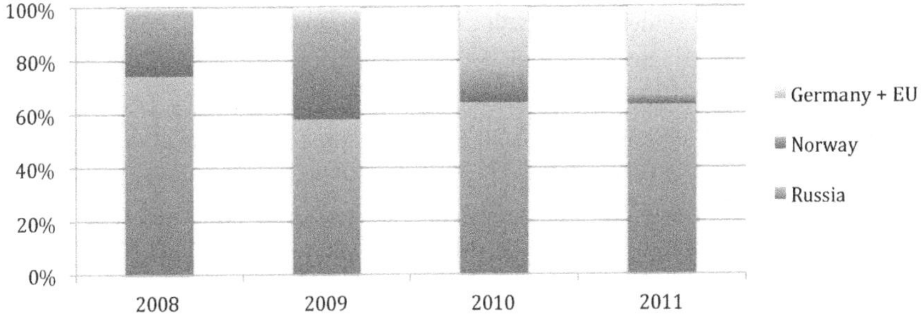

Graph 25: Share of supplier in annual Czech imports (2008–2009)[103]

However, in March 2013, with RWE still suffering from the negative financial impact of Germany's nuclear phase-out and the low margins for conventional fossil fuel–fired power stations, the German utility opted to sell the now re- branded Czech transmission system operator Net4Gas to a consortium of private equity buyers, Allianz and Borealis Infrastructure, for €1.6 billion.[104] The announced sale

---

101 Ministry of Industry and Trade of the Czech Republic, 'PREVENTIVE ACTION PLAN Required for Removing or Mitigating Identified Risks for Providing Deliveries of Natural Gas in the Czech Republic', 2012, p. 15.

102 Gaz-System, 'THE OPENING OF THE POLAND - CZECH REPUBLIC GAS PIPELINE', 2016 <http://en.gaz-system.pl/press-centre/news/information-for-the-media/artykul/201276/> [accessed 25 June 2016]. The so-called Bidirectional Austrian–Czech Interconnector is unlikely before 2020.

103 Ministry of Industry and Trade of the Czech Republic, 'PREVENTIVE ACTION PLAN Required for Removing or Mitigating Identified Risks for Providing Deliveries of Natural Gas in the Czech Republic', 2012, p. 17.

104 RWE, *RWE Verkauft NET4GAS*, 28 March 2013 <https://www.rwe.com/web/cms/en/113648/rwe/press-news/press-release/?pmid=4009093> [accessed 18 June 2015].

stoked fears in Prague that a ‘Trojan Horse’ would be used to purchase the company and increase the influence of main external supplier Gazprom, a narrative that had dated back to previous privatisations.[105]

On 9 December 2013, the Central European Gas Hub that operates the Baumgarten storage centre in Austria launched a gas futures market in Prague, with a futures trading platform started in 2015 alongside Czech-based Power Exchange Central Europe.[106] However, with a pipeline directly connecting the Czech and Austrian networks through the border village of Reintal not yet built, access between the two systems was dependent on Slovakia’s transmission system operator Eustream. A project named Bidirectional Austrian–Czech Interconnector, or BACI, aims to interconnect the Czech and Austrian market areas, but as of 2014 no decision on its construction had yet been taken.[107] The earliest the pipeline would be brought into service would be 2020.

In its April 2015 Statement of Objections against Gazprom under the case launched in 2012, the European Commission argued that the Russian supplier was “hindering competition in the gas supply markets” of eight countries. The Czech Republic was one of those identified, although only in the case of the imposition of territorial restrictions on onward gas trading.[108] RWE Supply & Trading had earlier begun delivering gas back through the Czech network through Slovakia into Ukraine. In September 2014, flows from the Czech Republic into Slovakia over the Lanžhot border point saw an increase of 42% as Net4Gas added new capacity to host greater demand.[109] The opening up of reverse-flow links to Ukraine accounted for some of the increase as a loop system emerged that allowed Nord

---

105 Stratfor/Wikileaks, ‘GERMANY/EUROPE-Czech Energy Expert Fears RWE-Gazprom Deal Could Focus on RWE’s Czech Gas Assets’, 2011 <https://wikileaks.org/gifiles/docs/25/2587105_germany-europe-czech-energy-expert-fears-rwe-gazprom-deal.html> [accessed 15 June 2016].

106 CEGH, ‘CEGH Czech Gas Futures Market Successfully Launched on 9 December 2013’, 2013 <http://www.cegh.at/cegh-czech-gas-futures-market-successfully-launched-9-december-2013> [accessed 25 June 2015].

107 Austria’s Gas Connect Austria and Net4Gas were developing a market demand survey as of early 2015 for a pipeline that would run 61 km, mostly on Austrian territory. The pipeline would link Baumgarten with Břeclav and cross the border into the Czech Republic at the village of Reintal.

108 European Commission, ‘Antitrust: Commission Sends Statement of Objections to Gazprom for Alleged Abuse of Dominance on Central and Eastern European Gas Supply Markets’, 2015 <http://europa.eu/rapid/press-release_IP-15-4828_en.htm> [accessed 12 May 2015].

109 ‘Czech to Slovakia Natural Gas Flows Increase after Lanzhot Capacity Expansion’ <http://www.icis.com/resources/news/2014/09/23/9823215/czech-to-slovakia-natural-gas-flows-increase-after-lanzhot-capacity-expansion/> [accessed 17 June 2015].

Stream imports to the German coast at Greifslwald to be sent through OPAL and Gazelle via the Lanžhot border station into Slovakia, whence deliveries could be made back out of the EU into Ukraine. The Czech network would act as one of the key facilitators for these flows owing to its geographical location, renewing its position as a regional pivot for gas supply.

5.5 Czech Republic policy review

The Czech Republic's approach to the formation of new gas LTC supply arrangements in the 1989 to 2014 period was defined by the concerted attempt to diversify in the early years of transition under successive Klaus administrations. This was based on uncertainty over the stability of Russian deliveries and in response to increased security pressures from Moscow over issues such as NATO membership. It was also because of a lengthy negotiation process that saw final agreement on a commercial LTC with Gazprom that could replace the Soviet-era Yamburg and Orenburg agreements delayed into 1998. Subsequently, despite the fact that Gazprom deliveries under either its 1998 LTC, and through Vemex or Gaz-Invest from the 2000s, amounted to around 80% of annual consumption for much of the period of investigation, the availability of an alternative option from Norway provided a security of supply premium.

Stern described the 1997 agreement between Transgas and Norwegian gas exporting group GFU as the "major breakthrough" in diversification across Central Europe, with Prague the only major importer in the region to resist Gazprom as a sole LTC supplier in the immediate transition period.[110] A regional dynamic was recognised in the 1990s, with the Czech Minister of Industry and Trade that signed the Norway deal, Vladimír Dlouhý, saying at the time that "it is not any secret that for Norwegian gas this is an historical moment, because it means the entry not only to the Czech Republic but into the Central European gas market."[111] Furthermore, a transportation system that held throughput capacity in excess of national consumption maintained the country's position as a transit state for Russian gas to Germany, even after the separation with Slovakia in 1993, boosted security. The development of the Gazela pipeline, which was brought on-stream in 2013, has

---

[110] Stern, *The Future of Russian Gas and Gazprom*, p. 115.

[111] Alexander Wöstmann, 'Norwegian-Czech Gas Deal — Alexander's Gas and Oil Connections', 18 March 1997 <http://www.gasandoil.com/news/europe/1e2abd4c1e8b5cb0fb5b474578ccaede> [accessed 28 June 2016].

helped to cement the Czech Republic as a key conduit for gas supplies from Nord Stream, with that project motivated as much by German internal delivery needs as by Czech security of supply, as already mentioned.

The 2008 Ministry of Industry and Trade statement on security of gas supply explains this point best:

> The security of deliveries also arises from the reality that the Czech Republic is a significant transit country. Annually, 28 bcm of gas is transported through the Czech Republic to other European Union states. This represents a significant security guarantee that the Czech Republic's gas supply will not be threatened, because it would mean threatening several other significant gas consumers in large EU states, at the same time.[112]

Crucially, in negotiating multiple contracts through the 1990s with different suppliers, Czech importing agencies did not get tied into a single LTC with excessive take-or-pay commitments. As shown in Graph 26, oversupply of Russian gas in the mid 1990s had been reduced by the early 2000s, with a persistent gap emerging in which excess demand could be met by cheaper alternatives like Norwegian gas. The Russian contract envisaged supplies of 8 bcm/y until 2006, with 7.2 bcm in theory mandatory under the 90% take-or- pay clause. Additionally, 3 bcm/y was available under the Norway contract, bringing total contracted volumes to around 10.2 bcm – more than consumption, but with added flexibility to mix and match as needed while utilising the 3.5 bcm of national storage capacity.

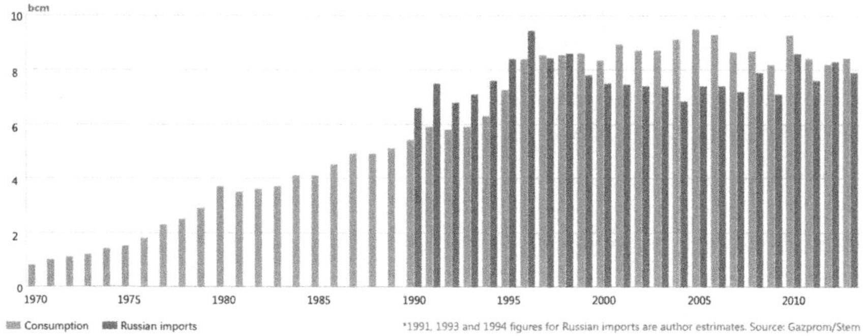

Graph 26: Czech Republic's consumption and imports (1970–2013)[113]

---

[112] Czech Ministry of Industry and Trade, *Securing Delivery of Natural Gas to the Czech Republic*, 3 June 2008 <http://www.mpo.cz/zprava41367.html> [accessed 10 June 2016].

[113] Data from Gazprom and BP, *Statistical Review of World Energy* energy.html>

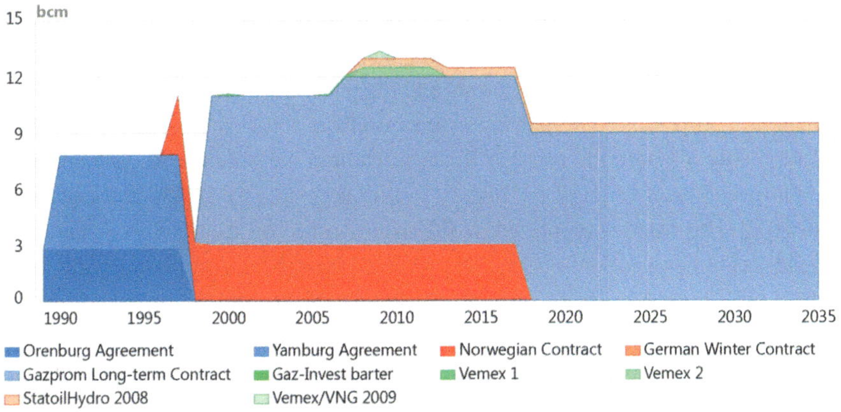

Graph 27: Czech Republic's actual contracted gas (1989–2014)[114]

In a review of potential supply disruption scenarios in 2012, the Czech Ministry of Industry and Trade identified only the collapse of operations at the Waidhaus border transfer station as being of severe risk – and even then mainly to consumers in southern Germany.[115] Both the 2006 and 2009 supply crises had a limited impact on supply to Czech consumers, and by refusing to use a joint marketing company through which to channel exports, the Czech government insulated itself from the opaque trade in natural gas that undermined supply stability in other countries. Vemex could be seen as one potential intermediary, but its share of Russian imports is only a tenth compared to that of RWE Supply & Trading. Gaz-Invest has been able to obtain a very limited position on the Czech market.

National policy on gas has also been determined by its relative lack of importance in the overall energy mix. Successive Czech governments retained a hands-off approach to gas as a fuel, preferring instead to generate power from domestically abundant lignite coal and nuclear. The latest long-term national energy strategy released by the government in May 2015 envisaged an even greater role for nuclear, leaving only a 15% share of the power production mix for gas by

[114] Graph uses all data as reported in Chapter 5 of contracts under an aggregated scenario.

[115] Ministry of Industry and Trade of the Czech Republic, *Preventative Action Plan Required for Removing or Mitigating Identified Risks for Providing Deliveries of Natural Gas in the Czech Republic*, 30 November 2012, p. 32.

2040.[116] The government has also had less of an influence on gas LTC policy, given the private ownership of Transgas since 2002. It can also be argued that under the ownership of Germany's second biggest utility, RWE, it could count on a balanced portfolio of alternatives to draw on from across the border.

Crucially, though, the price of Russian wholesale gas deliveries to the Czech Republic had been amongst the highest in Europe, rising by 53.4% between 2010 and 2012. This trend – supported by the rising cost of oil from 2009 – means the Czech Republic is not only decreasing its use of gas, but also moving away from LTCs, which are now more expensive than traded gas on neighbouring hubs, to which RWE Supply & Trading has access. With the collapse of Russian imports by 10% in 2011, Norwegian contracted volumes were instead sold in other markets.[117] The take-or-pay case against Gazprom, launched concurrently with the price re-negotiation, has ostensibly set a precedent in contract negotiations, facilitating a situation whereby RWE has substantially reduced its import volumes in 2014, despite falling under the take-or-pay requirement.

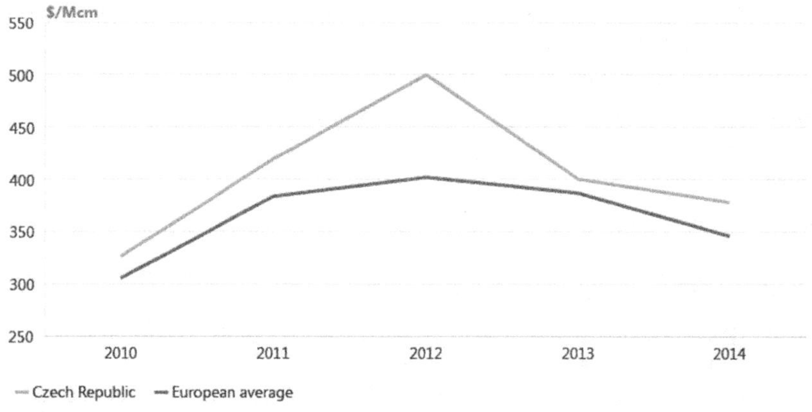

Graph 28: Price of Czech wholesale Russian gas imports (2010–2014)[118]

[116] Ministerstvo průmyslu a obchodu České republiky, *STÁTNÍ ENERGETICKÁ KONCEPCE ČESKÉ REPUBLIKY*, 2014, p. 44.

[117] Ministry of Industry and Trade of the Czech Republic, *Preventative Action Plan Required for Removing or Mitigating Identified Risks for Providing Deliveries of Natural Gas in the Czech Republic*, 30 November 2012, p. 16.

[118] As cited earlier, data from: Novikov, Alexey, *TABLE: How Prices Fell for Russian Gas* (Interfax, 6 March 2015).

Table 7: Gas supply contracts effective in Czech Republic (1989–2014)[119]

	Importer	Exporter	Contract signed	Start of deliveries	End of deliveries	Total volume	Yearly volume	Re-negotiations
Orenburg Agreement	Czechoslovakia	Soviet Union	June 1974	1978 (Scaled up to plateau by 1980)	1998	56 bcm	2.6 bcm or 2.8 bcm	
Yamburg Agreement	Czechoslovakia	Soviet Union	January 1987	1990	2010	57.5 bcm	5 bcm (2.5 bcm estimate following Velvet Divorce)	Protocol in August 1991.
Norwegian Contract	RWE Transgas	Norwegian Gas Negotiating Committee	September 1996	1 May 1997	2017	53 bcm	3 bcm	Arbitration win for RWE Transgas in 2006
German Winter Contract	RWE Transgas	VNG-Verbundnetz Gaz / BEB	November 1997	1 November 1997	28 February 1998	25-30 mcm	12.5 mcm	Extended in 1998 to include stopgap deliveries of 3 mcm/d.
Gazprom Long-term Contract	RWE Transgas	Gazprom	15 October 1998	1 January 1999	2035	325 bcm	8 bcm 1999-2006, 9 bcm 2006 onwards	Extended to 2035 in 2006
Gaz-Invest barter	RWE Transgas	Gaz-Invest	December 1999	December 1999	December 2000	100 mcm	100 mcm	
Vemex 1	Vemex	Gazprom	March 2006	March 2006	October 2007	186 mcm		
Vemex 2	Vemex	Gazprom	10 October 2007	2008	2012 (Five year extenstion possible)	2.5 bcm	500 mcm	Extended in
StatoilHydro 2008	Ceský plynárenský	StatoilHydro	April 2008	1 May 2008	?	475 mcm	475 mcm	January 2009 extra 1 mcm/d made available from 15 January and offered to RWE Transgas.
Vemex/VNG 2009	Vemex	VNG-Verbundnetz Gaz	January 2009	8 January 2009	20 January 2009	39 mcm	3 mcm/d	

Russia	Diversification	Barter/Third-party

[119] Data compiled by author from Gazprom, RWE, Statoil, VNG, data and various news and analyst reports. All information included herein is cited and referenced in the preceding case study chapter.

5.6 Czech Republic policy conclusions

In reference to the hypotheses presented earlier, the evidence collected in the preceding chapter on the Czech Republic's gas sector between 1989 and 2014 gives us some restricted hints as to state behaviour and its role in forming energy security policy. Though the process of separating utility companies in the Czech Republic began in the 1990s, full privatisation did not occur until 2002, giving the state decision-making influence in the early stage of transition with which to manage the formation of gas supply arrangements.[120] Hypothesis 1, or H1, posits that right-wing governments, such as those led by the ODS party between 1992 and 1998, and those in office between 2006 and 2013 post– Transgas privatisation, sought diversification and energy security–boosting measures, while left-wing governments, such as ČSSD-led administrations between 1998 and 2006, and then again from 2014, tend to prioritise cooperation with already dominant suppliers of natural gas like Gazprom. H2 suggests that left-wing governments are motivated to maintain downward pressure on retail prices for consumers that in turn prioritise lower wholesale costs as a strategic goal in LTC talks. H3 argues that in the LTC re-negotiation process state-owned utilities under left-wing governments opt for short-term price discounts over the long-term structural change that right-wing governments and private utilities seek. Significantly, in the case of the Czech Republic, privatised utilities are argued to be most effective at pursuing structural change in LTCs and easing dependence.

Figure 13 illustrates the governments in place during key gas market events in the Czech Republic. Under the ODS-led coalition governments of Klaus, new import contracts were signed, firstly on a small-scale basis with Germany's Ruhrgas, and later with BEB/VNG, and also on a large-scale with Norway's GFU for the 15-year deal. The absence of a full new Russian supply contract in this time is interpreted as evidence that the right-wing administration chose to prioritise gas supply diversification. Conversely, under the following four successive ČSSD governments with Zeman, Špidla, Gross and Paroubek as Prime Minister, only new Russia-related gas supply contracts were agreed, either between Transgas and Gazprom for the 1998 LTC, or with intermediary Gaz- Invest for the smaller 1999

[120] This is illustrated in the agreement with Norway being signed by the Minister for Trade and Industry during a bilateral summit, rather than purely between the importing and exporting companies.

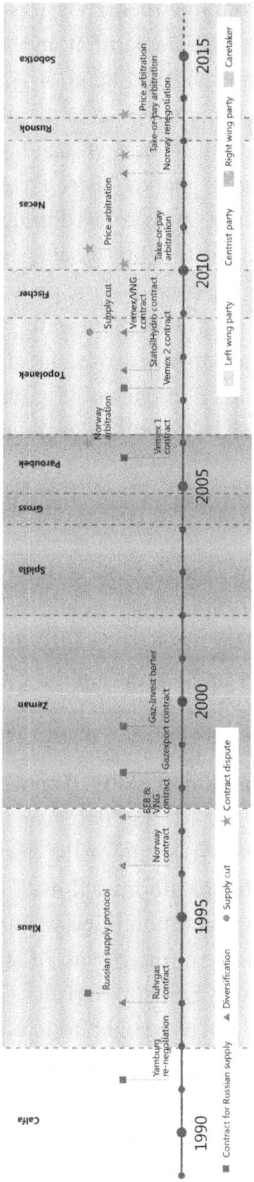

Figure 13: Czech political timeline with gas LTC milestones (1989–2014)

barter contract. The Vemex deal, which saw the Gazprom intermediary act as importer, was agreed just before the end of the Paroubek ČSSD-coalition, but with neither import/export agency responsible to the Czech state, the extent to which domestic political structure played a role in its formation cannot be determined.

The further development of Vemex contracts in the following year can be interpreted as an attempt by Gazprom to seek to ensure its market share through commercial activities, having seen its avenue for political engagement through a state-owned utility restricted. Though the Czech political timeline is congested with varying administrations and Prime Ministers over the course of the period of inquiry, its structural stability in terms of party cleavages (ODS representing the leading right-wing party and ČSSD the left-wing) and length of time in office (though regular elections took place, both parties remained in control of government for minimum stretches of six-years) make the Czech Republic a useful case study, especially until privatisation took place in 2002. No contracts were signed in either of the caretaker administrations of Fischer or Rusnok, making them irrelevant for the purposes of this analysis.

Nonetheless, although state control of the key utilities that could execute LTC arrangements was missing after 2002, the ODS-led right-wing coalitions of Topolánek and Nečas also illustrate a policy commitment to supply source diversification in reaction to the Gazprom transportation cut in 2009 during the Czech presidency of the EU. Topolánek in effect helped launch institutional- backing for the Southern Corridor initiative before the Prague Summit in May 2009, while Nečas publicly backed the initiative while in office. In January 2009, Topolánek also offered Slovakia's Prime Minister Robert Fico 20 MMcm/d of capacity through the Lanžhot border point in order to ease the crisis south of the border, while political impetus was given to the development of cross-border flows.

Assessing the applicability of H2, it is clear that the provision of new sources of gas allowed Transgas to secure lower prices generally in the period of state-ownership. As noted by Nosko and Lang, and according to Eurostat statistics from 1997 when the Norway contract came into effect until 2006, "neighboring countries imported natural gas at prices cheaper than in the Czech Republic only three times on an annual basis."[121] Though further analysis will be made of retail prices

[121] The three exceptions were 2001 and 2003 in Slovakia, and 2003 in Hungary. See: Andrej Nosko, and Petr Lang, 'Lessons from Prague: How the Czech Republic Has Enhanced Its Energy Security | European Dialogue', 2010 <http://www.eurodialogue.eu/Lessons-from-Prague-How-the-Czech-

comparatively in the Conclusion, no costly infrastructure projects weighed on the importer's budget and transit fees have also helped to mitigate import costs. Nevertheless, in the period for which price data is available (2010 to 2014), as shown in Table 2, Czech import costs for wholesale gas were consistently above the European average, as illustrated in Graph 28.

This brings us to H3, and the tendency for state-owned companies to behave in different ways during re-negotiations with the dominant supplier. In 2010, Czech costs were the lowest among the case study countries, at $333 per mcm, jumping to $419 per mcm in 2011 as arbitration cases began and oil-indexation costs boomed. Between 2010 and 2014, the numerous arbitration cases and appeals in courts located in Paris, Stockholm and Vienna effectively restructured the terms of the 1998 LTC, which was further extended in 2006, taking prices to a Europe-wide high in 2012 of $500 per mcm as RWE Supply & Trading refused to take a temporary price discount, like many of its neighbours had. Instead, the company opted to sue for structural change at the Stockholm courts. Arbitration proceedings during the following years were carried out under private ownership of the importing utility and its behaviour cannot be attributed to government agenda. However, the result provides a useful exception to the behaviour of other state-owned utilities in the region during re-negotiations. Instead of deriving policy from electoral agendas, in the case of RWE Supply & Trading, we must instead suppose commercial motivations for the decision to push the case to a legal resolution in 2013 and 2014, seeing Czech import costs first peak before settling to a regional low of $400 per mcm in 2013, then dropping further in 2014 (though not as low as other importers').

Naturally, private companies have unrelated commercial interests to protect, distinct from politics, often longer in outlook than electoral cycles, and transnational with respect to trade interests and portfolio optimisation. In June 2013, parent company RWE reported its own judgment from the Stockholm arbitration court, securing a reimbursement for fees paid since 2010 in addition to a deal that "adjusted the purchase price formula of the contract by introducing a gas market indexation, which according to the arbitral tribunal reflects the relevant conditions on the gas market at the time of the price revision in May 2010."[122]

Republic-Has-Enhanced-Its-Energy-Security-> [accessed 29 June 2016].

[122] RWE, *Arbitration Court Rules in Favour of RWE on Price Revision of Its Long-Term Gas Supply Contract with Gazprom*, 27 June 2013 <https://www.rwe.com/web/cms/mediablob/en/2402176/

In sum, H1 is illustrated through a clear policy of diversification in the early ODS governments, followed by a period of establishing new LTCs with the dominant supplier under the following four ČSSD governments. There is little evidence to ascertain whether either party prioritised lower retails prices based on the collected data under H2, but for H3 it can be noted that a private company secured major structural changes to its contract formula, illustrated not only by the statements of the companies following the ruling in both the Paris-based take-or-pay debt case and the Stockholm price re-negotiation case, but also through the sharp reduction in Russian deliveries post–court ruling, which would have been outlawed under the take-or-pay clause in the LTC set to run until 2035. These changes loosened dependence on Russian gas and added flexibility.

data/1360742/2/rwe-supply-trading/press/press-archive/Arbitration-court-rules-in-favour-of-RWE-on-price-revision-of-its-long-term-gas-supply-contract-with-Gazprom.pdf> [accessed 15 June 2016].

6 Slovakia

The Slovak Republic has received Russian gas since 1967 and has continued to do so since becoming independent as part of the 'Velvet Divorce' settlement that separated Czechoslovakia in 1993, as discussed in the preceding chapter. The Brotherhood pipeline enters EU territory at Slovakia's frontier with Ukraine before splitting into two directions, one via the Czech Republic and into Germany, and the other into Austria towards the markets of Italy and France. A transport capacity of over 100 bcm/y gives the Slovak market strategic value to Gazprom and is a valuable source of transit fees for the government-owned transmission system operator in Bratislava.[1] Annual consumption first moved over 5 bcm/y in 1989 and did not dip back under this total until the financial crisis damped demand 20 years later. A consumption peak of 6.9 bcm in 2001 has since given way to a total of 5.4 bcm in 2013, roughly in line with previous years, before a steep fall to 3.7 bcm in 2014.[2]

Gas production is minimal, catering to only 2% of demand in 2010 and expected to diminish further rapidly.[3] The Slovak Ministry for Economics reported production at 92 MMcm in 2011 and expects output to remain beneath 100 MMcm/y in the future. Additionally, the ministry has reported that the extraction of shale gas reserves is "problematic," suggesting little hope for any future output growth.[4] Without any alternatives, Slovakia is in effect 100% dependent on imports for its gas supply, with the fuel constituting 26.6% of total primary energy

---

1 Jonathan P. Stern, *The Future of Russian Gas and Gazprom* (Oxford: Oxford University Press, 2005), p. 243.

2 BP, *Statistical Review of World Energy 2014* <http://www.bp.com/en/global/corporate/about-bp/energy-economics/statistical-review-of-world-energy.html> [accessed 29 April 2015].

3 IEA, *Energy Policies of IEA Countries: Slovak Republic 2012* (Paris: Organisation for Economic Co-operation and Development, 2012) <http://www.oecd-ilibrary.org/content/book/9789264173507-en> [accessed 17 January 2015], p. 75.

4 Ministry of Economy of the Slovak Republic, 'Energy Policy of the Slovak Republic', 2014 <http://www.economy.gov.sk/energy-policy-of-the-slovak-republic_october-2014-qci/145533s> [accessed 2 June 2015], p. 56.

J. Posaner, *Held Captive by Gas*, Energiepolitik und Klimaschutz. Energy Policy and Climate Protection, https://doi.org/10.1007/978-3-658-27518-1_6

supply in 2009. That year, residential demand covered 27%, industry 23%, transport 9%, and power and heat generation a further 20% of the total share.

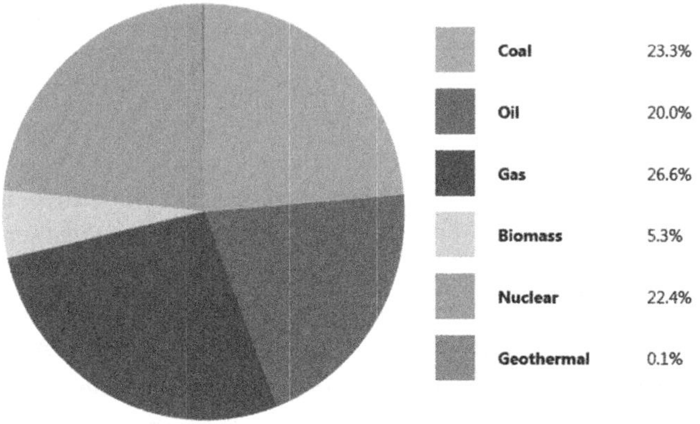

Figure 14: Slovakia's total primary energy supply in 2009[5]

Following the separation of the Czech Republic and Slovakia, gas transmission and importing activities in Slovakia were bundled into Slovensky plynarensky priemysel (SPP). After being part privatised in a 2002 deal that saw France's GDF Suez and Germany's E.On Ruhrgas take a managing stake in the company, SPP span off its transmission system management responsibilities into SPP-preprava in July 2006 under EU unbundling rules. The transportation company was re-branded as Eustream in 2008, responsible for the management of the national distribution network and compressor stations, including the Veľké Kapušany site on the border with Ukraine, the largest such facility in the EU.[6] SPP remains the major national gas utility, responsible for importing gas under LTC contracts. It has essentially been re-nationalised since 2014, with the Ministry of Economy of the Slovak Republic holding 100% of shares.[7] According to CV1 as shown in Figure 1,

5 IEA, *Energy Policies of IEA Countries: Slovak Republic 2012* (Paris: Organisation for Economic Co-operation and Development, 2012) <http://www.oecd-ilibrary.org/content/book/9789264173507-en> [accessed 17 January 2015], p. 75.

6 Eustream, 'MORE THEN 40 YEARS OF SAFE AND RELIABLE GAS TRANSMISSION SERVICES' <http://www.eustream.sk/en_company-eustream/en_history> [accessed 28 June 2016].

7 EPH, *THE REORGANISATION OF THE SPP GROUP WAS COMPLETED TODAY*, 4 June 2014 <http://www.epholding.cz/en/press/the-reorganisation-of-the-spp-group-was-completed-today/> [accessed 2 July 2015].

private ownership and management of the main importer from 2002 to summer 2014 effectively restricted government control over SPP's decision- making processes, which in turn limited the manifestation of domestic structures on overall gas import policy. The period before 2002 saw gas import policy still under the control of state structures.

By the end of 2014 the Slovak pipeline network had three major interconnection points with gas coming through mainline pipelines from Ukraine (Velké Kapušany) and exiting the Slovak system into the Czech Republic (Lanžhot) and Austria (Baumgarten), with reverse-flow possible on both the Lanžhot and Baumgarten interconnections, and the Vojany pipeline able to loop gas back into the Ukrainian system from Velké Kapušany as of September 2014. A number of smaller pipelines could send small quantities of gas back into the Slovak grid from Austria by the end of 2014, but the corridor from Ukraine is by far the highest capacity connection. Total Slovak import capacity was 313.11 MMcm/d through the various entry points in 2014, though Russian supply routes through Velké Kapušany accounted for 212.57 MMcm. The majority of the remaining capacity, including reverse-flow capability through Lanžhot, has only been developed in the post-2009 period. Choice over how and from whom to contract gas as outlined under CV2 in Figure 1 had previously been restricted, owing to the absence of alternative capacity beyond the Brotherhood pipeline system that runs through Velké Kapušany.

Storage capacity in Slovakia was 2.9 bcm as of 2014, although this is expected to rise to approximately 3.1 bcm in 2015 once the Gajary-Báden facility is completed. All facilities are located in the Láb complex near Bratislava, although the Dolní Bojanovice facility in the Czech Republic is also connected to the Slovak system and used for balancing the grid during peaks and troughs in demand. The Czech Republic correspondingly uses part of the capacity at the Láb complex, as outlined in the previous chapter.[8] Further infrastructure projects have been planned, including interconnectors with Hungary and Poland, though the former was only brought on-stream in 2015 after long delays, and the latter remains in planning in 2016. Eustream is also promoting Eastring, a project aimed at increasing circulation of gas and easing dependence on Russia.[9]

---

8 IEA, *Energy Policies of IEA Countries: Slovak Republic 2012* (Paris: Organisation for Economic Co-operation and Development, 2012) <http://www.oecd-ilibrary.org/content/book/9789264173507-en> [accessed 17 January 2015], p. 78.

9 Further information on the project can be found here: <http://www.eastring.eu/>.

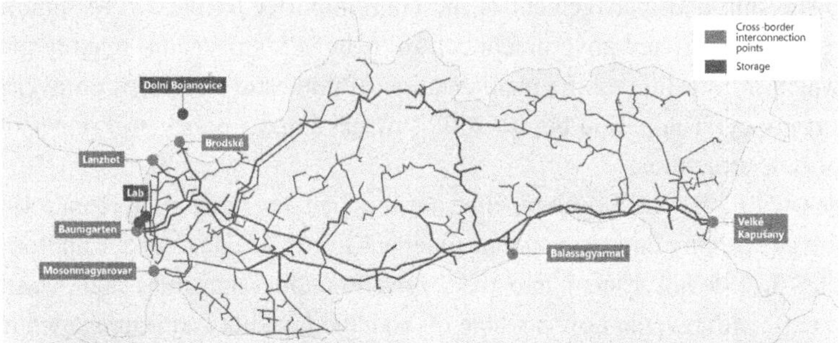

Storage capacity, existing		
	Operator	Target capacity
Láb I, II, III and Gajary-Baden	Nafta	2.5 bcm
Láb IV	Pozagas	655 MMcm
Dolní Bojanovice	SPP Storage (in Czech Republic)	576 MMcm
Total		3.73 bcm

Source: Company data

Mainline pipeline entry and exit points			
	Operators	Capacity	Flow
Lanzhot (to Czech Republic)	Net4Gas	64.66 MMcm/d	Bidirectional
	Eustream		
Lanzhot (from Czech Republic)	Eustream	49.24 MMcm/d	
	Net4Gas		
Baumgarten (from Austria)	BOG	23.04 MMcm/d	Bidirectional
	Eustream		
	Gas Connect Austria		Firm one way
	Eustream		Bidirectional
	TAG		Firm one way
	Eustream		Bidirectional
Baumgarten (to Austria)	Eustream	150.76 MMcm/d	Bidirectional
	BOG		
	Eustream		Bidirectional
	Gas Connect Austria		Firm one way with virtual in the other
	Eustream		Bidirectional
	TAG		Firm one way
Mosonmagyarovar (from Austria)	Gas Connect Austria	12.00 MMcm/d	Firm one way with virtual in the other
	FGSZ		
Brodské (from Czech Republic)	SPP Storage		Bidirectional
	Eustream		
Brodské (to Czech Republic)	Eustream		Bidirectional
	SPP Storage		
Lab (from Austria)	Gas Connect Austria	16.26 MMcm/d	Bidirectional
	Pozagas		
Lab (to Austria)	Gas Connect Austria	16.26 MMcm/d	Bidirectional
	Pozagas		
Velké Kapušany (from Ukraine)	Ukrtransgaz	212.57 MMcm/d	Firm one way
	Eustream		Bidirectional

*All data for April 2014. Source: ENTSO-G

Slovakia's annual consumption

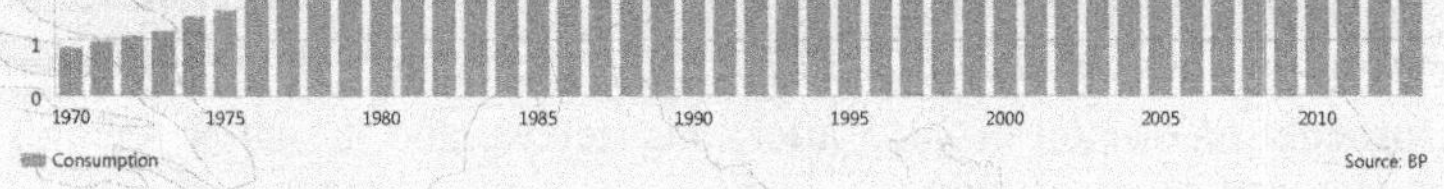

Figure 15: Slovakia market snapshot[10]

[10] Data taken from ENTSO-G, Pozagas, Nafta, Eustream, BP Statistical Review of World Energy and IEA, *Energy Policies of IEA Countries: Slovak Republic 2012* (Paris: Organisation for Economic Co-operation and Development, 2012) <http://www.oecd-ilibrary.org/content/book/9789264173507-en> [accessed 17 January 2015].

6.1 Post–Velvet Divorce: 1993–1998

Until 1 January 1993, Slovakia's gas sector had been inextricably interlinked with that of the Czech Republic, with a single integrated national transport network linking the Veľké Kapušany border station on the frontier with Ukraine to the exit points at the German and Austrian borders. The country imported gas under the Yamburg and Orenburg Soviet-era agreements agreed by the Czechoslovak regime and, with post-independence annual demand at just 5.2 bcm in 1993,[11] the first year of independence, this was already met by the existing supply arrangements. This meant that the conservative government of Prime Minister Vladimír Mečiar, who had already been the Prime Minister of Slovakia within the federal Czechoslovak structure from 1990, could put off signing a new LTC with Gazprom. Mečiar's People's Party–Movement for a Democratic Slovakia (ĽS- HZDS) was in office until losing its parliamentary majority in March 1994 and being replaced by an opposition coalition of the liberal Democratic Union of Slovakia (DEÚS), the conservative Christian Democratic Movement (KDH) and the left-wing Party of the Democratic Left (SDL) until elections were called and ĽS-HZDS was returned to office in coalition with the right-wing Slovak National Party (SNS) and the left-wing Union of the Workers of Slovakia (ZRS) in December.

The construction of the Lanžhot border point technically separated the Czech and Slovak gas systems from 1994 and companies wishing to supply through the former Czechoslovak corridor would now need to agree transit rights with two national system operators: Transgas, north of the border, and SPP in Slovakia. Under the eventual accord of separation, the Czech Republic took gas being delivered under contract through the CIS at a 2:1 ratio, while also agreeing to pay Slovakia a transit fee of $1.30 per mcm over 100 km, staving off losses for the Slovak operator[12] The Lanžhot border metering transfer station was inaugurated in January 1994, lying along the mainline rail connection between Bratislava and Prague.[13]

In February 1995, during Mečiar's second term as Prime Minister, Gazprom offered a 'gas for food' barter deal that would have seen a joint venture company

---

[11] BP, *Statistical Review of World Energy 2015* <http://www.bp.com/en/global/corporate/about-bp/energy-economics/statistical-review-of-world-energy.html> [12 June 2015].

[12] Robert A. Young, and Queen's University (Kingston ON) Institute of Intergovernmental Relations, *The Breakup of Czechoslovakia* (IIGR, Queen's University, 1994) p. 61. The transit fee was thought to be significantly under market rates.

[13] Net4Gas, 'History: Separation of Czechoslovakia' <http://www.net4gas.cz/en/history/> [accessed 10 June 2016]

set up to manage exports through the country.[14] Little progress was announced immediately following this offer, but during the visit of Russia's Prime Minister Viktor Chernomyrdin to Bratislava in April 1997, a new 10-year contract was unexpectedly announced as one of eight separate agreements. The new LTC deal would see 50/50 joint venture Slovrusgas launched to manage imports and the transit of Russian gas through Slovak territory.[15] The total volume of imports Gazprom subsidiary Gazexport would supply directly to SPP was to be 6.5 bcm/y[16] and the Russian exporter agreed to spend 40% of what it earned from gas sales on Slovak goods to be sold in Russia.[17] An initial 400 MMcm was scheduled to be delivered in surplus gas via Slovrusgas during 1998, with reports suggesting the price of the intermediary's imports through Veľké Kapušany was $75 MMcm.[18]

In addition to importing surplus supplies of gas to the Slovak market during winter peaks in demand, Slovrusgas would also handle gas transit for any new pipeline project, transferring potentially lucrative future revenue from SPP into Russian hands.[19] Meanwhile, as it had already done that month with Czech operator CPP, German importer VNG signed a deal with SPP and Kerametal in Bratislava in August 1997, ensuring the transit of 7 bcm/y of Russian via Slovak territory, with capacity made available for further supplies if needed.[20] However, soon after the contract was agreed, conflict over the goods that Russia would purchase as part of the agreement began to surface. Russia wanted foodstuff that it could sell on the domestic market, while Slovak officials preferred to supply higher value industrial goods and medicines.[21] For example, in 1997 the Slovak Docks and

---

[14] Anita Orbán, *Power, Energy, and the New Russian Imperialism*, PSI Reports (Westport, Conn: Praeger Security International, 2008), p. 45.

[15] Janusz Bugajski, *Cold Peace: Russia's New Imperialism* (Westport, Greenwood Publishing Group, 2004), p. 164. LOCATION?

[16] Ministry of the Economy of the Slovak Republic, 'NEGOTIATING POSITION OF THE SLOVAK REPUBLIC', 2004 <www.mhsr.sk/index/open_file.php?ext_dok=123264&idc=121492> [accessed 29 June 2016].

[17] Orbán, *Power, Energy, and the New Russian Imperialism*, p. 51.

[18] 'Slovrusgas Podpísal Kontrakt Na Dovoz Ruského Plynu', *Www.etrend.sk* <http://www.etrend.sk/trend-archiv/rok-/cislo-August/slovrusgas-podpisal-kontrakt-na-dovoz-ruskeho-plynu.html> [accessed 26 June 2015].

[19] 'V Apríli Dovezie Slovrusgas Na Slovensko Prvých 50 Mil. Kubických Metrov Plynu', 24 September 1998, *Www.etrend.sk* <http://www.etrend.sk/trend-archiv/rok-/cislo-Apríl/v-aprili-dovezie-slovrusgas-na-slovensko-prvych-50-mil-kubickych-metrov-plynu.html> [accessed 26 June 2015].

[20] 'VNG/WIEH Seal Further 1 Bcm/yr', *International Gas Report*, 16 September 1994, p. 10.

[21] Orbán, *Power, Energy, and the New Russian Imperialism*, p. 57.

Shipping Company based at Slovakia's principle Danube port-town of Komárno said it could supply up to five ships in part-payment for Slovak gas imports.[22]

The Slovrusgas deal was finalised with the registration of the company in Bratislava during March 1998, just months before Mečiar left office and was replaced by Mikuláš Dzurinda from the electoral multi-party coalition the Slovak Democratic Coalition (SDK), later replaced by the conservative-liberal Slovak Democratic and Christian Union–Democratic Party (SDKÚ-DS). As Prime Minister in his first four-year term, Dzurinda governed from a coalition that also included a Hungarian minority rights party and a centre-left party with reforms key on its agenda.

Nonetheless, even following the signature of the Czech Republic's 20-year gas contract with Norwegian producers in 1997, and Poland's push for the development of a physical import link from Scandinavia, Slovak officials insisted existing Russian supplies would suffice, and that diversification was not a necessary venture for SPP. "The existing agreements with Russian gas companies are beneficial for Slovakia, at least as beneficial as the ones the Czech Republic has... We do not see it as realistic that diversification of gas sources will take place within our term," Ľudovít Černák, Slovakia's Minister of Economics and a former SNS leader, said in December 1998.[23]

6.2 State sell-off: 1999–2005

As reforms under the first liberal conservative Dzurinda government gathered pace in 1999, Economy Minister Černák said that the gas sector would need to be kept under state control, apparently ruling out the prospect of an imminent privatisation of SPP.[24] The comments came shortly after a controversy in Slovak politics over the murder of Ján Ducký, a former economy minister under the Mečiar government and head of SPP from April 1997 to November 1998. Černák had announced a case against Ducký for alleged mishandling company finances at SPP. The media also alleged that Ducký was close to Russian interests, having been the co-signatory on the Slovrusgas gas deal in 1997.[25]

---

22 'National Shipyard May Repay Natural Gas Supplies To Slovakia.', *TASR - Tlacova Agentura Slovenskej Republiky*, 8 December 1997.

23 'Slovakia Will Continue Importing Russian Gas', *Reuters News*, 21 December 1998.

24 Orbán, *Power, Energy, and the New Russian Imperialism*, p. 89.

25 Jolyon Naegele, 'Slovakia: Politics Unsettled By Ducky Murder', *RadioFreeEurope/RadioLiberty*, 9 January 1999, <http://www.rferl.org/content/article/1090328.html> [accessed 29 June 2016].

The gas business was proving lucrative for state interests in the 1990s, with transit revenues for Russian gas flowing through the five mainlines of the Brotherhood system into Slovakia, with a combined annual throughput capacity of 90 bcm/y accounting for $600 million annually, a key component of state revenue.[26] In 2000, Slovrusgas supplied an additional 370 MMcm to the Slovak market in excess of SPP contracted volumes, yet its future as an intermediary remained unclear.[27] By January 2005 the company had been placed into liquidation, but in its review of the Slovak national energy sector that year, the IEA noted that Slovakia had received 1.9 bcm of Central Asian gas from Turkmenistan via Russia in 2004, "presumably delivered to Slovrusgaz by Eural Trans Gas."[28]

However, in 2000, the Dzurinda government decided to begin the part- privatisation process of SPP, looking for bids for a 49% managing stake that would leave the monopoly in overall state control, but with a clause in place ensuring any decision the company took must have at least 52% backing from the shareholders.[29] Gazprom officially signalled its intention to join the bidding process in November 2001 following a meeting in Moscow between Russian President Vladimir Putin and Slovakia's then-President Rudolf Schuster.[30] Although the Slovak government appeared to welcome Gazprom's interest, the public outcry over the sale of a 49% stake with managing rights in oil pipeline operator Transpetrol to Russia's Yukos that year appeared to rule out a deal that would have seen Slovakia's big two energy transport companies controlled by Russian interests.[31]

The final registered bid for SPP in February 2002 came from only one consortium – that of Germany's Ruhrgas and France's Gaz de France, with Gazprom holding a standby option.[32] The Russian major would retain the choice of taking on a 16.3% stake within two years but, by February 2004, Gazprom had still not taken on its reserved stake, and the parties agreed to postpone the deadline back

26 Orbán, *Power, Energy, and the New Russian Imperialism*, p. 89.

27 'Slovrusgas Supplies Slovakia with 370 mcm of Gas in 2000', *Platts Commodity News*, 22 August 2001.

28 IEA, *Slovak Republic Energy Policy Review 2005*, 2006 <https://www.iea.org/publications/freepublications/publication/slovak.pdf> [accessed 26 June 2015], p. 138.

29 Orbán, *Power, Energy, and the New Russian Imperialism*, p. 92.

30 Interfax, *Gazprom to Participate in Privatization of Slovakian Gas Company*, 13 November 2001.

31 Orbán, *Power, Energy, and the New Russian Imperialism*, p. 92. The Slovak government agreed to buy back the stake in Transpetrol in March 2009 following the take-over of Yukos, allowing it to control the Druzhba oil pipeline that transferred Russian oil exports through the country.

32 'SPP - SDĽ vyjadrila sklamanie z výsledku tendra na kúpu SPP', *SITA Slovenska Tlacova Agentura*, 1 March 2002.

until December 2005.[33] In June 2005, with the North-European Gas Pipeline project gathering momentum into what would eventually become the first two strings of the Nord Stream pipeline, Gazprom announced it would not be acquiring the SPP stake after all.[34] Under Dzurinda's second administration from 2002 – a coalition of his SDKÚ, the conservative KDH, liberal Alliance of the New Citizens (ANO) and minority interests group Party of the Hungarian Community (SMK) – Slovakia's move towards NATO and EU membership in March and May 2004 is notable in that there appeared to be little resistance from Russia. Gazprom had expressed an interest in buying the 49% stake in SPP as part of a strategy to ensure markets for Russian gas, and at that stage Bratislava would have accepted investment.

6.3 Crisis mode: 2006–2009

The 2006 gas supply crisis had only a moderate impact on Slovak supplies, with a 30% drop in deliveries on 2 January mitigated by storage inventories as Russia and Ukraine's contract stalemate turned into a stand-off.[35] The agreement between Moscow and Kiev on 4 January saw flows return to normal and allayed fears over the impact a bilateral conflict between Europe's biggest gas supplier and its key transit partner would have. In elections that year, Robert Fico's left- wing Direction–Social Democracy (SMER-SD) party took office as a breakaway faction from the SDL, in coalition with the former ruling parties from the other side of the electoral divide, ĽS-HZDS and SNS. Crucially, SMER-SD maintained control over the Ministry of Economy during this period, which had overall control of the state's 51% stake in SPP.

Meanwhile, after two years of negotiations on an LTC to replace the expiring 1998 deal SPP and Gazprom announced in late 2008 – just weeks before the existing deal was to come to an end – that a further 20-year contract had been agreed. The deal would see 130 bcm delivered to SPP over the 20-year period leading up to 2028, with a parallel transit contract for 1 trillion cubic metres of gas through the Slovak network agreed with recently re-branded and unbundled transmission

33 Orbán, *Power, Energy, and the New Russian Imperialism*, p. 147.
34 Interfax, *Gazprom Drops SPP Option*, 10 June 2005.
35 'UPDATE 1-Slovaks Say Russian Gas Supplies down 30 Pct', *Reuters News*, 2 January 2006.

system operator Eustream, still a subsidiary of SPP.[36] SPP's chairman at the time, Bernd Wagner, said the deal "ensures stability for us and secures reliable and at the same time competitive gas deliveries to Slovakia also after 2008" during the signing announcement in November.[37]

The two-week disruption in Russian supplies to Slovakia through Ukraine in January 2009 caused a major deficit in national energy supply. Between 7 and 20 January gas supplies were completely cut off, leaving Slovakia without its contracted supplies from the east.[38] A state of emergency was announced by SPP at 2 pm on 6 January after imports dropped by 70% overnight.[39] The measures meant that all companies with an annual consumption of more than 60 MMcm/y were forced either to stop consuming or to reduce economic activity during the crisis.[40] Over following days, Czech utility RWE Transgas agreed to dispatch 4 MMcm/d from its capacity at the Láb gas storage facility near Bratislava, usually reserved for use north of the border in the Czech Republic.[41] VNG also released 100 MMcm of its gas reserved in Slovak gas storage facilities.[42] Talks between the EU, Russia and Ukraine continued, meanwhile, with a proposal from Fico rejected by Kiev that would have provided a 'swap' solution to Slovakia's import deficit. This would have seen Russia supply 20 MMcm/d to eastern Ukraine and Naftogaz would have subsequently sent the same volume from its storage reserves in the west of the country to Slovakia, thus bypassing use of the mainline transit pipelines.[43]

---

36 SPP, *Predstavitelia Spoločností Skupiny SPP a Gazprom Export Sa Stretli v Bratislave*, 3 December 2008 <http://www.spp.sk/sk/vsetky-segmenty/o-spp/media/46-predstavitelia-spolocnosti-skupiny-spp-a-gazprom-export-sa-stretli-v-bratislave/> [accessed 29 June 2015].

37 Interfax, *Gazprom Extends Gas Supply Contract with Slovakia until 2028 (Part 2)*, 21 November 2008.

38 European Commission, *THE JANUARY 2009 GAS SUPPLY DISRUPTION TO THE EU: AN ASSESSMENT*, 2009 <http://ec.europa.eu/danmark/documents/alle_emner/energi/2009_ser2_autre_document_travail_service_part1_ver2.pdf> [accessed 29 June 2015], p. 4.

39 The state of emergency was not lifted until 23 January, meaning restrictions on consumption within Slovakia and delivery outside the country were in place for 17 days. Eustream, *Gas Crisis in January 2009 – Review and Outlook - Presskit*, 27 January 2009, p. 9.

40 Alexander Duleba, 'Slovakia's Relationship with Russia and Eastern Neighbours', in *EU-Russian Relations and the Eastern Partnership: Central-East European Member-State Interests and Positions*, ed. Gábor Fóti and Ludwig Zsuzsa, *East European Studies*, No. 1 (Hungarian Academy of Sciences. Institute for World Economics), p. 31.

41 Interfax, *Slovakia May Offset Russian Gas Halt by 'Swap' with Ukraine or Switch to Yamal Pipeline – SPP*, 15 January 2009.

42 Marlen Ristola, 'VNG liefert Erdgas in die Slowakei', *Energie & Management/Powernews.org*, 20 January 2009, section GASMARKT.

43 Duleba, 'Slovakia's Relationship with Russia and Eastern Neighbours', p. 39.

Without imports from the east, for the first time Slovakia looked to import gas from the west. On 16 January, Fico announced that Czech tranporter RWE Transgas was ready to allow the flow to be reversed through the Lanžhot border transfer station at a rate of 20 MMcm/d.[44] Small supply contracts with E.On Ruhrgas, GDF Suez and RWE Transgas utilising on-going flows through the Yamal pipeline looped back through Germany and into the Czech network were to provide 6.3 MMcm/d through this route, helping Slovakia to meet what would have usually been 15.5 MMcm/d of daily demand. However, with temperatures low in the peak of the winter season, consumption on 16 January reached 24 MMcm, despite savings of 3.5 MMcm made through the emergency regulatory measures.[45]

On 18 January, Slovakia received its first supplies of German gas, just hours before flows from the east returned and the new contracts from the west were due to come into force.[46] Even after normal service had resumed, diversification efforts were quickly expanded and, in February 2009, SPP said it had agreed emergency supply arrangements with two German suppliers, VNG and E.On Ruhrgas.[47] Slovakia is estimated to have lost €100 million per day throughout the January disruption, with overall losses equal to between 1-1.5% of annual gross domestic product.[48] Approximately 1,000 local enterprises were closed, according to the government.[49] In response, by June 2009, the utility had announced that it was in

44 'ENERGETIKA: Firma RWE Transgas je pripravená dodať SR plyn z Jamalu', *SITA Slovenska Tlacova Agentura*, 16 January 2009.

45 Of this total, E.On Ruhrgas supplied 6.5 mcm, GDF Suez 5.25 MMcm and RWE Transgas 3.75 MMcm, according to SPP. SPP, *Situácia v Dodávkach Zemného Plynu Na Slovensku*, 17 January 2009 <http://www.spp.sk/sk/vsetky-segmenty/o-spp/media/59-situacia-v-dodavkach-zemneho-plynu-na-slovensku/> [accessed 26 June 2015].

46 'Russian Gas Started Flowing to Slovakia from the Czech Republic', *SITA Slovenska Tlacova Agentura*, 18 January 2009.

47 SPP, *SPP Podniká Kroky Na Zaistenie Bezpečnosti Dodávok Zemného Plynu Pre Slovensko S E.ON Ruhrgas a VNG*, 19 February 2009 <http://www.spp.sk/sk/vsetky-segmenty/o-spp/media/66-spp-podnika-kroky-na-zaistenie-bezpecnosti-dodavok-zemneho-plynu-pre-slovensko-s-e-on-ruhrgas-a-vng/> [accessed 26 June 2009].

48 Alexander Duleba, 'Poučenia z plynovej krízy v januári 2009 Analýza príčin vzniku, pravdepodobnosti opakovania a návrhy opatrení na zvýšenie energetickej bezpečnosti SR v oblasti dodávok zemného plynu', *Slovak Foreign Policy Association*, October 2009, <http://www.old.sfpa.sk/dokumenty/publikacie/281> [accessed 20 June 2016] p. 4.

49 Ministry of Economy of the Slovak Republic, 'Government Responses to the Impact of the Financial Crisis on Energy Industries and Energy Security of the Slovak Republic', 2009 <http://www.unece.org/fileadmin/DAM/energy/se/pp/EnComm18_Nov09/18Nov/12_Jurasek.pdf> [accessed 2 July].

negotiations with VNG, E.On Ruhrgas and GDF Suez over LTCs. A contract with E.On was expected soon, the company said.[50]

Then, in late June, the company agreed a 10-year contract with E.On that would see Germany's biggest utility import 500 MMcm/y into the Slovak market, starting on 1 July that year.[51] In announcing the new contract and on-going negotiations with GDF Suez over a similar deal, SPP said that Gazprom Export would remain Slovakia's primary gas supplier, but new suppliers would ensure stable supplies in the case of another disruption to gas supplies from the east.[52] In August, SPP followed up with a contingency contract with VNG that would see the German trader deliver 30 MMcm of gas in the event of further supply disruption.[53] Finally, on 5 October, a GDF Suez LTC was announced by SPP that would see the French company also deliver up to 500 MMcm/y for five-years. E.On had also agreed a supplementary 350 MMcm/y contract bringing its total annual contracted volume for delivery to SPP to a potential 850 MMcm/y.[54] Pricing on each of the contracts would be pegged to the Russian contract formula, meaning SPP had no price advantage over its existing Gazprom LTC and would also need to cover further transit costs through the Czech system.[55]

However, in the event of renewed long-term supply disruption from Russia, Slovakia would now be able to count on 1.38 bcm/y of alternative contracted gas flowing through pipelines on its western flank or from within storage. Without high-capacity connections to the west, though, daily volume capacity would be limited. The Slovak government also moved to enact a new Energy Act at the end of January that would force storage operators to maintain 30 days of supply, in

---

50 SPP, *SPP Je Pripravený Zvládnuť Prípadné Prerušenie Dodávok Plynu Z Ukrajiny Bez Obmedzení Pre Odberateľo*, 23 June 2009 <http://www.spp.sk/sk/vsetky-segmenty/o-spp/media/80-spp-je-pripraveny-zvladnut-pripadne-prerusenie-dodavok-plynu-z-ukrajiny-bez-obmedzeni-pre-odberatelov/> [accessed 26 June 2015].

51 'Slovak Firm SPP Signs Contract on Gas Supplies with E.ON', *CTK Business News*, 29 June 2009.

52 SPP, *SPP Vstupuje Do Diverzifikačných Kontraktov S E.ON Ruhrgas a GDF SUEZ*, 29 June 2009 <http://www.spp.sk/sk/vsetky-segmenty/o-spp/media/81-spp-vstupuje-do-diverzifikacnych-kontraktov-s-e-on-ruhrgas-a-gdf-suez/> [accessed 27 June 2009].

53 'SPP Signs Gas Supply Contract with GDF Suez', *Cedigaz News Report*, 19 October 2009, p. 11.

54 'ZZ: SPP uzavrel kontrakty s GDF SUEZ a E.ON Ruhrgas', *SITA Slovenska Tlacova Agentura*, 5 October 2009.

55 The GDF Suez contract was scheduled to see deliveries made to the Lanžhot station, but the E.On contract stipulated Waidhaus as the delivery point, and the VNG contract Sayda – both on the German/Czech border. Slovakia Secures Emergency Gas', *International Gas Report*, 12 October 2009, section EUROPE, MIDDLE EAST & AFRICA, p. 22.

addition to giving the state control over whether gas in storage could be exported abroad in the event of crisis.[56] SPP objected to the proposals, claiming it would undermine the commercial relationship it had built up with suppliers in Austria, the Czech Republic and elsewhere during the disruption.[57]

6.4 Brotherhood reversed: 2010–2014

In response to the costly consequences of the disruption to supply in January 2009, SPP had lodged a case at the International Court of Arbitration of the International Chamber of Commerce in Paris during December that year, aiming to recoup some of the losses. Compensation for 300 MMcm of non-delivered gas from its contracted volume was the key request.[58] However, in April 2010, SPP confirmed it had withdrawn the case, while also announcing that it had reached agreement with Gazprom to lower the amount of gas it received as part of the 2008 LTC. With consumption lower following the financial crisis, SPP needed to reduce its annual import burden. Reports suggested the volume reduction was 10% for two years, but that SPP would then purchase a further 5% for the four following years under the agreement.[59] The withdrawal of arbitration proceedings and accord on gas supply reduction were not connected, SPP said.[60]

On 24 October 2010, work was completed on reversing the flow of gas back into Slovakia from the Baumgarten storage and trading hub in Austria. Dzurinda – now foreign minister under the SDKÚ-DS-led coalition of smaller parties elected in 2010 under Prime Minister Iveta Radičová, which took office in July that year

56 ICIS, 'Slovak SPP Signs Letter of Intent with E.ON, VNG on Alternative Supplies', 19 February 2009, <http://www.icis.com/resources/news/2009/02/19/9309850/slovak-spp-signs-letter-of-intent-with-e-on-vng-on-alternative-supplies/> [accessed 26 June 2015].

57 SPP, *Tlačové Vyhlásenie SPP*, 30 January 2009 <http://www.spp.sk/sk/vsetky-segmenty/o-spp/media/63-tlacove-vyhlasenie-spp/> [accessed 1 June 2016].

58 Interfax, *Slovakia's SPP Agrees New Gas Supply Terms with Gazprom, Drops Damages Claim*, 7 April 2010.

59 'SPP Drops Complaint against Gazprom', *Spectator.sme.sk*, 2010 <http://spectator.sme.sk/c/20035836/spp-drops-complaint-against-gazprom.html> [accessed 29 June 2015].

60 "After a thorough analysis and review of the options, risks and high costs associated with reaching a satisfactory result in an adequate timeframe, SPP decided against action at the Court of Arbitration," SPP said in a statement. SPP, *Stanovisko SPP K Obchodnej Dohode S Gazprom Export*, 1 April 2010 <http://www.spp.sk/sk/vsetky-segmenty/o-spp/media/103-stanovisko-spp-k-obchodnej-dohode-s-gazprom-export/> [accessed 1 July 2015].

to replace Fico – was in Austria to see the pipeline brought on-stream.[61] The project was Slovakia's second reverse-flow interconnection and reversed the flow of gas from the Brotherhood pipeline. It also gave the potential for Slovakia to link with the mooted Nabucco pipeline project that, under contemporary planning, would have shipped Caspian gas to Austria via Hungary, Romania, Bulgaria and Turkey.[62] By December 2010, Eustream was actively moving ahead with more interconnector projects that would form part of the EU's North-South Gas Corridor initiative.[63]

By 2011, Gazprom's market activities in Central Europe had come under the gaze of the European Commission. SPP had its offices raided by EU inspectors in September 2011[64] as Brussels gathered evidence for a full investigation against the Russian monopoly's practices in Central Europe, which was launched in September 2012.[65] The first line of Nord Stream had been brought on-stream earlier in November 2010, allowing Gazprom to re-route supplies to Germany away from the Slovak corridor despite the transit agreement being in place until 2028. However, speaking in Bratislava two weeks after the Commission raids, Gazprom Export's director general, Alexander Medvedev, sought to allay fears that Slovak transit fees would end:

---

61 Koller Jan, 'Opening the Gas Junction in Baumgarten, Austria on Oct. 24, 2010. - Inventing Europe', ČTK, <http://www.inventingeurope.eu/infrastructures/energy-brotherhood-reversed-after-1989&object> [accessed 29 June 2016].

62 "A strategic dimension of this arrangement is that it will also enable connection to the planned Nabucco gas pipeline, which should end right at the Baumgarten terminal. Once the Nabucco project is launched, Slovakia will have diversified both the transport route and sources of its gas supplies. A solution to connect the oil transport systems of the two countries is also being sought," the Ministry of Foreign Affairs of the Slovak Republic said in its annual report. Ministry of Foreign Affairs of the Slovak Republic, *Foreign Policy in 2010*, 2011, p. 13.

63 This strategy envisaged the development of a ladder of interconnectors connecting the Polskie LNG terminal in Poland with the planned Adria LNG import terminal in Croatia through Central Europe. Eustream, *Slovensko – Maďarské Prepojenie Plynovodov: Eustream Je Pripravený Investovať*, 22 December 2012 <http://www.eustream.sk/sk_media/sk_tlacove-spravy/slovensko--madarske-prepojenie-plynovodov-eustream-je-pripraveny-investovat/20> [accessed 30 June 2015].

64 'EU Inspectors "Raid" Slovak Gas Firm over Suspected Cartel with Russia's Gazprom', *BBC Monitoring European*, 1 October 2011.

65 "The Commission is investigating three suspected anti-competitive practices in Central and Eastern Europe. First, Gazprom may have divided gas markets by hindering the free flow of gas across Member States. Second, Gazprom may have prevented the diversification of supply of gas. Finally, Gazprom may have imposed unfair prices on its customers by linking the price of gas to oil prices," the European Commission said while launching the case. European Commission, *Antitrust: Commission Opens Proceedings against Gazprom*, 4 September 2012 <http://europa.eu/rapid/press-release_IP-12-937_en.htm> [accessed 26 June 2015].

> Surely, everyone here is concerned about the future of gas contracts after the commissioning of the Nord Stream and South Stream gas pipelines. May I assure you that all commitments under these contracts shall be met. Commitments on gas transit through Slovakia are secured by the 'ship-or-pay' condition.

Therefore, you can be assured that your country will not be left without transit fees.[66]

Like take-or-pay, ship-or-pay would oblige Gazprom to pay if it did not use the pipeline.

Under continued pressure to justify steeply rising oil-indexed contract prices in January 2012 Gazprom announced a contract renegotiation with SPP in addition to similar so-called "price correction" deals with Germany's Wingas, Italy's Sinergie Italiane, Austria's EconGas and French developer GDF Suez.[67] The price reductions were reported to be 10% for each of the companies.[68] Fico's return as Prime Minister following a vote of no-confidence in Radičová over the Eurozone crisis in 2012 heralded a renewed focus on state intervention in the energy sector as his left-wing populist SMER-SD party gained an outright majority in the National Council legislative house. Applications for retail price hikes for consumers had prompted an earlier open conflict between Fico and SPP's foreign owners, GDF Suez and E.On Ruhrgas, during the Prime Minister's earlier term up to 2010.[69] Slovakia's Regulatory Office for Networks Industries (URSO) had turned down attempts for retail price rises from SPP in 2008.[70]

Fico's desire to wrestle SPP back under state control – whilst GDF Suez and E.On Ruhrgas sought to sell their stake, faced with declining margins and political

---

66 Alexander Medvedev - Director General of Gazprom Export, 'GAZPROM AND SLOVAKIA: ANNIVERSARIES OF COOPERATION IN ENERGY SECTOR' (Bratislava, Slovakia, 2012).

67 Gazprom Export, *Достигнуты Договоренности Об Адаптации Цен С Рядом Европейских Партнеров*, 17 January 2012 <http://www.gazpromexport.com/presscenter/news/446/> [accessed 1 July 2015].

68 Guy Chazan, 'Gazprom Bows to Demand with Gas Price Cut', *Financial Times*, 16 February 2012 <http://www.ft.com/intl/cms/s/0/2e57f4c4-58ad-11e1-9f28-00144feabdc0.html#axzz3eetppqAy> [accessed 1 July 2015].

69 "Lords of Ruhrgas and Gaz de France, if you do not like that you earned in 2007 only $16.7 billion, so [sic] give it back," Fico is reported to have said after the utility lodged a request to increase prices by 20%, owing to what they claimed were the costs of rising oil-indexed gas imports. 'E.ON a GdF: Podiel v SPP Naspäť Nepredáme', *Www.sme.sk*, 10 September 2012 <http://www.sme.sk/c/4069072/eon-a-gdf-podiel-v-spp-naspat-nepredame.html> [accessed 2 July 2015].

70 'UPDATE 2-Slovakia Rejects Company's Plea for Gas Price Hike', *Reuters*, 15 October 2008 <http://www.reuters.com/article/2008/10/15/slovakia-gas-idUSLF59825220081015> [accessed 2 July 2015]. One initial application was made in August and another request for a 19.8% bill increase in October that year.

pressure to keep already regulated retail prices low – opened a broader conflict in SMER-SD's second term in office. However, the state, the sellers were told, did not have the funds to buy the 49% managing stake back. Instead, GDF Suez and E.On sold their interest to Czech power company Energetický a Průmyslový Holding (EPH) in January 2013 for €1.3 billion.[71] A company re-organisation then saw SPP brought back under Slovak state control in June 2014, with EPH retaining a minority share in the holding company, but with the utility company itself controlled 100% by the National Property Fund of the Slovak Republic.[72]

Just before EPH ceded full-control to the state, SPP completed a contract renegotiation with Gazprom Export in March 2014 that saw a "modification of the purchase price and contract terms of the long-term contract for the supply of natural gas in order to more closely reflect current trends in the market price of gas."[73] Meanwhile, gas traders in the region complained about a sharp increase in Slovak network tariffs into the Lanžhot and Baumgarten entry points enforced by URSO in May 2013. The changes made it more costly for new players to enter the wholesale supply market from western import routes and made plans for regional trading integration more difficult owing to a rise of 300% in fees at Lanžhot and 50% at Baumgarten, in effect since January that year.[74]

---

[71] GDF Suez, *GDF SUEZ Cède Sa Participation de 24,5 % Dans La Société Gazière Slovaque SPP*, 15 January 2013 <http://www.gdfsuez.com/journalistes/communiques-de-presse/gdf-suez-cede-sa-participation-de-245-dans-la-societe-gaziere-slovaque-spp/> [accessed 2 July 2015].

[72] "We are delivering SPP into the hands of the state with a good feeling and in a much better condition than we accepted it from the former shareholders. We have successfully renegotiated the parameters of the contract with Gazprom, slashed operating costs, and enhanced the company's strategic position in the market," EPH's chairman, Daniel Křetínský, said in statement. EPH, *THE REORGANISATION OF THE SPP GROUP WAS COMPLETED TODAY*, 4 June 2014 <http://www.epholding.cz/en/press/the-reorganisation-of-the-spp-group-was-completed-today/> [accessed 2 July 2015].

[73] SPP, *SPP Ukončil Rokovania so Spoločnosťou Gazprom Export*, 28 March 2014 <http://www.spp.sk/sk/vsetky-segmenty/o-spp/media/303/> [accessed 2 July 2015].

[74] Chris Johnstone, 'Slovak Supplier Queries Charges', *Platts European Gas Daily*, 29 May 2013. Eustream responded: "The situation in gas transmission through the Slovak transmission network has significantly changed in recent years, resulting in a completely new gas flows scheme we are facing today. Restructuring of the tariff system of Eustream is linked to the efforts of the regulatory authority to encourage the utilisation of existing available gas infrastructure [...]. [The] current fee for daily capacity at Lanžhot is still well below the tariffs in Veľké Kapušany entry point. Compared with other European TSO-s we can state, that actual tariffs of Eustream are competitive and appropriate." Email to the author from Eustream spokesman Vahram Chuguryan, 'Cross Border Entry Tariff', 11 December 2013.

With Gazprom and Ukraine once again in conflict over the terms and payment for gas imports following the change in government brought about by the Euromaidan protests in early 2014 and Russia's annexation of Crimea, Eustream inaugurated a new pipeline loop system on 2 September, re-directing gas out of Velké Kapušany and back through a refurbished pipeline that had previously serviced a nearby power station at Vojany. The pipeline would initially allow exports back into Ukraine of 6.4 bcm/y from October that year, making it the largest capacity route back out of the EU, bigger than that from Hungary and from Poland.[75] However, Ukraine's Naftogaz Ukrainy persistently requested a larger connection that would convert one of the five mainline Brotherhood pipelines crossing from Uzhgorod in Ukraine. Eustream had claimed before the crisis that there was little interest in a Ukraine interconnection, but the crisis had created demand, with fears that transit from the east would once again cease.

A month after the so-called Vojany pipeline was brought on-stream in 2014, on 2 October SPP reported a cut in Gazprom deliveries of 51.5% beneath nominations. Throughout September European importers had announced smaller falls and an emergency government session was called to address the disruption, with Fico announcing a new five-year contract between SPP and E.On that would allow deliveries of 2 MMcm/d.[76] That contract would replace the earlier agreement signed following the gas cut in 2009. SPP also made emergency gas purchases on the Austrian market to cover any potential disruption in the final quarter of 2014 and first quarter of 2015.[77]

Slovakia's Economy Minister Pavol Pavlis travelled to Moscow in October 2014 seeking answers from Russia's Energy Minister, Alexander Novak, on the continued disruption to supply that was denied by Gazprom. The Slovak side had made nominations of 12.4 MMcm/d under the Gazprom contract, but only 6.4 MMcm/d was being received, Pavlis said before leaving for the Russian capital.[78]

---

[75] Eustream, *Plynovod Vojany-Užhorod Je Spustený Do Komerčnej Prevádzky*, 2 September 2009.

[76] Vláda Slovenskej republiky, *Polovičný Pokles Dodávok Plynu Pokračoval Aj Dnes, Mimoriadne Zasadla Vláda*, 2 October 2014 <http://www.vlada.gov.sk/polovicny-pokles-dodavok-plynu-pokracoval-aj-dnes-mimoriadne-zasadla-vlada/> [accessed 26 June 2015].

[77] SPP, *SPP Uzavrel Nový Diverzifikačný Kontrakt S E.ON Global Commodities*, 2 October 2014 <http://translate.google.de/translate?hl=en&sl=sk&tl=en&u=http%3A%2F%2Fwww.spp.sk%2Fsk%2Fvsetky-segmenty%2Fo-spp%2Fmedia%2F324%2F&anno=2> [accessed 26 June 2015].

[78] 'INTERVIEW-Slovak Minister to Meet Russian Counterpart over Gas Supplies', *Reuters News*, 16 October 2014.

The reduction, according to the Slovak Ministry of Economy, was because Gazprom had to replenish Russian storage facilities ahead of the winter.[79] Deliveries continued at below nominated rates through November and December, with transmission at 40% below nominated volumes in December.[80]

SPP also said in October that it was seeking to reduce the quantity of its LTC imports from Gazprom by 10-15%, in addition to securing a price cut and lowering the take-or-pay threshold.[81] At the same time, executives at Eustream began presenting a new pipeline concept called Eastring that would connect up Gazprom's mainline spurs heading from Velké Kapušany and the Brotherhood pipeline, in addition to those pipelines transiting Ukraine to Romania and Bulgaria. This 570 km network, Eustream argued, would mean transmission capacities could be interlinked, allowing European shippers to utilise Ukraine's storage facilities around Uzhgorod and better to circulate both existing supplies from Russia and new imports from the Caspian, due at the end of the decade.[82] Former Czech Prime Minister Mirek Topolánek – instrumental in resolving the 2009 crisis – was hired to lobby formally for the project on behalf of Eustream.[83]

Meanwhile, the company also renewed its focus on an interconnection with Poland that would help to link the North-South Corridor and bring supplies of LNG from the Świnoujście terminal south. However, by the end of 2014 the Eustream/Gaz-System joint venture had made little progress beyond cost allocation.[84] Repeated delays to the commissioning of the Hungary interconnector were overcome, however, and on 1 July 2015 the 4.5 bcm/y– capacity link was opened,

---

79 Ministrovo hospodárstva SR, *Ruský Minister Energetiky Prisľúbil Intervenciu Za Obnovenie Dodávok Plynu Na Zmluvnej Úrovni*, 23 October 2014 <http://www.economy.gov.sk/aktuality-rusky-minister-energetiky-prislubil-intervenciu-za-obnovenie-dodavok-plynu-na-zmluvnej-urovni/10s143983c?stxt=novak&sekcia=&oblast=&sfrom=31.07.2014&sto=21.11.2014&page=1> [accessed 2 July 2015].

80 'SPP Keeps Receiving Less Gas from Russia', *CTK Business News*, 19 December 2014.

81 Interfax, *SPP in Talks with Gazprom on Cutting Purchases 10%-15%, on Price (Part 2)*, 22 October 2014.

82 Tomáš Mareček, Chairman of the Board of Directors, Eustream, 'Usual Questions, Unusual Answers' (presented at the Central European Energy Conference 2014, Bratislava, Slovakia, 2014) <http://ceec.sk/wp-content/uploads/2014/12/Mare%C4%8Dek-OK.pdf> [accessed 2 July 2015].

83 Georgi Gotev, 'Former Czech PM Promotes Eastring Gas Pipeline', *EurActiv*, 2015 <http://www.euractiv.com/sections/energy/former-czech-pm-promotes-eastring-gas-pipeline-314394> [accessed 2 July 2015].

84 URE, *Step Closer to the Development of the Polish-Slovak Gas Interconnector*, 3 March 2015 <http://www.ure.gov.pl/en/communication/news/223,Step-closer-to-the-development-of-the-Polish-Slovak-gas-interconnector.html> [accessed 2 July 2015].

connecting the Slovak transmission network at Veľké Zlievce with the Hungarian system at Vecsés in the suburbs to the east of Budapest.[85] However, at least initially, the pipeline was almost idle.[86] In its April 2015 Statement of Objections against Gazprom under the case launched in 2012 following the raids on importers, the European Commission argued that the Russian supplier was "hindering competition in the gas supply markets" of eight countries, including Slovakia. The imposition of territorial restrictions on onward delivery of gas to third parties was the only part of Commission's case in which Slovakia was specifically identified.[87] Gazprom denied the charges.

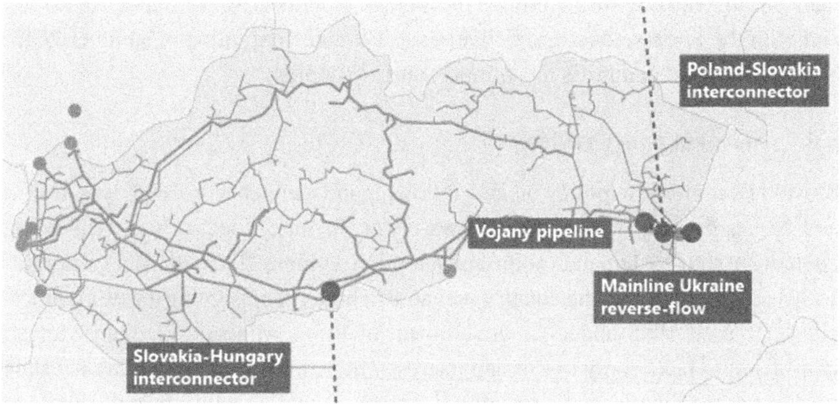

Figure 16: Slovakia's planned pipeline interconnector projects in 2014

In a letter to the three heads of EU institutions in June 2015, Ukraine's Prime Minister Arseniy Yatsenyuk reiterated Kiev's complaint that the unclear contractual arrangement surrounding ownership of the mainline Brotherhood pipeline system as it crossed the border from Ukraine into the EU was a "major obstacle"

85 Eustream, *Slovensko-Maďarský Plynovod Je Uvedený Do Komerčnej Prevádzky*, 1 July 2015 <http://www.eustream.sk/sk_media/sk_aktuality/slovensko-madarsky-plynovod-je-uvedeny-dokomercnej-prevadzky> [accessed 2 July 2015].

86 'No Capacity Nominated on New Hungary-Slovakia Pipe', 2 July 2015 <http://www.icis.com/resources/news/2015/07/02/9900530/no-capacity-nominated-on-new-hungary-slovakia-pipe/> [accessed 2 July 2015].

87 European Commission, 'Antitrust: Commission Sends Statement of Objections to Gazprom for Alleged Abuse of Dominance on Central and Eastern European Gas Supply Markets', 2015 <http://europa.eu/rapid/press-release_IP-15-4828_en.htm> [accessed 12 May 2015].

to reverse-flow deliveries. Yatsenyuk was clear that Kiev interpreted this as a breach of EU regulations:

> Eustream […] has declined to enter into an interconnection agreement with Ukrtransgaz […] because it claims Gazprom Export holds exclusive rights under a legacy agreement regulating the utilisation of the interconnection point […]. Under this agreement, Gazprom Export is given the exclusive right to control the pipelines between the Uzhgorod and Velké Kapušany gas metering stations.[88]

Eustream claimed in response that ownership of the border infrastructure around Velké Kapušany was not governed by the 2008 transmission contract, but under the terms of a separate deal. Eustream argued that Ukraine was not utilising more than half of available flows through the Vojany pipeline's 40 MMcm/d capacity,[89] and with the impasse over gas deliveries to Ukraine continuing in summer 2015, Slovakia was the country's most important EU supplier.

6.5 Slovakia policy review

Slovakia's immediate policy on gas, following independence in 1993, was a 'wait and see' approach, with existing flows under Soviet-era legacy contracts being enough to satisfy demand. With consumption volume fluctuations in the mid-1990s relatively stable, the country was able to hold off on signing a new commercial LTC until 1998 under the government of Prime Minister Vladimír Mečiar, considered to be friendly to Russian interests. Slovakia's role as a key transit state for Gazprom deliveries to Germany and Austria – coupled with a friendly bilateral relationship cultivated by the administration and illustrated through its acceptance of a trading intermediary, Slovrusgas, and Gazprom's approach to take ownership of SPP – made it one of Moscow's key regional allies in the 1990s.

Supply diversification was clearly not a policy priority either for the Dzurinda, Moravčík or earlier Mečiar administrations. In December 1998, Czech Economy Minister Ľudovít Černák made this point by saying that "we do not see it as realistic that diversification of gas sources will take place within our term."[90] However, the profound impact of the 2009 gas crisis on Slovak energy supply sparked

[88] Prime Minister of Ukraine Arseniy Yatsenyuk, 'Letter to the President's of EU Institutions', June 2015.

[89] Eustream, *Reakcia Eustreamu Na List Ukrajinského Premiéra Adresovaný Orgánom EÚ*, 24 June 2015.

[90] 'Slovakia Will Continue Importing Russian Gas.', *Reuters News*, 21 December 1998.

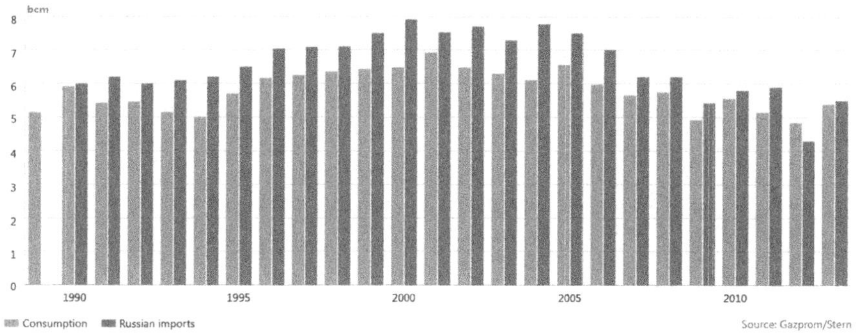

Graph 29: Slovakia's consumption and imports (1970–2013)[91]

a swift review of public policy changes on energy. Fico's administration – elected in 2006 on a pledge to keep a lid on retail prices – quickly opted to build out reverse-flow links with western neighbours Austria and the Czech Republic after January 2009 and to break the pattern of dependence that saw Slovak demand met almost 100% by Gazprom supplies. A number of new contracts were also signed with Western suppliers in the immediate post-crisis period that would not only be sufficient to cover any future temporary cut-off but would also eat into Gazprom's market share. The availability of up to 1.38 bcm/y of alternative contracted gas by 2010 through new contracts with GDF Suez, E.On and VNG allayed fears over a future supply cut.

A broader debate on how best to deal with dependence on Russian gas also began in 2009, and though an arbitration case was dropped in 2010 that sought compensation for the earlier supply disruption, SPP sought further re- negotiations on price and take-or-pay in 2011 and 2014. This more robust approach to energy security policy is illustrated by the state's swift reaction to subsequent supply disruption in October 2014, with the confirmation of a renewed contract with E.On Global Commodities as SPP settled back under state ownership. Slovak energy expert Alexander Duleba writes: "The gas crisis in January 2009 has compelled

91 Data from Stern, Gazprom and BP, *Statistical Review of World Energy 2015* <http://www.bp.com/en/global/corporate/about-bp/energy-economics/statistical-review-of-world-energy.html> [12 May 2015].

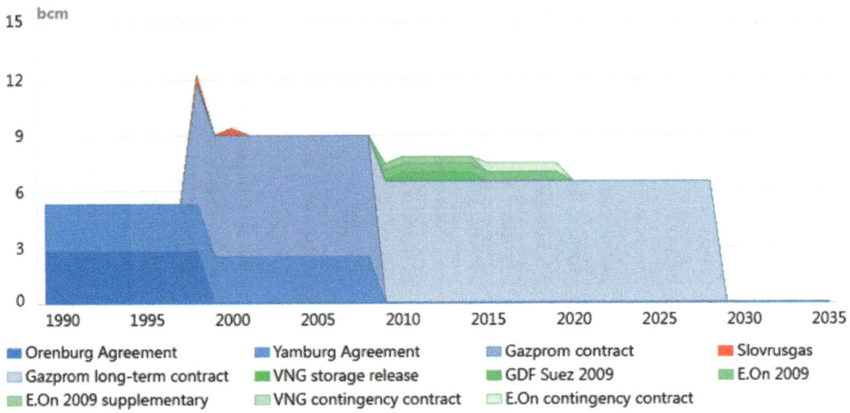

Graph 30: Slovakia's actual contracted gas (1989–2014)[92]

the Fico government to approach the issue of energy security much seriously, including a quest for alternative ways to secure natural-gas supply to Slovakia. "[93] The Energy Act also sought to give the government direct operational control over gas supplies in the event of crisis, and by October 2009, SPP's then-chairman Jean Jacques Ciazynski said that the new LTC deals with E.On and GDF Suez had "significantly reduce[d] the Slovak Republic's dependence on a single source of natural gas. In the event of any extraordinary situation, we are now able to cover up to about one fifth of the annual consumption of natural gas from diversified sources."[94]

The crisis can also be seen to have laid the foundations for the Slovak state to gain direct control over SPP once again, 12 years after the partial privatisation by the Dzurinda administration in 2002. Days after the national security council met with officials of Eustream to discuss the threat of a gas supply crisis in May 2014,[95] Fico announced that after months of negotiations, 100% of SPP had been brought under state control in June:

---

92 Graph uses all contract data as reported so far in Chapter 6 under an aggregated scenario.

93 Duleba, ,'Slovakia's Relationship with Russia and Eastern Neighbours', p. 19.

94 'SPP Signs Gas Supply Contract with GDF Suez', *Cedigaz News Report*, 19 October 2009, p. 11.

95 Vláda Slovenskej republiky, *Mimoriadne Rokovanie Bezpečnostnej Rady SR*, 23 May 2014 <http://www.vlada.gov.sk/mimoriadne-rokovanie-bezpecnostnej-rady-sr/> [accessed 2 July 2015].

> As a result, there can be no repeat of a situation when a foreign shareholder that privatised SPP filed nonsensical proposals with the energy regulator ÚRSO on increases in gas rates for households and small companies. As of this moment, we as a state have control over pricing proposals, and I believe, and it's no secret to repeat it, that we guaranteed price stability between 2006 and 2010, and we're aiming to guarantee it between 2014 and 2016 too.[96]

As shown in Graph 31, Slovakia's wholesale import costs from Gazprom fell beneath the European average in 2011 as the temporary discount assured under the deal with Gazprom that coincided with the closure of the compensation case took effect. Slow development of high-capacity interconnections and the insistence on raising the entry tariff for operators to send gas into Slovakia has since also served to defend SPP's position as monopoly supplier. It seems unlikely this policy will end soon.

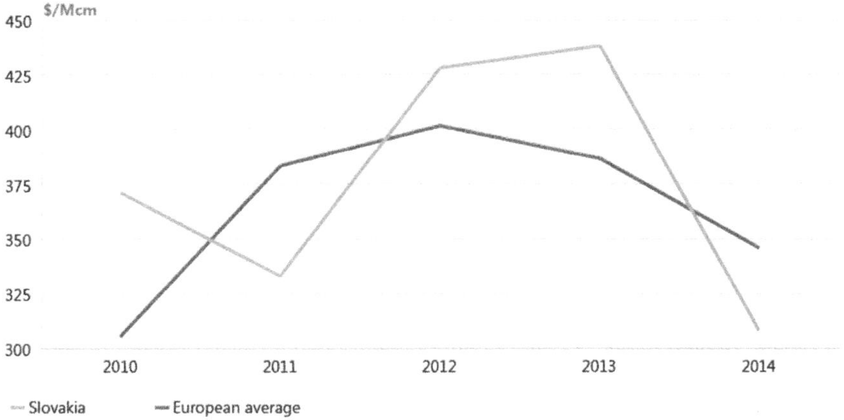

Graph 31: Price of Slovakia's wholesale Russian gas imports (2010–2014)[97]

[96] Vláda Slovenskej republiky, *R. FICO: Štát Dnes Získal 100-% Podiel v Materskej Spoločnosti SPP*, 4 June 2015 <http://www.vlada.gov.sk/r-fico-stat-dnes-ziskal-100-podiel-v-materskej-spolocnosti-spp/> [accessed 2 July 2015].

[97] As cited earlier, data from: Alexey Novikov, *TABLE: How Prices Fell for Russian Gas* (Interfax, 6 March 2015).

Table 8: Gas supply contracts effective in Slovakia (1989–2014)[98]

Slovakia contract database

	Importer	Exporter	Contract signed	Start of deliveries	End of deliveries	Total volume	Yearly volume	Re-negotiations
Orenburg Agreement	Czechoslovakia	Soviet Union	June 1974	1978 (Scaled up to plateau by 1980)	1998	54.6 bcm (combined yearly rate of 2.6 bcm average)	2.6 bcm or 2.8 bcm	
Yamburg Agreement	Czechoslovakia	Soviet Union	January 1987	1989	2008	45 bcm	2.5 bcm	
Gazprom contract	SPP	Gazprom	April 1997	1998	2008	65 bcm	6.5 bcm	
Slovrusgas	Slovrusgas	Gazprom	March 1998	1998	2005		400 mcm in 1998, 370 mcm in 2000	
Gazprom long-term contract	SPP	Gazprom	November 2008	1 January 2009	2028	130 bcm	6.5 bcm	2010, 2014
VNG storage release	SPP	VNG	January 2009	January 2009	2009	100 mcm	100 mcm	
GDF Suez 2009	SPP	GDF Suez	October 2009	October 2009	October 2014	2.5 bcm	500 mcm	
E.On 2009	SPP	E.On Ruhrgas	June 2009	1 July 2009	1 July 2019	5 bcm	500 mcm	
E.On 2009 supplementary	SPP	E.On Ruhrgas	July 2009	July 2009	July 2014	1.75 bcm	350 mcm	
VNG contingency contract	SPP	Verbundnetz-Gas	August 2009	August			30 mcm	
E.On contingency contract	SPP	E.On Global Commodities	October 2014	October 2014	October 2019	2.5 bcm	500 mcm	

Russia	Diversification	Barter/Third-party

98 Data compiled by the author from Gazprom, SPP and various news and analyst reports. All information included herein is cited and referenced in the preceding case study chapter.

6.6 Slovakia policy conclusions

The evidence collected in the preceding chapter on the Slovak Republic's gas sector between 1989 and 2014 provides further evidence with which to test the hypotheses presented in Chapter 2. Part privatisation under a co-ownership structure that saw minority private shareholders given management rights between 2002 and 2014 provides an interesting hybrid example for analysis. The state maintained full decision-making influence before the privatisation, during which it signed only a single LTC, with Gazprom. Hypothesis 1, or H1, posits that right-wing governments, such as those under Mečiar, Dzurinda, or Moravčík, would proritise new contracts with non-dominant suppliers, while left-wing governments, such as the Fico SMER-SD administrations of 2006 to 2010 and from 2012 onwards, would tend to prioritise cooperation with already dominant suppliers of natural gas like Gazprom. H2 suggests that left-wing governments are motivated to maintain downward pressure on retail prices for consumers and in turn make price a strategic priority in LTC talks with suppliers. Finally, H3 argues that in the LTC renegotiation process state-owned utilities under left-wing governments opt for short-term price discounts over the long- term structural change that right-wing governments and private utilities seek.

Figure 17 illustrates the governments in place during key gas market events in Slovakia during the period of inquiry. The assumptions made as part of H1 fail the test immediately, with right-wing administrations shown as keen to pursue increased and sustained contractual dependence on the already dominant supplier. Not a single LTC was agreed with a non-Russian supplier until the 2009 gas supply crisis and the imposition of Slovrusgas gave the dominant supplier a conduit for further increasing market share outside the main Gazprom LTC. When diversification-granting contracts were signed, they were done so mostly with the shareholders in privatised SPP, GDF Suez and E.On under the left-wing Fico government following January 2009. This evidence contradicts that collected in the previous two case study chapters. Alternative theories on why state behavior is so differentiated in Slovakia could lie in alleged clientelism in the 1990s that saw the Mečiar governments move ever closer to Russia. Explanation could also lie in Slovakia's comparatively late ascension to NATO, which potentially eased security pressures on Bratislava at the time.[99]

[99] Slovakia joined the transatlantic security alliance in 2004, while the other three case studies had done so in 1999.

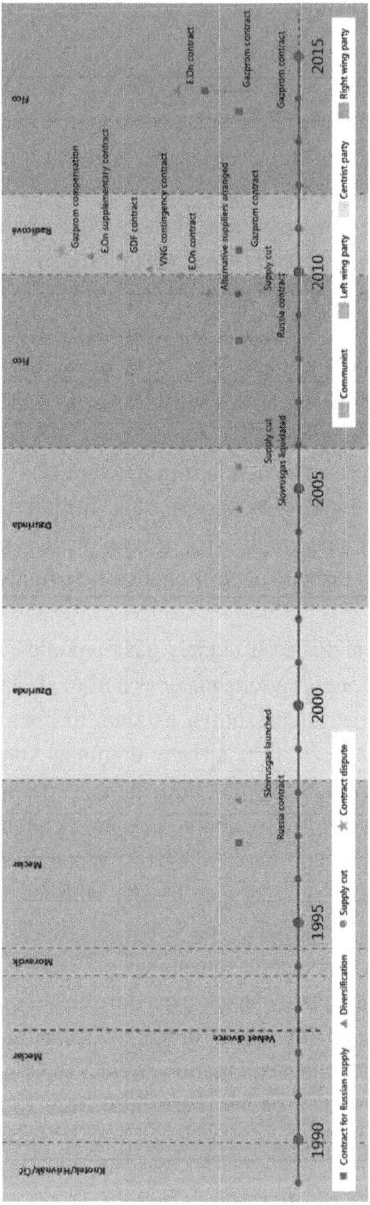

Figure 17: Slovak political timeline with gas LTC milestones (1989–2014)

Crucially, another state grab for control over energy policy came under the SMER-SD government in 2009 through the Energy Act, which, as noted in section 6.3, called for further decision-making powers over how and when to draw down from storage and alternative sources of gas during a crisis. Fico's struggle to take back control of SPP after his left-wing party was re-elected in 2012, and SMER-SD's commitment to lowering utility bills during its earlier 2006 to 2010 term in office, appear to support H2's argument that governments under a left-wing electoral agenda prioritise the provision of low energy prices for consumers.

Furthermore, Fico claimed in 2006 that "everything the previous [Dzurinda 2002–2006 coalition, which included the privatisation period] government did in the energy sector in Slovakia was energy treason."[100] Once control of SPP was re-asserted in 2014, Fico made further comments about the price-setting power the state would now wield: "we as a state have control over pricing proposals, and I believe, and it's no secret to repeat it, that we guaranteed price stability between 2006 and 2010, and we're aiming to guarantee it between 2014 and 2016 too."[101]

In reference to the argument made in H3, the tendency for state-owned import companies to behave in different ways during the re-negotaition process for which data is collected is once again inverted. Though the SPP lodged the compensation claim in the Paris court against Gazprom in late 2009 under SMER-SD and Fico, it was the Radičová centre-right coalition that was in office when SPP dropped the claim and announced a concurrent re-negotiation on volumes and discount the following year. Radičová's SDKÚ-DS party–led coalition was also in office when SPP agreed a 10% price discount with Gazprom. The left-wing single-party SMER-SD government that returned to office in 2012 has subsequently been more robust in its re-negotiations with the dominant supplier, especially since returning control via EPH in 2014, seeking both structural change in the total volumes of gas that SPP is obligated to offtake under the 2008 LTC contract and also cutting the price of imports.

---

100 Lowering utility bills for consumers was a major campaign promise for SMER-SD during the run-up to the 2006 election. spectator.sme.sk, 'Monopolies Reject Lower Fuel and Energy Prices', 14 August 2006 <http://spectator.sme.sk/c/20003083/monopolies-reject-lower-fuel-and-energy-prices.html> [accessed 1 July 2016].

101 Vláda Slovenskej republiky, *R. FICO: Štát Dnes Získal 100-% Podiel v Materskej Spoločnosti SPP*, 4 June 2015 <http://www.vlada.gov.sk/r-fico-stat-dnes-ziskal-100-podiel-v-materskej-spolocnosti-spp/> [accessed 2 July 2015].

In sum, H1 is not proven in the analysis of the Slovak gas sector, with right-wing governments sustaining dependence on the dominant supplier and new supply contracts only signed after January 2009 in response to a major supply crisis, rather than party policy as derived from an electoral agenda. There is some evidence to suggest the SMER-SD governments from 2006 onwards prioritised lower household bill prices over security of supply, and this will be addressed further in the conclusion chapter. Slovakia has not had a single LTC arbitration case made public, but its search for compensation in the case with Gazprom lodged in Paris was settled out of court, and a subsequent discount was also granted under the Radičová government. The only tangible evidence in relation to H3 is that state-owned companies seek to negotiation out of court, though no conclusion can be drawn on the behaviour of different governments. The analysis will expand on these possible alternative explanations in the concluding two chapters.

7 Hungary

The Magyars have long drawn on their own indigenous supplies of natural gas, but Hungary itself has not been self-sufficient since 1973, when demand first outstripped local output.[1] The first deliveries of Russian gas started two years later in 1975, through a 130 km spur to the Bratsvo, or Brotherhood, pipeline system, running through from Uzhgorod in Ukraine.[2] After that, in 1989, the year 'red gas' first arrived in Hungary, demand rose exponentially from 4.8 bcm to 10.2 bcm, before falling back beneath 10 bcm/y around 1990 as industry slowed following the collapse of the Soviet Union and its control economy. A steady increase from 1995 onwards to a peak of 14.7 bcm/y in 2005 precipitated a collapse back to just 9.2 bcm in 2013 and then a further fall to 8.4 bcm in 2014, according to BP statistics.[3]

Hungary has a legacy of gas production stretching back to the 1800s in territory lost following the post-WW1 Treaty of Trianon, signed in 1920, specifically at sites based in the Romanian region of Transylvania and close to the Adriatic Sea in modern-day Croatia. The discovery of a number of new reserves in the Great Hungarian Plain during the 1960s – notably the Algyő field, which was brought on-stream in 1965 – served to reinvigorate the Hungarian upstream sector during the communist period.[4] However, output has since shrunk to around 2 bcm/y, with the country's flagship oil and gas developer, Magyar Olaj-és Gázipari Nyilvánosan működő Részvénytársaság (MOL), battling to mitigate a 5% year-on-year

1 IEA, *Energy Policies of IEA Countries: Hungary 2006*, Energy Policies of IEA Countries (Paris: OECD Publishing, 2007) p. 100.

2 Per Högselius, *Red Gas: Russia and the Origins of European Energy Dependence* (New York: Palgrave, 2013), p. 171.

3 BP, *Statistical Review of World Energy 2014* <http://www.bp.com/en/global/corporate/about-bp/energy-economics/statistical-review-of-world-energy.html> [accessed 29 April 2015].

4 Janos Toth, 'A SHORT REVIEW OF THE HUNGARIAN PETROLEUM AND NATURAL GAS INDUSTRY FROM THE BEGINNINGS UP TO THE PRESENT DAY' (Museum of the Hungarian Petroleum Industry, 1988), p. 80.

J. Posaner, *Held Captive by Gas*, Energiepolitik und Klimaschutz. Energy Policy and Climate Protection, https://doi.org/10.1007/978-3-658-27518-1_7

decrease from outflow at mature fields.[5] Potential for unconventional gas has not yet been seriously explored in Hungary, but conventional reserves of 95 bcm were estimated to remain in place in 2012, giving the country some stock yet to be drawn upon.[6] Despite the decline in overall annual consumption from 2005, gas still plays a key role in Hungary's total primary energy consumption, holding a 38% share in 2010.[7] The residential and commercial sectors covered a combined 50% of demand with 15% also taken by industry and 31% for power generation, according to IEA statistics for 2012.[8] Around 90% of Hungarian homes are connected to the gas grid.[9]

A Gazprom/MOL joint venture called Panrusgas was set up in 1997 to manage the country's LTC agreement with Russia as an intermediary. MOL had otherwise acted as sector monopoly through a vertically-integrated structure until the Hungarian market was liberalised in 2004 in accordance with EU rules. Germany's E.On acquired MOL's wholesale trading and storage units in 2006 on the condition that a gas release programme be launched each year whereby the utility would auction off 1 bcm annually until 2013.[10] MOL also retained the transmission system operator Földgázszállító (FGSZ) that manages the 5782 km national network and six compressor stations.[11] Various utilities and management of the country's storage facilities have been brought back under the state's control since 2010. According to CV1 as shown in Figure 1, this gives the state partial control over the importing entity in its decision-making processes through MOL's stake in Panrus-

5 MOL, *Annual Report*, 2014 <http://annualreport2014.mol.hu/en/our-businesses/upstream> [accessed 8 July 2015].

6 IEA, *Oil and Gas Security: Emergency Response of IEA Countries (Hungary)*, 2012 <http://www.iea.org/publications/freepublications/publication/hungary_2012.pdf> [accessed 8 July 2015], p. 16.

7 IEA, *Energy Policies of IEA Countries: Hungary 2011* (Paris: Organisation for Economic Cooperation and Development, 2011) <http://www.oecd-ilibrary.org/content/book/9789264098237-en> [accessed 17 January 2015], p. 57.

8 IEA, *Natural Gas Information: Hungary* <http://www.iea.org/gtf/index.asp> [accessed 9 July 2015].

9 András Deák, 'Diversification in Hungarian Manner: The Gyurcsány Government's Energy Policy.', *International Issues & Slovak Foreign Policy Affairs*, 15 (2006) p. 46

10 Sophie Moonen, Miguel de la Mano, Alessandro Paolicchi, Pierre Lahbabi, and Csilla Bartok, 'A Combination of Gas Release Programmes and Ownership Unbundling as Remedy to a Problematic Energy Merger: E.ON / MOL', *Competition Policy Newsletter*, Competition Directorate-General of the European Commission, 2006, p. 73.

11 IEA, *Energy Policies of IEA Countries: Hungary 2011* (Paris: Organisation for Economic Cooperation and Development, 2011) <http://www.oecd-ilibrary.org/content/book/9789264098237-en> [accessed 17 January 2015], p. 60.

gas, though in turn direct state ownership of MOL has receded to 25% in recent years.[12]

As of 2014, Hungary's natural gas network had four major system entry points – one with Ukraine (Beregdaróc), one with Austria (Mosonmagyaróvár), one with Romania (Csanádpalota) and a single interconnection point with Croatia (Drávaszerdahely), open since 2011. Gas can be re-directed out of the Hungarian network through the Beregdaróc and Csanádpalota border crossings or through dedicated export lines on the Serbian and Croatian borders. As of 2014, total import capacity was 94.22 MMcm/d, with 90.56 MMcm/d through the two crossings used to deliver Russian gas via Ukraine and Romania. This gives Hungarian importers some limited capacity with which to arrange alternative non-Russian supply contracts from Austria, as also outlined under CV2 in Figure 1.

Gas storage capacity in Hungary totals 5.43 bcm split across five facilities. The Szőreg-1 site was brought into service in 2010 in part of the decommissioned Algyő field near the city of Szeged. It is the country's strategic storage site, mandated after the 2009 supply crisis and with a total capacity of 1.9 bcm/y. The site was managed by the state through MMBF Földgáztároló as of 2014.[13] The other four facilities are controlled by a subsidiary of state power company MVM Hungarian Electricity after it bought out E.On in 2013.[14] All of the entry points – barring the Beregdaróc border point opened in 1975 to supply the first flows of Soviet gas – have been developed since 1989. The Hungaria-Austria-Gasleitung, or HAG Pipeline, was brought on- stream in 1996 opening up the Mosonmagyaróvár crossing with a capacity of 4.4 bcm/y. The bi-directional Arad–Szeged pipeline (2010) with Romania and the Városföld–Slobodnica export pipeline (2011) to Croatia were brought on-stream after the 2009 crisis. Another link with Slovakia was brought on-stream on 1 July 2015, leaving Slovenia as the only neighbour with which Hungary is not yet interconnected. The original Soviet transport system was extended through Hungary to the current Serbian border in 1978, making the country a transit

12 MOL, *Ownership Structure: MOL Capital and Shareholder Structure* (MOL) <https://molgroup.info/en/investor-relations/share-information/ownership-structure> [accessed 21 June 2016].

13 MMBF Földgáztároló Zártkörűen Működő Részvénytársaság, *Cégtörténet* <http://mmbf.hu/hu/web/guest/cegismerteto/cegtortenet> [accessed 9 July 2015].

14 E.On, *E.ON Veräußert Ungarische Gasgesellschaften E.ON Földgáz Trade Und E.ON Földgáz Storage*, 28 March 2013. <http://www.eon.com/de/presse/pressemitteilungen/pressemitteilungen/2013/3/28/eon_veraeussert_ungarische_gasgesellschaften_eon_Foeldgaz_trade_und_eon_foeldgaz_storage.html> [accessed 9 July 2015].

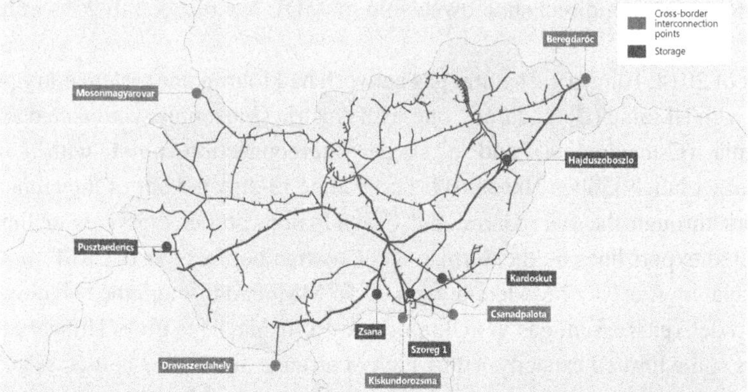

Storage capacity, existing	Operator	Capacity
Szoreg 1 (Strategic storage)	MMBF	1.9 bcm
Pusztaederics	Magyar Foldgaztarolo	340 MMcm
Zsana Nord	Magyar Foldgaztarolo	2.17 bcm
Kardoskut Pusztaszolos	Magyar Foldgaztarolo	
Hajduszoboszlo	Magyar Foldgaztarolo	1.64 bcm

Source: Company data

Mainline pipeline entry and exit points	Operators	Capacity	Flow
Mosonmagyarovar (from Austria)	Gas Connect Austria FGSZ	3.66 MMcm/d	Firm one way with virtual in the other
Kiskundorozsma (to Serbia)	FGSZ Srbijagas	3.97 MMcm/d	Firm one way -
Csanadpalota (to Romania)	FGSZ Transgaz	1.4 MMcm/d	Firm one way
Csanadpalota (from Romania)	Transgaz GSZ	73.6 Mcm/d	Firm one way
Dravaszerdahely (to Croatia)	FGSZ Plinacro	2.15 MMcm/d	Firm one way
Beregdaróc (from Ukraine)	Ukrtransgaz FGSZ	16.56 MMcm/d	- Firm one way

*All data for April 2014. Source: ENTSO-G

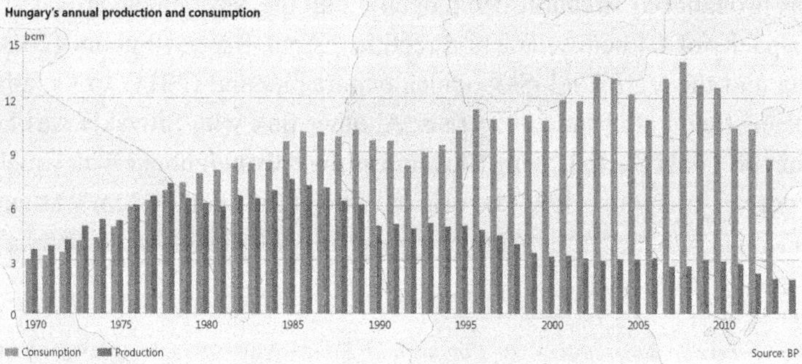

Figure 18: Hungary market snapshot[15]

[15] Data taken from ENTSO-G, FGSZ, MMBF, BP Statistical Review of World Energy and IEA, *Energy Policies of IEA Countries: Hungary 2011* (Paris: Organisation for Economic Co-operation and Development, 2011) <http://www.oecd-ilibrary.org/content/book/9789264098237-en> [accessed 17 January 2015].

state for Russian gas supplies to the Balkans.[16] Hungary is also likely to benefit from LNG imports once a planned regasification terminal on the Croatian island of Krk is built, although this has been beset by delays and has remained in the early stages of development in 2014.[17] A number of other major pipeline projects have been proposed that would have transited Hungarian territory, with the EU-backed Nabucco project and Gazprom's South Stream being the most notable.

7.1 Back to Europe: 1989–1997

From the late 1980s Hungary covered annual gas demand through supply arrangements structured under the Orenburg and Yamburg intergovernmental agreements signed with the Soviet Union in 1974 and 1985, respectively. Under the terms of the Orenburg arrangement, Hungary imported 2.8 bcm/y and under Yamburg, 2 bcm/y.[18] In return, Hungarian engineers had joined those from East Germany, Bulgaria, Romania, Poland and Czechoslovakia in helping to construct Soviet export infrastructure, while Hungarian workers had also assisted in the development of the Tengiz oil field in western Kazakhstan throughout the 1980s.[19]

József Antall took office as Prime Minister in Hungary's first democratically elected government in May 1990, at the top of a right-wing coalition that included his Hungarian Democratic Forum (MDF), the Independent Smallholders, Agrarian Workers and Civic Party (FKgP) and the Christian Democratic People's Party (KDNP). Subsequent attempts to re-negotiate the terms of the Yamburg agreement in Moscow in June 1990 were initially unsuccessful,[20] but an agreement was reached a year later clarifying payment terms for 14.6 bcm of total deliveries and

---

16 Božidar Mijović - Srbijagas, 'Natural Gas Distribution in Serbia' <https://www.energy-community.org/pls/portal/docs/142190.PDF> [12 June 2016].

17 András Deák, 'Hungary: Collecting the First Dividends of Interconnectivity?' in Dariusz Kałan and Jarosław Ćwiek-Karpowicz, eds., *North–South Gas Corridor. Geopolitical Breakthrough in Central Europe* (PISM, 2013), pp. 20–25, p. 23.

18 *Energy Policies of IEA Countries: Hungary 1999*, Energy Policies of IEA Countries (Paris: OECD Publishing, 2000), p. 59. The Orenburg Agreement was signed on 21 June 1974 and the Yamburg contract on 30 December 1985.

19 The repayment of Hungary's contribution to the Tengiz project would be a cause for continual negotiations throughout the 1990s, with Kazakhstan agreeing to supply gas to cover its debt. However, despite agreements being reached in 1992 and 1995, the debt was not settled by the time of the visit of Hungary's President Árpád Göncz to Kazakhstan in 1997. 'Kazakhstan Pledges to Supply Gas to Hungary as Debt Repayment', *BBC Monitoring Service: Central Europe & Balkans*, 13 November 1997.

20 'Ryzhkov/Antall - Hungarian-Soviet Gas Agreement on the Agenda', *MTI - Econews*, 8 June 1990.

ensuring its possible extension past the original expiry date of 1998.[21] First gas supplies had arrived under Yamburg at a rate of 500 MMcm in 1989, 1 bcm in 1990 and 1.5 bcm in 1991, with a 2 bcm/y level approved from 1992 onwards. The Yamburg contract was later extended on 9 September 1991 to run until 31 December 2008.[22]

However, while negotiating with Russia over Yamburg, from May 1990 Antall's administration and MOL were also looking to build an interconnection with the gas network of Austria beyond the old iron curtain, in addition to bolstering broader diversification measures.[23] In February 1994, following Antall's death in office but before new elections had been called, MOL also agreed a cooperation deal with Germany's Ruhrgas that would see the two seek to jointly procure gas from non-Russian sources under the temporary Prime Minister Péter Boross.[24] The HAG pipeline to Baumgarten an der March in Austria would not be commissioned until 1996, but it in effect it acted as the first high capacity connection from the region to western Europe once onstream. The 46 km pipeline was developed as a joint venture between MOL and Austria's OMV, with the cost split between the two parties.

Following elections in 1993, the left-wing communist legacy party the Hungarian Socialist Party (MSZP) governed in coalition with the Alliance of Free Democrats (SZDSZ) under Prime Minister Gyula Horn. According to an agreement announced at the opening ceremony in October attended by Horn and Austrian Chancellor Franz Vranitzky, an annual 3 bcm/y would be provided by OMV until the end of December 2016.[25] No further reference is made to this contract

---

21 'Agreement on Yamburg Settlement Initialled', *MTI - Econews*, 20 June 1991.

22 OECD, *Energy Policies of IEA Countries: Hungary 2003* (Paris: Organisation for Economic Co-operation and Development, 2003) <http://www.oecd-ilibrary.org/content/book/9789264014718-en> [accessed 7 July 2015], p. 88.

23 András Deák, 'Diversification in Hungarian Manner: The Gyurcsány Government's Energy Policy', *International Issues & Slovak Foreign Policy Affairs*, 15 (2006), p. 46. Plans considered in Budapest also appear to have included discussions with Austrian, Czechoslovakian and Yugoslavian partners on joint LNG purchasing. 'Hungary to Diversify Long-Term Natural Gas Imports', *MTI - Econews*, 19 October 1990.

24 'Ruhrgas/MOL Seal New Gas Cooperation Deal', *International Gas Report*, 5 February 1994, p. 1.

25 'Horn, Vranitzky Open Hungary-Austria Gas Pipeline', *Reuters News*, 29 October 1996. European Press Agency, 'Austrian Chancellor Franz Vranitzky (center R) and Hungarian Prime Minister Gyula Horn (center L, Others Are Unidentified) Walk Together during the Opening Ceremony of the Joint Gas Pipeline in Mosonszolnok, Hungary', *Epa.eu*, 29 October 1996 <http://www.epa.eu/economy-business-and-finance-photos/energy-resources-photos/gas-pipeline-opening-photos-51064411> [accessed 1 July 2016].

after the pipeline was brought on-stream, suggesting the deal was never ratified. However, the new infrastructure route would allow Ruhrgas to begin deliveries under its own separate LTC.

By the end of the Horn government's first year in office, a jointly-owned intermediary would be set-up to manage expanded exports of Russian gas deliveries to Hungary.[26] Ownership of Panrusgas was originally split between Gazprom subsidiary Gazexport with 50%, MOL with 30%, and the final 20% share split between oil services company DKG-East (15%) and Hungary's state foreign trade agency Mineralimpex (5%). Gazprom's partial control of DKG-East essentially gave it a majority interest.[27] Panrusgas took over the function previously undertaken by Mineralimpex in the communist era, which had purchased gas and then resold it to MOL for distribution within Hungary. MOL had been required to take over Mineralimpex's duties in December 1994, meaning Panrusgas took over as direct intermediary from 1995 onwards. The supply of gas under the Yamburg agreement became part of its mandate. By the time of price re-negotiation on the Orenburg agreement in February 1995, Panrusgas was also included as a signatory on that deal.[28]

A full commercial LTC was signed in November 1996 that formalised Panrusgas as the main long-term intermediary for Russian-imported gas into Hungary. Under the terms of the agreement, Panrugas would buy 225 bcm up to 2015 through both the traditional Ukrainian corridor and also through the HAG pipeline.[29] The volume included both annual quantities totalling around 194 bcm and an additional option for an extra 2 bcm/y to be purchased between 2000 and the maturity of the contract in 2015. On average, this would have seen around 10.2 bcm/y imported under the base case scenario.[30] According to the IEA, this supply arrangement is split across five different contracts.[31] The day before the agreement

[26] Anita Orbán, *Power, Energy, and the New Russian Imperialism*, PSI Reports (Westport, Conn: Praeger Security International, 2008), p. 45. Until 2009, the company would effectively hold a monopoly over all Gazprom deliveries into Hungary. See: Jonathan P. Stern, *The Future of Russian Gas and Gazprom* (Oxford: Oxford University Press, 2005), p. 114.

[27] Orbán, *Power, Energy, and the New Russian Imperialism*, p. 46.

[28] 'NEW GAS PRICE AGREEMENT REACHED WITH RUSSIA', *BBC Monitoring Service: Central Europe & Balkans*, 9 February 1995.

[29] Denes Albert, 'Hungary MOL Signs Record Gas Deal with Panrusgaz', *Reuters News*, 8 November 1996.

[30] IEA, *Energy Policies of IEA Countries: Hungary 1999*, Energy Policies of IEA Countries (Paris: OECD Publishing, 2000), p. 59.

[31] IEA, *Energy Policies of IEA Countries: Hungary 2006*, Energy Policies of IEA Countries (Paris: OECD Publishing, 2007), p. 101.

was announced, Gazprom closed a $160 million loan facility with three Hungarian banks to pre-finance the gas supplies, the first debt the Russian export monopoly had taken out with lenders in the region.[32] In addition to raising annual imports, the new Panrusgas contract would also consolidate Gazprom's direct exports to Hungary through the integration of the Orenburg and Yamburg intergovernmental agreements.[33]

However, despite the acceptance of a Gazprom-owned third party intermediary to channel supply, Horn's government restricted Russia's direct market access, effectively vetoing any Russian ownership of Hungarian transmission or distribution infrastructure as talks of a privatisation drive began in the mid- 1990s.[34] Although Panrusgas did not own any infrastructure directly, and therefore could not extract fees for the transportation of its parent company's gas, the company planned to develop a transit pipeline running through the Transdanubia region of western Hungary from Slovakia that would deliver gas onwards to northern Italy via Slovenia by 2000.[35] An initial deal on the development of the project was reached in October 1995.[36] The Horn government was also in place during the development of alternative contracts by MOL for gas imports from Gaz de France and Ruhrgas to be conducted through the HAG pipeline and worked out almost concurrently to the Panrusgas LTC.

The LTC with Ruhrgas had been signed in July 1995, expanding on the 1994 cooperation agreement. The supply arrangement ensured the delivery of 500 MMcm/y for 10 years, starting in October 1996.[37] The Gaz de France deal was signed in Budapest in December 1996 and covered the delivery of 400 MMcm/y to the Austrian terminus of the HAG pipeline.[38] Later this was extended to 600

32 'GAZPROM BORROWS FROM HUNGARIAN BANKS', *MTI - Econews*, 6 November 1996.

33 *Energy Policies of IEA Countries: Hungary 2003* (Paris: Organisation for Economic Co-operation and Development, 2003) <http://www.oecd-ilibrary.org/content/book/9789264014718-en> [accessed 7 July 2015], p. 88.

34 Deák, 'Diversification in Hungarian Manner', p. 46.

35 'Hungary, Russia to Build New Gas Pipeline', *Reuters News*, 18 October 1995. The pipeline would have been developed under a joint venture between Panrusgas and MOL.

36 Orbán, *Power, Energy, and the New Russian Imperialism*, p. 47. The failure of Panrusgas to agree terms with Italian energy companies Edison and Snam eventually led to the project being scrapped soon after 1998.

37 'Hungary, Germany Sign Gas Import Deal', *Agence France-Presse*, 10 June 1995.

38 'NATURAL GAS CONTRACT SIGNED WITH FRANCE', *BBC Monitoring Service: Central Europe & Balkans*, 2 January 1997.

MMcm/y, set for expiry in 2012.[39] Each contract in practice included only swap trading, with Russian gas molecules still constituting the physical deliveries from Austria, but by 1997 roughly 1.6 bcm of gas was delivered via the HAG pipeline, of which 900 MMcm were under contract with western suppliers.[40] The non-Russian supplies were believed to be up to 30% more expensive than Gazprom-contracted gas, but supplied an alternative source for gas-dependent Hungary in the event of supply disruption.[41] In the late 1990s, MOL estimates for future Hungarian demand pitched total consumption at 16–18 bcm by 2010, and, when declining production was taken into account, this warranted the additional supply arrangements through HAG alongside the Gazprom/Panrusgas LTC.[42]

7.2 Enter Orbán: 1998–2004

In July 1998, Viktor Orbán, from the conservative Alliance of Young Democrats (Fidesz), became Prime Minister in a coalition with the old right-wing ruling parties of the early 1990s, MDF and FKgP. MOL said in December 1998 that it had agreed to pay 10% of the cost of its imports from Gazprom in food and pharmaceutical products as the Russian financial crisis gathered pace.[43] A follow-up deal reached in March 1999 would see MOL import an additional 1 bcm/y from Gazprom over a five-year period under a barter deal. Payment would be made in Hungarian products, including technology. The annual value of the products to be exported was $60 million, with further talks on at least doubling that volume underway before the millennium.[44] However, by September 2000 Gazprom was threatened with legal action by Hungarian food-packaging company Globus,

---

39 IEA, *Energy Policies of IEA Countries: Hungary 2011* (Paris: Organisation for Economic Co-operation and Development, 2011) <http://www.oecd-ilibrary.org/content/book/9789264098237-en> [accessed 17 January 2015], p. 57.

40 IEA, *Energy Policies of IEA Countries: Hungary 1999*, Energy Policies of IEA Countries (Paris: OECD Publishing, 2000), p. 61.

41 Deák, 'Diversification in Hungarian Manner', p. 48.

42 IEA, *Energy Policies of IEA Countries: Hungary 1999*, Energy Policies of IEA Countries (Paris: OECD Publishing, 2000), p. 59.

43 MOL would reportedly pay the purchase price for gas to Gazprom's bank in Budapest – General Banking and Trust Co Ltd, AEB – which would then handle the barter trade. Gazprom was expected to direct the goods to its employees. 'HUNGARY-RUSSIA', *Platt's Oilgram News*, 30 December 1998, section NEWS BRIEFS: INTERNATIONAL, p. 6.

44 'Government Backs Mol-Gazprom Barter Deal', *MTI - Econews*, 26 March 1999.

which claimed the Russian exporter had not paid it for its services under the terms of the March 1999 deal.[45]

Political relations between Budapest and Moscow had soured during the final years of the Yeltsin Presidency in Russia and the early months following the election of Orbán and his Fidesz party in Hungary. A dispute over supplies to Serbia through Hungary during the NATO bombing campaign of 1999 stoked hostility in spring that year, leading to the cancellation of talks between Orbán and Russia's Prime Minister Yevgeny Primakov.[46] Orbán's suggestion that Hungary might consider the deployment of nuclear weapons on its territory during a crisis situation, citing uncertainties about the future of Russia during an interview in Canada, further raised tensions in the winter of 1999/2000 as Hungary closed in on NATO membership in 1999.[47]

Meanwhile, in 2001, MOL said it had ensured cheaper terms on its Ruhrgas contract as the German supplier began circling the gas markets of Central Europe for possible acquisition targets.[48] In October that year, a consortium of four Hungarian banks provided a new $130 million loan to Gazprom that would be partly used to increase Russian import capacity into the country. As in the earlier deal, gas deliveries would act as collateral for the lenders.[49] Russian companies had also tracked Hungarian energy assets, with Gazprom competing against its Panrusgas joint venture partner MOL to gain control of chemical company BorsodChem through a series of indirect deals in 2000.[50] BorsodChem and its ethylene supplier TVK counted on an interconnected set of supply chain interests that also relied on MOL to supply petrochemical feedstock. A change in ownership of BorsodChem, a successful enterprise and the biggest company of its kind in the region at the time, would potentially undermine the interests of both TVK and, strategically, Hungarian government-owned MOL.[51]

---

45 'Globus Considers Legal Action against Gazprom, Eyes Moscow Market', *MTI - Econews*, 28 September 2000.

46 Orbán, *Power, Energy, and the New Russian Imperialism*, p. 55.

47 Jeff Sallot, 'Activist Past Lives on in Hungary's PM Viktor Orban's pro-NATO Stand Is in Keeping with His Long-Time Anti-Communist Views', *The Globe and Mail*, 29 October 1999, Metro edition, section International News, p. A15.

48 'MOL Renegotiates Gas Contract with Ruhrgas', *Reuters News*, 28 March 2001.

49 'HUNGARIAN BANKS SIGN USD 130 MILLION SYNDICATED LOAN TO GAZPROM', *Interfax Hungary Weekly Business Report*, 30 October 2001.

50 Marlene Laruelle, *Eurasianism and the European Far Right: Reshaping the Europe–Russia Relationship* (Lexington Books, 2015), p. 187.

51 Orbán, *Power, Energy, and the New Russian Imperialism*, p. 93.

Acting through ownership of Russian petrochemicals company Sibur and Ireland-registered Milford Holdings, among others, Gazprom attempted to tie up majority ownership of BorsodChem through a hostile takeover. Gazprom also saw the opportunity further to consolidate control over the supply chain through ownership of a Ukrainian company, Oriana, specialising in TVK's feedstock, which MOL had supplied.[52] By avoiding admitting ownership of some of the vehicles through which shares in BorsodChem were acquired, Gazprom also avoided having to make a public offer in late 2000 for the entire company, necessary under Hungarian law once 33% of the company was secured.[53]

Hungary's security services warned that, if allowed, the take-over could harm the national economy.[54] In reaction to the hostile takeover, BorsodChem sought to sell its share in TVK to MOL, in order to restrict Gazprom from controlling both companies through the ownership of one.[55] Gazprom objected to the fire sale and Milford Holdings chief executive (and, coincidentally, chief executive of Panrusgas and Gazprom's Hungarian banking operation Általános Értékforgalmi Bank), Megdet Rahimkulov, explicitly referenced the plan to use Ukraine's Oriani as feedstock supplier to both BorsodChem and TVK once an expansion programme was complete.[56] As the wrangle over what essentially constituted control of the lucrative Hungarian petrochemicals sector continued, Rahimkulov explicitly referenced the terms of import that could also have affected the barter deal for natural gas signed with MOL in 1999. "If Gazprom's interests are not considered with regard to buying shares in Hungarian chemical companies, we will reconsider how to shape our policy regarding purchases of meat, vegetables, fruits and pharmaceuticals from Hungary," Rahimkulov said in October 2000, although he maintained that gas supplies would continue.[57]

52 Alexander Wöstmann, 'Gazprom Acquires Stake in Hungary's Borsodchem — Alexander's Gas and Oil Connections' 26 September 2000 <http://www.gasandoil.com/news/russia/11fbb67bcd6fa454894aff8af00b5687> [accessed 10 July 2015].

53 Orbán, *Power, Energy, and the New Russian Imperialism*, p. 94.

54 'A Terjeszkedés Nemzetbiztonsági Kockázatai', Világgazdaság <http://www.vg.hu/kozelet/tarsadalom/a-terjeszkedes-nemzetbiztonsagi-kockazatai-3513> [accessed 10 July 2015].

55 ICIS, 'Gazprom to Block BorsodChem Plan to Sell TVK Stake to MOL', 21 September 2000 <http://www.icis.com/resources/news/2000/09/21/122091/gazprom-to-block-borsodchem-plan-to-sell-tvk-stake-to-mol/> [accessed 12 July 2015].

56 Orbán, *Power, Energy, and the New Russian Imperialism*, p. 94.

57 'GAZPROM MAY REVISE POLICY ON HUNGARIAN IMPORTS OVER BORSODCHEM ISSUE', *Interfax Hungary Weekly Business Report*, 9 October 2000.

Hungary's National Financial Supervisory Agency (PSzAF) launched an investigation into the issue, eventually dropping a further probe into unethical market practices by a Budapest-based bank after the chief executive resigned in December 2001.[58] Gazprom eventually took control of BorsodChem through its proxy stock buyers and, despite Orbán deploying rhetoric to support state interests, the Hungarian government did not intervene to force a full tender for the shares.[59] The impending privatisation of MOL, however, would no longer be open to Russian bidders.

The MSZP/SZDSZ left-wing coalition partnership was elected back into office in 2002 under Prime Minister Péter Medgyessy. As Hungary's EU membership was approved for 2004, gas market liberalisation efforts needed to be stepped up, though another new supply company was registered in Hungary during 2003 that would further entrench Russian gas supply interests. Emfesz, wholly-owned by a holding company in turn controlled by Ukrainian businessman Dmytro Firtash, signed a 3 bcm/y import contract with RosUkrEnergo in Gazprom's office in December 2004 that would commence the next year and was due to expire in 2015. The shipper – a Swiss-registered joint-venture between Gazprom and another company also owned by Firtash called Centragas – would deliver Central Asian gas under a transit guarantee with Ukraine's Naftogaz Ukrainy to both Poland and Hungary.[60]

Medgyessy resigned in 2004 to avoid a no-confidence vote in parliament and would be replaced as Prime Minister by Ferenc Gyurcsány, with the MSZP/SZDSZ coalition going on to win the next election in 2006. Meanwhile, in documents released as part of court cases over the ownership of Emfesz and its liability to RosUkrEnergo, it is clear that the former often failed to make timely payments for gas imports almost as soon as the contract became effective in 2005. There were a number of other irregularities about the terms of the contract initially signed. For example, RosUkrEnergo (RUE) had the obligation to supply gas but

---

58 'BorsodChem Board Says PSzAF Ruling Justified Postponement of EGM', *MTI - Econews*, 24 November 2000. It had been alleged that the subsidiary of Italy's Intesa Banca Commerciale Italaina had purchased a 24.8% stake in BorsodChem and transferred it to Sibur without notifying the authorities in January 2001. The Budapest Metropolitan Court had found the bank guilty in June. 'PLATT'S - Hungary Drops Borsodchem Probe after Bank Chief Resigns', *Platts Commodity News*, 13 December 2001.

59 Orbán, *Power, Energy, and the New Russian Imperialism*, p. 98.

60 Arbitration Institute of the Stockholm Chamber of Commerce, Arbitration between Rosukrenergo and Emfesz (V 183/2009), 2011 <http://www.xn--skiljedomsfreningen-06b.se/file/rosukrenergo-ag-vs-emfesz.pdf> [accessed 9 July 2015], p. 22.

Emfesz held no parallel obligation to nominate any quantity of gas for delivery as is usual under LTC arrangements. A discount was also incorporated from 2006 of 15% beneath the base price, although how much this was is not specified. No re-negotiation clause was included either, meaning there was no contingency for dispute resolution as would usually be the case in a commercial LTC.[61]

Emfesz's quick capture of gas market share in Hungary precipitated plans to expand into Poland and also to use the cheaper stocks of imports to facilitate the development of a gas-fired power station on the Ukraine–Hungary border.[62] In order to do this, Emfesz began working on a plan for a new 2 bcm/y capacity pipeline in 2007 that would have allowed it to supply directly the gas necessary to fuel a 1.5 GW power generation facility in north-western Hungary from the Bohorodchany gas storage facility in Ukraine.[63] However, as companies like RUE and Emfesz made plans locally to increase their own revenue from the lucrative gas business, the dispute between Russia and its key transit partner, Ukraine, intensified in 2005, raising the prospect of a supply disruption.

7.3 The drama of Nabucco: 2005–2009

One evening in 2002 the heads of five European energy companies had met in Vienna to discuss the development of a new pipeline project that would link the gas riches of the Caspian region and the Middle East with their import dependent markets. Hosted by OMV, executives from MOL, Bulgaria's Bulgargaz, Romania's Transgas and Turkey's BOTAŞ agreed a protocol on the development of a project that would be christened Nabucco over the post-summit dinner, named after the Verdi classic they had seen at the opera that evening just 50 km from the tanks, pipelines and compressors of the Baumgarten storage centre envisaged as the final terminus of the project, once it had wound its way 3,300 km from Erzurum in Turkey into the heart of Europe.[64] The pipeline would become part of a new 'fourth' corridor for external gas to reach EU markets and along with Bulgaria, Hungary would be a key transit state for the scheme.

61 *ibid.*, p. 23.

62 'Gazprom Eyes Emfesz', *Platts Energy in East Europe*, 6 July 2007, section OIL & GAS NEWS; Hungary, p. 26.

63 'Emfesz to Build 2 Gm3/yr Link from Ukraine to Hungary', *European Gas Markets*, 16 April 2007.

64 'The Great Pipeline Opera', *Foreign Policy*, 22 August 2009 <https://foreignpolicy.com/2009/08/22/the-great-pipeline-opera/> [accessed 10 July 2015].

Hungary's large storage capacity, its proximity to the Balkans and Baumgarten, and the slow fall in the country's own domestic production made it an ideal candidate for a new pipeline system. By 2004, when the Nabucco project company was set up to manage development of the project, E.On deliveries to Hungary were ramping up to 800 MMcm to cover the loss of indigenous gas supplies as consumption rose above 13 bcm that year.[65] Meanwhile, MOL's gas downstream business was eventually sold off to E.On, including the 50% stake in Panrusgas, in 2006. The deal had been set since November 2004, with the now- combined E.On Ruhrgas agreeing to receive a 75% stake in MOL Földgázellátó (wholesale, marketing and trading) and in MOL Földgáztároló (storage). With the European Commission approving the deal in late 2005, the two companies set the closing of the deal for March 2006.[66]

The brief disruption to Russian supply through Ukraine during January 2006 caused a drop in deliveries to Hungary of around 40% on Sunday 2 January, with some consumers instructed to switch to oil.[67] Although supplies were quickly returned to normal through the breakthrough deal agreed between Gazprom and Naftogaz that would see RosUkrEnergo take on the role of intermediary, deliveries to Hungary were again reduced by 25% in response to a peak in Russian domestic demand later in the month.[68] The result was an increased awareness of the impact of reliance on external suppliers in Budapest and the Act on Strategic Storage of Natural Gas, which passed through the parliament during March, mandated the construction of a strategic gas storage facility with a capacity of 1.2 bcm that would have a withdrawal rate of 20 MMcm/d and cater to 45 days of demand in the event of crisis. The Szőreg-1 well in the Algyő field was chosen as the location.[69]

---

65 E.On, 'MOL Gas acquisition update', 2004 <https://www.eon.com/content/dam/eon-com/download/dwn-news/601_5/20041111_MOL_Gas_Transaction_Handout.pdf> [accessed 6 July 2015].

66 MOL, *A MOL És Az E.ON-Ruhrgas International Megállapodtak a Gáztranzakció Zárásáról*, 13 January 2006.

67 Jonathan Stern, *The Russian-Ukrainian Gas Crisis of January 2006* (Oxford Institute for Energy Studies, 16 January 2006), p. 8.

68 'Hungary's Gas Imports Still 20-25pc under Normal Levels because of Cold in Russia', *MTI - EcoNews*, 19 January 2006.

69 Hungarian Energy Office, *Hungarian Energy Office Annual Report to the European Commission*, August 2011 <http://www.mekh.hu/gcpdocs/52/HEO%20Annual%20Report%20to%20EC%202011.pdf> [accessed 12 July 2015], p. 42. Work would not be completed on the project until 2010. In the meantime, a minimum level of 300 MMcm of capacity was set between 1 October 2007 and 31 December 2009 in existing commercial storage facilities. A further 700 MMcm of capacity at Szőreg-1 is approved for commercial use.

With funding sought to build the new storage site, Gyurcsány welcomed potential Russian investment ahead of a visit to Budapest of Russian President Vladimir Putin in late February 2006.[70] During the summit in Budapest, Putin referenced the development of another new pipeline system that would transport gas through southern and central Europe, using the Hungarian system as a "distribution hub" according to Gyurcsány.[71] New gas storage facilities totalling a potential 10 bcm capacity in Hungary were also discussed during the talks.[72] Then, on 21 June, Gazprom chief executive Alexey Miller signed a cooperation agreement with his MOL counterpart Zsolt Hernádi whereby a project company would be founded on a 50/50 basis to develop and manage gas transmission and storage projects in Hungary.[73] In 2007, Gazprom and Italy started talks on the development of a transit pipeline circumventing Ukraine and flowing through Central Europe before forking into two route, one heading towards Baumgarten via the Great Hungarian Plain and the other sending gas out through Slovenia into Italy along a path potentially similar to the route to the earlier Panrusgas/MOL joint-venture concept from the 1990s.[74]

The so-called 'South Stream' project was immediately seen as a competitor to Nabucco, and as the sister project to Nord Stream running through the Baltic Sea to the north. Hungary stood to benefit, with increased transit fees and ensured flows as demand continued to rise, peaking at an all-time high of 14 bcm in 2008. Gyurcsány signed the intergovernmental agreement on South Stream in Moscow on 28 February 2008, shortly before Putin temporarily left office to take up the Prime Minister role for four years. "Hungary has realised that there is no alternative to cooperating with Russia," Gyurcsány said.[75] Budapest had become used to

70 'Hungary PM Says Russia Welcome as Energy Investor', *Reuters News*, 27 February 2006.

71 'Russia's Putin Proposes South Europe Gas Pipeline', *Reuters News*, 28 February 2006.

72 Deák, 'Diversification in Hungarian Manner', p. 50.

73 Gazprom, *«Газпром» И MOL Group Подписали Соглашение О Сотрудничестве*, 21 June 2006 <http://www.gazprom.ru/press/news/2006/june/article55771/> [accessed 11 July 2015].

74 A number of plans for South Stream were discussed with no clear definitive routing confirmed before the project's cancellation in December 2014. Early designs had the pipeline forking once it reached landfall in Bulgaria, with one spur heading south through Greece and the Adriatic before reaching Italy. The other line would continue onwards through Central Europe to Baumgarten.

75 'CORRECTED - UPDATE 1-Hungary Joins Russia's South Stream Gas Pipeline', *Reuters News*, 28 February 2008.

playing a balancing game with Russia, with former MSZP Prime Minister Medgyessy a regular visitor to Moscow during his time in office.[76]

However, further disruption was to come. At 4 pm on Monday 5 January 2009, FGSZ began to record declining flows through the pipelines coming from Ukraine, from the usual 38 MMcm/d down to 30 MMcm/d.[77] By Tuesday, Russian deliveries via Austria also sharply declined as reduced transit through Slovakia came into effect.[78] From Wednesday, consumption restrictions were put in place for companies consuming up to 2,500 cubic metres per hour in Hungary, but the impact on households was generally mitigated by storage reserves and domestic production.[79] E.On agreed to supply 2.5 MMcm/y via the HAG pipeline for 10 days in addition to the capacity it could withdraw from storage sites in Hungary through subsidiary E.ON Földgáz Storage.[80]

The European Commission estimated a 45% cut to supply for Hungary but reported that officials had managed to secure Norwegian gas in addition to relying on storage inventories and alternative fuel supply through a switch to oil.[81] Hungary was also able to supply some of its gas in storage to Serbia having also benefited from increased German flows via Austria.[82] MOL and E.On agreed to supply gas jointly to Bosnia Herzogovina and Croatia from 10 January, the former receiving 1.5 MMcm/d through the Kiskundorozsma border transfer point with

---

76 Medgyessy held five summits with Russian President Vladimir Putin, or other senior leadership figures, in 2003 and 2004, with Gyurcsány continuing that trend during his time in office. Orbán, *Power, Energy, and the New Russian Imperialism*, p. 192.

77 'Gas Deliveries from Ukraine Reduced at 4 P.m. on Monday - Wrap up', *MTI - EcoNews*, 5 January 2009.

78 'Russian Gas Imports via Slovakia-Austria Drop - E.ON's Hungarian Unit', *MTI - EcoNews*, 6 January 2009.

79 Among those industrial concerns affected, carmaker Suzuki was forced to halt production at its site in Esztergom near the Slovak border. Tile manufacturer Tondach also had to reduce output at five plants. Budapest Ferihegy International Airport switched from gas to oil usage. Budapest Times, *Hungary Further Limits Industrial Gas Use after Ukraine Cuts Supplies*, 7 January 2009 <http://budapesttimes.hu/2009/01/07/hungary-further-limits-industrial-gas-use-after-ukraine-cuts-supplies/> [accessed 11 July 2015].

80 'Ruhrgas Can Supply Hungary with Daily 2.5m Cubic Meters of Gas', *Budapest Business Journal* <http://bbj.hu/energy/ruhrgas-can-supply-hungary-with-daily-25m-cubic-meters-of-gas--_46185> [accessed 11 July 2015].

81 European Commission, 'Member State General Situation According the Significance of Impact', 2009 <http://europa.eu/rapid/press-release_MEMO-09-3_en.htm> [accessed 11 July 2015].

82 European Commission, *Gas Coordination Group: Solidarity Works and the EU's Gas Market Adapts to Challenges of Gas Crisis*, 19 January 2009 <http://europa.eu/rapid/press-release_IP-09-75_en.htm> [accessed 11 July 2015].

Serbia and the latter 1 MMcm/d at Baumgarten. Both deals were to last an initial five days.[83] Meanwhile, plans had also been put in place to supply Slovakia with gas and power from state company MVM.[84]

Normal service returned to Hungary at 13:20 on 20 January after a two-week outage, with an initial 11 MMcm supplied that afternoon through Ukraine.[85] MOL had already been able to lift restrictions on gas use from 15 January as cold weather abated.[86] However, weeks later a return to winter temperatures regionally led to further shortfalls in supply according to FGSZ.[87] Although not as critically affected as Slovakia, which was totally dependent on Russian gas, Hungary saw its industrial production drop by 22.9% year-on-year in January, partially on account of to the gas crisis.[88] The cut to gas transit via Ukraine in January 2009 effectively also severed the business relationship between Emfesz and RUE. Late payments had been a constant feature of the trade relationship since the first months of supply in 2005, with the offtaker leaving a shortfall of $150 million in unpaid fees out of the $330 million worth of gas nominated for 2005 alone.[89]

Just days after the 2009 crisis started, Emfesz announced it had filed a court case against Naftogaz, the Ukrainian transiter and guarantor of Central Asian gas through which it was buying RUE. In a statement, Emfesz accused Naftogaz of failing "to deliver to the Hungarian firm the natural gas it owns, which was supplied by Russia through Ukraine for Hungary and was partially kept at the Ukrainian gas storage facilities, and of using someone else's gas as if it was its own."[90] By late April, Emfesz had also announced that it had switched its gas supply arrangement to RosGas, a shell company registered in Zug, Switzerland, but with an

83 MOL, *A MOL És Az E-ON Ruhrgas Gázt Szállít Horvátországba És Boszniába*, 10 January 2009.
84 'UPDATE 1-Hungary Ready to Supply Power, Gas to Slovakia', *Reuters News*, 15 January 2009.
85 FGSZ, *SAJTÓKÖZLEMÉNY - SIÓFOK, 2009. JANUÁR 20. 17.00*, 20 January 2009 <https://fgsz.hu/hir/sajtokozlemeny-siofok-2009-januar-20-1700> [accessed 12 July 2015].
86 FGSZ, *SAJTÓKÖZLEMÉNY - SIÓFOK, 2009. JANUÁR 15. 11.30*, 15 January 2009 <https://fgsz.hu/hir/sajtokozlemeny-siofok-2009-januar-15-1130> [accessed 12 July 2015].
87 'Hungary's Gas Imports from Ukraine Drop', *Reuters News*, 30 April 2009.
88 Output had already trended downwards in December, causing a greater fall for output in year-on-year statistics. 'INSTANT VIEW 4-Hungary's Jan Output Falls as Exports down', *Reuters News*, 6 March 2009.
89 Arbitration Institute of the Stockholm Chamber of Commerce, Arbitration between RosUkrEnergo and Emfesz (V 183/2009), 2011 <http://www.xn--skiljedomsfreningen-06b.se/file/rosukrenergo-ag-vs-emfesz.pdf> [accessed 9 July 2015], p. 26.
90 Interfax, *Hungary's Emfesz Files Lawsuit against Naftogaz Ukrainy*, 9 January 2009.

opaque management structure. Emfesz's claim at the time that RosGas was in Gazprom's "network of business interests" was denied by the Russian monopoly.[91]

It quickly emerged that RosGas had also bought out Emfesz from its direct parent company Mabofi Holding for a reported $1 fee, though allegations quickly surfaced that questioned the legitimacy of the sale. István Góczi, Emfesz's managing director, was believed to have used an old power of attorney to transfer ownership of the company to RosGas, essentially locking Dmytro Firtash's Group DF, which owned Cyprus-based Mabofi Holding, out of Emfesz. The exchange in ownership was approved within a swift 24 hours by the Hungarian regulator, MEKH, raising further questions.[92]

However, Emfesz said it would receive gas from E.On Földgáz Trade in the short- term before RosGas deliveries could begin, albeit it at a higher price than it had received on discount from RUE.[93] RUE lodged a case in the Stockholm arbitration court in 2009, accusing Emfesz of non-payment for gas delivered and claiming compensation. A counter claim was subsequently initiated. Emfesz was discovered to have still been able to receive gas between January and April 2009, even as the transit of gas from Russia into Ukraine was cut and the arbiters ruled against its claim that it did not know the source of deliveries to the Beregdaróc point. The court ruled against Emfesz in March 2011, with that decision upheld during appeal in 2013. The arbitration demanded Emfesz pay $527 million to its former supplier in compensation.[94] Although Dmytro Firtash's Group DF was eventually restored as sole owner of Emfesz in 2013, the company was by then no longer active.[95] As recently as 2011, MEKH maintained that a contract for annual imports of 900 MMcm/y from Swiss-

91 Global Witness, *How a Fifth of Hungary's Gas Supply Came into the Hands of an Unknown Shell Company* (May 2009), p. 3.

92 Chris Bryant, 'Firtash Remains Frozen out of Hungary', *Financial Times*, 9 March 2011 <http://www.ft.com/intl/cms/s/0/99796846-4986-11e0-b051-00144feab49a.html#axzz3fkqN9Sk5> [accessed 13 July 2015].

93 Világgazdaság, 'EMFESZ: MEH-Bírság És Gázszerződés Az Év Végéig', *VG*, 2009 <http://www.vg.hu/vallalatok/energia/emfesz-meh-birsag-es-gazszerzodes-az-ev-vegeig-298670> [accessed 13 July 2015].

94 According to the court judgement, Emfesz owed $269.5 million for gas imported from RUE in 2008, $151.2 million to cover 2009 and $106.2 million for delayed payments in the three-year period 2005- 2007. Arbitration Institute of the Stockholm Chamber of Commerce, Arbitration between RosUkrEnergo and Emfesz (V 183/2009), 2011 <http://www.xn--skiljedomsfreningen-06b.se/file/rosukrenergo-ag-vs-emfesz.pdf> [accessed 9 July 2015], p. 77.

95 'Gazdaság - Ismét Felszámolják Az EMFESZ-T', *NOL.hu* <http://nol.hu/gazdasag/ismet_felszamoljak_az_emfesz-t-1443713> [accessed 7 July 2015] and 'Website Says Court Rules Again Liquidation of Hungarian Gas Company', *BBC Monitoring European*, 18 June 2013.

registered Bothli Trade – another company bound up in the complex web of ownership structures around RUE and Emfesz – was in effect until 2014.[96] However, the murky ownership structures around these companies, and their interlinked business interests, make a precise evaluation of the share of Russian gas in the Hungarian market hard to determine. In Graph 32, the IEA estimates the share of supply for each kind of gas in Hungary's national consumption that year.

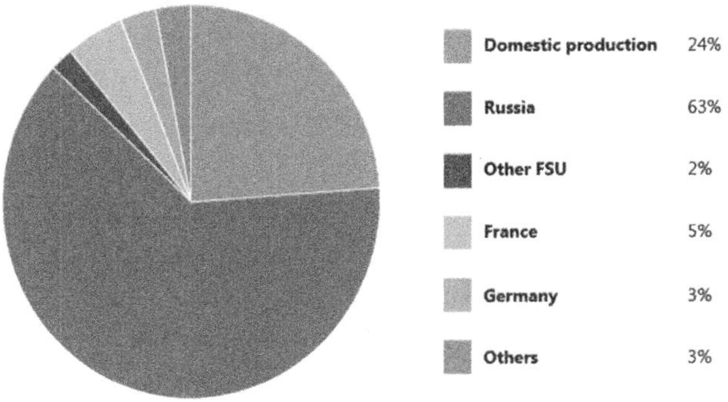

Graph 32: Hungary gas supply by source (2009)[97]

Meanwhile, as court cases escalated and contingency measures to shore up security of supply were put in place after the supply disruption, another crisis was brewing in domestic politics, with Gyurcsány resigning as Prime Minister in March 2009 after a no-confidence motion, eventually bringing down the left- wing MSZP/SZDSZ coalition that had been in office since 2002. Facing a continued drop in support, leading back to an infamous speech at Balatonőszöd on the banks of Lake Balaton two-and-a-half years earlier, Gyurcsány first lost support of the junior coalition partner SZDSZ and was eventually replaced by Gordon Bajnai, who took office until new elections were called.[98] After putting his name to the IGA deal on South Stream in Moscow almost a year earlier, in March 2009, just

96 Hungarian Energy Office, *Hungarian Energy Office Annual Report to the European Commission*, August 2011, p. 37.

97 IEA, *Energy Policies of IEA Countries: Hungary 2011* (Paris: Organisation for Economic Co-operation and Development, 2011) <http://www.oecd-ilibrary.org/content/book/9789264098237-en> [accessed 17 January 2015] p. 58.

98 The Gyurcsány speech was not connected to the gas trade, but rather a private meeting of the governing MSZP. In a bizarre turn of events, recorded and subsequently aired on Hungarian radio in September 2006, the Prime Minister had admitted to lying about policies before the elections that year.

days before leaving office, Gyurcsány visited Moscow. Furthermore, in late November, as plans for Nabucco and a series of other diversification-promoting rivals gathered pace in response to the January crisis, the former Prime Minister was treated to a private dinner in Moscow with Putin.[99]

7.4 Orbánistan and the pipeline graveyard: 2010–2014

The return to office of Viktor Orbán and his conservative Fidesz party, in coalition with the peripheral KDNP that had not been in power since 1994, following the April 2010 election, precipitated a sharp lurch to the right in Hungarian politics.[100] The re-nationalisation of energy companies became a central part of the process of re-asserting state control over key utility providers as the government began to push for a 'not-for-profit' energy retail sector. One of its first successes was the acquisition by the state of a 21.2% stake in MOL from Russia's Surgutneftegas in May 2011, which typified a more robust policy toward Russian energy interests. "Today Hungary has reacquired a 21.2% stake in MOL from Russia [...]. It was more than a purchase, it was a tough struggle. From a national strategic point of view, we have managed to place one of the most important corporations into safe hands," Orbán said of the acquisition.[101]

By 2012, the re-nationalisation of E.On's gas businesses in Hungary had become another objective for the Fidesz government. In March 2013 state power company MVM announced the buy-out of E.On's storage and wholesale concerns for €870 million. The deal also gave the buyer the option to buy E.On's stake in Panrusgas. in turn allowing the state to negotiate directly through the intermediary with Gazprom.[102] In February 2015, MVM eventually exercised that option,

---

[99] Government of the Russian Federation, *Prime Minister Vladimir Putin Met Informally with Former Hungarian Prime Minister Ferenc Gyurcsány at a Moscow Ukrainian Restaurant*, 24 November 2009 <http://archive.government.ru/eng/docs/8337/index.html> [accessed 11 July 2015].

[100] *The Economist* described the Fidesz government as "constructing a top-down, over-centralised state that fuses elements of welfare socialism with nationalist rhetoric," 'Viktor Goes to London', *The Economist*, 8 October 2013 <http://www.economist.com/blogs/easternapproaches/2013/10/hungary-and-britain> [accessed 13 July 2015].

[101] 'Hungary Bought Back Surgut's Stake in MOL -PM Orban', *Reuters*, 24 May 2011 <http://www.reuters.com/article/2011/05/24/mol-surgut-idUSTST00206120110524> [accessed 14 July 2015].

[102] MVM, *Az MVM Aláírta Az E.ON Magyarországi Gázipari Érdekeltségeinek Megvásárlásáról Szóló Szerződést*, 28 March 2015 <http://www.mvm.hu/hu/hirek/SitePages/newsDetails.aspx?NewsID=371> [accessed 14 July 2015].

allowing the government to deal directly with its main external supplier and manage contract terms at a political level.[103] With an election to contest in 2014 and the Russia LTC through Panrusgas due to expire in 2015, Hungary's Minister for National Development in the Fidesz government, Tamás Fellegi, said in a reply to question from the opposition in 2011 that Gazprom was against re- negotiating the contract before its expiry but that the Hungarian side would prefer to start talks in 2012. The Minister was also reported to have noted that contract talks would need to consider private stakeholder interests, but that an IGA should be signed additionally on the terms of supply at a state level. "The Russian side's categorical stand is that they do not want to negotiate on questions of price, and they are only prepared to put on the agenda talks on the extension of the contract which runs out at the end of 2014 in the year it expires," Fellegi said.[104]

However, during 2012 and 2013 the issue of gas supply contracts was inextricably linked to the two major and competing pipeline projects, South Stream and Nabucco. In opposition, Orbán and Fidesz had been strong opponents of prioritising South Stream over Nabucco after the 2009 crisis, in contrast to government policy under Gyurcsány.[105] However, in practice, support for the South Stream pipeline intensified during the 2010–2014 period and Hungary's shareholder in the Nabucco project, FGSZ, withheld management fees before the project was eventually scrapped in 2013 after it failed to secure any gas supply from its key targets.[106] Owing to politics, Iranian gas was off the table, no prospect of volumes from Iraqi Kurdistan could be determined and without a Trans-Caspian Pipeline Turkmeni gas could not reach Turkey, leaving only Azerbaijan as a potential

103 MVM, *Az MVM Csoport Tulajdonába Került a Panrusgáz 50%-A*, 13 February 2015 <http://www.mvm.hu/hu/hirek/SitePages/newsDetails.aspx?NewsID=541> [accessed 14 July 2015].

104 'Hungary Seeks to Renegotiate Russian Gas Contract from 2012', *MTI - EcoNews*, 1 February 2011.

105 In a statement during July 2009 the party's soon to be appointed Minister for Foreign Affairs, Zsolt Németh, spoke of the abundance of Caspian gas supplies in Azerbaijan and Turkmenistan that needed to be exploited and delivered to Europe through Nabucco, instead of pushing ahead with South Stream. Fidesz, *FÜGGESSZÉK FEL A DÉLI ÁRAMLAT MUNKÁLATAINAK ELŐKÉSZÍTÉSÉT*, 13 July 2009 <http://www.fidesz.hu/hirek/2009-07-13/fuggesszek-fel-a-deli-aramlat-munkalatainak-el337kesziteset/> [accessed 14 July 2015].

106 The company first opted to freeze its quarterly contributions in 2012 seeing its shareholding drop from 16.7% to 14.4%. The project's other shareholders: OMV, RWE, BOTAŞ, Bulgarian Energy Holdings and Transgaz subsequently saw their interest rise to 17.6%. 'Hungarian Natural Gas TSO FGSZ's Nabucco Shareholding Falls as Payments Withheld', 25 September 2012 <http://www.icis.com/resources/news/2012/09/25/9598541/hungarian-natural-gas-tso-fgsz-s-nabucco-shareholding-falls-as-payments-withheld/> [accessed 14 July 2015].

supplier, with the consortium behind development of the second phase of the off-shore Shah Deniz field launching a competition to pick a project from a crowded field to transmit the first 10 bcm/y of Caspian gas to Europe from 2019.

Nabucco's initial design had factored in capacity of 31 bcm/y, and with both EU support and the addition of RWE to the consortium in 2008, progress on the project had looked assured, despite a raft of rival schemes starting up.[107] However, Orbán had warned in April 2012 that the Nabucco project was "in trouble" and that the Hungarian shareholder planned to leave.[108] Despite reducing the pipeline to a truncated 'Nabucco West' version that would begin only at the Bulgarian/Turkish border with a capacity of just 10 bcm/y compared to the original 31 bcm/y, a lack of firm supply contracts had in effect left Nabucco's shareholders without gas to channel and a strategy in trouble. The decision of the Shah Deniz consortium in August 2013 to supply the available 10 bcm/y to the Trans-Adriatic Pipeline (TAP) running through Greece and the Balkans put an end to Nabucco officially.[109] Within weeks the project website had been shut down and key staff released from the Vienna headquarters.

No Hungarian company was on the list of purchasers of gas from the Shah Deniz 2 field that the TAP project would transmit, but E.On (1.6 bcm/y) and GDF Suez (1.6 bcm/y) did sign 25-year export agreements starting in 2019.[110] With a direct link to the 'fourth corridor' initiative impossible without Nabucco, Budapest signalled strongly in favour of South Stream. Market rumour in summer 2012 that Gazprom would re-route the pipeline through Croatia to avoid slow administrative progress in Budapest appeared to help force a final investment decision from the

---

[107] Other pipeline concepts that emerged over this period included White Stream, ITGI, and the eventual winner of the Shah Deniz competition, the Trans-Adriatic Pipeline, in addition to the AGRI LNG scheme that proposed to link Georgia and Romania across the Black Sea.

[108] Guy Chazan, 'MOL to Drop Share in Nabucco Pipeline', *Financial Times*, 26 April 2012 <http://www.ft.com/intl/cms/s/0/bb333a08-8fbb-11e1-beaa-00144feab49a.html#axzz3fs7iG7bb> [accessed 14 July 2015].

[109] OMV, *Ad Hoc Meldung: Entscheidung Über Nabucco West*, 26 June 2013 <http://www.omv.com/portal/generic-list/display?lang=de&contentId=12557536930446l> [accessed 14 July 2015].

[110] BP, *Shah Deniz Major Sales Agreements with European Gas Purchasers Concluded*, 19 September 2013 <http://www.bp.com/en/global/corporate/press/press-releases/shah-deniz-major-sales-agreements-with-european-gas-purchasers-c.html> [accessed 10 July 2015]. The full list of buyers for 10 bcm include Axpo Trading, Bulgargaz, DEPA, Enel, E.On Global Commodities, Gas Natural Aprovisionamientos SDG, GDF Suez, Hera Trading and Shell. In total, 1 bcm was reserved for buyers in Greece and Bulgaria.

Hungarian shareholder MVM on a 229 km line, skirting the south of the country and costing €600 million, in October that year.[111]

Hungary had already began work on an interconnector with Slovakia in 2012 after bringing on-stream cross-border interconnections with both Romania and Croatia in 2010 and 2011, respectively, as part of post-2009 efforts to ensure circulation of existing gas supplies around the region. However, by 2014, Orbán had clearly signalled willingness to increase cooperation with Russia on energy issues broadly. In November 2013 Gazprom said it had completed talks with Panrusgas and another of its subsidiaries that in turn owned a stake in the intermediary Centrex on contract re-negotiations that would see price revisions incorporated.[112] A controversial €10 billion loan agreement with Moscow to pay for a Russia-contracted expansion of the Paks nuclear power station on the Danube was announced in January 2014, just weeks before the annexation of Ukraine's Crimea.[113]

With the April 2014 national election giving Fidesz an even greater mandate to govern alongside the KDNP again, the new Russia-focused policy direction gained momentum. Gazprom chief executive Alexei Miller visited Budapest in September 2014. ostensibly to discuss the development of South Stream.[114] On 26 September FGSZ announced that reverse-flow deliveries to Ukraine, which had started after Russian supplies to its neighbour had been stopped yet again, would cease "indefinitely" owing to "the demand for incoming delivery" over the Beregdaróc delivery point.[115] Gazprom had booked a further 700 MMcm of Hungarian

---

111 Interfax, *Hungary Takes FID on Gazprom's South Stream*, 1 November 2012.

112 Interfax, *Gazprom Revises Gas Contracts with Hungarian Cos*, 14 November 2013.

113 'UPDATE 2-Russia to Increase Hungary's Nuclear Power', *Reuters*, 14 January 2014 <http://www.reuters.com/article/2014/01/14/russia-hungary-idUSL6N0KO28L20140114> [accessed 14 July 2015].

114 Gazprom, *Проектировщик Венгерского Участка «Южного Потока» В Направлении Баумгартена Будет Выбран До Конца Октября*, 22 September 2014 <http://www.gazprom.ru/press/news/2014/september/article201737/> [accessed 8 July 2015].

115 FGSZ, *AZ FGSZ ZRT. ÁTMENETILEG SZÜNETELTETI A FÖLDGÁZSZÁLLÍTÁST UKRAJNA IRÁNYÁBA*, 25 September 2014 <https://fgsz.hu/content/az-fgsz-zrt-atmenetileg-szunetelteti-foldgazszallitast-ukrajna-iranyaba> [accessed 6 July 2015], Ukraine's Naftogaz said in a counter- statement following the announcement of a cessation in deliveries: "FGSZ was not available to provide any additional information about the reasons and the duration of the interruption to either Ukrtransgaz or Naftogaz. According to Naftogaz information, the Western European gas suppliers have not received any plausible explanation of the current situation from FGSZ either." Naftogaz Ukrainy, *Після Зустрічі З Газпромом Угорщина Зупиняє Потік Газу В Україну*, 25 September 2014 <http://www.naftogaz.com/www/3/nakweb.nsf/0/68C29121CE52AE2EC2257D5E00784649?OpenDocument&year=2014&month=09&nt=%D0%9D%D0%BE%D0%B2%D0%B8%D0%BD%D0%B8&> [accessed 6 July 2015].

storage capacity, MVM announced in early October, as the prospect of renewed disruption to transit through Ukraine heightened.[116] In November 2014, a law aiming to bypass EU obstacles to South Stream by allowing any gas company to push forward with developing a pipeline project once approval from the national regulator had been received was forced through, paving the way for construction to start.[117]

However, during a state visit to Turkey alongside Gazprom's Miller in December 2014, Putin announced South Stream would be scrapped. Despite progress on Hungary, Bulgaria was still seeking EU approval before allowing work to begin. With no breakthrough on whether Gazprom would allow third party access under EU rules for the onshore segment of the pipeline, South Stream would instead be replaced with the so-called Turk Stream design that would ship the same 63 bcm/y under the Black Sea to the Turkish–Greek border, from where European importers would need to collect the gas.[118] Hungary's reaction was to seek new options for increased gas supply, according to Minister of Foreign Affairs and Trade, Péter Szijjártó. During a trip to Moscow later in December to meet with Russia's Minister for Energy, Alexander Novak, Szijjártó said attention would now turn to shoring up import opportunities through Greece and the Balkans to ensure offtake from Gazprom's replacement project.[119]

Putin's visit to Budapest in February 2015 would deal directly with the issue of the expiring LTC. Instead of a full re-negotiation, a stop-gap scenario was announced that would cover Hungarian imports for the next few years. Under the 'extension' mechanism, Hungary would ostensibly no longer be charged under take-or-pay rules but would instead have the option of importing the unused portion of the 225 bcm total contracted amount from the 1996 contract at a later date

---

116 MVM, *Újabb Jelentős Lépés Magyarország Földgáz-Ellátásbiztonságának Növelése Érdekében*, 10 October 2014 <http://www.mvm.hu/hu/hirek/SitePages/newsDetails.aspx?NewsID=496> [accessed 14 July 2015].

117 'Hungary Bypassing EU Concerns with South Stream Law', *Interfax Global Energy* <http://interfaxenergy.com//gasdaily/article/14116/hungary-bypassing-eu-concerns-with-south-stream-law> [accessed 14 July 2015].

118 'Putin Drops South Stream Gas Pipeline to EU, Courts Turkey', *Reuters*, 2 December 2014 <http://www.reuters.com/article/2014/12/02/us-russia-gas-gazprom-pipeline-idUSKCN0JF30A20141202> [accessed 10 July 2015]. The contracts for construction work and development of the offshore pipeline would not be cancelled until July 2015.

119 Minister of Foreign Affairs and Foreign Economic Relations, *Szijjártó Péter Az Orosz Energiaügyi Miniszterrel Tárgyalt Moszkvában*, 22 December 2014 <http://www.kormany.hu/hu/kulgazdasagi-es-kulugyminiszterium/hirek/szijjarto-peter-az-orosz-energiaugyi-miniszterrel-targyalt-moszkvaban> [accessed 14 July 2015].

while paying for it directly upon receipt of the gas. Putin also suggested part of the deal could see Gazprom expanding its use of Hungarian storage facilities.[120] The leaders claimed at the summit that only technical issues needed to be arranged,[121] with Hungary avoiding €3 billion in take-or-pay fees by striking the deal on postponed delivery at a price of $260 per mcm.[122]

Orbán said in an interview with Russian daily *Kommersant*:

> The current restructuring […] organizes Hungary's gas supply for about four or five years. Well, I think we decided that not to sign a new long-term contract, because no one knows what will happen to international prices. Today there is a nervous and volatile market and you have to wait until it calms down, be it a year or two, and then we'll see whether you can negotiate a long-term agreement on what basis.[123]

A week following Putin's visit, Orbán outlined the need to bring new gas to Hungary in order to secure supply after 2020 during the visit of Turkey's Prime Minister Ahmet Davutoğlu to Budapest. "Hungary has been cornered" by the collapse of the South Stream and Nabucco pipelines and by the failure of Croatia and Romania to provide options for delivering gas back along the lines constructed by Hungary, Orbán said.[124] Budapest was keeping its options open.

In April 2015, the European Commission outlined its Statement of Objections against Gazprom for alleged abuse of its dominance in the gas supply markets of Central and Eastern Europe.[125] Hungary was one of the markets being probed under the investigation launched in 2012, with Gazprom denying the charges.[126]

---

120 Interfax, *Gazprom to Increase Flexibility in New Gas Contract with Hungary (Part 3)*, 18 February 2015. Sources suggest Hungary would be able to draw upon 22 bcm of unused gas.

121 Hungarian Government, *Megerősítettük Az Együttműködést Oroszországgal*, 17 February 2015 <http://www.kormany.hu/hu/a-miniszterelnok/hirek/vlagyimir-putyint-fogadta-orban-viktor> [accessed 6 July 2015].

122 Reuters, *UPDATE 1-Hungary Can Use Gas from Russian Contract over next 4-5 Years - PM*, 18 February 2015.

123 Hungarian Government, *Orbán Viktor Interjúja a Kommerszant Című Orosz Napilapnak*, 20 February 2015 <http://www.kormany.hu/hu/a-miniszterelnok/beszedek-publikaciok-interjuk/a-minszki-megallapodas-alapjan-rendezni-lehet-az-eu-es-oroszorszag-kapcsolatait> [accessed 6 July 2015].

124 Hungarian Government, *Az a Cél, Hogy Érkezzen Gáz Törökországból Magyarországra*, 24 February 2015 <http://www.kormany.hu/hu/a-miniszterelnok/hirek/elo-kozvetites-orban-viktor-es-ahmet-davutoglu-sajtotajekoztatoja> [accessed 6 July 2015].

125 European Commission, 'Antitrust: Commission Sends Statement of Objections to Gazprom for Alleged Abuse of Dominance on Central and Eastern European Gas Supply Markets', 2015 <http://europa.eu/rapid/press-release_IP-15-4828_en.htm> [accessed 12 May 2015].

126 Gazprom, 'Statement of OAO "Gazprom" with Respect to the Adoption of "statement of Objections" by the European Commission under the Antitrust Investigation', 2015 <http://www.gazprom.com/press/news/2015/april/article224444/> [accessed 12 May 2015].

Gazprom representative Sergei Kupriyanov said in reaction to the case being launched in 2012:

> The EC's actions at the beginning of the formal investigation in relation to Gazprom, as was the case with the raids performed at firms affiliated with the company last year, can be regarded as pressure by the EC on Gazprom with the goal of influencing prices and the results of business negotiations, which obviously contradicts market principle...Right now a number of relatively weak economies in the European Union are continuing to demand that Gazprom make unilateral concessions on gas prices. That can only be regarded as support by the EC to subsidize Eastern European countries at Gazprom's expense. This is an attempt to solve the EU's economic problems at Russia's expense.[127]

7.5 Hungary policy review

Hungary's gas policy under the country's first democratically elected government was immediately to prioritise a new physical connection westwards to Austria through the HAG pipeline while clarifying the terms of the Yamburg and Orenburg Soviet-era deals. One explanation for the prioritisation of gas supply security through diversification efforts in Hungary comes in the overall predominance of the fuel in the total primary energy supply. The share of gas in Hungary's energy mix stood at 35.4% in 2013, the highest in the region and more than double that of coal-consuming Poland and the Czech Republic, despite declining consumption overall.[128] Historically, Hungary has also used gas for power generation. Analyst András Deák has argued that, with almost 90% of households connected to the grid, gas supply has become a "major social issue," with public policy factors overshadowing security. "Hungarian energy must first of all be cheap and only subsequently secure," Deak has argued.[129] The HAG pipeline provided not only more security, but also secured sufficient supply.

Rather than seeking to raise import volumes drastically under a single take-or-pay LTC to meet rising national demand in the 1990s, shorter term contracts with Gaz de France and Ruhrgas served to open up new delivery options via HAG. From 1998, approximately 1 bcm in total could run into Hungary through three separate contracts expiring in 2012 at the latest, in addition to the 9 bcm/y contracted to flow under LTC with Panrusgas. With domestic production factored in, this provided plentiful alternatives to Russian supply. Additionally, Hungary has

---

[127] Interfax, *EC's Actions Regarding Gazprom Are Pressure Aimed at Influencing Gas Prices - Company (Part 2)*, 9 November 2012.

[128] IEA figures.

[129] Deák, 'Diversification in Hungarian Manner', p. 45.

never been a major transit country for Russian gas, despite Soviet-era suggestions of a pipeline route to Italy, meaning it could not count on transit fees and could not guarantee that Russian gas would continue to flow through its territory. Subsequently, the policies pursued in the first decade of independence ensured alternative quantities that effectively covered annual demand, and, owing to falling demand after 2005, did not require further auxiliary agreements later on.

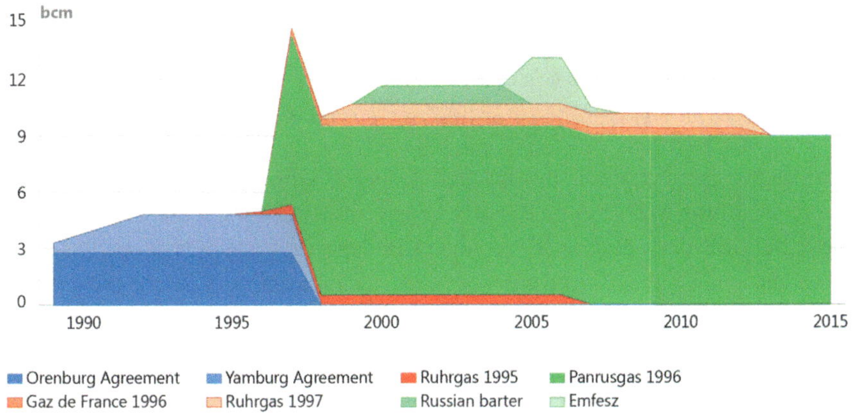

Graph 33: Hungary's actual contracted gas (1989–2014)[130]

However, MOL was forced to sell its gas imports at regulated prices that did not secure sufficient revenue to support investment in infrastructure and production projects. This posed inevitable and serious risks to supply around the millennium, owing to the lack of investment, most aptly illustrated with the explosion at the aging Pusztaszőllős storage facility in August 2000 that cost over HUF 5 billion to repair[131] and saw up to 70 MMcm/d flared over the first few weeks.[132]

The process of privatisation also inevitably raised fears over Russian investment through Gazprom. Policy on the issue changed markedly between the early governments of Antall and Horn, and Viktor Orbán's first term in office between 1998 and 2002, during which the Fidesz leader took a stand on the BorsodChem

130 Graph uses all data as reported in this chapter far regarding contracts signed under an aggregated scenario based on figures collated in Table 9.

131 MOL, *A Pusztaszőlősi Gázkitörés Sikeres Elfojtása*, 23 November 2000.

132 MOL, *A Pusztaszőlősi Gázkitörés Várható Költségei*, 12 September 2000.

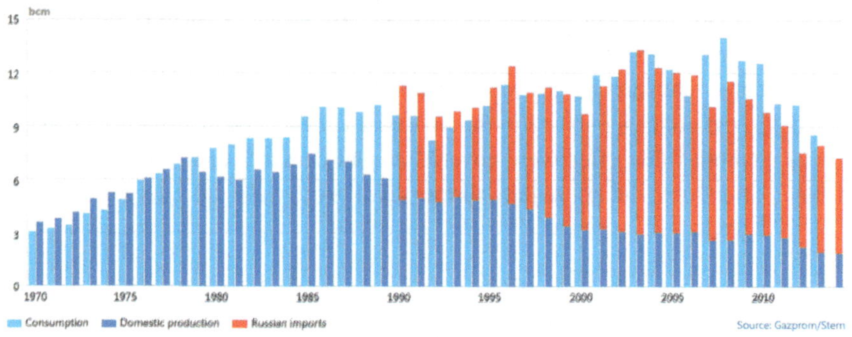

Graph 34: Hungary consumption, production and imports (1970–2013)[133]

deal, as discussed earlier in this chapter. A similar swing can be identified during the return of the MZSP socialist party to government between 2002 and 2010 as close political ties between Moscow and Budapest's leaders developed and accords on South Stream's construction were signed even as Nabucco moved forward. Meanwhile, a number of new intermediary companies became active in Hungary, with Emfesz, Centrex and RusUkrEnergo joining Panrusgas in holding some stake in the national gas supply market. In a May 2009 paper, the Jamestown Foundation was sharply critical of the RosGas acquisition of Emfesz:

> The immediate suspicion is that RosGas AG is yet another in a long line of shadowy intermediary companies created by Firtash and Gazprom. However, in the case of RosGas this may mask a possible attempt by Gazprom to cut gas supplies to Firtash's Emfesz, as a precursor to a company takeover - vastly increasing its share of the Hungarian domestic gas distribution network.[134]

Nevertheless, Hungary is the only case study to have avoided direct arbitration cases with Gazprom and was able to extract policy concessions in the final renegotiation of 2015 (when the Panrusgas deal expired) that other companies were not able to. Through Gazprom subsidiaries and intermediaries the country was also able to secure a discount on import prices in 2013, as shown in Table 1 and Table 2. This saw Hungary's wholesale import price for Russian gas drop below the European average in 2014 for the first time in the time period under consideration.

---

133 Data from Gazprom, IEA and BP, *Statistical Review of World Energy 2015* <http://www.bp.com/en/global/corporate/about-bp/energy-economics/statistical-review-of-world-energy.html> [accessed 12 May 2015].

134 Roman Kupchinsky, 'Gazprom's Murky Games in Hungary', *The Jamestown Foundation* <http://www.jamestown.org/programs/edm/single/?tx_ttnews%5Btt_news%5D=34948&cHash=eece94b606> [accessed 13 July 2015].

Panrusgas and other import intermediaries paid approximately $338 per mcm against an annual EU average of $346 per mcm that year.

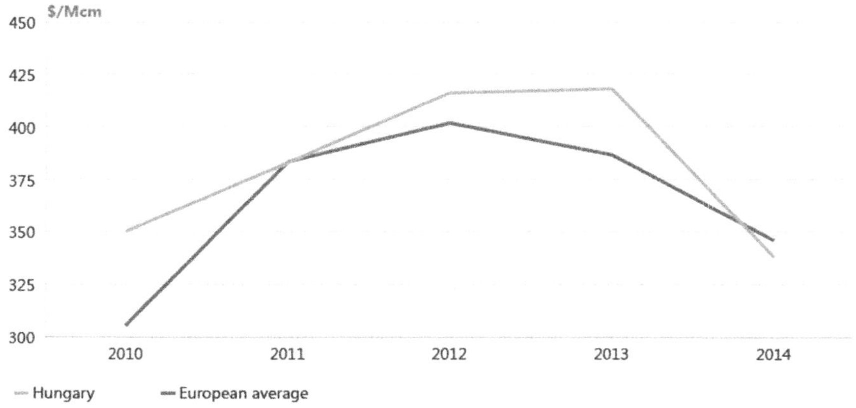

Graph 35: Price of Hungary wholesale Russian gas imports (2010–2014)[135]

Conversely, despite the relative separation between state and utility during the period under review, because of the intermediary companies and privatisation of MOL's gas business, by the end of the 1989–2014 period the government had secured direct control over its LTC negotiations, with the deal to extend the expiring contract signed off on during a summit between Orbán and Russian President Vladimir Putin in Budapest during early 2015. Concern over the costs paid to foreign utilities to regain control over storage management rights, distribution networks and import arrangements were dismissed by the Ministry for National Development, which said in a statement that "several independent assessments showed the economic justifiability of the purchase in the long run.

The state ownership guarantees the secure gas supply of Hungary and it serves as a solid foundation for future economic growth."[136]

By the end of the period under review, Hungary was without the burden of an LTC contract with take-or-pay terms, and it also held significant interconnection capacity to establish deliveries of gas to meet demand in the event of crisis. New

135 As cited earlier, data from: Alexey Novikov, *TABLE: How Prices Fell for Russian Gas* (Interfax, 6 March 2015).

136 'NFM: Független Vagyonértékelések Alapján Vette Meg Az állam Az E.on-T | Mandiner', <http://mandiner.hu/cikk/20140814_nfm_fuggetlen_vagyonertekelesek_alapjan_vette_meg_az_allam_az_e_on_t> [accessed 2 July 2016]

Table 9: Gas supply contracts effective in Hungary (1989–2014)[137]

	Importer		Contract signed	Start of deliveries	End of deliveries	Total volume	Yearly volume	Re-negotiations
Orenburg	Hungary/Mineralimpex/Panrusgas	Russia	21 June 1974	1978	31 December 1997	56 bcm	2.8 bcm/y	1994
Yamburg	Hungary/Mineralimpex/Panrusgas	Russia	30 December 1985	1989	1998	15 bcm	500 mcm in 1989, 1 bcm in 1990, 1.5 bcm in 1991 then 2 bcm in 1992 onwards	Extended in 1991 until 2008
Ruhrgas	MOL	Ruhrgas	10 May 1995	October 1996	October 2006	5 bcm	150 mcm/y in 1996 then 500 mcm/y	
Panrusgas 1996	Panrusgas	Gazprom Export	7 November 1996	1 October 1996	31 December 2015	225 bcm	9 bcm/y	2014
Gaz de France 1996	MOL	Gaz de France	16 December 1996	1 January 1997	2012	6 bcm	400 MMcm/y	
Ruhrgas 1997	MOL	Ruhrgas	October 1997	1998	2012	5.4 bcm	100 MMcm/y in 1998 up to 760 mcm from 2006 onwards	
Barter	MOL	Gazprom	March 1999	1999	2004	5 bcm	1 bcm/y	
Emfesz	Emfesz	RUE	23 December 2004	2005	April 2009	10.35 bcm	Up to 3 bcm/y (2.5 bcm in 2005 and 2006 and 350 mcm in 2009)	

Russia	Diversification	Barter/Third-party

[137] Data compiled by author from Gazprom, E.On, FGSZ, IEA information and various news and analyst reports. All information included herein is cited and referenced in the preceding case study chapter.

infrastructure projects – whether they be the Eastring project presented in the preceding Slovakia chapter, or a revived version of either Nabucco or South Stream – will almost certainly transit the country, and its storage inventory was courted by Gazprom as a forward delivery point for the Balkans.

7.6 Hungary policy conclusions

How does the information outlined in the preceding chapter and the data collected on Hungary's gas sector between 1989 and 2014 align with the hypotheses presented in Chapter 2? To re-cap, hypothesis 1, or H1, posits that left-wing governments, under the communist legacy MZSP party in Hungary, for example, tend to prioritise cooperation with the already-dominant supplier of natural gas, such as Gazprom, in this case. Conversely, right-wing governments, such as the first Antall MDF-led coalition government and the following Fidesz administrations from 1998 to 2002, and again from 2010, seek security-boosting diversification measures through LTCs with non-dominant suppliers.

A further hypothesis, H2, suggests that left-wing governments are motivated to maintain downward pressure on retail prices as part of their electoral agenda, and therefore prioritise lower wholesale import costs as a strategic priority in LTC talks by seeking ways in which to achieve the absolute best price in the short-term through a utility. Right-wing governments, meanwhile, pursue greater supply security and are willing to pay a premium for gas from sources that re-enforces that security through diversification of supply options. Finally, H3 argues that in the LTC re-negotiation process utilities under state-ownership behave in different ways from privately-owned utilities.

Of the case studies under review here, Hungary's party system has been the most stable, with a clear cleavage between the MSZP on the left and the MDF and the Fidesz party on the right. In the case of Hungary, there is clear evidence that the right-wing government in the early phase of transition sought to build new physical and contractual links westwards. Under the MDF-led coalition of Prime Minister Antall, plans were put in place to build the HAG pipeline to Austria and MOL signed an agreement with Ruhrgas that would see the two companies seek to procure gas jointly from non-Russian sources. However, the fruits of these initiatives were signed off on during the succeeding Horn left-wing government of the MSZP. Under Horn's four-year term in office, the HAG pipeline was brought onstream and diversification-granting contracts were signed with Ruhrgas and Gaz

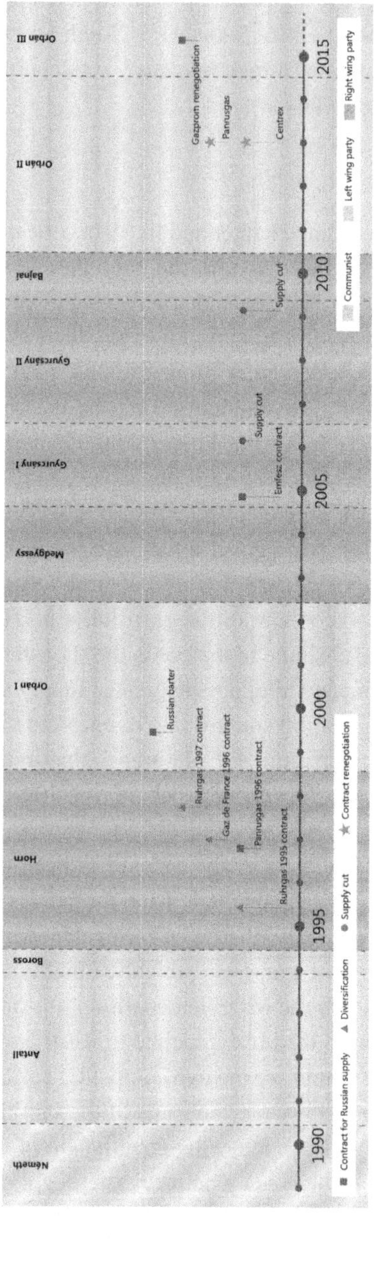

Figure 19: Hungary political timeline with gas LTC milestones (1989–2014)

de France. However, under the MSZP/SZDSZ coalition, Panrusgas was also registered as an intermediary that would handle the 20-year LTC to supply Hungary with Gazprom gas, indicating the proclivity of left-wing governments for making policy concessions to Russian energy supply interests assumed under H1, because intermediaries provide no added value to the gas they transited but rather served to increase the supplier's share of ownership in the chain of delivery. A barter deal was also agreed shortly before the left-wing government was replaced in 1998 that would see Hungarian goods used as payment for gas under further contract with Russian suppliers.

Under Orbán's first conservative Fidesz-led government from 1998, Hungary took a markedly more sceptical position on Russian investment, with a long- running dispute emerging over ownership of key Hungarian petrochemicals companies such as BorsodChem, which eventually served to rule out any further Russian investment in the later privatisation of MOL. With LTC arrangements few and far between after the flurry of activity in the mid-1990s, as shown in Figure 19, the 2000s instead provide evidence for party behaviour based on support for new infrastructure developments, such as those that favoured new alternative supplies of gas from the Caspian or Middle East against those that prioritised new Russian import routes like South Stream. The Medgyessy and Gyurcsány governments had close ties to Moscow, with repeated bilateral summits during the eight years of MSZP governance.

Despite MSZP backing for South Stream, which would support the thesis that left-wing parties prioritise cooperation with the dominant supplier, once again the policy of one government continued into the next, with Orbán appearing to move forward with state support for South Stream after his re-election in 2010, at odds with his own government's earlier policy of robust opposition to Russian investment in BorsodChem. The decision to prioritise new Russian import routes after Nabucco's prospects were diminished by the lack of supply guarantees can be explained by the Hungarian government's desire to position itself as a potential future transit state, being at present the only case study country not to channel a major Russian export pipeline.

Assessing the applicability of H2, it is clear that the right-wing Fidesz government under Orbán from 2010 opted to prioritise cheaper utility rates as part of its populist-conservative electoral agenda. Orbán said in 2013:

> We are going to mobilise against the large, foreign-owned energy service providers and the political powers behind them. However, we must once and for all bring an end to the era where energy providers can ride roughshod over people. We must therefore pass a utility service law that eliminates profits from the supply of utilities to Hungarian households.[138]

Though this does not clearly support H2 in its assumption that a right-wing government would be less concerned with retail prices under its electoral agenda, it can also be interpreted as part of an overarching state strategy to regain the levers of control necessary for consolidating energy security itself. The absence of any new LTC arrangements or re-negotiations during the earlier MZSP governments dating back to 2002 makes further conclusions on H2 unfeasible.

On H3 and the tendency for state-owned companies to behave in different ways during re-negotiations with the dominant supplier between 2010 and 2014, the lack of arbitration cases between Hungarian importers and Gazprom as supplier over the course of inquiry means there is no evidence on which to draw. Instead, I am led to assume that Gazprom's part-ownership of Panrusgas and Centrex, another utility active on the Hungarian market, means that the supplier was incentivised to provide ample re-negotiations, as shown in the 2013-announced contractual amendments to terms.

In sum, H1 is anecdotally illustrated through the prioritisation of energy security–boosting measures under the first MDF Antall government, the later battle against Russian investment in the 'strategic' petrochemicals sector by the first Orbán government, and by the rapid consolidation of energy utilities during Orbán's second and third terms, which allowed it negotiate directly with Russia over gas supply as the Panrusgas contract expired in 2014. Additionally, little evidence is found to support the assertion made in H2, but further investigation of retail prices during different governments is made in the Conclusion. As an additional note, the Fidesz government's construction of "a top-down, over- centralised state that fuses elements of welfare socialism with nationalist rhetoric," as *The Economist* put it in 2013, subverts the system of party cleavages as defined earlier.[139] There is very limited evidence to test H3, indicating only the lack of arbitration on account of Gazprom's ownership of the intermediary companies that buy its gas.

---

138 Budapest Times, 'Hungary Declares War', 2013 <http://budapesttimes.hu/2013/09/20/hun%C2%ADgary-declares-war/> [accessed 3 July 2016].

139 Adam LeBor, 'Viktor Goes to London', *The Economist*, 8 October 2013 <http://www.economist.com/blogs/easternapproaches/2013/10/hungary-and-britain> [accessed 13 July 2015].

8 Evaluation

Having presented the evidence collected on each of the four case study markets under review, it is now necessary to aggregate and discuss the findings while returning once again to the hypotheses, theory, methodology and accompanying central arguments as outlined in the first three chapters. Specifically, this chapter will discuss the relationship between price and dependence, to what extent differing government policy has determined import priority under the process- tracing mechanism shown in Figure 3, and how different utilities have behaved in arbitration. It will also return to the 'energy weapon' thesis, and how the evidence collected in earlier chapters supports the case for a broader understanding of how contracts and dependence structures can form part of an inconspicuous 'weapon' open to exploitation by dominant suppliers.

This chapter also draws brief conclusions on the theoretical elements of domestic structure as posited in Chapter 2 and its position as an explanatory variable for the international system –, specifically here, the trade in energy products. The literature tells us that the domestic structure is an important variable in explaining the way states' foreign policies function, while Katzenstein's contention that foreign economic policies are attempts to harmonise the domestic structure with the international political economy chimes with our understanding here of a state's policy preferences as derived from its internal characteristics but restricted by the status quo in the international system.[1] In this setting, the largely land-locked small-states of Central Europe are construed as born import-reliant consumers in 1989, needing to project their status quo–amending interests on an already structured supply circuitry between Russia and its major clients in Western Europe. To paint this picture, however, a short collation of the evidence collected in the preceding four chapters is necessary in order to understand to what extent there has

---

[1] As discussed earlier, see: Peter J. Katzenstein, 'Introduction: Domestic and International Forces and Strategies of Foreign Economic Policy', *International Organization*, 31 (1977), 587–606, p. 587.

J. Posaner, *Held Captive by Gas*, Energiepolitik und Klimaschutz. Energy Policy and Climate Protection, https://doi.org/10.1007/978-3-658-27518-1_8

been any difference in output between right and left–wing governments over the course of this inquiry.

8.1 Aggregating contract evidence

Of the 47 supply arrangements valid for importers in Poland, the Czech Republic, Slovakia and Hungary between 1989 and 2014 listed in Tables 6, 7, 8 and 9, after excluding the 8 agreements arranged before 1989 under the Yamburg and Orenbug Soviet-era labour-for-gas supply deals, 39 separate contracts remain. In the case of Poland there are 16, Slovakia 9, the Czech Republic 8 and Hungary just 6. When contracts signed by fully privatised importers are also excluded, the locally-focused Naftogaz/Hrubieszów contract that was implemented temporarily to gasify a local Polish community near the Ukrainian border is set aside, and further secondary contracts signed by intermediary importers with no state ownership on the demand side (Vemex/Emfesz) are discarded. This leaves 33 separate gas supply contracts signed by utilities that were either partially or fully state-owned between 1990 and 2014. Furthermore, there are 5 instances of arbitration/compensation cases being lodged by importers in the case study countries during the 2009 to 2014 period of inquiry.

Table 10: Aggregated gas supply arrangements/arbitration results[2]

	Left-wing	Right-wing
Total supply arrangements signed after 1989	14 (10)	19 (16)
LTCs signed directly with Russia	3	2 (1)
LTCs signed through Russian intermediary/barter	2	4
LTCs signed with alternative supplier	9 (4)	13 (11)
Arbitration cases between 2009 and 2014	1	4

Statistics show that under right-wing governments 36% more gas contracts were signed overall than under left-wing governments, while right-wing governments also appear to have prioritised the signing of LTCs with alternative non-dominant suppliers, agreeing 44% more in the period under review than their left-wing counterparts. Meanwhile, three LTCs were agreed directly with Gazprom under left-wing governments, but right-wing governments oversaw four supply contracts

2 Brackets are included to denote the number of contracts signed after excluding those signed in the 'crisis' period shown in Table 11 later in this section.

arranged through intermediaries or as barter deals. It can also be shown that companies under right-wing governments were more likely to begin arbitration proceedings against Gazprom than left-wing governments, with only Slovakia's 2009 request for compensation being an example of an attempt by a left-wing government to settle a dispute through court.

Controlling for the time in office that each side of the electoral divide has had, it is clear that right-wing governments have been favoured by voters over their left-wing counterparts. In total, left-wing administrations in the four case studies constituted 420 months in office over the 25-year period of review, or 37% the total 1,140 combined months. Meanwhile, right-wing administrations were in office for 693 months and caretaker administrations in the Czech Republic held power for 27 months to complete the total. Data from Table 10 illustrates that under right-wing governments 58% of supply contracts were signed, near enough equal to the 61% of time they were in office. Right-wing governments also signed their approximate share of diversifying contracts while in office, at 59%. Though arbitration proceedings were predominantly lodged under right- wing governments, the data concerning the absolute quantity of contracts signed appears to suggest an even split between the behaviour of parties on each side of the electoral divide.

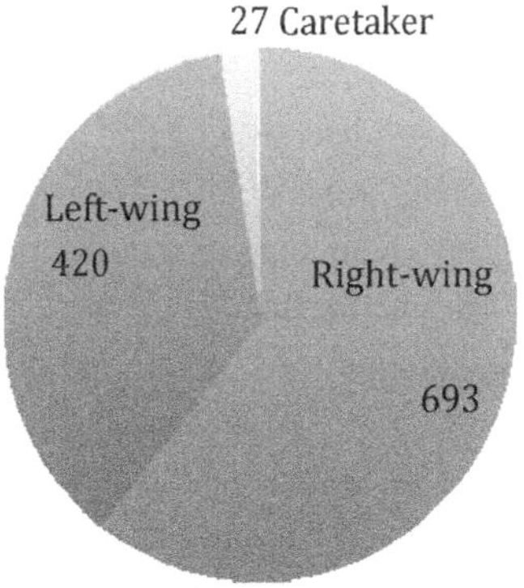

Graph 36: Share of right/left-wing in 25-year review period (months)[3]

[3] Based on a calculation of the months in office of each administration on the left-to-right spectrum between January 1990 and December 2014 in the case of Poland and Hungary and July 1992 to December 2014 in the case of the Czech Republic and Slovakia. This totals 1,140 months.

On timing, it is clear that new gas supply contracts were principally signed during two periods – that of the 'late transition' 1994–1999 era, and the crisis period between 2005–2009, which included the two transit disruptions via Ukraine that caused disruption to supply across CEE. Of the 39 post-Soviet contracts, 30 were signed in these two periods, as shown in Table 11. This helps support the argument that there have been two broad rationales underpinning the pursuit of new gas supply arrangements by governments and their importing agencies: firstly, to secure adequate supply to meet demand over what has traditionally been seen as the 'long-term' scenario of LTCs and demand-side management; and secondly, to cover shortfalls in supply caused by 'short-term' crises.[4] These crisis-era contingency contracts have typically been far shorter in tenure than the LTCs arranged with Gazprom and have been signed in multiple deals in combination, rather than in a single contract outlining a fixed volume under take-or-pay.

Table 11: Supply contracts agreed by time period

	pre-1990 (Soviet-era)	1990-1994 (Early transition)	1995-1999 (Late transition)	2000-2004 (Privatisations)	2005-2009 (Gas Wars)	2010-2014 (Arbitration)
Total	6	1	14	5	16	3
Poland	2	1	3	4	6	2
Czech Republic	2	-	4	-	4	-
Slovakia			2	-	6	1
Hungary	2	-	5	1	-	-

A clearer divide between right and left becomes apparent if we seek to control for the effect of 'crisis contracts' in governments' gas import policy formation and exclude those 'short-term' contingency deals agreed by any of the case study countries in the first 12 months after the Ukraine/Russia dispute in January 2009, instead focusing on deals signed under the assumption of 'normal' flows. Now, under the scenario replacing the contract numbers with the bracketed figures in Table 10, right-wing governments can be shown to have agreed 74% of the total alternative import arrangements, above their share expected based on time in office, and the only example of a right-wing government seeking a new import LTC directly with Gazprom is Slovakia's Mečiar government of the mid-1990s, which was itself accused of being affected by high levels of clientelism in its dealings with Russia.

4 Jonathan Stern, *Security of European Natural Gas Supplies: The Impact of Import Dependence and Liberalization* (The Royal Institute of International Affairs, July 2002*)*, p. 4.

The four landmark LTC agreements signed in the mid 1990s by each of the V4 case studies with the dominant supplier Gazprom to transform the Yamburg and Orenburg agreements formally into commercial contracts were all signed under left-wing parties with the single exception of Mečiar and his ĽS-HZDS party. In the case of Hungary, the 20-year LTC contract was signed by the socialist MSZP coalition under Horn, the ČSSD coalition under Zeman in the Czech Republic agreed the LTC with Russia after the earlier right-wing government had agreed the Norway import contract, and, in the case of the Yamal contract in Poland, the SLD government of Cimoszewicz closed the initial deal. In contrast, the main diversification-granting contracts were each arranged under right-wing governments: the Norway contract was signed under Klaus's ODS government in the Czech Republic and the similar 'big' and 'little' Norway contracts (plus the DONG supply contract) were signed by PGNiG under Poland's AWS-led Buzek government in the late 1990s, albeit cancelled before they came into force. Graph 37 shows the volume of gas envisaged for delivery in contracts signed each year, coded by the government in office at the time.

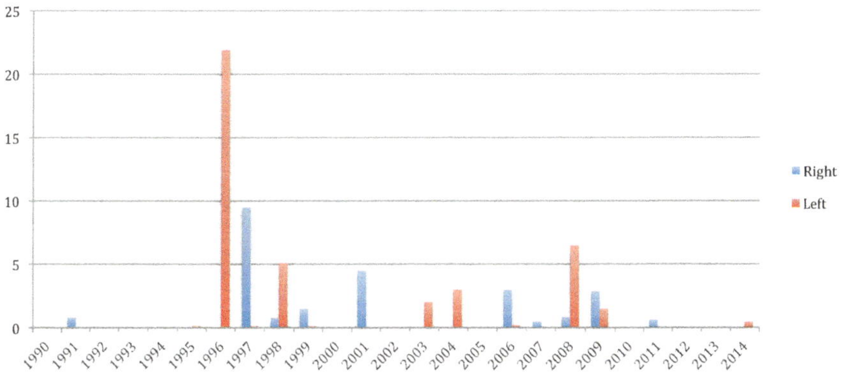

Graph 37: Total yearly contracted volume by right/left (bcm)[5]

8.2 Dependence as proxy for price

In reviewing the central argument it is also important to return to its key assumptions, most importantly: does level of dependence on the supplier to meet annual

[5] Including all contracts signed after 1989 in Tables 6–9.

demand determine the price of a country's gas imports and, if so, are more dependent states charged more? Graph 38 illustrates data from 2012, the middle year in the post-2009 period for which data is available and the point at which the oil-price rise from 2009 had fully followed through into Gazprom's LTC contract formula calculation. What is immediately clear from Graph 38 is that those importers that are the least dependent – such as the Netherlands, Switzerland and Denmark – paid the lowest rates for their gas imports, despite being situated further along the supply chain and therefore, it could be assumed, subject to greater transportation costs. Major consumers in Western Europe such as Germany and France paid more, but beneath the rate paid by the most dependent consumers, such as those in CEE. Each of the case studies paid beyond that year's European average price of $401.74, as shown earlier in Table 2.

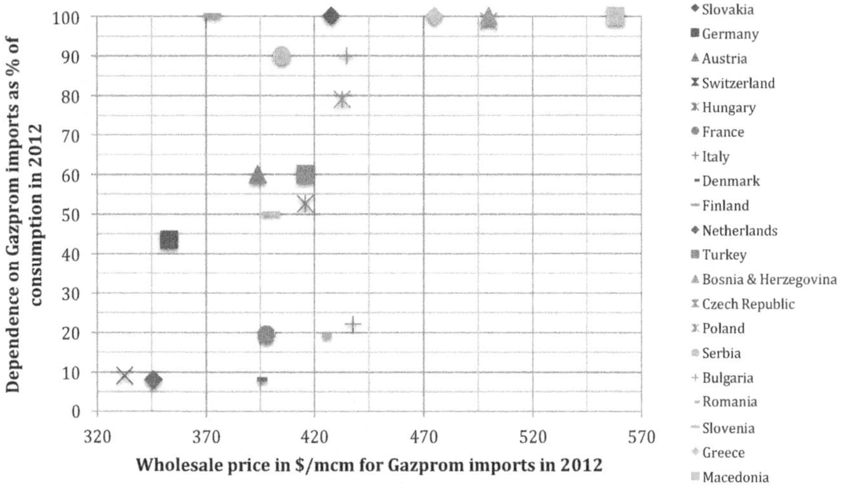

Graph 38: Dependence on Gazprom and wholesale price (2012)[6]

However, simply to interpret the level of reliance in a given year as illustrative of a dependence structure is to oversimplify the predicament in which the CEE importers placed on Graph 38 find themselves. Two further factors must be presented

6 Gazprom, BP data and prices from Alexey Novikov, *TABLE: How Prices Fell for Russian Gas* (Interfax, 6 March 2015).

as evidence of the cost of prolonged dependence: the absence of alternative supply routes and dependence on LTC gas supplies.

To deal with the first factor initially, the availability of import routes westwards has provided some of the case study countries (Hungary and the Czech Republic especially) with insulation from the threat of gas supply disruption, ensuring an open channel to the German market or Austria. Even if the importing country is already dependent on Russia as the dominant supplier, alternative supply corridors allow both 'short-term' relief from supply disruptions, such as that experienced in January 2009, and 'long-term' competition to LTC gas in the bargaining process between supplier and consumer during re-negotiations processes. Table 12 illustrates how many network entry points have been installed during different periods, with only those pipelines collated that can cater to 10% of annual consumption or more.

Owing to its position along the transit route for Soviet gas to be delivered into Germany, Czechoslovakia (later the Czech Republic) emerged as an independent state already connected to a western neighbour with which it could arrange large capacity contracts via the Waidhaus border interconnection point. Hungary's decision to push ahead with the HAG pipeline in the early 1990s also gave it access to alternative sources from Austria. Poland, meanwhile, nervous about its lack of transit pipelines and facing estimates of steeply rising demand, opted to commit to the Yamal pipeline in a bid to secure larger volumes of stable Russian supply under LTC. Slovakia's government's did nothing.

Table 12: Entry point with capacity of >10% annual demand by time period

	pre-1990 (Soviet-era)	1990-1994 (Early transition)	1995-1999 (Late transition)	2000-2004 (Privatisations)	2005-2009 (Gas Wars)	2010-2014 (Arbitration)	Total (2014)
Poland	2		1	-	-	(3)	6
Cz. Rep.	1 (1)	-	-	-	-	(1)	3
Slovakia	1	-	-	-	(1)	(2)	4
Hungary	1	-	(1)	-	-	(1)	3

Secondly, there is an important difference between states dependent on a supplier but with the choice either to fuel-switch away from gas or to reduce contracted volumes at short notice and those that are locked into take-or-pay LTCs that outstretch consumption and estimates of future demand, as was the case with Poland's PGNiG and the Yamal contract agreed in 1996. Graph 39 illustrates the case study countries envisaged annual LTC supply volumes from Gazprom with demand rates according to BP statistics and domestic production subtracted leaving either the oversupply or demand surplus visible per year.

What becomes clear is that the LTC agreements signed in the mid 1990s (and the additional 2008 contract signed to replace the earlier expiring deal in Slovakia) all settled at an excess volume by the time of their conclusion or, in the case of Poland's Yamal LTC, after a European Commission–brokered re-negotiation in 2010 gave the importing agency PGNiG an annual demand gap of 2 bcm with which to source alternative volumes. In the case of both Poland and Hungary these surplus volumes were the result of over-exaggerated forecasts for demand, coupled with the excessive length of the contract agreement signed in the mid 1990s.

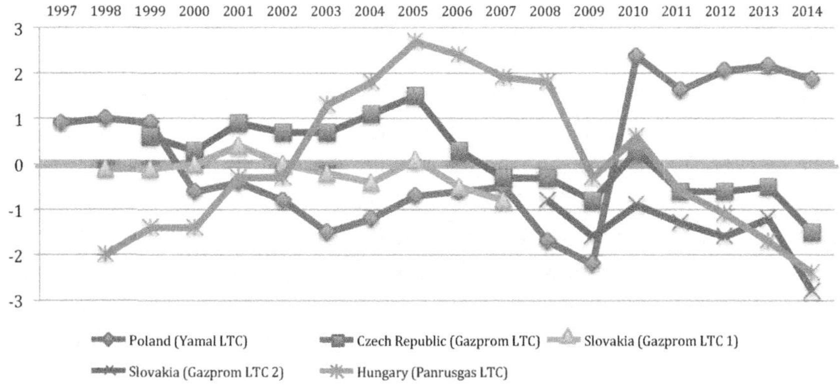

Graph 39: LTC volume in annual demand for case studies scenario[7]

However, over contracting LTC gas is not a phenomenon confined to the countries of Central Europe. In 2002, Stern concluded that "many of the major companies on the European continent have a surplus of long-term contract gas over and above their national requirements."[8] In fact, the major utilities that did overcontract, such as Eni, Gaz de France and Ruhrgas, were also the utilities that arranged the diversification-granting contracts to Hungary and Slovakia in the mid-2000s. It was these companies' ability to reach out to new markets in Central Europe that

7 Using contract data collected and presented in Tables 6-9. This uses approximate averaged-out yearly LTC rates from the main Russia contracts set against BP and IEA production and consumption data.

8 Jonathan Stern, *Security of European Natural Gas Supplies,* p. 8.

allowed them to circulate excess volumes and remove the obligation to pay for unwanted gas and/or receive fines under take-or-pay agreements embedded in LTC arrangements. The importers in CEE under review here had neither the access to alternative markets where demand was strong nor the diversified supply portfolios to manage. Instead, a combination of early transition period fears over supply stability, grossly exaggerated forecasts for demand growth, poor negotiating with the dominant supplier and a lack of infrastructure conspired to 'lock-in' the case study countries into what became burdensome LTCs.

It is thus not only the cost per mcm that should be interpreted as the price of dependence. Instead, a legacy cost-burden from the failure to open up alternative supply lines to conduit competing gas upholds dependence structures in case study markets like Slovakia and Poland. Where diversifying infrastructure had been put in place, it provided valuable competing alternatives to Russian gas, warranting less of a contractual dependence on the dominant supplier. Taken in tandem, these two auxiliary factors supporting a 'cost to dependence' thesis create the antecedent condition through which 1,000 businesses are forced to halt production and up to 1.5% of GDP is wiped from a state's annual output owing to a two-week cut to deliveries under a single contract through the only high-capacity import route.[9] There is a price to dependence, as shown, but is there also a price to the politics of gas supply policy formation?

8.3 Politics as a variable

Having identified and discussed the cost of a country's dependence on gas imports from a dominant supplier, it is also necessary further to illustrate the relationship between the state and gas import policy: in short, does a government decide why, when, with whom and for how long an LTC supply arrangement is signed? Examples of state intervention in the gas import sector have been given throughout the case study chapters, from summits yielding new supply contracts and intermediary companies during Mečiar's second term as Slovak Prime Minister to Hungary's Prime Minister Viktor Orbán seemingly acting as the lead negotiator on the extension of his country's Russian import arrangement in early 2015. Both Poland's

---

9 Alexander Duleba, *Poučenia Z Plynovej Krízy v Januári 2009 Analýza Príčin Vzniku, Pravdepodobnosti Opakovania a Návrhy Opatrení Na Zvýšenie Energetickej Bezpečnosti SR v Oblasti Dodávok Zemného Plynu'* (Slovak Foreign Policy Association, October 2009) <http://www.old.sfpa.sk/dokumenty/publikacie/281> [accessed 20 June 2015].

Jerzy Buzek and Václav Klaus were kindred spirit Prime Ministers of Poland and the Czech Republic, respectively, in their pursuit of diversification-boosting measures.

Table 13 illustrates the instances mentioned already in the case study chapters where direct state intervention in the terms and supply of gas is clear. The process-tracing mechanism presented in Figure 3 was also designed to provide a way of understanding the historical qualitative data presented in the case study chapters. This investigation is not a full discourse analysis, so a clear and scientific appraisal of each importing country's predominant motivation for importing gas cannot be ascertained for certain without delving through parliamentary minutes and ministerial speeches. However, in Table 13 we can make some attempt to encode the instances of state intervention. Importing country governments and Prime Ministers have been assumed in this analysis to have sought supply arrangements based on a policy driver derived from their electoral agenda. Right-wing governments tend to opt more for security, while left-wing governments have prioritised the provision of lower prices. Right-wing governments pursue diversification, left-wing governments closer political ties with the dominant supplier to achieve price discounts.

A number of the instances from each country illustrate a tendency for governments to act as the selector of import priority, as posited in Figure 3, and then to work through the state-owned utility to bargain out an LTC agreement (based on what the supplier is able to offer), often supported by an IGA between the heads of government. In total, 14 of the collated instances show governments acting on an issue pertaining to gas supply directly, with a further four related to infrastructure developments such as South Stream. As negotiations take place at the transnational level between state actors, the domestic structure is therefore argued to have a determinative influence on the international system and the foreign economic policies of the case study countries.

Putman's two-tier game helps us explain the disparity in some countries between what a government projects at home as its interests and what it pursues in the range of options open to it in the international system.[10] Gourevitch's proposal that the international system acts as an intervening variable helping to shape domestic

---

[10] Robert D. Putnam, 'Diplomacy and Domestic Politics: The Logic of Two-Level Games', *International Organization*, 42 (1988), 427–60.

Table 13: Instances of political influence on gas supply in CE (1989-2015)

Date	Country	Event	Government	Motivation
August 1993	PL	Yamal Pipeline IGA	Suchocka (centre-right)	Fears over the continued stable supply of Russian gas to Poland.
February 1994	PL	Yamal LTC trade ministers protocol	Pawlak II (centre-right)	Reduced demand forecast warranted downward volume negotiation.
September 1996	CZ	Norway LTC signed by Minister of Industry and Trade	Klaus II (right)	Reduce dependence on Russian gas supply.
April 1997	SK	Slovakia LTC 1 signed during Russia's Prime Minister's visit to Bratislava	Mečiar (right)	Ensure long-term Russian gas supply.
December 1998	CZ	Moscow visit by Deputy Prime Minister discuses barter supply contract.	Zeman (left)	Aimed at securing deal for Russian gas paid for in Czech goods through intermediary.
July 2001	PL	DONG contract signing	Buzek (right)	Ensure alternative non-Russian supply of gas.
September 2001	PL	'Big' Norway contract signing	Buzek (right)	Ensure alternative non-Russian supply of gas.
February 2003	PL	Deputy Prime Minister's Yamal LTC protocol	Miller (left)	Re-negotiate volume/terms of Yamal LTC to meet requirements.
February 2006	HU	Budapest summit discusses new storage developments and a gas pipeline project (South Stream)	Gyurcsány (left)	Aimed at securing Russian investment and gas transit.
January 2009	SK	Proposal to send 'swap' gas supplies from Ukraine to Slovakia	Fico (left)	Aimed at restoring some delivery of Russian gas during 2009 crisis.
February 2008	HU	South Stream IGA	Gyurcsány (left)	Aimed at securing Russian investment and gas transit.
January 2009	SK	Western supply contracts announced by Prime Minister	Fico (left)	Aimed at restoring some delivery of Russian gas during 2009 crisis.
January 2009	CZ	Joint EU/Czech government statement on gas crisis	Topolánek (right)	Statement under EU presidency "demands" gas supply return to normal.
April 2013	PL	PGNiG/cabinet dismissals over Yamal-2 Memorandum of Understanding	Tusk (centre-right)	Government sought to keep new Russian gas supply infrastructure investment at bay.
April 2014	PL	Energy Union editorial on joint gas purchasing	Tusk (centre-right)	Attempt to advocate joint purchasing of gas from Russia across EU to bring fairer prices.
October 2014	SK	Economy Minister travels to Moscow for talks on gas supply	Fico (left)	Attempt to secure stable Russian gas supplies.
September 2014	HU	Gazprom CEO meets with Prime Minister in Budapest	Orbán (right)	Aimed at securing favour from Gazprom on South Stream.
October 2014	SK	Western emergency supply contract announced by Prime Minister	Fico (left)	Contingency contract to replace temporarily disrupted Russian gas flow.
December 2014	HU	Foreign Minister travels to Moscow for talks on gas supply post-South Stream	Orbán (right)	Aimed at securing favour from Gazprom post-South Stream cancellation.
February 2015	HU	Panrusgas LTC extension	Orbán (right)	Ensured extension of Russian gas supply at summit in Budapest.

structures within the state comes back into relevance at this stage.[11] Import dependence and the contractual relationship on energy with the major external supplier in Gazprom has likely had a formative influence on how governments have been able to project themselves at home as security providers. The critical undermining of Slovakia's notional energy security following the 2009 crisis precipitated a change of government in 2010 as Fico's SMER-SD was unable to form a coalition. As Krasner has identified, "some catalytic external event seems necessary to move states to dramatic policy initiatives in line with state interests," rather than day-to-day political routine internally providing its own impetus for great policy reform.[12] The MSZP administration's ties with Russia and Gazprom over South Stream also played heavily at home in the domestic debate, as has been discussed in the Hungarian case study chapter.

Gourevitch's proposes four tests to ascertain a state's internal form in determining its foreign economic policy: (i) the position of the country in relation to the global economy, (ii) the beneficiaries of policy inside the domestic structure, (iii) who defines the policy alternative (the state apparatus or an external actor able to co-opt policy-making) and (iv) how the policy can be legitimised and how it is successful. Each test provides useful clarity and helps to avoid confusion over who has led on policymaking.[13] Dealing with each in turn, the case study countries, as small-powers, can be assumed to have often had a "perception of vulnerability," whether that be related to economic threats or otherwise, according to Katzenstein, who argues that this has served to strengthen a domestic front in such small states.[14]

The predominant beneficiaries of energy policy choices are considered to be consumers, except in the case of regimes captured by private interests and clientelism during the 1990s where alternative interests can be seen to have co- opted government policy-making. Meanwhile, the policy alternatives (where available) appear to have been forwarded by the right-wing governments observed to have proposed diversification-seeking projects, with little policy input from private interests coming into play in the case studies' development owing to their largely

---

11 Peter Gourevitch, 'The Second Image Reversed: The International Sources of Domestic Politics', *International Organization*, 32 (1978), 881-912, p. 911.

12 Stephen D. Krasner, 'State Power and the Structure of International Trade', *World Politics*, 28 (1976), 317-347, p. 341.

13 *ibid.*, p. 906f.

14 Peter Katzenstein, 'Small States and Small States Revisited', *New Political Economy*, 8 (2010), 9–30.

state-owned utility structures. However, where supplier intermediaries infiltrated markets in the late 1990s and earlier 2000s, there can be seen to be some private interests relevant to gas contract formation. Finally, it is assumed herein that policy is legitimised and made successful by the lowering of dependence on the external supplier, in turn providing relief from the cost of dependence.

8.4 Re-appraising the 'energy weapon'

An additional objective of this work has been to propose a broader understanding of the 'energy weapon' thesis, confined not simply to threats and disruption of supply but also including the contractual arrangements and market-based instruments such as 'gas dumping' and the use of leverage by the dominant supplier to keep out competitors, isolate consumers and restrict their access to alternative gas. In her compartmentalisation of the stages of control necessary for a state to wield an energy weapon, Stegen argues that consolidation of reserves, acquisition of transportation means and use of energy resources either to secure political objectives through punishment, threats or rewards constitutes an ability to use the weapon.[15] In the case of Russia, its government holds a clear dominion over each of these elements, making it a natural case study for assessing whether such a weapon exists in practice.

Counter claims argue that interdependence and reputational issues make any energy weapon that Russia (and Gazprom as the world's largest gas reserve holder) may theoretically wield blunt anyway. If it were to cut supplies, as it did in January 2006 and January 2009 with Ukraine, it would be forgoing market share, with no replacement buyer in sight. Therefore, the concept "barely exists, and arguably never did," according to Boersma.[16] However, evidence has pointed to the contrary, with Russia identified in a 2007 Swedish government report to have in at least 55 instances since 1991 deployed cuts, threats or pricing policy with "strategic underpinnings in almost every case,", with disruptions largely concentrated in the former Soviet Union countries.[17] Though strategically the

---

15 Karen Smith Stegen, 'Deconstructing the "Energy Weapon": Russia's Threat to Europe as Case Study', *Energy Policy*, Sustainability of biofuels, 39 (2011), 6505–13, p. 6506.

16 'The End of the Russian Energy Weapon (that Arguably Was Never There)', *The Brookings Institution* <http://www.brookings.edu/blogs/order-from-chaos/posts/2015/03/05-end-of-russian-energy-weapon-boersma> [accessed 2 July 2016].

17 Robert L. Larson, *Nord Stream, Sweden and Baltic Sea Security* (Swedish Defence Research Agency, 2007), p. 80.

argument against using such an instrument is persuasive, evidence points to some continued political usage of energy supply to force through objectives by Russian agencies after 2007. In the case study chapters, for example, Gazprom restricted flows to the countries in order, it was claimed at the time, to halt their utilities' onward sale of gas back into Ukraine through reverse-flow interconnections in 2014.[18] Additionally, Gazprom's position as a dominant supplier in a number of other markets grants it assumed leverage with alternative potential suppliers to its captive markets. In 2009, PGNiG chairman Michał Szubski said in an interview that companies had refused to trade directly with PGNiG without first seeking the permission of Gazprom

> Western energy firms refuse to go into business with us without Gazprom's blessing and there is nothing we can do about it. All of them are doing business with Gazprom on a much larger scale than they could with us and will not risk their negotiating position to sell Poland 1 bcm of gas.[19]

In contending that Russia's foreign energy policy has drawn on a limited toolkit over the decade leading up to 2010, Orttung and Overland provided a number of contentious topics over which disputes in the energy sector could arise, be they connected with price, volume of sales, asset ownership, transit pipelines or broader political goals. They also open up the toolbox with which the dominant supplier can seek to leverage its position, be it through the use of subsidies, pipeline shutdowns, pipeline explosions or the construction of alternative transportation infrastructure.[20] However, though each of these tools is persuasive, they do not assist in understanding the contractual element to the energy weapon as posited here.

Högselius takes us closer to a holistic understanding, urging readers not to neglect more nuanced measures the dominant supplier can take and the way in which hydrocarbon exports were used to divide the capitalist world during the Cold War era, in addition to West Germany's vulnerability to 'gas dumping,' which would have undermined its coal industry. Högselius also recognises that the energy

---

18 Although not officially confirmed by Gazprom, analysts consistently claimed that the timing of disruption and quantity of volumes cut indicated an attempt by Gazprom to halt reverse-flow deliveries to Ukraine. Russian state media also actively pursued the line that deliveries back into Ukraine were illegal while Gazprom CEO Alexey Miller described the reverse-flow deliveries as a "half-fraud mechanism." 'Gas Supplies from Poland, Hungary to Ukraine Contradict Contract with Gazprom - Miller', *Interfax*, 6 December 2014.

19 'Szubski: Poland Cannot Afford to Wage War on Gazprom', *Polish News Bulletin*, 23 December 2009.

20 Robert W. Orttung and Indra Overland, 'A Limited Toolbox: Explaining the Constraints on Russia's Foreign Energy Policy', *Journal of Eurasian Studies*, 2 (2011), 74–85, p. 79.

weapon only exists to the extent "that it is believed to exist," and that "perception rather than objective reality" is the more pressing force influencing states' import policies.[21] It is in reaction to this perceived threat that companies have taken very real mitigating measures, such as building out new pipelines and configuring gas storage capacity to be able to respond to disruption as and when it occurs.

In this analysis there have been examples of where a traditional energy weapon has been deployed, such as in the case of the 1997 comments by Russia's ambassador to Prague, Nikolai Ryabov, linking gas supply to the country's impending NATO membership as it negotiated new contracts with both Gazprom and Norwegian suppliers.[22] Additionally, this work posits a market-based approach to interpreting the 'energy weapon' that recognises Gazprom's sophisticated ability to operate in an increasingly globalised gas market behind the scenes and out of the headlines. In the case of Poland, under the terms of the 1996 Yamal LTC, PGNiG found itself under pressure to import take-or-pay volumes of gas either in excess of demand or at a quantity restrictive to the implementation of competition in the supply market as shown in Graph 39. Here, structural aspects of the gas trade dating back to the early Soviet-era contracts for exporting gas to western Europe in the 1960s provided instruments of leverage for the exporter, giving it a structural advantage. Högselius argues that, though often exaggerated, the energy weapon does exist and requires an understanding that "reaches beyond the much debated nightmare of politically motivated supply disruptions."[23] In essence, not only does dependence on external supply provide leverage to the supplier, but the very nature of the gas system, its composition of east-to-west pipeline flows and the concentration of small-import markets placed in between the dominant supplier and its major consumers in Western Europe put the countries under review here in the secondary transit space identified in Chapter 3 in peril. The argument here is that, by failing to adapt to modern trading practices and insisting on maintaining oil-indexation pricing and take-or-pay clauses, the gas supply circuitry has been rigged to favour the producer.

---

21 Per Högselius, *Red Gas: Russia and the Origins of European Energy Dependence* (New York: Palgrave, 2013), p. 221.

22 'Russia Hints at Reprisals If Czechs Join NATO', *Reuters News*, 16 March 1997 [accessed 16 June 2015]. "Agreements fundamental to the Czech Republic, such as gas deliveries and nuclear energy, create a basis for future problems that our countries would face," Ryabov is reported to have said.

23 Högselius, *Red Gas*, p. 7f.

A counter argument would be that Gazprom is only pursuing its logical aim as a profit-maximising vehicle in markets where it has enjoyed a monopoly since the early system-building endeavours of the Soviet era. However, the European Commission's announcement of its 2012 competition case against Gazprom enforces the suspicion of unfair practices and what the EC calls the supplier's potential abuse of its "dominant market position" in the European supply market. The Commission pointed to three practices in CEE that were of concern:

> The Commission is investigating three suspected anti-competitive practices in Central and Eastern Europe. First, Gazprom may have divided gas markets by hindering the free flow of gas across Member States. Second, Gazprom may have prevented the diversification of supply of gas. Finally, Gazprom may have imposed unfair prices on its customers by linking the price of gas to oil prices.[24]

These allegations – principally the causal effect the first two practices have on the third – indicate the effect dependence has on the case studies under review here. If there is a single narrative thread to the case study chapters beyond the testing of the hypotheses, it is that Gazprom's insistence on maintaining its norms of business under contract structure from the 1990s in the 2010s has in effect cost it market share in otherwise captive markets. It has been illustrated already that calls for energy security-boosting diversification measures in Prague, Budapest, Warsaw and Bratislava go back to the early stages of transition, but without the ambassador's comments in Prague in 1997, or without the cut to transit to Slovakia in 2009, or without the furore over the management of the Yamal pipeline project company EuRoPol Gaz, perhaps governments would not have been incentivised to pay the premium cost of opening up Polskie LNG, or the Norwegian corridor, or the numerous reverse-flow pipelines.

---

24 'European Commission, *Antitrust: Commission Opens Proceedings against Gazprom*, 4 September 2012 <http://europa.eu/rapid/press-release_IP-12-937_en.htm> [accessed 26 June 2015].

9 Conclusion

This analysis began with a proposal to investigate the persistent differential in wholesale gas import prices within a group of neighbouring countries, each reliant on deliveries from Russia to meet annual demand. It did so by setting forward a research puzzle in Chapter 1, that being: why do some states under comparable conditions pay more for their gas imports than others, and which factors determine how equitable the terms under which the gas is priced and supplied are? The analysis proposed to focus on domestic structure (political parties in government and their policy drivers as derived from electoral agenda across the right/left spectrum) as an intervening variable in determining how dependent states were on a single dominant supplier, using this as a proxy for price, while also setting forward three related hypotheses to be tested using evidence collected and presented in the case study chapters 4 through to 7.

The case studies used were four import-dependent Central European EU member states, previously Soviet satellites that had all been dependent on the former hegemon, Russia, as their single foreign source of gas upon independence in 1989, but having since taken diverging policy courses on gas supply and hence variously dependent during the final period of inquiry. The countries analysed were Poland, the Czech Republic, Slovakia and Hungary over the time period 1989 to 2014. This final, concluding chapter will seek to answer the research question and reflect on the three hypotheses as presented again below:

- H1: Left-wing governments tend to prioritise cooperation with already dominant suppliers of natural gas through LTCs, while right-wing governments seek security-boosting diversification measures (see Figure 1).
- H2: Left-wing governments are motivated to maintain downward pressure on retail prices for consumers, making lower wholesale costs a strategic priority. Right-wing governments seek greater supply security (see Figure 1).

J. Posaner, *Held Captive by Gas*, Energiepolitik und Klimaschutz. Energy Policy and Climate Protection, https://doi.org/10.1007/978-3-658-27518-1_9

- H3: In LTC re-negotiation processes, state-owned utilities under left-wing governments prioritise short-term price discounts over the structural change that right-wing governments and private utilities seek (see Figure 2).

9.1 Results

There is evidence to support the claim in H1 that right-wing governments favour energy security-boosting LTCs with non-dominant suppliers. In the case of Poland, the conservative Buzek government (1997-2001) was responsible for pushing forward a diversification-seeking agenda that included the signing of three new high-capacity supply contracts (two with Norway and one with Denmark) and the promotion of a new pipeline link called BalticPipe that would have allowed new volumes from the west to reach Poland. The later PiS and PO conservative governments from 2005, principally under Kaczyński and then Tusk, also promoted new supply arrangements, supporting and then executing the construction of an LNG terminal and an associated import contract.

In the Czech Republic, the right-wing ODS-led Klaus government pursued and signed an LTC agreement with Norwegian suppliers that allowed the country to downgrade its need for Russian gas in the 1990s. Although Hungary's leaders have often been observed to have hedged their bets on strategic gas infrastructure projects over the second half of the course of this inquiry, the policy of the early Antall government (1990-1993) to push ahead with the HAG pipeline project and the later insistence during each of Orbán's three periods in office (1998-2002, 2010-2014, 2014 onwards) either to challenge Russian investment in the national energy sector or to take back state control of the agencies that deal directly with Gazprom (and hence to allow direct state-level negotiations on supply terms) appear to concur with the assumption presented in H1.

The case of Slovakia provides an exception, where dependence was maintained, with Russia as the dominant supplier throughout the 1990s, despite the period being dominated by the conservative governments of Mečiar (1992-1994 and then 1994-1998). Alternative supply contracts were not signed until they became necessary as a response to the supply crisis of 2009, during which Slovak supply was catastrophically disrupted, as discussed in the relevant case study chapter. Though this exception runs contrary to the argument of this analysis, there remains a potential explanation of the anomaly in Slovakia's murky politics of the 1990s. Where governments in Poland, Hungary and the Czech Republic were by this stage seeking to build political, security and trade structures outside the structures of the former Soviet system, Slovakia under Mečiar has been observed to have continued a system of reliance on Russia through a network of illicit business arrangements and shadowy deals.[1]

Left-wing governments have been observed to have prioritised and preserved dependence on the dominant supplier over the period of enquiry. With the exception of Slovakia again, each of the three landmark LTC contracts signed by Czech, Hungarian and Polish importers in the mid-1990s to commercialise their import arrangements with Russia's Gazprom were agreed through a state-owned utility under a left-wing government (Zeman's ČSSD and Transgas in the case of the Czech Republic in 1998, Cimoszewicz's SLD and PGNiG in Poland in 1996 and MSZP's Horn through MOL in Hungary, also in 1996). Furthermore, each of these contracts were for long-term periods in excess of 10-years, locking Russian supply volumes in under take-or-pay and destination clause provisions until at least the 2010s: 25 years in the case of the PGNiG Yamal LTC up to 2022, 20 years in the case of Hungary's Panrusgas LTC through to 2015, and, following the contracts extension in 2006, up to 2035 for the Czech Republic.

This is illustrated through a number of key events in the case study chapters, be it through the apparent cancellation of Buzek's diversification-granting contracts under the successor SLD Miller administration in Poland (2001-2004) or the Hungarian government's close ties to Russian political leaders during the 2000s under the Medgyessy (2002-2006) and then Gyurcsány MSZP governments (2006-2009), which heralded an IGA on Gazprom's South Stream pipeline and the proliferation of opaque intermediary companies operating in the national gas import market, such as Emfesz, Rosgas and RosUkrEnergo. In the Czech Republic the process of privatisation may have taken the key importing agency out of state-ownership and placed it under the direction of Germany's RWE, but the period of left-wing ČSSD governance from 1998 to 2006 saw a barter contract signed with Russia and the inauguration of Vemex as a part–Gazprom owned intermediary importer into the country.

1 Bugajski concludes that during "the Mečiar period, pro-Russian officials and businessmen accumulated sizable assets through dubious privatization schemes in banking, energy, steel, telecommunications." Janusz Bugajski, *Cold Peace: Russia's New Imperialism* (Westport, Conn: Greenwood Publishing Group, 2004), p. 166.

Again, Slovakia provides contrary evidence concerning H2, with the gas supply crisis of 2009 leading to a policy of diversification visibly carried out by the left- wing SMER-SD administration of Fico (2006-2010 and 2012 onwards). However, during Fico's first term in office, the expiring LTC arrangement with Gazprom, reached under Mečiar in 1998, was replaced by utility SPP, under partial state- ownership at that time. However, throughout 2009 a number of diversification- granting alternative supply contracts were signed with SPP's own private managing shareholders, E.On Ruhrgas and GDF Suez, in addition to a rapid roll-out of reverse-flow capacity links with Austria and the Czech Republic. The policy anomaly in the case of Slovakia, where a left-wing government prioritises energy security–boosting measures that reduce the market share of the dominant supplier, is therefore explained by the impact of the crisis on the domestic political structure, forcing the governing left-wing administration to respond to its absolute dependence on Russian gas through rapid policy change in a time of crisis that left few alternative options open. Under a normal scenario, the SMER-SD government was observed to have continued the relationship with Russia's Gazprom in the 2008 LTC, only amending this outlook during a crisis.

In sum, significant evidence is found to support H1's claim that left-wing governments prioritise ties with the dominant supplier, therefore maintaining dependence structures and the associated cost to security. Conversely, right- wing governments opt for new supply arrangements that cut into the dominant supplier's market share and give it relief from reliance, despite the potentially higher cost of building new import routes and channelling gas from more distant sources. Though Slovakia provides partially conflicting evidence, its internal context under the Mečiar governments of the 1990s and the radical impact of the 2009 gas supply crisis on the national economy that year, as discussed in Chapter 6 and evaluated in Chapter 8, provide mitigating evidence to explain the divergence.

Moving on to H2, only anecdotal evidence is available in this analysis to support the claim that left-wing governments are motivated to maintain downward pressure on retail prices for consumers, while right-wing governments seek greater supply security and are therefore willing to pay a premium for alternative sources of gas. In the case of right-wing administrations, the Buzek government's (1997-2001) support for a proposal to build the BalticPipe project linking Scandinavia with Poland would have made the Norwegian and Danish gas supply contracts more expensive than the Russian gas it would have competed against, but the security premium of having an alternative option would have justified the cost. In 2003, PGNiG confirmed this in a statement saying that "gas purchased from Denmark would be much more expensive" than Russian gas.[2]

Additionally, the LNG cargoes contracted under the Qatargas arrangement in 2009 by the Tusk PO administration (2006-2010) were by 2013 understood to be expected to cost a third more than existing pipeline gas into the Polskie LNG terminal.[3] In the Czech Republic, Norwegian gas was potentially able to compete on price owing to existing infrastructure capability through Germany, but the ODS government under Klaus (1992-1998) evidently prioritised security benefits in the pursuit of a new supply line after the Russian ambassador's comments linking Prague's pursuit of NATO membership with gas supply, as discussed in Chapter 5. During Orbán II (2010-2014) and Orbán III (2014 onwards) the policy of renationalisation of energy companies was implemented with the express aim of ensuring a direct negotiating position with Russia's state-owned supplier Gazprom in order to seek to secure a better price, an example of a conservative government pursuing a policy ascribed here more often to socialist administrations, but generally conducive to the hands-on centralised structure pursued in Hungary during this period. Left-wing administrations under Miller in Poland (2001-2004) have been shown to have prioritised the pursuit of lower prices over security and diversification, perhaps hoping to achieve a political settlement with Gazprom that would achieve a discount and provide electorally lucrative utility bill cuts. Following the Miller government's cancellation of the Buzek administration's Norwegian gas contracts, a further 10-year extension to the Yamal contract was signed, tying PGNiG into longer-term dependence on the dominant supplier in exchange for apparent reductions in volumes. In Slovakia, the provision of low-cost utility prices to consumers was a major part of Fico's SMER-SD election campaign in 2006 and the chairman of the partially state-owned SPP said, after ensuring the country's second Gazprom LTC was signed in 2008, that it "secures reliable and

---

2 PGNiG, 'Komunikat PGNiG S.A. W Sprawie Artykułów We "Wprost" Opublikowanych 3.11.2003 R.' <http://www.pgnig.pl/aktualnosci/-/news-list/changeYear/2003?_newslistportlet_WAR_newslistportlet_urlTitle=komunikat-pgnig-s-a-w-sprawie-artykulow-we-wprost-opublikowanych-3-11-2003-r-&_newslistportlet_WAR_newslistportlet_newsGroupId=10184&_newslistportlet_WAR_newslistportlet_action=newsDetails&_newslistportlet_WAR_newslistportlet_currentPage=1> [accessed 2 June 2015].

3 'Poland's Energy Security Strategy Comes at High Cost', *Reuters*, 9 September 2013 <http://www.reuters.com/article/poland-energy-lng-idUSL6N0H22WR20130909> [accessed 7 July 2016].

at the same time competitive gas deliveries to Slovakia," though the level of state intervention in this contract negotiation is unclear.[4]

To wrap up the findings associated with H2, only anecdotal evidence serves to support the conclusion on the behaviour of left-wing governments and their prioritisation of cheaper wholesale import costs. However, right-wing governments can be repeatedly shown to have pursued security-boosting measures, whether these be new contracts with alternative suppliers or new pipeline projects that could open up new gateways for gas supply from Western Europe and beyond. Indeed, all the major diversification-granting LTC arrangements can be traced back to import policy under right-wing governments, with the exception of the flurry of LTCs signed by Slovakia following the 2009 supply crisis, as discussed. Though the absence of data restricts access to long-term wholesale gas price figures, the behaviour of left- wing governments in supporting dependency structures in regards to the dominant supplier can be observed as counter-productive, given that although the apparent aim is often to negotiate lower prices in the short-term, the inherent security cost to dependence-enforcing agreements to extend contract duration or maintain take-or-pay obligations leaves the country vulnerable in the long-term. An example can be given in the case of the Miller governments' decision to renegotiate the Yamal LTC in 2003 rather than further commit to Buzek's diversification plans, leaving PGNiG prone to prolonged dispute over contracting of Russian gas for the rest of the period under review.

Addressing H3 in reference to Table 1 and the data collected on re-negotiations and arbitration case processes in the 2009-2014 period, it is clear that there is some difference in behaviour between different utilities under various ownership structures, though the lack of a large enough dataset restricts the ability to draw firm conclusions applicable beyond the contextual confines of CEE. In the period of enquiry there were a number of arbitration cases including out-of-court settlements and judgments as illustrated by Figure 2. Specifically, Gazprom intermediaries active in Hungary (Panrusgas, Centrex in 2013) and the Czech Republic (Vemex in 2012) were granted price cuts in private negotiations, while the Polish state-owned importer (PGNiG in 2012, 2014) sued in the Stockholm arbitration court but settled before a ruling in the first case. Only the privatised Czech importer

[4] Interfax, Gazprom Extends Gas Supply Contract with Slovakia until 2028 (Part 2), 21 November, 2008.

(RWE Supply & Trading in 2010, 2011) persevered to judgements, achieving significant amendments, as shown in Chapter 5. State- owned importers agreed to short-term discount/volume deals.

In conclusion, H1 is found to have sufficient evidence to supports the claim that left-wing governments pursue persistent ties with the dominant supplier while right-wing governments instead place greater importance on diversification. Less evidence is found to support the presence of inherent policy drivers in each government's outlook as shown in H2, though anecdotal evidence points towards this trend. For example. there is certainly evidence to support the claim that some governments have been willing to pay a premium for new non-Russian sources of gas and/or corridors through which these supplies can arrive. Finally, analysis of H3 supports the conclusion that privately-owned importers are less incentivised to take short-term deals on price/volume that could prove electorally useful (utility price cuts, for example) and push instead for long-term structural change to unprofitable contracts through court cases that ultimately ease their dependence on LTC gas. The central research puzzle question will be addressed in the final segment of this conclusion.

9.2 Further research

There is significant room for further research on the topic of gas supply contracts and the interplay between politics and the trade in energy products more generally. Firstly, further discourse analysis of state-level dynamics in policy- making circles is necessary to determine how the selection and prioritisation of energy security policies is made within government. There has been some work on this already, but the subject remains theoretically undeveloped. Additionally, such an analysis could help the reader better understand the way in which some governments choose to focus on short-term price objectives rather than long- term security benefits.

Another interesting area for further scholarship is on the supply-side, and the role the Russian state plays in determining Gazprom policy output. The apparent politicisation of Russia's energy resources under President Vladimir Putin has served to heighten interest in the topic of oil and gas supply over recent years, in reference to themes such as the 'energy weapon' discussed herein. However, in focusing on domestic structure and the demand-side characteristics of the importing states, Gazprom's interests and policy in some of its most important captive market areas has been assumed to be static – that of a market share– maximising state-vehicle energy company with a high degree of penetration from political interests. Whether that has been the case during the entire 25-year review period is open to further analysis, as is the contention that Gazprom is, as some have claimed, a quasi-ministerial entity.

This analysis has looked at just four countries, but better use of data across Europe could provide an interesting angle for a review of contract terms continentally or throughout CEE. Staying with those assessed here, the V4 structure that has provided them with a discussion platform since 1991 could also be examined for signs of policy convergence or divergence over the first 25- years of its existence. Though often discussed as an irrelevant sub-institutional structure, the V4 has had some relevance in promoting gas market integration, and this subject has so far not been addressed in the literature.

9.3 Policy outcome

One morning in October 2014, off the coast of Klaipeda on Lithuania's Baltic coast, a hulking vessel approached its dock under the watch of a jubilant crowd. Named 'Independence,' the South Korean-built floating regasification, storage and unloading vessel, or FRSU for short, would open up the Baltic region's first non-Russian gas supply route, enabling deliveries of Norwegian gas to start in 2015 as LNG cargoes. The crowd gathered that morning were not only celebrating the technical achievement of replacing pipelines with an open door to the global LNG trade, but also the prospect of cheaper heating bills during the coming Baltic winters. In the eyes of some, Lithuania had become independent once more, almost twenty-five years after its re-establishment as an independent state in post-communist Central Europe. However, beyond the geopolitical benefit, there was also a practical business case. Months before the arrival of 'Independence FRSU' into national waters, as Gazprom's LTC with Lithuanian importer Lietuvo dujos neared expiry and arbitration cases mounted up between Vilnius and Moscow, details emerged of a discount in the price Gazprom was charging. With a new supplier on the scene, the dominant supplier would have to compete for price, Lithuanians crowed.

The general argument that diversification is better for price than single supplier dependence has been a theme throughout this work and it is not novel, dating back a century or more. However, in addressing the central research puzzle presented in Chapter 1 – why do some states under comparable conditions pay more for their gas imports than others, and which factors determine how equitable the terms under which the gas is priced and supplied are? – it is first necessary to understand that the absence of alternatives for many of the countries under review provides an added cost beyond the figure represented in dollar or euro signs next to an mcm abbreviation. Single supplier dependence has its own price – whether that be illustrated in Graph 38, or through the equivalent loss of up to 1.5% of GDP in the case of Slovakia during the two-week outage of gas supplies in January 2009, or the enforced offtake of gas under the terms of the Yamal LTC owing to the imposition of take-or-pay clauses negotiated far in excess and for far too long in advance during the 1990s.

To provide a broader answer to the first part of the question, this analysis has argued that domestic structures have helped determine dependence, with structural dependence largely maintained by left-wing governments in the 1990s, apart from the instances in the Czech Republic, partially in Hungary, and partly in Poland, where right-wing governments were able to seize the moment and build out new contractual and infrastructural routes westwards. The second part of the question is harder to answer, but in part the same reasons persist. Poor importer negotiating and a supply system in favour of the producer meant that the terms agreed in 1990s LTCs were the subject of a European Commission investigation in 2012. As much as a high price, a high import obligation under take-or-pay rules, with the ability to re-sell locally outlawed, put its own pressures on importers. This analysis has illustrated the role of domestic structure as an independent variable in the process of gas contract formation by looking at four import dependent countries. Lithuania may lie outside the remit of this analysis, but there again, state policy has had a formative influence on shifting dependence levels through a state utility. However, by the end of 2014 contracts were expiring and markets liberalising and with these developments, accelerated in the post-2009 era, import-dependent countries have become less and less beholden to single large suppliers.

In terms of clear policy proposals, two 'price'-reducing factors are predominant in this research: voters should elect right-wing or centre-right liberal governments and they in turn should sell off the national importer to a large diversified European utility with the portfolio to swap and trade gas around the continent. But could there be another way? In 2014, the final year of this period of analysis, Hungary paid \$338/mcm for Gazprom gas on average, almost \$8/mcm cheaper than the continental average rate that year. With the Orbán/Putin LTC-extending deal just weeks away, Hungary was continuing to bargain and balance the dominant supplier, as small-powers have at times learnt to do in politics and trade, learning that there can be benefits. The question that remains is: does this tactic work in the long-term or is it only an illusory kind of short-term energy security?

Bibliography

Various news reports were compiled and cross-referenced for statistics in order to generate the dataset used in Tables 6-9. For reasons of space these are not individually listed here; detailed citations can be found in each case study chapter. However, the news agencies and newspapers referenced in the compilation of this analysis form a broad selection and include: Reuters, Interfax, Bloomberg, Wprost, BBC Monitoring, Rzeczpospolita, Gazeta Wyborcza, Hospodářské noviny, CTK, SME, Polish Press Agency, MTI, Népszabadság, Financial Times, Világgazdaság and Izvestia.

ACER, 'European Gas Target Model Review and Update', 2015 <http://www.acer.europa.eu/Events/Presentation-of-ACER-Gas-Target-Model-/Documents/European%20Gas%20Target%20Model%20Review%20and%20Update.pdf> [accessed 17 June 2016].

Arbitration Institute of the Stockholm Chamber of Commerce, Arbitration between Rosukrenergo and Emfesz (V 183/2009), 2011 <http://www.xn-skiljedomsfreningen-06b.se/file/rosukrenergo-ag-vs-emfesz.pdf> [accessed 9 July 2015].

Arentsen, M. and R. Kunneke, *National Reforms in European Gas* (Gulf Professional Publishing, 2003).

Ash, Timothy Garton, 'Does Central Europe Exist?', *The New York Review of Books*, 9 October 1986 <http://www.nybooks.com/articles/archives/1986/oct/09/does-central-europe-exist/> [accessed 11 February 2015].

———, 'The Puzzle of Central Europe', *The New York Review of Books*, 18 March 1999 <http://www.nybooks. com/articles/archives/1999/mar/18/the-puzzle-of-central-europe/> [accessed 11 February 2015].

Asia Pacific Energy Research Centre, *A Quest for Energy Security in the 21st Century: Resources and Constraints*, 2007 <http://aperc.ieej.or.jp/file/2010/9/26/APERC_2007_A_Quest_for_Energy_Security.pdf> [accessed 30 July 2015].

Baev, Pavel K., 'From European to Eurasian Energy Security: Russia Needs and Energy Perestroika', *Journal of Eurasian Studies*, 3 (2012), 177–84.

Bennett, Colin J., 'What Is Policy Convergence and What Causes It?', *British Journal of Political Science*, 21 (1991), 215–33.

BP, *Statistical Review of World Energy 2015* <http://www.bp.com/en/global/corporate/about-bp/energy-economics/statistical-review-of-world-energy.html> [12 August 2015].

Bugajski, Janusz, *Cold Peace: Russia's New Imperialism* (Westport, Conn: Greenwood Publishing Group, 2004).

Busch, Per-Olof and Helge Jörgens, 'The International Sources of Policy Convergence: Explaining the Spread of Environmental Policy Innovations', *Journal of European Public Policy*, 12 (2005), 860–84

J. Posaner, *Held Captive by Gas*, Energiepolitik und Klimaschutz. Energy Policy and Climate Protection, https://doi.org/10.1007/978-3-658-27518-1

Buzan, Barry, Ole Wæver and Jaap de Wilde, *Security: A New Framework for Analysis* (Lynne Rienner Publishers, 1998).

Byrnes, Robert F. and Oscar Halecki, *East-Central Europe Under the Communists: Poland* (Atlantic Books, 1957).

Cherp, Aleh and Jessica Jewell, 'The Three Perspectives on Energy Security: Intellectual History, Disciplinary Roots and the Potential for Integration', *Current Opinion in Environmental Sustainability*, 3 (2011), 202–12.

Cofala, Janusz, 'Energy Reform in Central and Eastern Europe', *Energy Policy*, 22 (1994), 486–98.

Collier, David, 'Understanding Process Tracing', *PS: Political Science & Politics*, 44 (2011), 823–30.

Correlje, A., C. Van der Linde and T. Westerwoudt, *Natural Gas in the Netherlands. From Cooperation to Competition?* (Oranje-Nassau Groep, 2003) <http://inis.iaea.org/Search/search.aspx?orig_q=RN:34066235> [accessed 24 August 2015].

Creti, Anna, *The Economics of Natural Gas Storage: A European Perspective* (Springer Science & Business Media, 2009).

Creti, Anna and Bertrand Villeneuve, 'Longterm Contracts and Take-or-Pay Clauses in Natural Gas Markets', *Energy Studies Review*, 13 (2004), 75–94.

Crocker, Keith J. and Scott E. Masten, 'Mitigating Contractual Hazards: Unilateral Options and Contract Length', *The RAND Journal of Economics*, 19 (1988), 327– 43.

Czech Ministry of Foreign Affairs, 'CASPIAN REGION HAS SIGNIFICANT POTENTIAL WHICH MUST BE USED', 2012 <http://www.mzv.cz/file/946031/> [accessed 3 June 2016].

Czech Ministry of Industry and Trade, *Securing Delivery of Natural Gas to the Czech Republic*, 3 June 2008 <http://www.mpo.cz/zprava41367.html> [accessed 10 June 2016].

Dariusz Kałan and Jarosław Ćwiek-Karpowicz, eds., *North–South Gas Corridor. Geopolitical Breakthrough in Central Europe* (PISM, 2013).

Deák, András, 'Diversification in Hungarian Manner: The Gyurcsány Government's Energy Policy', *International Issues & Slovak Foreign Policy Affairs*, 15 (2006).

———, 'Hungary: Collecting the First Dividends of Interconnectivity?' in Dariusz Kałan and Jarosław Ćwiek-Karpowicz, eds., *North–South Gas Corridor. Geopolitical Breakthrough in Central Europe* (PISM, 2013), pp. 20–25.

Duleba, Alexander, *Poučenia Z Plynovej Krízy v Januári 2009 Analýza Príčin Vzniku, Pravdepodobnosti Opakovania a Návrhy Opatrení Na Zvýšenie Energetickej Bezpečnosti SR v Oblasti Dodávok Zemného Plynu'* (Slovak Foreign Policy Association, October 2009) <http://www.old.sfpa.sk/dokumenty/publikacie/281> [accessed 20 June 2015].

———, 'Slovakia's Relationship with Russia and Eastern Neighbours', in *EU-Russian Relations and the Eastern Partnership: Central-East European Member-State Interests and Positions*, ed. Gábor Fóti and Ludwig Zsuzsa, East European Studies; No. 1 (Hungarian Academy of Sciences. Institute for World Economics, 2012).

Edoli, Enrico, Stefano Fiorenzani, Samuele Ravelli and Tiziano Vargiolu, 'Modeling and Valuing Make-up Clauses in Gas Swing Contracts', *Energy Economics*, Quantitative Analysis of Energy Markets, 35 (2013), 58–73.

Euratom, 'Consolidated Version of the Treaty Establishing the European Atomic Energy Community' <http://eur-lex.europa.eu/legal-content/EN/TXT/?uri=CELEX:12012A/TXT> [accessed 17 June 2016].

European Commission, 'Antitrust: Commission Sends Statement of Objections to Gazprom - Factsheet' <http://europa.eu/rapid/press-release_MEMO-15-4829_en.htm> [accessed 7 April 2016].

———, 'COMMUNICATION FROM THE COMMISSION TO THE COUNCIL AND THE EUROPEAN PARLIAMENT Report on Progress in Creating the Internal Gas and Electricity Market', 2005 <http://ec.europa.eu/transparency/regdoc/rep/1/2005/EN/1-2005-568-EN-F1-1.Pdf> [accessed 12 June 2016].

———, *Country Report: Czech Republic*, 2014 <https://ec.europa.eu/energy/sites/ener/files/documents/2014_countryreports_czechrepublic.pdf> [accessed 24 May 2016].

———, *Glossary of Terms Used in EU Competition Policy Antitrust and Control of Concentrations*, 2002 <http://ec.europa.eu/translation/spanish/documents/glossary_competition_archived_en.pdf> [accessed 5 August 2015].

———, ed., 'In-Depth Study of European Energy Security: Commission Staff Working Document' (European Commission, 2014) <http://ec.europa.eu/energy/doc/20140528_energy_security_study.pdf> [14 April 2015].

———, 'Member State General Situation According the Significance of Impact', 2009 <http://europa.eu/rapid/press-release_MEMO-09-3_en.htm> [25 June 2015].

———, 'Prague Summit Declaration: "Southern Corridor"', 2009 <https://www.consilium.europa.eu/uedocs/cms_data/docs/pressdata/en/misc/107598.pdf> [accessed 15 June 2016].

———, *Quarterly Report on European Gas Markets (volumes 6 and 7)*, 2014 <https://ec.europa.eu/energy/sites/ener/files/documents/201410_q3-4_quaterly_report_gas_market.pdf> [accessed 28 August 2015].

———, *The January 2009 Gas Supply Disruption to the EU: An Assessment*, 2009 <http://ec.europa.eu/danmark/documents/alle_emner/energi/2009_ser2_autre_document_travail_service_part1_ver2.pdf> [accessed 29 June 2015].

European Commission (DG Energy), *Quarterly Report on European Gas Markets (fourth* <https://ec.europa.eu/energy/sites/ener/files/documents/quarterly_report_on_european_gas_markets_2014_q4.pdf> [accessed 28 July 2015].

European Community, Protocole d'accord relatif aux problèmes énergétiques intervenu entre les gouvernements des États membres des Communautés européennes, à l'occasion de la 94e session du Conseil spécial de ministres de la Communauté européenne du charbon et de l'acier tenue le 21 avril 1964 à Luxembourg, 1964 <http://eur-lex.europa.eu/legal-content/EN/TXT/?qid=1440423481217&uri=CELEX:41964A0430(01)> [accessed 24 August 2015].

European Council, '1999/280/EC: Council Decision of 22 April 1999 Regarding a Community Procedure for Information and Consultation on Crude Oil Supply Costs and the Consumer Prices of Petroleum Products', 1999 <http://eur-lex.europa.eu/legal-content/EN/TXT/?uri=CELEX%3A31999D0280> [accessed 17 June 2016].

———, 'Council Regulation (EC) No 736/96 of 22 April 1996 on Notifying the Commission of Investment Projects of Interest to the Community in the Petroleum, Natural Gas and Electricity Sectors', 1996 <http://eur-lex.europa.eu/legal-content/EN/TXT/?uri=celex%3A31996R0736> [accessed 17 June 2016].

———, '"Maastricht Treaty" on European Union', 1992 <http://europa.eu/eu-law/decision-making/treaties/pdf/treaty_on_european_union/treaty_on_european_union_en.pdf> [accessed 12 June 2016].

European Parliament, 'Directive 2003/55/EC of the European Parliament and of the Council of 26 June 2003 Concerning Common Rules for the Internal Market in Natural Gas and Repealing Directive 98/30/EC', 2003 <http://eur-lex.europa.eu/legal-content/EN/TXT/?uri=celex:32003L0055> [accessed 15 July 2015].

European Union, 'Directive 98/30/EC of the European Parliament and of the Council of 22 June 1998 Concerning Common Rules for the Internal Market in Natural Gas', 1998 <http://eur-lex.europa.eu/legal-content/EN/TXT/?uri=celex%3A31998L0030> [accessed 17 June 2016].

———, 'Directive 2003/55/EC of the European Parliament and of the Council of 26 June 2003 Concerning Common Rules for the Internal Market in Natural Gas and Repealing Directive 98/30/EC', 2003 <http://eur-lex.europa.eu/legal-content/GA/ALL/?uri=CELEX:32003L0055> [accessed 17 June 2016].

———, 'Regulation (EU) No 994/2010 of the European Parliament and of the Council of 20 October 2010 Concerning Measures to Safeguard Security of Gas Supply and Repealing Council Directive 2004/67/EC Text with EEA Relevance', 2010 <http://eur-lex.europa.eu/legal-content/EN/ALL/?uri=CELEX%3A32010R0994> [accessed 17 June 2016].

Eurostat Statistical Books, *Energy Balance Sheets: 2013 Data* (Eurostat, 2015) <http://ec.europa.eu/eurostat/documents/3217494/6898731/KS-EN-15-001-EN-N.pdf/e5851c73-9259-462e-befc-6d037dc8216a> [accessed 11 August 2015].

Eustream, *Gas Crisis in January 2009 – Review and Outlook - Presskit*, 27 January 2009.

Evera, Stephen Van, *Guide to Methods for Students of Political Science*, Reprint edition (Ithaca: Cornell University Press, 1997).

Filip Černoch and Tomáš Vlček, *The Energy Sector and Energy Policy of the Czech Republic* (Brno: Masaryk University, 2013).

Franza, Luca, *Long-Term Gas Import Contracts in Europe: The Evolution in Pricing Mechanisms* (Clingendael International Energy Programme, 2014) <http://www.clingendaelenergy.com/publications/publication/long-term-gas-import-contracts-in-europe> [20 September 2015].

Fukuyama, Francis, *The End of History and the Last Man*, Re-issue edition (London: Penguin, 1992).

Gazprom Export, *Annual Corporate Brochure 2010*, 2011.

———, *Blue Fuel: Gazprom Export Global Newsletter*, April 2013.

Ginsburg, George and Robert Melville Slusser, *A Calendar of Soviet Treaties: 1958- 1973* (BRILL, 1981).

Global Witness, *How a Fifth of Hungary's Gas Supply Came into the Hands of an Unknown Shell Company* (May 2009).

———, *It's a Gas: Funny Business in the Turkmen-Ukraine Gas Trade*, April 2006. Goldthau, Andreas, ed., *The Handbook of Global Energy Policy*, Handbooks of Global Policy Series (Chichester: Wiley-Blackwell, 2013).

———, *The Politics of Natural Gas Development in the European Union* (Harvard University's Belfer Center, October 2013) <http://belfercenter.ksg.harvard.edu/files/MO-CES-pub-GeoGasEU-102513.pdf> [accessed 12 May 2015].

Goldthau, Andreas and Jan Martin Witte, eds., *Global Energy Governance: The New Rules of the Game* (Berlin, Germany/Washington, D.C: Brookings Institution Press and Global Public Policy Institute, 2010).

Golonka, Jan and Frank J. Picha, *The Carpathians and Their Foreland: Geology and Hydrocarbon Resources, AAPG Memoir 84* (AAPG, 2006).

Gorska, Joanna Agnieszka, *Dealing with a Juggernaut: Analyzing Poland's Policy towards Russia; 1989 - 2009* (Lanham ua: Rowman & Littlefield, 2010).

Gourevitch, Peter, 'The Second Image Reversed: The International Sources of Domestic Politics', *International Organization*, 32 (1978), 881–912.

Grzymala-Busse, Anna, 'Coalition Formation and the Regime Divide in New Democracies: East Central Europe', *Comparative Politics*, 34 (2001), 85–104.

Gustafson, Thane, *Wheel of Fortune: The Battle for Oil and Power in Russia* (Cambridge, Mass: Belknap Press of Harvard University Press, 2012).

Halecki, Oscar, *Poland (East-Central Europe under the Communists).* (London: 1957).

Heather, Patrick and James Henderson, *Lessons from the February 2012 European Gas 'crisis'* <http://www.oxfordenergy.org/2012/04/lessons-from-the-february-2012-european-gas-%e2%80%9ccrisis%e2%80%9d/> [accessed 12 May 2015].

Henderson, James and Simon Pirani, eds., *The Russian Gas Matrix: How Markets Are Driving Change* (Oxford: Oxford Institute for Energy Studies, 2014).

Henderson, Karen and Neil Robinson, *Post-Communist Politics: An Introduction* (London: Prentice Hall, 1997), Reading Hall II / Political Science 320.9/42 HEN. Hintze, Otto, *The Historical Essays of Otto Hintze* (Oxford: Oxford University Press, 1975).

Hoberg, George, Jr., 'Technology, Political Structure and Social Regulation: A Cross- National Analysis', *Comparative Politics*, 18 (1986), 357–76.

Hodgson, Geoffrey M., 'What Is the Essence of Institutional Economics?', *Journal of Economic Issues*, 34 (2000), 317–29.

Högselius, Per, *Red Gas: Russia and the Origins of European Energy Dependence* (New York: Palgrave, 2013).

———, 'The European Natural Gas Industry and the Oil Crisis of 1973/74', 2013 <https://networks.h-net.org/system/files/contributed-files/henergy-p-hogselius-natural-gas-and-oil-crisis-1973.pdf> [accessed 16 December 2015].

Huntington, Samuel P., *The Clash of Civilizations and the Remaking of World Order* (New York: Simon & Schuster, 1996).

IEA, *Energy Policies of IEA Countries: Czech Republic 2010* (Paris: Organisation for Economic Co-operation and Development, 2010) <http://www.oecd-ilibrary.org/content/book/9789264094710-en> [accessed 17 January 2015].

———, *Energy Policies of IEA Countries: Hungary 1999*, Energy Policies of IEA Countries (Paris: OECD Publishing, 2000).

———, *Energy Policies of IEA Countries: Hungary 2003* (Paris: Organisation for Economic Co-operation and Development, 2003) <http://www.oecd-ilibrary.org/content/book/9789264014718-en> [accessed 7 July 2015].

———, *Energy Policies of IEA Countries: Hungary 2006*, Energy Policies of IEA Countries (Paris: OECD Publishing, 2007).

———, *Energy Policies of IEA Countries: Hungary 2011* (Paris: Organisation for Economic Co-operation and Development, 2011) <http://www.oecd-ilibrary.org/content/book/9789264098237-en> [accessed 17 January 2015].

———, *Energy Policies of IEA Countries: Poland 2011* (Paris: Organisation for Economic Co-operation and Development, 2011) <http://www.oecd-ilibrary.org/content/book/9789264098190-en> [accessed 17 January 2015].

———, *Energy Policies of IEA Countries: Slovak Republic 2012* (Paris: Organisation for Economic Co-operation and Development, 2012) <http://www.oecd-ilibrary.org/content/book/9789264173507-en> [accessed 17 January 2015].

———, *Energy Supply Security: The Emergency Response of IEA Countries - 2014 Edition* (IEA, 2014).

———, *Slovak Republic Energy Policy Review 2005*, 2006 <https://www.iea.org/publications/freepublications/publication/slovak.pdf> [accessed 26 June 2015].

International Gas Union, *Wholesale Gas Price Survey - 2015 Edition: A Global Review of Price Formation Mechanisms 2005 - 2014*, May 2015 <http://www.igu.org/sites/default/files/node-page-field_file/IGU%20Whole%20Sale%20Gas%20Price%20Survey%20Report%20%202015%20Edition.pdf> [accessed 27 July 2015].

Jacques de Jong, Jean-Michel Glachant, Manfred Hafner, Nicole Ahner and Simone Tagliapietra, 'A New EU Gas Security of Supply Architecture?', *European Energy Journal*, 2 (2012) <http://www.clingendaelenergy.com/inc/upload/files/A_new_EU_gas_SoS_architecture_2_1.pdf> [accessed 4 August 2015].

Jankowski, Dominik P. and Małgorzata Grzegrzółka, 'Toward an Effective Minilateralism: The Polish Experience in the Visegrad Group after 2004', *DGAP e.V.*, 2014 <https://dgap.org/en/think-tank/publications/dgapanalysis/toward-effective-minilateralism> [accessed 17 January 2015].

Jaspal, Rusi, Brigitte Nerlich and Szczepan Lemańcyzk, 'Fracking in the Polish Press: Geopolitics and National Identity', *Energy Policy*, 74 (2014), 253–61.

Jensen, Robert G., Theodore Shabad and Arthur W. Wright, *Soviet Natural Resources in the World Economy* (University of Chicago Press, 1983).

Jessica Jewell, *The IEA Model of Short-Term Energy Security (MOSES) Primary Energy Sources and Secondary Fuels* (IEA, 2011) <https://www.iea.org/publications/freepublications/publication/moses_paper.pdf> [accessed 22 July 2015].

Johnson, Lonnie, *Central Europe: Enemies, Neighbors, Friends*, 3rd ed (New York: Oxford University Press, 2011).

Kancelaria Prezesa Rady Ministrów, 'Lech Kaczyński Patronem Terminala LNG W Świnoujście', 2016 <https://www.premier.gov.pl/wydarzenia/aktualnosci/lech-kaczynski-patronem-terminala-lng-w-swinoujsciu.html> [accessed 23 June 2016].

Katzenstein, Peter J., 'International Relations and Domestic Structures: Foreign Economic Policies of Advanced Industrial States', *International Organization*, 30 (1976), 1–45.

———, 'Introduction: Domestic and International Forces and Strategies of Foreign Economic Policy', *International Organization*, 31 (1977), 587–606.

———, ed., *Mitteleuropa: Between Europe and Germany* (Providence, RI: Berghahn Books, 1997).

Keohane, Robert O., 'Lilliputians' Dilemmas: Small States in International Politics', *International Organization*, 23 (1969), 291–310.

Kissinger, Henry A., 'Domestic Structure and Foreign Policy', *Daedalus*, 95 (1966), 503–29.

Kitschelt, Herbert, 'Formation of Party Cleavages in Post-Communist Democracies Theoretical Propositions', *Party Politics*, 1 (1995), 447–72.

———, *Post-Communist Party Systems: Competition, Representation and Inter-Party Cooperation*, 1. publ. (Cambridge ua: Cambridge UnivPress, 1999).

Komlev, Sergei, 'European Gas Market State and Prospects: View from Gazprom Export' (presented at the Flame Conference, Amsterdam, 2015).

———, 'Pricing the "Invisible" Commodity' (Contracts Structuring and Pricing Directorate, Gazprom Export, 2013).

Konoplyanik, A. A., 'Evolution of Gas Pricing in Continental Europe: A View From Russia - Modernization of Indexation Formulas versus Gas-to-Gas Competition', *Oil, Gas & Energy Law Journal (OGEL)*, 9 (2011) <https://www.ogel.org/article.asp?key=3077> [accessed 24 August 2015].

Kovacevic, Aleksandar, 'The Impact of the Russia–Ukraine Gas Crisis in South Eastern Europe', *Oxford Institute for Energy Studies* <http://www.oxfordenergy.org/2009/03/the-impact-of-the-russia%e2%80%93ukraine-gas-crisis-in-south-eastern-europe/> [accessed 5 March 2015].

Krasner, Stephen D., 'State Power and the Structure of International Trade', *World Politics*, 28 (1976), 317–47.

Kruyt, B., D. P. van Vuuren, H. J. M. de Vries and H. Groenenberg, 'Indicators for energy security', *Energy Policy*, 37 (2009), 2166–88.

Kundera, Milan, 'The Tragedy of Central Europe', *The New York Review of Books*, 26 April 1984, p. 33.

Kupchinsky, Roman, *Gazprom's European Web* <http://www.jamestown.org/single/?tx_ttnews%5Btt_news%5D=34516&no_cache=1> [accessed 2 February 2015].

Larson, Rober L., *Nord Stream, Sweden and Baltic Sea Security* (Swedish Defence Research Agency, 2007).

Laruelle, Marlene, *Eurasianism and the European Far Right: Reshaping the Europe– Russia Relationship* (Lexington Books, 2015).

Lenschow, Andrea, Duncan Liefferink and Sietske Veenman, 'When the Birds Sing. A Framework for Analysing Domestic Factors behind Policy Convergence', *Journal of European Public Policy*, 12 (2005), 797–816.

'Lessons from Prague: How the Czech Republic Has Enhanced Its Energy Security | European Dialogue' <http://www.eurodialogue.eu/Lessons-from-Prague-How-the-Czech-Republic-Has-Enhanced-Its-Energy-Security-> [accessed 29 June 2016].

Lijphart, Arend, 'Comparative Politics and the Comparative Method', *The American Political Science Review*, 65 (1971), 682–93.

Lipson, Charles and Benjamin J. Cohen, *Theory and Structure in International Political Economy: An International Organization Reader* (MIT Press, 1999).

Long, David, Geoff Moore and Gay Wenban-Smith, *Gas Trading Manual: A Comprehensive Guide to the Gas Markets* (Elsevier, 2001).

Luttwak, Edward N., 'From Geopolitics to Geo-Economics: Logic of Conflict, Grammar of Commerce', *The National Interest*, 1990, 17–23.

Makholm, Jeff D., *The Political Economy of Pipelines: A Century of Comparative Institutional Development* (University of Chicago Press, 2012).
Mareček, Tomáš, 'Usual Questions, Unusual Answers' (presented at the Central European Energy Conference, Bratislava, Slovakia, 2014) <http://ceec.sk/wp-content/uploads/2014/12/Mare%C4%8Dek-OK.pdf> [accessed 25 August 2015].
Marušiak, Juraj, 'Slovakia's Eastern Policy – from the Trojan Horse of Russia to "Eastern Multivectoralism"' <http://www.academia.edu/6005353/Slovakia_s_Eastern_policy_from_the_Trojan_horse_of_Russia_to_Eastern_multivectoralism_> [accessed 26 June 2015].
Masten, Scott E. and Keith J. Crocker, 'Efficient Adaptation in Long-Term Contracts: Take-or-Pay Provisions for Natural Gas', *The American Economic Review*, 75 (1985), 1083–93.
Mearsheimer, John J., 'Back to the Future: Instability in Europe after the Cold War', *International Security*, 15 (1990), 5–56.
———, *The Tragedy of Great Power Politics*, The Norton Series in World Politics (New York, NY: Norton, 2001), Potsdamer Straße 1 A 505091.
Melling, Anthony J., *Natural Gas Pricing and Its Future: Europe as a Battleground* (Washington, D.C.: Carnegie Endowment for International Peace, 2010).
Mez, Lutz, 'Germany's Merger of Energy and Climate Change Policy', *Bulletin of the Atomic Scientists*, 68 (2012), 22–29.
———, 'The Transformation of the German Gas Supply Industry', in *National Reforms in European Gas*, ed. by Maarten J. Arentsen and Rolf W. Künneke, Elsevier Global Energy Policy and Economics Series (Oxford: Elsevier Science, 2003), pp. 213–43 <http://www.sciencedirect.com/science/article/pii/B9780080436876500122> [accessed 4 August 2015].
Mill, John Stuart, *A System of Logic, Ratiocinative and Inductive: Being a Connected View of the Principles of Evidence and the Methods of Scientific Investigation* (John W. Parker, 1843).
Milner, Helen V., *Interests, Institutions and Information: Domestic Politics and International Relations* (Princeton, N.J.: Princeton University Press, c1997), Reading Hall II / International Relations 327 MIL.
Milner, Helen V. and Benjamin Judkins, 'Partisanship, Trade Policy and Globalization: Is There a Left-Right Divide on Trade Policy?', *International Studies Quarterly*, 48 (2004), 95–119.
Milton Friedman, 'The Methodology of Positive Economics', in *Essays in Positive Economics* (University of Chicago Press, 1953), pp. 3–43.
Ministerstvo životního prostředí, *SUROVINOVÉ ZDROJE ČESKÉ REPUBLIKY NEROSTNÉ SUROVINY 2014 - Statistické údaje Do Roku 2013*, 2014 <http://www.geology.cz/extranet/publikace/online/surovinove-zdroje/SUROVINOVE-ZDROJE-CESKE-REPUBLIKY-2014.pdf> [accessed 22 May 2015].
Ministry of Economy of the Slovak Republic, 'Energy Policy of the Slovak Republic', 2014 <http://www.economy.gov.sk/energy-policy-of-the-slovak-republic_october-2014-qci/145533s> [accessed 2 June 2015].
———, 'Government Responses to the Impact of the Financial Crisis on Energy Industries and Energy Security of the Slovak Republic', 2009 <http://www.unece.org/fileadmin/DAM/energy/se/pp/EnComm18_Nov09/18Nov/12_Jurasek.pdf> [12 June 2015].
Ministry of Industry and Trade of the Czech Republic, 'PREVENTIVE ACTION PLAN Required for Removing or Mitigating Identified Risks for Providing Deliveries of Natural Gas in the Czech Republic', 2012.
Ministry of the Economy of the Slovak Republic, 'NEGOTIATING POSITION OF THE SLOVAK REPUBLIC', 2004 <www.mhsr.sk/index/open_file.php?ext_dok=123264&idc=121492> [accessed 29 June 2016].
Mitchell, Wess, 'The Mice That Roared: How Central Europe Is Reshaping Global Politics' <http://www.cepa.org/content/report-no-16-mice-roared-how-central-europe-reshaping-global-politics> [accessed 6 August 2015].

Morgenthau, Hans Joachim, *Politics among Nations* (New York Knopf, 1967), Potsdamer Straße 358274.

Mulherin, J. Harold, 'Complexity in Long-Term Contracts: An Analysis of Natural Gas Contractual Provisions', *Journal of Law, Economics and Organization*, 2 (1986), 105–17.

Naimski, Piotr, 'Energy Diversification Strategy for Poland' (Secretary of State at the Ministry of Economy Republic of Poland / Colombia University, 2007) <http://www.columbia.edu/cu/ece/academics/regional/conf/Piotr_Naimski_at_Columbia%20University070917_.pdf> [accessed 12 June 2016].

Najwyższa Izba Kontroli, *Informacja O Wynikach Kontroli Zaopatrzenia W Gaz Ziemny*, 2004.

Net4Gas, *40 Years of Natural Gas Transit through the Czech Republic*, 24 March 2015 <http://www.net4gas.cz/en/media/brozury/N4G_40_year_history_brochure_EN.pdf?jis=20150324133252> [accessed 21 May 2015].

Neumann, Anne, Sophia Rüster and Christian von Hirschhausen, *Long-Term Contracts in the Natural Gas Industry – Literature Survey and Data on 426 Contracts (1965- 2014)*, Data Documentation (Deutsches Institut für Wirtschaftsforschung, 2015).

Neumann, Iver B., 'Russia as Central Europe's Constituting Other', *East European Politics & Societies*, 7 (1993), 349–69.

Noël, Pierre, *EU Gas Supply Security: Unfinished Business* (EPRG, Faculty of Economics, University of Cambridge, 1 April 2013) <https://www.repository.cam.ac.uk/handle/1810/244756> [accessed 30 June 2016].

Nosko, Andrej, *Energy Security in Transition: Coping with Energy Import Dependence in the Czech Republic, Slovakia and Hungary*, CEU Political Science Department PhD Theses, 2013/2 (Budapest: CEU, Budapest College, 2013).

Nosko, Andrej and Petr Lang, 'Lessons from Prague: How the Czech Republic Has Enhanced Its Energy Security | European Dialogue', 2010 <http://www.eurodialogue.eu/Lessons-from-Prague-How-the-Czech-Republic-Has-Enhanced-Its-Energy-Security-> [accessed 29 June 2016].

Novikov, Alexey, 'Russia-Europe Gas Prices Vary', *Interfax Global Energy* </gasdaily/article/5754/russia-europe-gas-prices-vary> [accessed 21 January 2015].

———, *TABLE: How Prices Fell for Russian Gas* (Interfax, 6 March 2015).

Olav Bjerkholt, Eystein Gjelsvik and Øystein Olsen, 'Gas Trade Demand in Northwest Europe: Regulation, Bargaining and Competition', *Norwegian Central Bureau of Statistics*, 1989.

Orbán, Anita, *Power, Energy and the New Russian Imperialism*, PSI Reports (Westport, Conn: Praeger Security International, 2008).

Orttung, Robert W. and Indra Overland, 'A Limited Toolbox: Explaining the Constraints on Russia's Foreign Energy Policy', *Journal of Eurasian Studies*, 2 (2011), 74–85.

Patnaik, Laxmi Kanta, 'MODEL BUILDING IN POLITICAL SCIENCE', *The Indian Journal of Political Science*, 50 (1989), 234–50.

Pełczyńska-Nałęcz, Katarzyna and Agata Loskot-Strachota, *Gazprom's Expansion in the EU – Co-Operation or Domination?*, April 2008 <http://aei.pitt.edu/57997/1/gp_eu_en_.pdf> [accessed 20 May 2015].

Pirani, Simon, 'Ukraine's Gas Sector', *Oxford Institute for Energy Studies* <http://www.oxfordenergy.org/2007/06/ukraine%e2%80%99s-gas-sector/> [accessed 12 March 2015].

Pirani, Simon, Jonathan P. Stern, Katja Yafimava and Oxford Institute for Energy Studies, *The Russo-Ukrainian Gas Dispute of January 2009: A Comprehensive Assessment* (Oxford Institute for Energy Studies, 2009).

Polish Geological Institute, *Zasoby Gazu Z łupków W Polsce – Gwarancja Z Zapasem*, 21 March 2012 <http://www.pgi.gov.pl/pl/instytut-geologiczny-informacje-prasowe/4109-zasoby-gazu-z-lupkow-w-polsce> [accessed 13 May 2015].

Putnam, Robert D., 'Diplomacy and Domestic Politics: The Logic of Two-Level Games', *International Organization*, 42 (1988), 427–60.

Risse-Kappen, Thomas, 'Ideas Do Not Float Freely: Transnational Coalitions, Domestic Structures and the End of the Cold War', *International Organization*, 48 (1994), 185–214.

Rittberger, Volker, *German Foreign Policy since Unification: Theories and Case Studies*, Issues in German Politics (Manchester: Manchester University Press, 2001), Reading Hall II / International Relations 327./43 RIT.

Rogers, Howard, 'The Interaction of LNG and Pipeline Gas Pricing: Does Greater Connectivity Equal Globalisation' in Jonathan Stern, ed., *The Pricing of Internationally Traded Gas* (Oxford/New York: Oxford Institute for Energy Studies, 2012), pp. 375–423.

Sanford, George, 'Overcoming the Burden of History in Polish Foreign Policy', *Journal of Communist Studies and Transition Politics*, 19 (2003), 178–203.

Schreurs, Miranda A., Stacy VanDeveer and Henrik Selin, eds., *Transatlantic Environment and Energy Politics: Comparative and International Perspectives* (Farnham, UK and Burlington, VT: Ashgate Press, 2009).

Sinnhuber, Karl A., 'Central Europe, Mitteleuropa, Europe Centrale: An Analysis of a Geographical Term', *Transactions and Papers (Institute of British Geographers)*, 1954, pp. 15–39.

Sitter, Nick, 'Cleavages, Party Strategy and Party System Change in Europe, East and West', *Perspectives on European Politics and Society*, 2002, 425–51.

Smith Stegen, Karen, 'Deconstructing the "Energy Weapon": Russia's Threat to Europe as Case Study', *Energy Policy*, Sustainability of biofuels, 39 (2011), 6505–13.

Sovacool, Benjamin K., ed., *The Routledge Handbook of Energy Security* (London: Routledge, 2011).

Sovacool, Benjamin K. and Ishani Mukherjee, 'Conceptualizing and Measuring Energy Security: A Synthesized Approach', *Energy*, PRES 2010, 36 (2011), 5343–55.

Spykman, Nicholas John, *America's Strategy in World Politics: The United States and the Balance of Power* (Transaction Publishers, 1942).

Stern, Jonathan, *Gas Pipeline Co-Operation between Political Adversaries: Examples from Europe* (Royal Institute of International Affairs (Chatham House), January 2005) <https://www.chathamhouse.org/sites/files/chathamhouse/public/Research/Energy,%20Environment%20and%20Development/jsjan05.pdf> [accessed 22 August 2015].

———, 'Is There a Rationale for the Continuing Link to Oil Product Prices in Continental European Long Term Gas Contracts?', *Oxford Institute for Energy Studies*, 2007 <http://www.oxfordenergy.org/2007/04/is-there-a-rationale-for-the-continuing-link-to-oil-product-prices-in-continental-european-long-term-gas-contracts/> [accessed 5 August 2015].

———, *Security of European Natural Gas Supplies: The Impact of Import Dependence and Liberalization* (The Royal Institute of International Affairs, July 2002).

———, 'Pricing of Gas in International Trade: An Historical Survey', in Jonathan Stern, ed., *The Pricing of Internationally Traded Gas* (Oxford/New York: Oxford Institute for Energy Studies, 2012), pp. 40-84.

———, *The Russian-Ukrainian Gas Crisis of January 2006* (Oxford Institute for Energy Studies, 16 January 2006).

———, 'Norwegian Troll Gas: The Consequences for Britain, Continental Europe and Energy Security', *The World Today*, 43 (1987), 1–4.

———, 'Specters and Pipe Dreams', *Foreign Policy*, 1982, 21–36.

———, *The Future of Russian Gas and Gazprom* (Oxford University Press, 2005).

Stern, Jonathan, Simon Pirani and Katja Yafimava, 'The Russo-Ukrainian Gas Dispute of January 2009: A Comprehensive Assessment', *Oxford Institute for Energy Studies* <http://www.oxfordenergy.org/2009/02/the-russo-ukrainian-gas-dispute-of-january-2009-a-comprehensive-assessment/> [accessed 27 July 2015].

Stern, Jonathan and Howard Rogers, 'The Transition to Hub-Based Pricing in Continental Europe - A Response to Sergei Komlev of Gazprom Export', *Oxford Institute for Energy Studies* <http://www.oxfordenergy.org/2013/02/the-transition-to-hub-based-pricing-in-continental-europe-a-response-to-sergei-komlev-of-gazprom-export/> [accessed 28 August 2015].

Stoecker, Randy, 'Evaluating and Rethinking the Case Study', *The Sociological Review*, 39 (1991), 88–112.

Supreme Audit Office of Poland, *Informacja O Wynikach Kontroli Zaopatrzenia W Gaz Ziemny*, 2004 <http://www.cire.pl/pliki/2/2003083.pdf> [accessed 10 October 2016].

———, 'NIK O Budowie Terminalu LNG - Najwyższa Izba Kontroli', 2015 <https://www.nik.gov.pl/aktualnosci/nik-o-budowie-terminalu-lng.html> [accessed 23 June 2016].

———, *NIK O Poszukiwaniach Gazu łupkowego - Najwyższa Izba Kontroli*, 2012 <https://www.nik.gov.pl/aktualnosci/nik-o-poszukiwaniach-gazu-lupkowego.html> [accessed 23 June 2016].

Szurlej, Adam, 'The State Policy for Natural Gas Sector / Sektor Gazu Ziemnego W Polityce Państwa', *Archives of Mining Sciences*, 58 (2013), 925–40.

Timera Energy, 'Hub Pricing in a Converging Global Gas Market', 2015 <http://www.timera-energy.com/a-converging-gas-price-world/> [accessed 17 June 2016].

Toth, Janos, 'A Short Review of the Hungarian Petroleum and Natural Gas Industry from the Beginnings up to the Present Day' (Museum of the Hungarian Petroleum Industry: Museum of the Hungarian Petroleum Industry, 1988).

Tulmets, Elsa, *East Central European Foreign Policy Identity in Perspective: Back to Europe and the EU's Neighbourhood* (Palgrave Macmillan, 2014).

URE, *National Reports* (URE, 2013, 2012, 2011, 2010, 2009, 2014) <http://www.ure.gov.pl/pl/urzad/informacje-ogolne/sprawozdania/2916,Sprawozdania.html> [accessed 2 June 2015].

Victor, David G., Amy M. Jaffe and Mark H. Hayes, *Natural Gas and Geopolitics From 1970 to 2040* (Cambridge: Cambridge University Press, 2006).

Waltz, Kenneth N., 'Evaluating Theories', *The American Political Science Review*, 91 (1997), 913–17

———, *Theory of International Politics* (Boston: McGraw-Hill, 1979).

———, *Man, the State and War: A Theoretical Analysis* (New York/Columbia University Press, 1959).

Wendt, Alexander, *Social Theory of International Politics* (Cambridge University Press, 1999) [accessed 8 August 2015].

Whitefield, Stephen, 'Political Cleavages and Post-Communist Politics', *Annual Review of Political Science*, 5 (2002), 181–200.

Williamson, Oliver E., 'Transaction-Cost Economics: The Governance of Contractual Relations', *Journal of Law and Economics*, 22 (1979), 233–61.

World Bank, *Caspian Development Corporation: Final Implementation Report* (The World Bank, 1 December 2010) <http://documents.worldbank.org/curated/en/2010/12/16286570/caspian-development-corporation-final-implementation-report> [accessed 1 February 2016].

Yafimava, Katja, 'European Energy Security and the Role of Russian Gas', *IAI Istituto Affari Internazionali*, 2016 <http://www.iai.it/en/pubblicazioni/european-energy-security-and-role-russian-gas> [accessed 27 January 2016].

———, *The Transit Dimension of EU Energy Security: Russian Gas Transit Across Ukraine, Belarus and Moldova* (Oxford/New York: Oxford Institute for Energy Studies, 2011).

Yergin, Daniel, *The Prize: The Epic Quest for Oil, Money & Power*, Reissue edition (New York: Free Press, 2008).

———, *The Quest: Energy, Security and the Remaking of the Modern World*, Re-edition (New York: Penguin Books, 2012).

Young, Robert A. and Queen's University (Kingston ON) Institute of Intergovernmental Relations, *The Breakup of Czechoslovakia* (IIGR, Queen's University, 1994).

Youngs, Richard and Senior Associate Carnegie Endowment for International Peace and Professor of International Relations Richard Youngs, *Energy Security: Europe's New Foreign Policy Challenge* (London: Routledge, 2009).

Zawisza, Aleksander, *Gaz dla Polski. Zarys historii sektora gazu ziemnego w ostatnich dwóch dekadach w Polsce* (Instytut Sobieskiego) <http://www.sobieski.org.pl/gaz-dla-polski/> [accessed 5 May 2015].

Zeniewski, Peter, 'Poland's Energy Security and the Origins of the Yamal Contract with Russia', *The Polish Quarterly of International Affairs*, 38–62. <https://basepub.dauphine.fr/bitstream/handle/123456789/5372/long_term_authorized.PDF?sequence=1> [accessed 30 June 2016].

Made in the USA
Las Vegas, NV
11 November 2024

11558018R00164